ECONOMIC ISSUES, PROBLEMS AND PERSPECTIVES

FINANCIAL ALARM AND FEDERAL RESERVE RESPONSE

ECONOMIC ISSUES, PROBLEMS AND PERSPECTIVES

Additional books in this series can be found on Nova's website
under the Series tab.

Additional E-books in this series can be found on Nova's website
under the E-books tab.

AMERICA IN THE 21ST CENTURY: POLITICAL AND ECONOMIC ISSUES

Additional books in this series can be found on Nova's website
under the Series tab.

Additional E-books in this series can be found on Nova's website
under the E-books tab.

ECONOMIC ISSUES, PROBLEMS AND PERSPECTIVES

FINANCIAL ALARM AND FEDERAL RESERVE RESPONSE

ALEXANDER L. CLARK
AND
MASON R. WILLIAMS
EDITORS

Nova Science Publishers, Inc.
New York

Copyright © 2012 by Nova Science Publishers, Inc.

All rights reserved. No part of this book may be reproduced, stored in a retrieval system or transmitted in any form or by any means: electronic, electrostatic, magnetic, tape, mechanical photocopying, recording or otherwise without the written permission of the Publisher.

For permission to use material from this book please contact us:
Telephone 631-231-7269; Fax 631-231-8175
Web Site: http://www.novapublishers.com

NOTICE TO THE READER

The Publisher has taken reasonable care in the preparation of this book, but makes no expressed or implied warranty of any kind and assumes no responsibility for any errors or omissions. No liability is assumed for incidental or consequential damages in connection with or arising out of information contained in this book. The Publisher shall not be liable for any special, consequential, or exemplary damages resulting, in whole or in part, from the readers' use of, or reliance upon, this material. Any parts of this book based on government reports are so indicated and copyright is claimed for those parts to the extent applicable to compilations of such works.

Independent verification should be sought for any data, advice or recommendations contained in this book. In addition, no responsibility is assumed by the publisher for any injury and/or damage to persons or property arising from any methods, products, instructions, ideas or otherwise contained in this publication.

This publication is designed to provide accurate and authoritative information with regard to the subject matter covered herein. It is sold with the clear understanding that the Publisher is not engaged in rendering legal or any other professional services. If legal or any other expert assistance is required, the services of a competent person should be sought. FROM A DECLARATION OF PARTICIPANTS JOINTLY ADOPTED BY A COMMITTEE OF THE AMERICAN BAR ASSOCIATION AND A COMMITTEE OF PUBLISHERS.

Additional color graphics may be available in the e-book version of this book.

Library of Congress Cataloging-in-Publication Data

Financial alarm and Federal Reserve response / editors, Alexander L. Clark and Mason R. Williams.
   p. cm.
  Includes index.
  ISBN 978-1-62100-582-7 (hardcover)
 1. Federal Reserve banks. 2. Monetary policy--United States. 3. Fiscal policy--United States. I. Clark, Alexander L. II. Williams, Mason R.
  HG2563.F56 2011
  332.1'10973--dc23
                          2011035668

Published by Nova Science Publishers, Inc. † New York

CONTENTS

Preface		vii
Chapter 1	Financial Turmoil: Federal Reserve Policy Responses *Marc Labonte*	1
Chapter 2	Federal Reserve System: Opportunities Exist to Strengthen Policies and Processes for Managing Emergency Assistance *United States Government Accountability Office*	53
Index		233

PREFACE

The Federal Reserve (Fed) has been central in the policy response to the financial turmoil that began in August 2007. It has sharply increased reserves to the banking system through open market operations and lowered the federal funds rate and discount rate on several occasions. Through new credit facilities, the Fed first expanded the scale of its lending to the banking system and then extended direct lending to non-bank financial firms. The latter marked the first since the Great Depression that firms that are not banks or members of the Federal Reserve System have been allowed to borrow directly from the Fed. This book explores the financial crisis and Federal Reserve Policy responses with a focus on the opportunities that exist to strengthen policies and processes for managing emergency assistance.

Chapter 1 - The Federal Reserve (Fed) has been central in the policy response to the financial turmoil that began in August 2007. It has sharply increased reserves to the banking system through open market operations and lowered the federal funds rate and discount rate on several occasions. Since December 2008, it has allowed the federal funds rate to fall close to zero. As the crisis deepened, the Fed's focus shifted to providing liquidity directly to the financial system through new policy tools. Through new credit facilities, the Fed first expanded the scale of its lending to the banking system and then extended direct lending to non-bank financial firms. The latter marked the first time since the Great Depression that firms that are not banks or members of the Federal Reserve System have been allowed to borrow directly from the Fed. After the crisis worsened in September 2008, the Fed began providing credit directly to markets for commercial paper and asset-backed securities. All of these emergency facilities had expired by the end of June 2010, but central bank liquidity swap lines were reopened in May 2010 in response to the crisis in Greece. The Fed also provided emergency assistance to Bear Stearns, AIG, and Citigroup over the course of the crisis; the Fed still holds assets from and loans to AIG and assets from Bear Stearns.

Chapter 2 - The Dodd-Frank Wall Street Reform and Consumer Protection Act directed GAO to conduct a one-time audit of the emergency loan programs and other assistance authorized by the Board of Governors of the Federal Reserve System (Federal Reserve Board) during the recent financial crisis. This report examines the emergency actions taken by the Federal Reserve Board from December 1, 2007, through July 21, 2010. For each of these actions, where relevant, GAO's objectives included a review of (1) the basis and purpose for its authorization, as well as accounting and financial reporting internal controls; (2) the use, selection, and payment of vendors; (3) management of conflicts of interest; (4) policies in place to secure loan repayment; and (5) the treatment of program participants. To meet these objectives, GAO reviewed program documentation, analyzed program data, and interviewed officials from the Federal Reserve Board and Reserve Banks (Federal Reserve System).

In: Financial Alarm and Federal Reserve Response
Editors: Alexander L. Clark and Mason R. Williams
ISBN: 978-1-62100-582-7
© 2012 Nova Science Publishers, Inc.

Chapter 1

FINANCIAL TURMOIL: FEDERAL RESERVE POLICY RESPONSES

Marc Labonte

SUMMARY

The Federal Reserve (Fed) has been central in the policy response to the financial turmoil that began in August 2007. It has sharply increased reserves to the banking system through open market operations and lowered the federal funds rate and discount rate on several occasions. Since December 2008, it has allowed the federal funds rate to fall close to zero. As the crisis deepened, the Fed's focus shifted to providing liquidity directly to the financial system through new policy tools. Through new credit facilities, the Fed first expanded the scale of its lending to the banking system and then extended direct lending to non-bank financial firms. The latter marked the first time since the Great Depression that firms that are not banks or members of the Federal Reserve System have been allowed to borrow directly from the Fed. After the crisis worsened in September 2008, the Fed began providing credit directly to markets for commercial paper and asset-backed securities. All of these emergency facilities had expired by the end of June 2010, but central bank liquidity swap lines were reopened in May 2010 in response to the crisis in Greece. The Fed also provided emergency assistance to Bear Stearns, AIG, and Citigroup over the course of the crisis; the Fed still holds assets from and loans to AIG and assets from Bear Stearns.

These programs resulted in an increase in the Fed's balance sheet of $1.4 trillion at its peak in December 2008, staying relatively steady since then. The Fed's authority and capacity to lend is bound only by fears of the inflationary consequences, which have been partly offset by additional debt issuance by the Treasury. High inflation has not materialized yet because most of the liquidity created by the Fed is being held by banks as excess reserves, but after the economy stabilizes, the Fed may have to scale back its balance sheet rapidly to avoid it. Asset sales could be disruptive, but the Fed has argued that it can contain inflationary pressures through the payment of interest on bank reserves, which it was authorized by Congress to do in 2008.

The statutory authority for most of the Fed's recent actions is based on a clause in the Federal Reserve Act to be used in "unusual or exigent circumstances." All loans are backed by collateral that reduces the risk of losses. Any losses borne by the Fed from its loans or asset purchases would reduce the income it remits to the Treasury, making the effect on the federal budget similar to if the loans were made directly by Treasury. It is highly unlikely that losses would exceed its other income and capital, and require revenues to be transferred to the Fed from the Treasury. To date, the Fed's crisis activities have increased its net income.

Two policy issues raised by the Fed's actions are issues of systemic risk and moral hazard. Moral hazard refers to the phenomenon where actors take on more risk because they are protected. The Fed's involvement in stabilizing Bear Stearns, AIG, and Citigroup stemmed from the fear of systemic risk (that the financial system as a whole would cease to function) if they were allowed to fail. In other words, the firms were seen as "too big (or too interconnected) to fail." The Fed regulates member banks to mitigate the moral hazard that stems from access to government protections. Yet Bear Stearns and AIG were not under the Fed's regulatory oversight because they were not member banks.

Some Members of Congress have expressed concern that certain details of the Fed's lending activities are kept confidential. H.R. 4173 adds conditions to the Fed's emergency lending authority, removes most GAO audit restrictions, and requires disclosure of the identities of borrowers with a delay. It also changes the Fed's role in the financial regulatory system.

INTRODUCTION

On August 9, 2007, liquidity abruptly dried up for many financial firms and securities markets. Suddenly some firms were able to borrow and investors were able to sell certain securities only at prohibitive rates and prices, if at all. The "liquidity crunch" was most extreme for firms and securities with links to subprime mortgages, but it also spread rapidly into seemingly unrelated areas.[1] The Federal Reserve (Fed) was drawn into the liquidity crunch from the start. On August 9, it injected unusually large quantities of reserves into the banking system to prevent the federal funds rate from exceeding its target. In a series of steps between September 2007 and December 2008, the Fed reduced the federal funds rate from 5.25% to a target range of 0% to 0.25%.

It has been observed that the most unusual aspect of the crisis is its persistence over time. Over that time, the Fed has aggressively reduced the federal funds rate and the discount rate in an attempt to calm the waters. When this proved not to be enough, the Fed greatly expanded its direct lending to the financial sector through several new lending programs, some of which can be seen as adaptations of traditional tools and others which can be seen as more fundamental departures from the status quo.[2]

The Fed's decision to assist specific troubled financial institutions sparked controversy. In March 2008, the Fed helped the investment bank Bear Stearns avoid bankruptcy, even though Bear Stearns was not a member bank of the Federal Reserve system (because it was not a depository institution), and, therefore, not part of the regulatory regime that accompanies membership.[3] At the same time, it created two lending facilities for other non-bank primary dealers. In September, the investment bank Lehman Brothers filed for bankruptcy (it did not receive emergency government assistance), and the financial firm American International Group (AIG), which was also not a member bank, received a credit line from the Fed in order to meet its obligations. (Additional aid to AIG was extended on three subsequent occasions.) The Fed then began directly assisting the markets for commercial paper and asset-backed securities. More recently, the Fed and federal government has guaranteed losses on assets owned by Citigroup. This marked the first time in more than 70 years that the Fed had lent to non-members, and it did so using emergency statutory authority (Section 13(3) of the Federal Reserve Act).[4] The Dodd-Frank Wall Street Reform and Consumer Protection Act (H.R. 4173) adds conditions to the Fed's emergency lending authority. The House passed the conference report for H.R. 4173 on June 30, 2010, and the Senate passed the conference report on July 15, 2010.

In September 2008, the housing government-sponsored enterprises (GSEs) Fannie Mae and Freddie Mac were taken into conservatorship by the government. On November 25, 2008, the Fed announced that it would make large-scale purchases of the direct obligations and mortgage-backed securities (MBS) issued by the housing GSEs.

As financial conditions have improved in 2009, the Fed's focus, in turn, has shifted from stabilizing financial markets to stabilizing the housing market. As fewer financial firms have accessed Fed lending facilities, direct assistance has been replaced on the Fed's balance sheet by purchases of debt and MBS issued by the housing GSEs. This has kept relatively constant the overall amount of liquidity the Fed has provided to the economy. The Fed purchased about $175 billion of GSE debt and $1.25 trillion of MBS by the spring of 2010. Most emergency facilities were allowed to expire in February 2010, but the central bank liquidity swap lines were reopened in May 2010 to provide dollar liquidity to foreign countries needed as a result of the economic crisis in Greece.

One of the original purposes of the Federal Reserve Act, enacted in 1913, was to prevent the recurrence of financial panics. To that end, the Fed has been given broad authority over monetary policy and the payments system, including the issuance of federal reserve notes as the national currency. Because this authority is delegated from Congress, the Fed's actions are subject to congressional oversight. Although the Fed has broad authority to independently execute monetary policy on a day-to-day basis, questions have arisen as to whether the unusual events of recent months raise fundamental issues about the Fed's proper role, and what role Congress should play in assessing those issues. S. 896, which was signed into law on May 20, 2009 (P.L. 111-22), allows Government Accountability Office (GAO) audits of a limited subset of Fed emergency activities. H.R. 4173 removes most GAO audit restrictions, calls for a GAO audit of emergency actions, and requires disclosure of the identities of borrowers with a delay.[5]

H.R. 4173 also made comprehensive changes to the financial regulatory system. The Fed's role in prudential regulation, consumer protection regulation, payment system regulation, and systemic risk regulation was modified by this legislation.

This report reviews the Fed's actions since August 2007 and analyzes the policy issues raised by those actions.

TRADITIONAL TOOLS

The Fed, the nation's central bank, was established in 1913 by the Federal Reserve Act (38 Stat. 251). Today, its primary duty is the execution of monetary policy through open market operations to fulfill its mandate to promote price stability and maximum employment. Besides the conduct of monetary policy, the Federal Reserve has a number of other duties: it regulates financial institutions and consumer financial products, issues paper currency, clears checks, collects economic data, and carries out economic research. Prominent in the current debate is one particular responsibility: to act as a lender of last resort to the financial system when capital cannot be raised in private markets to prevent financial panics. The next two sections explain the Fed's traditional tools, open market operations and discount window lending, and summarize its recent use of those tools.

Open Market Operations and the Federal Funds Rate

Open market operations are carried out through the purchase and sale of U.S. Treasury securities in the secondary market to alter the reserves of the banking system.[6] By altering bank reserves, the Fed can influence short-term interest rates, and hence overall credit conditions. The Fed's target for open market operations is the federal funds rate, the rate at which banks lend to one another on an overnight basis. The federal funds rate is market determined, meaning the rate fluctuates as supply and demand for bank reserves change. The Fed announces a target for the federal funds rate and pushes the market rate toward the target by altering the supply of reserves in the market through the purchase and sale of Treasury securities.[7] More reserves increase the liquidity in the banking system and, in theory, should make banks more willing to lend, spreading greater liquidity throughout the financial system.

When the Fed wants to stimulate economic activity, it lowers the federal funds target, in what is referred to as expansionary policy. Lower interest rates stimulate economic activity by stimulating interest-sensitive spending, which includes physical capital investment (e.g., plant and equipment) by firms, residential investment (housing construction), and consumer durable spending (e.g., automobiles and appliances) by households. Lower rates would also be expected to lead to a lower value of the dollar, all else equal. A depreciated dollar would stimulate exports and the output of U.S. import-competing firms. To reduce spending in the economy (called contractionary policy), the Fed raises interest rates, and the process works in reverse.

The Fed's actions with regards to open market operations have taken two forms in the crisis. First, a loss of liquidity in the interbank lending market has forced the Fed to inject unusually large volumes of reserves into the market on several occasions since August 2007. These actions have been necessary to maintain the availability of reserves at the existing federal funds target.

Second, the Fed has reduced the federal funds target on numerous occasions over the course of the crisis. On September 18, 2007, the Fed reduced the federal funds target rate by 0.5 percentage points to 4.75%, stating that the change was "intended to forestall some of the adverse effects on the broader economy that might otherwise arise from the disruptions in financial markets." Since then, the Fed has aggressively lowered interest rates several times.

The Fed decides whether to change its target for the federal funds rate at meetings scheduled every six weeks. In normal conditions, the Fed would typically leave the target unchanged or change it by 0.25 percentage points. From September 2007 to March 2008, the Fed lowered the target at each regularly scheduled meeting, by an increment larger than 0.25 percentage points at most of these meetings. It also lowered the target by 0.75 percentage points at an unscheduled meeting on January 21, 2008. Although financial conditions had not returned to normal, the Fed kept the federal funds rate steady from April 30, 2008, until October 9, 2008, when it again reduced the federal funds rate, this time by 0.5 percentage points, to 1.5%. Unusually, this rate reduction was coordinated with several foreign central banks. On December 16, 2008, the Fed established a target range of 0% to 0.25% for the federal funds rate.

Quantitative Easing

Even before December 2008, the Fed began supplying the federal funds market with a greater quantity of bank reserves than needed to reach the federal funds target, a policy that has been described as "quantitative easing."[8] Because the Fed has only one tool, it cannot meet more than one target at once. As long as the Fed was willing to create liquidity on demand, the federal funds rate was unlikely to meet its target. Therefore, after the Fed began focusing on meeting the financial sector's liquidity needs in September, the federal funds rate began undershooting the Fed's target on a regular basis.[9] In December 2008, the Fed began providing so much liquidity that the interest rate target often fell close to zero. The target range of 0% to 0.25% set in December can be seen as an acknowledgment by the Fed that targeting interest rates had been subordinated to the goal of providing ample liquidity to the financial system for the time being. Initially, quantitative easing was implemented through direct lending, but even after that liquidity was no longer sought by financial firms through the Fed's lending facilities, quantitative easing was continued through large purchases of Treasury securities, Agency securities, and Agency mortgage-backed securities in an attempt to continue stimulating the economy.[10] According to one estimate, the Fed purchased 22% of the entire available stock of these assets.[11]

The Discount Window

The Fed can also provide liquidity to member banks (depository institutions that are members of the Federal Reserve system) directly through discount window lending.[12] Discount window lending dates back to the early days of the Fed, and was originally the Fed's main policy tool. (The Fed's main policy tool shifted from the discount window to open market operations several decades ago.) Loans made at the discount window are backed by collateral in excess of the loan value. A wide array of assets can be used as collateral; loans and asset-backed securities are the most frequently posted collateral. Although not all collateral has a credit rating, those that are rated typically have the highest rating.[13] Most discount window lending is done on an overnight basis. Unlike the federal funds rate, the Fed sets the discount rate directly through fiat.

During normal market conditions, the Fed discouraged banks from borrowing at the discount window on a routine basis, believing that banks should be able to meet their normal reserve needs through the market. In 2003, the Fed made that policy explicit in its pricing by changing the discount rate from 0.5 percentage points below to 1 percentage point above the federal funds rate. A majority of member banks do not access the discount window in a typical year. Thus, the discount window has played a secondary role in policymaking to open market operations.

On August 17, 2007, the Fed began reducing the discount rate—about a month before it first reduced the federal funds rate. Since then, the discount rate has been lowered several times, typically at the same time as the federal funds rate. Over that period, the Fed has reduced the spread between the federal funds rate and the discount rate, but kept the spread positive. When the federal funds rate was allowed to fall to zero beginning in December 2008, the discount rate was set at 0.5%. From 1959 to 2007, discount window lending outstanding never surpassed $8 billion, and was usually well below $1 billion. Discount window lending (in the primary credit category) increased from a daily average of $45 million outstanding in July 2007 to $1,345 million in September 2007. Lending continued to increase to more than $10 billion outstanding per day from May 2008, and peaked at $111 billion in October 2008, but was superseded in economic significance by the creation of the "Term Auction Facility" in December 2007. Discount window lending fell steadily throughout 2009, and by mid-2010, it had returned to pre-crisis levels.

NEW TOOLS

The Fed's traditional tools are aimed at the commercial banking system, but current financial turmoil has occurred outside of the banking system as well. The inability of traditional tools to calm financial markets since August 2007 has led the Fed to develop several new tools to fill perceived gaps between open market operations and the discount window.[14]

Traditionally, the lender of last resort function has focused on the banking system, and the Fed's relationship with the banking system, encompassing costs and privileges, is prescribed in detail by the Federal Reserve Act. Many of the new facilities are aimed at other parts of the financial system, however, and the Federal Reserve Act is largely silent on the Fed's authority outside the banking system.[15] One exception is the broad emergency authority under Section 13(3) of the Federal Reserve Act, which the Fed has frequently invoked since the financial crisis began.

Term Auction Facility

A stigma is thought to be attached to borrowing from the discount window. In good times, discount window lending has traditionally been discouraged on the grounds that banks should meet their reserve requirements through the marketplace (the federal funds market) rather than the Fed. Borrowing from the Fed was therefore seen as a sign of weakness, as it implied that market participants were unwilling to lend to the bank because of fears of insolvency. In the current turmoil, this perception of weakness could be particularly damaging since a bank could be undermined by a run based on unfounded, but self-fulfilling fears. Ironically, this meant that although the Fed encourages discount window borrowing so that banks can avoid liquidity problems, at first banks were hesitant to turn to the Fed because of fears that doing so would spark a crisis of confidence. To overcome these problems, the Fed created the supplementary Term Auction Facility (TAF) in December 2007.[16]

Discount window lending is initiated at the behest of the requesting institution—the Fed has no control over how many requests for loans it receives. The TAF allows the Fed to determine the amount of reserves it wishes to make available to banks, based on market conditions. The auction process determines the rate at which those funds will be lent, with all bidders receiving the lowest winning bid rate. The winning bid may not be lower than the prevailing federal funds rate. Determining the rate by bid provides the Fed with additional information on how much demand for reserves exists.

Any depository institution eligible for discount window lending can participate in the TAF, and hundreds have accessed it or the discount window at a time since its inception. Auctions through the TAF have been held twice a month beginning in December 2007. The amounts auctioned have greatly exceeded discount window lending, which averages in the hundreds of millions of dollars outstanding daily in normal times and more than $10 billion outstanding since May 2008. The TAF initially auctioned up to $20 billion every two weeks, but this amount was increased on several occasions to as much as $150 billion (and currently up to $125 billion) every two weeks. Loans outstanding under the facility peaked at $493 billion in March 2009, and have fallen steadily since.[17] Like discount window lending, TAF loans must be fully collateralized with the same qualifying collateral. Loans and asset-backed securities are the most frequently posted collateral. Although not all collateral has a credit rating, those that are rated typically have the highest rating. As with discount window lending, the Fed faces the risk that the value of collateral would fall below the loan amount in the event that the loan was not repaid. For that reason, the amount lent diminishes as the quality of the collateral diminishes. Most borrowers borrow much less than the posted collateral.[18]

Loans mature in 28 days—far longer than overnight loans in the federal funds market or the typical discount window loan. (In July 2008, the Fed began making some TAF loans that matured in 84 days.) Another motivation for the TAF may have been an attempt to reduce the unusually large divergence that had emerged between the federal funds rate and interbank lending rates for longer maturities. This divergence, which can be seen as a sign of how much liquidity had deteriorated in spite of the Fed's previous efforts, became much smaller after December 2007. In subsequent periods of market stress, such as September 2008, the divergence reemerged. The evidence on the effectiveness of the TAF in reducing this divergence is mixed.[19]

The TAF program was announced as a temporary program (with no fixed expiration date) that could be made permanent after assessment. Given that the discount rate is set higher than the federal funds rate to discourage its use in normal market conditions, it is unclear what role a permanent TAF would fill, unless the funds auctioned were minimal in normal market conditions. A permanent TAF would seem to run counter to the philosophy governing the discount window that financial institutions, if possible, should rely on the private sector to meet their short-term reserve needs during normal market conditions. The Fed has not held a TAF auction since March 2010.

Term Securities Lending Facility

For many years, the Fed has allowed primary dealers (see box for definition) to swap Treasuries of different maturities or attributes with the Fed on an overnight basis through a program called the System Open Market Account Securities Lending Program to help meet the dealers' liquidity needs. (While all Treasury securities are backed by the full faith and credit of the federal government, some securities are more liquid than others, mainly because of differences in availability.) Securities lending has no effect on general interest rates or the money supply because it does not involve cash, but can affect the liquidity premium of the securities traded. Because the loans were overnight and collateralized with other Treasury securities, there was very little risk for the Fed.

> ### WHAT IS A PRIMARY DEALER?
>
> Primary dealers are about 20 large financial institutions who are the counterparties with which the Fed undertakes open market operations (buying and selling of Treasury securities). Because open market operations are very large, the Fed needs large counterparties to these transactions. To be a primary dealer, an institution must, among other things, meet relevant Basel or SEC capital requirements and maintain a good trading relationship with the Fed.

On March 11, 2008, the Fed set up a more expansive securities lending program for the primary dealers called the Term Securities Lending Facility (TSLF) using emergency authority under Section 13(3) of the Federal Reserve Act. Under this program, up to $75 billion (previously up to $200 billion) of Treasury securities could be lent for 28 days instead of overnight. Loans could be collateralized with private-label MBS with an AAA/Aaa rating, agency commercial mortgage-backed securities, and agency collateralized mortgage obligations.[20] On September 14, 2008, the Fed expanded acceptable collateral to include all investment-grade debt securities. Given the recent drop in MBS and other asset prices, this made the new lending program considerably more risky than the old one. But the scope for losses is limited by the fact that the loans are fully collateralized with a "haircut" (i.e., less money is loaned than the value of the collateral), and if the collateral loses value before the loan is due, the Fed can call for substitute collateral. In addition, most of the collateral that has been posted received a high rating from a credit rating agency.[21] The first auction on March 27 involved $75 billion of securities. In August 2008, the program was expanded to allow the primary dealers to purchase up to $50 billion of options (with prices set by auction) to swap for Treasuries through the TSLF. The TSLF was announced as a temporary facility. In July 2009, the Fed announced that primary dealers could also swap their assets for the Fed's Agency debt securities. Securities lent through all programs peaked at $260 billion on October 1, 2008. Since August 2009, no securities have been borrowed through this facility. The facility expired at the end of January 2010.

By allowing the primary dealers to temporarily swap illiquid assets for highly liquid assets such as Treasuries, "[t]he TSLF is intended to promote liquidity in the financing markets for Treasury and other collateral and thus to foster the functioning of financial markets more generally," according to the Fed.[22] According to research from the New York

Fed, the spreads between repos backed by GSE debt and MBS and repos backed by Treasuries fell from over 1 percentage point before the first TSLF auction to less than 0.2 percentage points by April 2008.[23] Given the timing of the announcement—less than a week before the failure of one of its primary dealers, Bear Stearns—critics have alleged that the program was created, in effect, in an attempt to rescue Bear Stearns from its liquidity problems. As will be discussed below, the Fed would take much larger steps to aid Bear Stearns later the same week.

EMERGENCY AUTHORITY UNDER SECTION 13(3) OF THE FEDERAL RESERVE ACT

The Fed has limited authority to assist non-member banks under the Federal Reserve Act. One exception where such authority is granted is under paragraph 3 of Section 13 of the Federal Reserve Act, and the Fed has used it to authorize many of its actions during the crisis. Prior to July 2010, it read,

In unusual and exigent circumstances, the Board of Governors of the Federal Reserve System, by the affirmative vote of not less than five members, may authorize any Federal reserve bank ... to discount for any individual, partnership, or corporation, notes, drafts, and bills of exchange ... secured to the satisfaction of the Federal Reserve Bank. Provided, that before discounting any such note, draft, or bill exchange ... the Federal reserve bank shall obtain evidence that such individual, partnership, or corporation is unable to secure adequate credit accommodations from other banking institutions.

It is noteworthy that this text allows emergencies to be identified by the Board of Governors and places few limits on what type of institution can receive financial assistance from the Fed or what form that assistance can take. The fact that the authority is justified only by unusual and exigent circumstances suggests that decisions made under 13(3), such as the creation of lending facilities, could not be made permanent under existing authority. Nevertheless, expiration dates were pushed back more than once for some new facilities. In 1991, Section 13(3) was amended to expand the collateral that the Fed could accept to back its lending; this was widely seen as making it easier for the Fed to lend to non-bank financial firms in an emergency. As will be discussed below, on a few occasions in 2008, Section 13(3) has been invoked to lend to an entity that the Fed created so that the entity could purchase private securities.

According to Hackley (1973), only 123 loans to businesses were made using 13(3) authority from 1932 to 1936. Until Bear Stearns, the authority had not been used for non-banks since. (The authority was superseded by Section 13b authority to lend to non-banks; Section 13b was revoked in 1958.) It has been invoked numerous times in 2008, including to authorize the Primary Dealer Credit Facility, the Fed's role in the Bear Stearns merger, and the Fed's extension of credit to AIG. Financial crises can spread quickly, and Section 13(3) makes a prompt response possible. But recent events have demonstrated that it vests the Fed with the ability to make large, wide-ranging financial commitments without congressional approval. It has voluntarily sought and received Treasury approval in each instance, however.

Section 13(3) was amended in October 2008. P.L. 110-343 requires the Fed to report to the House Financial Services Committee and the Senate Banking, Housing, and Urban

Affairs Committee on its justification for exercising Section 13(3), the terms of the assistance provided, and regular updates on the status of the loan.

H.R. 4173 requires the Fed to establish policies for lending under 13(3) that ensure that lending programs are broadly available for the purpose of providing liquidity to the financial system, and not used to assist specific firms or failing firms, and that emergency loans are sufficiently secured to protect taxpayers from losses. It also forbids "a program or facility that is structured to remove assets from the balance sheet of a single and specific company." It requires the Fed to seek approval from the Treasury Secretary before establishing a 13(3) program or facility.

For more information, see David Fettig, "The History of a Powerful Paragraph," Federal Reserve Bank of Minneapolis, *The Region*, June 2008; Howard Hackley, *Lending Functions of the Federal Reserve Banks: A History*, May 1973; Walker Todd, "FDICIA's Emergency Liquidity Provisions," *Federal Reserve Bank of Cleveland Review*, Third Quarter 1993, p. 16.

Primary Dealer Credit Facility

On March 16—a day too late to help Bear Stearns—the Fed announced the creation of the Primary Dealer Credit Facility (PDCF), a new direct lending program for primary dealers very similar to the discount window program for depository institutions. Loans are made through the PDCF on an overnight basis at the discount rate, limiting their riskiness. Acceptable collateral initially included Treasuries, government agency debt, and investment grade corporate, mortgage-backed, asset-backed, and municipal securities. On September 14, 2008, the Fed expanded acceptable collateral to include certain classes of equities. Many of the classes of eligible assets can and have fluctuated significantly in value. Fees will be charged to frequent users.

The program was announced as lasting six months, or longer if events warrant. The program is authorized under paragraph 3 of Section 13 of the Federal Reserve Act. The facility was subsequently extended, but allowed to expire at the end of January 2010.

Borrowing from the facility has been sporadic, with average daily borrowing outstanding above $10 billion in the first three months, and falling to zero in August 2008. Much of this initial borrowing was done by Bear Stearns, before its merger with J.P. Morgan Chase had been completed.[24] Loans outstanding through the PDCF peaked at $148 billion during the week of October 1, 2008. Since May 2009, outstanding loans through the PDCF have been zero, because of improvement in the financial system and because the largest investment banks converted into or were acquired by bank holding companies in late 2008, making them eligible to access other Fed lending facilities.

Although the program shares some characteristics with the discount window, the fact that the program was authorized under paragraph 3 of Section 13 of the Federal Reserve Act suggests that there is a fundamental difference between this program and the Fed's normal operations. The Fed is referred to as the nation's central bank because it is at the center of the banking system—providing reserves and credit, and acting as a regulator, clearinghouse, and lender of last resort to the banking system. The privileges for banks that come from belonging to the Federal Reserve system—access to Fed credit—come with the costs of regulation to ensure that banks do not take excessive risks. Although the primary dealers are subject to certain capital requirements, they are not necessarily part of the banking system, and do not fall under the same "safety and soundness" regulatory structure as banks.

Term Asset-Backed Securities Loan Facility

In November 2008, the Fed created the Term Asset-Backed Securities Loan Facility (TALF) in response to problems in the market for asset-backed securities (ABS). According to the Fed, "new issuance of ABS declined precipitously in September and came to a halt in October. At the same time, interest rate spreads on AAA-rated tranches of ABS soared to levels well outside the range of historical experience, reflecting unusually high risk premiums."[25]

Data support the Fed's view: issuance of non-mortgage asset backed securities fell from more than $175 billion per quarter from 2005 through the second quarter of 2007 to $5 billion in the fourth quarter of 2008, according to the Securities Industry and Financial Markets Association (SIFMA). The Fed fears that if lenders cannot securitize these types of loans, less credit will be extended to consumers, and eventually households will be forced to reduce consumption spending, which would exacerbate the economic downturn.

The TALF is intended to stimulate the issuance of new securities backed by pools of the following assets:

- auto loans or leases, including motorcycles, recreational vehicles (including boats), and commercial, rental, and government fleets;
- credit cards, consumer and corporate;
- student loans, private and government guaranteed;
- SBA-guaranteed small business loans;
- business equipment loans, including retail and leases;
- floorplan loans for inventories, including auto dealers;
- mortgage servicing advances;
- commercial mortgages; and
- insurance premium finance loans.

In May 2009, the Fed began accepting legacy commercial mortgage-backed securities (CMBSs). The Fed announced that the TALF may later be expanded to other classes of ABS. In March 2009, the Treasury announced that TALF may be expanded in the future to include private-label residential MBS, and collateralized debt and loan obligations. To date, most TALF loans have been backed by auto, credit card, and student loans.[26]

Rather than purchase ABS directly, the Fed will make non-recourse loans to any private U.S. company or subsidiary with a relationship with a primary dealer to purchase recently issued ABS receiving the highest credit rating, using the ABS as collateral. The minimum loan size will be $10 million. If the ABS lose value, the losses will be borne by the Fed and the Treasury (through the TARP program) instead of by the borrower—an unusual feature for a Fed lending facility. The Fed will lend less than the current value of the collateral, so the Fed would not bear losses on the loan until losses exceed the value of the "haircut" (different

ABS receive different haircuts). The loans will have a term of up to three years for most types of assets (and up to five years for some types of assets), but can be renewed. Interest rates will be set at a markup over different maturities of LIBOR or the federal funds rate, depending on the type of loan and underlying collateral.

If the loans are not repaid, the Treasury will bear the first $20 billion in total losses on the underlying collateral, and the Fed will bear any additional losses. Treasury will receive interest in return for bearing this risk. The Treasury's losses will be financed through the Troubled Asset Relief Program (TARP), authorized by P.L. 110-343. In addition, TARP has already loaned the TALF program $100 million to finance initial administrative costs. It was originally proposed that ABS issuers would be subject to TARP's executive compensation restrictions. Subsequently, in a letter to the Special Inspector General for TARP, the General Counsel of the Treasury reasoned that the Fed, not the TALF loan recipients nor the ABS issuers, is the recipient of TARP funds, and so executive compensation restrictions do not apply to TALF.[27]

TALF has some similarities to TARP as it was originally envisioned, with the primary differences being that the Fed is lending to purchase rather than directly purchasing assets, and the assets backing the loans are mostly newly or recently issued as opposed to "troubled" existing assets. Because the Treasury's funds will finance loan losses rather than asset purchases, the $20 billion will support a much larger volume of assets than would be possible through direct purchase via TARP.

In March 2009, Treasury announced a new Public-Private Partnership Investment Program (PPIP) within TARP.[28] Under this program, private investors will receive matching capital from TARP to purchase up to $500 billion to $1 trillion of legacy loans and securities. These legacy securities are defined as existing ABS backed by mortgages and other assets. Treasury has announced that private partners will be able to use loans from TALF (and other sources) to finance the purchase of these legacy securities. In May 2009, the Fed began accepting legacy commercial mortgage-backed securities (CMBSs) as the first class of legacy securities eligible for TALF. PPIP has also turned out to be much smaller than envisioned—as of May 2010, Treasury had pledged a maximum of $30 billion for PPIP-Securities.

The Fed originally announced TALF as a $200 billion program, and Treasury expressed the desire to see it increased to $1 trillion. As it turns out, TALF lending grew slowly after inception, and peaked at $48 billion on March 17, 2010. The low lending totals seem less indicative of the unpopularity of TALF, and more indicative of the continued depressed state of the private securitization market. According to data from SIFMA, non-mortgage ABS issuance rose to $52 billion per quarter in the first two full quarters that TALF was in operation, but fell to $32 billion per quarter in the next two quarters—a far cry from issuance of more than $175 billion per quarter before the crisis. Nevertheless, a review of the program by the Federal Reserve Bank of Dallas argues that TALF should be credited with a decline in ABS spreads against Treasury bonds and a rise in ABS issuance.[29] The facility expired at the end of June 2010 for loans against newly issued CMBS and March 2010 for loans against other assets.

Intervention in the Commercial Paper Market

Many large firms routinely issue commercial paper, which is short-term debt purchased directly by investors that matures in less than 270 days, with an average maturity of 30 days. There are three broad categories of commercial paper issuers: financial firms, non-financial firms, and pass-through entities that issue paper backed by assets. The commercial paper issued directly by firms tends not to be backed by collateral, as these firms are viewed as large and creditworthy and the paper matures quickly.[30]

Individual investors are major purchasers of commercial paper through money market mutual funds and money market accounts. The Securities and Exchange Commission regulates the holdings of money market mutual funds, limiting their holdings to highly rated, short-term debt; thus, investors widely perceived money market mutual funds as safe and low risk. On September 16, 2008, a money market mutual fund called the Reserve Fund "broke the buck," meaning that the value of its shares had fallen below face value. This occurred because of losses it had taken on short-term debt issued by Lehman Brothers, which filed for bankruptcy on September 15. Money market investors had perceived "breaking the buck" to be highly unlikely, and its occurrence set off a run on money market funds, as investors simultaneously attempted to withdraw an estimated $250 billion of their investments—even from funds without exposure to Lehman.[31] This run greatly decreased the demand for new commercial paper. Firms rely on the ability to issue new debt to roll over maturing debt to meet their liquidity needs.

Fearing that disruption in the commercial paper markets could make overall problems in financial markets more severe, the Fed announced on September 19 that it would create the Asset-Backed Commercial Paper Money Market Mutual Fund Liquidity Facility (AMLF). This facility would make non-recourse loans to banks to purchase asset-backed commercial paper. Because the loans were non-recourse, the banks would have no further liability to repay any losses on the commercial paper collateralizing the loan. On October 1, 2008, daily loans outstanding peaked at $152 billion. The AMLF would soon be superseded in importance by the creation of the Commercial Paper Funding Facility, and lending fell to zero in October 2009.[32] The temporary facility was authorized under Section 13(3) of the Federal Reserve Act, and was subsequently extended until the end of January 2010.

Although the creation of the AMLF and the Treasury's temporary guarantee of money market mutual fund deposits had eased conditions in the commercial paper market, the market remained strained. For example, commercial paper outstanding fell from more than $2 trillion outstanding in August 2007 to $1.8 trillion on September 7, 2008, to $1.6 trillion on October 1, 2008. The yield on 30-day, AA-rated asset-backed commercial paper rose from 2.7% on September 8, 2008, to 5.5% on October 7, 2008.

Because of the importance of commercial paper for meeting firms' liquidity needs, the Fed decided to take stronger action to ensure that the market was not disrupted. On October 7, it announced the creation of the Commercial Paper Funding Facility (CPFF), a special purpose vehicle (SPV) that would borrow from the Fed to purchase all types of three-month, highly rated U.S. commercial paper, secured and unsecured, from issuers.[33] The Fed argued that the assurance that firms will be able to roll over commercial paper at the CPFF will encourage private investors to buy commercial paper again. The interest rate charged by the CPFF was set at the three month overnight index swap plus 1 percentage point for secured corporate debt, 2 percentage points for unsecured corporate debt, and 3 percentage points for asset-backed paper. The CPFF can buy as much commercial paper from any individual issuer as that issuer had outstanding in the year to date. Any losses borne by the CPFF would ultimately be borne by the Fed. The Fed has hired the private company PIMCO to manage the SPV's assets. The facility is authorized under Section 13(3) of the Federal Reserve Act, and was subsequently extended until the end of January 2010.

At its peak in January 2009, the CPFF held $351 billion of commercial paper, and has fallen steadily since. Goldman Sachs reports that conditions in commercial paper markets improved significantly after the creation of the CPFF (although they remained worse than before the crisis), and in January 2009, the CPFF was holding far more commercial paper than the total that had been issued since its inception.[34]

The CPFF is notable on several grounds. First, it is the first Fed standing facility in modern times with an ongoing commitment to purchase assets, as opposed to lending against assets. Technically, the Fed is lending against the assets of the SPV, but the SPV was created by the Fed and is controlled by the Fed.[35] Second, in the case of non-financial commercial paper, it is the first time in 50 years that the Fed is providing financial assistance to non-financial firms.[36] (In practice, the Fed has bought very little commercial paper issued by non-financial firms.[37]) Third, in the case of commercial paper that is not asset backed, it is unusual for the Fed (through the SPV) to purchase uncollateralized debt. Indeed, the Federal Reserve Act would seem to rule out the direct purchase of uncollateralized debt.

On October 21, 2008, the Fed announced the creation of the Money Market Investor Funding Facility (MMIFF), and pledged to lend it up to $540 billion. The MMIFF will lend to private sector SPVs that invest in commercial paper issued by highly rated financial institutions. Each SPV will be owned by a group of financial firms and can only purchase commercial paper issued by that group. These SPVs can purchase commercial paper from money market mutual funds and similar entities facing redemption requests to help avoid runs such as the run on the Reserve Fund. The facility expired at the end of October 2009 without ever being used. The Fed's director of the Division of Monetary Affairs reported that money market funds were unwilling to use it because "investors would recognize that leverage would ... intensify their incentive to run."[38]

Mortgage-Backed Securities Purchase Program and Purchase of GSE Obligations

In July 2008, the stock prices of Fannie Mae and Freddie Mac, the housing GSEs, came under increasing pressure, leading to fears that they would be unable to roll over debt and become illiquid. On July 13, 2008, the Fed authorized lending to the housing GSEs, but this authority was not used at that point. On September 7, 2009, Treasury placed the two housing GSEs into conservatorship.[39] On September 19, 2008, the Fed announced that it would purchase debt obligations of Fannie Mae, Freddie Mac, and the Federal Home Loan Banks through open market operations.[40]

On November 25, 2008, the Fed announced it would purchase up to $100 billion of direct obligations (e.g., bonds) issued by these institutions and up to $500 billion of MBS guaranteed by Fannie Mae, Freddie Mac, and Ginnie Mae, a government agency. GSE obligations will be purchased through auctions and MBS will be purchased on the Fed's behalf by private investment managers. Adjustable rate MBS, collateralized mortgage obligations (CMOs), real estate mortgage investment conduits (REMICs), and mortgage derivatives would not be eligible for purchase under the program. Assets purchased under these programs will be held passively and long-term. On March 18, 2009 the Fed announced an increase in the purchase commitment of up to $1.25 trillion in MBS and $200 billion of GSE obligations. In September 2009, the Fed announced that it would complete these purchases by the end of the first quarter of 2010. In November 2009, the Fed announced that it would purchase only $175 billion of Agency debt securities due to limited availability.

The Fed argued that these programs would "reduce the cost and increase the availability of credit for the purchase of houses."[41] Support to mortgage markets through these programs can be seen as indirect and selective, however. The Fed is not providing or purchasing mortgages directly, nor is it purchasing newly issued MBS. By purchasing existing MBS from the secondary market, the price should rise, and that may induce more MBS to be issued. If more MBS are issued, then the increased availability of credit to mortgage markets would be expected to cause mortgage rates to fall. Further, the Fed is accepting MBS issued by GSEs but not by private firms, even though the GSEs have issued more MBS in 2008 than before the crisis started, while private-label issuance has dried up almost entirely, according to data from the Securities Industry and Financial Markets Association. Further, overall mortgage rates have been low during the crisis, but access has been limited to highly qualified lenders. Increasing the demand for GSE-issued MBS and GSE debt would be expected to primarily reduce already low mortgage rates, and increase borrower access only indirectly, at best. Mortgage rates fell noticeably after the Fed announced that the programs had begun, although the amounts of securities purchased by the Fed at that point were small. Subsequently, mortgage rates rose despite the Fed's purchases, presumably because of the economy's improvement. One concern is that mortgage rates could rise after the Fed's purchases are complete, and the housing market will not have recovered by then.

These programs did not require the use of Section 13(3) emergency authority. Transactions involving agency debt are authorized under Section 13(13) and 14b of the Federal Reserve Act. The Fed's programs are similar to two Treasury programs, the GSE MBS Purchase Program and the GSE Credit Facility, already in place. Since the Treasury programs were authorized to provide the GSEs with unlimited financial assistance through the end of 2009, it is not clear why the Fed felt that the Treasury programs needed to be supplemented.[42]

Swap Lines with Foreign Central Banks

In December 2007, the Fed announced the creation of temporary reciprocal currency agreements, known as swap lines, with the European Central Bank and the Swiss central bank.[43] These agreements let the Fed swap dollars for euros or Swiss francs for a fixed period of time. Since September 2008, the Fed has extended similar swap lines to central banks in several other countries. To date, most of the swaps outstanding have been with the European Central Bank and Bank of Japan.[44] In October 2008, it made the swap lines with certain countries unlimited in size. Interest is paid to the Fed on a swap outstanding at the rate the foreign central bank charges to its dollar borrowers. The temporary swaps are repaid at the exchange rate at the time of the original swap, meaning that there is no downside risk for the Fed if the dollar appreciates in the meantime (although the Fed also does not enjoy upside gain if the dollar depreciates). The swap lines are currently authorized through the end of January 2010. Except in the unlikely event that the borrowing country's currency becomes unconvertible in foreign exchange markets, there is no credit risk involved for the Fed. Swaps outstanding peaked at $583 billion in December 2008, and have fallen steadily since.

The swap lines are intended to provide liquidity to banks in non-domestic denominations. For example, many European banks have borrowed in dollars to finance dollar-denominated transactions, such as the purchase of U.S. assets. Normally, foreign banks could finance their dollar-denominated borrowing through the private inter-bank lending market. As banks have become reluctant to lend to each other through this market, central banks at home and abroad have taken a much larger role in providing banks with liquidity directly. But normally banks can only borrow from their home central bank, and central banks can only provide liquidity in their own currency. The swap lines allow foreign central banks to provide needed liquidity in dollars. As such, the swap lines directly benefit foreign borrowers who need access to dollars. But the swap lines indirectly benefit the United States by promoting the use of the dollar as the "reserve" currency, which results in more seigniorage (earnings from currency) for the United States, as well as intangible benefits. Initially, the swap lines were designed to allow foreign central banks to U.S. dollars. In April 2009, the swap lines were modified so that the Fed could access foreign currency to provide to its banks as well; to date, the Fed has not accessed foreign currency through these lines.

The swap lines were ended in February 2010, but reopened with five countries in May 2010 in response to the crisis in Greece.[45] To date, their use in 2010 was much more limited than in 2008 to 2009.

Payment of Interest on Bank Reserves

Banks hold some assets in the form of cash reserves stored in their vaults or in accounts at the Fed to meet daily cash-flow needs and required ratios imposed by the Fed. At times before the federal funds target was reduced to zero in December 2008, the Fed faced conflicting goals—it sought to ensure that banks have enough reserves to remain liquid, but it also sought to maintain its target for the federal funds rate to meet its economic goals. The federal funds rate is the market rate in the private market where a bank with excess reserves lends them overnight to other banks. At times, ensuring that all banks have adequate reserves has resulted in an overall level of reserves in the market that has pushed the federal funds rate below its target. In other words, the only way for the Fed to make sure that each bank has enough reserves has been to oversupply the banking system as a whole with liquidity at the given federal funds target.

To avoid this problem, Congress authorized the Fed to pay interest on bank reserves in the Emergency Economic Stabilization Act of 2008 (H.R. 1424/P.L. 110-343).[46] By setting an interest rate on bank reserves close to the federal funds rate, the Fed would in effect place a floor on the rate. In theory, the federal funds rate would not fall below the interest rate on reserves because banks would rather hold excess reserves to earn interest than lend them out to other banks at a lower interest rate.[47] Paying interest on reserves may also encourage banks to hold more reserves overall, which may somewhat reduce the likelihood that banks will have liquidity problems in the future.

Paying interest on reserves does not encourage banks to increase overall lending to firms and households, however, because it increases the attractiveness of holding reserves. Thus, it is not a policy that stimulates the economy, at least in any direct sense; on the contrary, it prevents the increase in liquidity to banks from stimulating the economy by preventing the federal funds rate from falling.

The interest rate on excess reserves was initially set at 0.75 percentage points less than the federal funds rate. In the short term, paying interest on reserves did not succeed in placing a floor under the federal funds target. Immediately after the Fed began paying interest, the federal funds rate was still falling below the target, and some days was even below the interest rate on reserves. In response, the Fed subsequently reduced the spread between the interest rate on reserves and the federal funds rate, but the actual federal funds rate continued to fall below the target rate.[48] When the Fed reduced the federal funds rate target to a range of 0% to 0.25% in December 2008, it set the interest rate paid on reserves to 0.25%, the high end of the target range. At that point, paying interest on reserves could no longer place a floor under the federal funds rate, the stated rationale for its authorization.

P.L. 110-343 gave the Fed permanent authority to pay interest on reserves. Once financial conditions return to normal, the liquidity benefits from paying interest will be less important (since banks will again be able to meet reserve needs through the federal funds market), and the primary remaining benefit would be a reduction in the volatility of the federal funds rate. The Fed previously intervened in the federal funds market on a daily basis to keep the market rate close to the target, sometimes unsuccessfully. The volatility partly resulted from banks devoting resources to activities that minimize reserves, such as "sweep accounts."

Paying interest on reserves reduces the Fed's profits, and thus reduces its remittances to the Treasury, thereby increasing the budget deficit, all else equal. It can be viewed as a transfer from the federal government to the banks, although in the long run, competition makes it likely that the banks will pass on the benefit to depositors in the form of higher interest paid on deposits. From Congress's perspective, the benefit of a less volatile target rate and less resources spent minimizing reserves would have to be weighed against the lost federal revenue, over time. The decision to pay interest on required, as well as excess, reserves also increases the cost of the policy without any additional benefit to liquidity or reduced volatility (because banks must keep required reserves even if no incentive is offered).

The growth in the Fed's balance sheet has raised concerns about the future implications for inflation. The Fed has argued that paying interest on reserves can help prevent its balance sheet growth from becoming inflationary.[49] It approved "term deposits" of up to six months for bank reserves in April 2010. The interest rate paid by term deposits will be determined by auction.

ASSISTANCE TO INDIVIDUAL FINANCIAL INSTITUTIONS

Over the course of the year, several financial firms that were deemed "too big to fail" received financial assistance from the Fed in the form of loans, troubled asset purchases, and asset guarantees. This assistance went beyond its traditional role of acting as a lender of last resort by providing loans to illiquid but solvent firms.[50] In a joint announcement in March 2009, the Treasury and Fed stated a desire in the long run to transfer assets acquired by the

Fed (via the Maiden Lane LLCs) from Bear Stearns and the American International Group (AIG) to the Treasury, but to date have not taken any steps to do so.[51] H.R. 4173 alters Section 13(3) authority in an attempt to prevent assistance to individual firms in the future.

The Fed's Role in the JPMorgan Chase Acquisition of Bear Stearns

The investment bank Bear Stearns came under severe liquidity pressures in early March 2008, in what many observers have coined a non-bank run.[52] On Friday, March 14, 2008, JPMorgan Chase announced that, in conjunction with the Federal Reserve, it had agreed to provide secured funding to Bear Stearns, as necessary. Through its discount window, the Fed agreed to provide $13 billion of back-to-back financing to Bear Stearns via JPMorgan Chase. It was a non-recourse loan, meaning that the Fed had no general claim against JPMorgan Chase in the event that the loan was not repaid and the outstanding balance exceeded the value of the collateral. Bear Stearns could not access the discount window directly because, at that point, only member banks could borrow directly from the Fed. This loan was superseded by the events of March 16, and the loan was repaid in full on March 17, 2008.

On Sunday, March 16, after negotiations between the two companies, the Fed and the Treasury, JPMorgan Chase agreed to acquire Bear Stearns. The Fed agreed to purchase up to $30 billion of Bear Stearns' assets through Maiden Lane I, a new Limited Liability Corporation (LLC) based in Delaware that it created and controls. After the merger was completed, the loan was finalized on June 26, 2008. Two loans were made to the LLC: the Fed lent the LLC $28.82 billion, and JPMorgan Chase made a subordinate loan to the LLC worth $1.15 billion, based on assets initially valued at $29.97 billion.[53] The Fed's loan will be made at an interest rate set equal to the discount rate (2.5% when the terms were announced, but fluctuating over time) for a term of 10 years, renewable by the Fed.[54] JPMorgan Chase's loan will have an interest rate 4.5 percentage points above the discount rate.

Using the proceeds from that loan, the LLC purchased assets from Bear Stearns worth $29.97 billion at marked to market prices by Bear Stearns on March 14, 2008. On its website, the New York Fed gives information on the current fair market value of the assets by type of asset, credit rating of the assets, and geographical location of the underlying assets. At the end of 2008, 44% of the portfolio consisted of agency collateralized mortgage obligations (CMOs), 6% was non-agency CMOs, 18% was commercial loans, 3% was residential loans, 8% was swap contracts, 7% was TBA commitments, and 8% was cash or cash equivalents. More than half of the non-agency CMOs had a credit rating of AAA; about one-fifth had a junk rating. (Agency CMOs are guaranteed by the GSE that issued them, and the Treasury has pledged to maintain the GSE's solvency.)

The CEO of JPMorgan Chase testified that JPMorgan Chase "kept the riskier and more complex securities in the Bear Stearns portfolio.... We did not cherry pick the assets in the collateral pool (for the LLC)."[55] These assets are owned by the LLC, which will eventually liquidate them to pay back the principal and interest owed to the Fed and JPMorgan Chase. The LLC's assets (purchased from Bear Stearns) are the collateral backing the loans from the Fed and JPMorgan Chase. A private company, BlackRock Financial Management, has been hired to manage the portfolio. Neither Bear Stearns nor JPMorgan Chase owes the Fed any principal or interest, nor are they liable if the LLC is unable to pay back the money the Fed lent it. The New York Fed explained that the LLC was created to "ease administration of the portfolio and will remove constraints on the money manager that might arise from retaining the assets on the books of Bear Stearns."[56] JPMorgan Chase and Bear Stearns did not receive the $28.82 billion from the LLC until the merger was completed.[57]

It was announced that the Fed is planning to begin liquidating the assets after two years. The assets will be sold off gradually, "to minimize disruption to financial markets and maximize recovery value."[58] As the assets are liquidated, interest will continue to accrue on the remaining amount of the loan outstanding. Thus, in order for the principal and interest to be paid off, the assets will need to appreciate enough or generate enough income so that the rate of return on the assets exceeds the weighted interest rate on the loans (plus the operating costs of the LLC). **Table 1** shows how the funds raised through the liquidation will be used. Any difference between the proceeds and the amount of the loans is profit or loss for the Fed, not JPMorgan Chase. Because JPMorgan Chase's $1.15 billion loan was subordinate to the Fed's $28.82 billion loan, if there are losses on the total assets, the first $1.15 billion of losses will be borne, in effect, by JPMorgan Chase, however. The interest on the loan will be repaid out of the asset sales, not by JPMorgan Chase. At the end of 2009, the value of the assets had already been written down by over $3.5 billion, exceeding the maximum losses borne by JPMorgan Chase.[59]

The CEO of JPMorgan Chase testified that "we *could* not and *would* not have assumed the substantial risks of acquiring Bear Stearns without the $30 billion facility provided by the Fed" (emphasis in original).[60] The primary risk was presumably that the value of mortgage-related assets would continue to decline. Had the transaction been crafted as a typical discount window loan directly to JPMorgan Chase, JPMorgan Chase would have been required to pay back the principal and interest, and it (rather than the Fed) would have borne the full risk of any depreciation in value of Bear Stearns' assets.

The Fed's statutory authority for its role in both Bear Stearns transactions comes from paragraph 3 of Section 13 of the Federal Reserve Act. In his testimony, Timothy Geithner, New York Fed president at the time, stated that the Fed did not have authority to acquire an equity interest in Bear Stearns or JPMorgan Chase.[61] Yet the LLC controlled by the Fed acquired assets from Bear Stearns, and the profits or losses from that acquisition will ultimately accrue to the Fed. It is unclear why the Fed decided to create and lend to a LLC to complete the transaction, rather than engaging in the transaction directly. Although the Fed did not buy Bear Stearns' assets directly, there are certainly important policy questions raised by the Fed's creation and financing of an LLC in order to buy Bear Stearns' assets. Typically, the Fed lends money to institutions and receives collateral in return to reduce the risk of suffering a loss. When the loan is repaid, the collateral is returned to the institution. In this case, the Fed made a loan, but to a LLC they created and controlled, not to a financial institution. From the perspective of JPMorgan Chase or Bear Stearns, the transaction was a sale (to the LLC), not a loan, regardless of whether the Fed or the LLC was the principal.

Assistance to American International Group (AIG)[62]

Initial Loan

On September 16, 2008, the Fed announced, after consultation with the Treasury Department, that it would lend up to $85 billion to the financial institution American International Group. AIG had experienced a significant decline in its stock price and was facing immediate demands for $14 billion to $15 billion in collateral payments due to recent downgrades by credit rating agencies, according to press reports.[63] The Fed and Treasury feared that AIG was also "too big to fail" because of the potential for widespread disruption to financial markets that would result.

The Fed announced that AIG could borrow up to $85 billion from the Fed over the next two years. On September 18, the Fed announced that it had initially lent $28 billion to AIG.[64] The interest rate on the funds drawn is 8.5 percentage points above the London Interbank Offered Rate (LIBOR), a rate that banks charge to lend to each other. A lower interest rate is charged on any funds that it is does not draw from the facility. In return, the government agreed to receive warrants that, if exercised, would give the government a 79.9% ownership stake in AIG. The Fed named three independent trustees to oversee the firm for the duration of the loan.

The lending facility is backed by the assets of AIG's non-regulated subsidiaries (but not the assets of its insurance company). In other words, the Fed can seize AIG's assets if the firm fails to honor the terms of the loan. This reduces the risk that the Fed (and ultimately, taxpayers) will suffer a loss. The risk still remains that if AIG turned out to be insolvent, its assets would be insufficient to cover the amount it had borrowed from the Fed. Since AIG has been identified as too big to fail, it is unclear how its assets could be seized in the event of non-payment without precipitating failure.

Second Loan

On October 8, 2008, the Fed announced that it was expanding its assistance to AIG and swapping cash for up to $37.8 billion of AIG's investment-grade, fixed-income securities. These securities, belonging to AIG's insurance subsidiaries, had been previously lent out and unavailable as collateral at the time of the original agreement. It has been reported that as AIG's loans matured, AIG realized losses on investments it had made with the collateral and some counterparties stopped participating in the lending program.[65] As a result, AIG needed liquidity from the Fed to cover these losses and counterparty withdrawals.

Although this assistance resembles a typical collateralized loan (the Fed receives assets as collateral, and the borrower receives cash), the Fed characterized the agreement as a loan of securities from AIG to the Fed in exchange for cash collateral. It appears the arrangement was structured this way because New York insurance law prevents AIG from using the securities as collateral in a loan.[66]

Table 1. Use of Funds Raised by Liquidation of Bear Stearns Assets.

Payments from the liquidation will be made in the following order:
(1) operating expenses of the limited liability corporation
(2) $29 billion principal owed to the Federal Reserve
(3) interest due to the Federal Reserve on the $29 billion loan
(4) $1 billion principal owed to JPMorgan Chase
(5) interest due to JPMorgan Chase on $1 billion subordinated note
(6) non-operating expenses of the limited liability corporation
(7) remaining funds accrue to Federal Reserve

Source: Federal Reserve Bank of New York.

Note: Each category must be fully paid before proceeding to the next category.

Revision to Agreement on November 10, 2008

On November 10, 2008, the Federal Reserve and the U.S. Treasury announced a restructuring of the federal intervention to support AIG. As evidenced by the additional borrowing after the September 16 loan, AIG had continued to see cash flow out of the company, particularly to post collateral for the credit default swaps that were arguably the primary cause of the financial problems in the company. The revised agreement points to the tension between making the terms of the assistance undesirable enough to deter other firms from seeking government assistance in the future, compared to making the terms of assistance so punitive that it exacerbates the financial problems of the recipient firm. It also points to the fact that once a firm has been identified as too big to fail, government assistance to the firm can become open-ended, as the original amounts offered were quickly revised upward.

The November 10 restructuring eased the payment terms for AIG and had three primary parts: (1) a $40 billion direct capital injection, (2) restructuring of the $85 billion loan, and (3) a $52.5 billion purchase of troubled assets.

Loan Restructuring

The initial $85 billion loan facility from the Federal Reserve was reduced to $60 billion, for a time period extended to five years, and the financial terms are eased considerably. Specifically, the interest rate on the amount outstanding is reduced by 5.5 percentage points (to Libor plus 3%) and the fee on undrawn funds is reduced by 7.75 percentage points (to 0.75%).

Purchase of Troubled Assets

While P.L. 110-343 provided for the government purchase of troubled assets, the purchases related to AIG are being done by LLCs created and controlled by the Federal Reserve. This structure is similar to that created by the Federal Reserve to facilitate the purchase of Bear Stearns by JPMorgan Chase in March 2008. There are two LLCs set up for AIG—one for residential mortgage-backed securities (RMBS) and one for collateralized debt obligations (CDO).

The agreement called for the RMBS LLC (Maiden Lane II) to be lent up to $22.5 billion by the Federal Reserve and $1 billion from AIG to purchase RMBS from AIG's securities lending portfolio. The AIG loan is subordinated and AIG will bear the first $1 billion in losses should there be future losses on these securities. AIG and the Federal Reserve will "share" in any future gains, with five-sixths of future profits accruing to the Fed and one-sixth accruing to AIG. As of March 2009, the assets had lost nearly $3 billion in value, more than AIG's total loss exposure. The previous $37.8 billion loan securities lending loan facility is to be repaid and terminated with the proceeds from this LLC plus additional AIG funds if necessary. At the end of 2008, about half of the RMBS purchased were backed by subprime mortgages, and about one quarter were backed by Alt-A mortgages. Thirteen percent of the portfolio's holdings had a credit rating of AAA and 65% had a junk rating. At the end of 2009, the Maiden Lane II assets had lost $1.1 billion in value, slightly exceeding the AIG's maximum loss sharing.

The agreement called for the CDO LLC (Maiden Lane III) to be lent up to $30 billion from the Federal Reserve and $5 billion from AIG to purchase CDOs on which AIG has written credit default swaps. The $5 billion loan from AIG is subordinated and AIG will bear the first $5 billion in future losses on these securities. As of March 2009, the assets had lost nearly $8.5 billion in value, more than AIG's total loss exposure. AIG and the Federal Reserve will "share" in any future gains, with five-sixths of future profits accruing to the Fed and one-sixth accruing to AIG. The Federal Reserve also indicates that the credit default swaps will be unwound at the same time that the CDOs are purchased. Many credit default swaps, however, are purchased by entities not holding the underlying CDOs; it is unclear how, or if, such credit default swaps written by AIG will be addressed. At the end of March 2009, 16% of the portfolio's holdings had a credit rating of AAA, and 72% had a junk rating. At the end of 2009, the Maiden Lane III assets had lost $0.9 billion in value, resulting in no losses to date for the Fed.

Direct Capital Injection

Through the TARP, the Treasury purchased $40 billion in preferred shares of AIG. In addition to $40 billion in preferred shares, the Treasury also receives warrants for common shares equal to 2% of the outstanding AIG shares. AIG was the first announced non-bank to receive TARP funds. The $40 billion in preferred AIG shares now held by the Treasury are slated to pay a 10% dividend per annum, accrued quarterly.[67] Participation in TARP triggers restrictions on executive pay as required by Congress, including a restriction on "golden parachutes" and a requirement for clawbacks on previously provided bonuses in the case of accounting irregularities. According to the November 10, 2008, AIG filings with the Securities and Exchange Commission, the amount of shares held in trust for the benefit of the U.S. Treasury will be reduced by the shares and warrants purchased under TARP, so the total equity interest currently held by the U.S. government equals 77.9% plus warrants to purchase another 2%. The warrants equal to 77.9% of AIG equity were exercised and transferred to the government on March 4, 2009.

Revision to Agreement on March 2, 2009

On March 2, 2009, the Treasury and Fed announced another revision of the financial assistance to AIG. On the same day, AIG announced a loss of more than $60 billion in the fourth quarter of 2008. In response to the poor results and ongoing financial turmoil, the ratings agencies were reportedly considering further downgrading AIG, which would most likely have resulted in further significant cash demands due to collateral calls.[68] According to the Treasury, AIG "continues to face significant challenges, driven by the rapid deterioration in certain financial markets in the last two months of the year and continued turbulence in the markets generally." The revised assistance is intended to "enhance the company's capital and liquidity in order to facilitate the orderly completion of the company's global divestiture program."[69]

The revised assistance includes the following:

- Exchange of the existing $40 billion in preferred shares purchased through the TARP program for preferred shares that "more closely resemble common equity," thus improving AIG's financial position. Dividends paid on these new shares will remain at 10%, but will be non-cumulative and only be paid as declared by AIG's board of directors. Should dividends not be paid for four consecutive quarters, the government has the right to appoint at least two new directors to the board.

- Commitment of up to $30 billion in additional preferred share purchases from TARP. As of October 2009, AIG had issued $3.2 billion of these shares.[70]
- Reduction of interest rate on the existing Fed loan facility by removing the current floor of 3.5% over the LIBOR portion of the rate. The rate will now simply be three month LIBOR plus 3%, which is approximately 4.25%.
- Limit on Fed revolving credit facility will be reduced from $60 billion to $25 billion.
- Up to $33.5 billion of the approximately $38 billion outstanding on the Fed credit facility will be repaid by asset transfers from AIG to the Fed. Specifically, (1) $8.5 billion in ongoing life insurance cash flows will be securitized by AIG and transferred to the Fed; and (2) $25 billion in preferred interests in two of AIG's large life insurance subsidiaries will be issued to the Fed. The transfer of the preferred interest in the life insurance subsidiaries was finalized in December 2009. This effectively transfers a majority stake in these companies to the Fed, but the companies will still be managed by AIG.

Assistance through the end of 2009 is summarized in **Table 2**. In addition to the new assistance, AIG announced that it was forming a new holding company to include its primary property/casualty insurance subsidiaries. Since the first assistance in September 2008, AIG has sought to sell subsidiaries, including those whose equity has been transferred to the Fed, to repay the loans and reduce its holdings to a core property/casualty business. Such sales have been difficult during the ongoing financial turmoil. By effectively transferring the two life insurance subsidiaries to the Fed and gathering property casualty subsidiaries in a new holding company, AIG is arguably progressing toward this goal.

CBO estimates that most of the expected government losses from assistance to AIG will accrue to TARP, in part because those claims are junior to the Fed's. In addition, CBO did not expect losses from the Maiden Lane asset purchases at the time of purchase because the Fed reported the assets were bought at current market value. It is unclear why it was necessary for the Fed to acquire the assets if they could have been sold at the same price in the private market, however.

Who Benefits from Assistance to AIG?

While billions of dollars in government assistance have gone to AIG, in many cases, it can be argued that AIG has essentially acted as an intermediary for this assistance. In short order after drawing on government assistance, substantial funds have flowed out of AIG to entities on the other side of AIG's financial transactions, such as securities lending or credit default swaps. If AIG had been allowed to fail and had entered bankruptcy, as was the case with Lehman Brothers, then these counterparties in many cases would have been treated as unsecured creditors and seen their claims reduced.

Seen from this view, the true beneficiaries of the billions in federal assistance that have flowed to AIG has not been AIG itself, but these counterparties. On March 15, 2009, AIG released information detailing the counterparties to many of its transactions.[71] The released information detailed $52.0 billion of direct support to AIG that went to AIGFP related transactions, $29.6 billion in Maiden Lane III CDS-related transactions, and $43.7 billion in payments to securities lending counterparties.

Legal Authority

All Fed assistance to AIG is authorized under Section 13(3) of the Federal Reserve Act, the same emergency authorization used for Bear Stearns. This authorization was needed because the Fed cannot normally lend to a financial firm that is neither primarily a depository institution (although it owns a small thrift) nor a primary dealer.

Guarantee of Citigroup's Assets

Similar to Bear Stearns and AIG, Citigroup faced a sudden drop in its stock price in late 2008. Its stock price fell from $23 per share on October 1, 2008, to $3.77 on November 21, 2008, amidst investor concern about its losses. Stepping in before a potential run began, the Federal Reserve and federal government announced on November 23 that they would purchase an additional $20 billion of Citigroup preferred shares through TARP and guarantee a pool of up to $306 billion of Citigroup's assets. (The assets were valued at $301 billion when the agreement was finalized on January 16, 2009.) Citigroup announced that the assets guaranteed include mortgages, consumer loans, corporate loans, asset backed securities, and unfunded lending commitments.[72] The guarantee was to be in place for 10 years for residential assets and five years for non-residential assets. Citigroup would exclusively bear up to the first $29 billion of losses on the pool. Any additional losses would be split between Citigroup and the government, with Citigroup bearing 10% of the losses and the government bearing 90%. The first $5 billion of any government losses would be borne by the Treasury using TARP funds; the next $10 billion would be borne by the FDIC; any further losses would be borne by the Fed through a non-recourse loan. Citigroup will pay the federal government a fee for the guarantee in the form of $7 billion in preferred stock with an 8% dividend rate and warrants to purchase common stock that were worth $2.7 billion at the time of the agreement. The assets will remain on Citigroup's balance sheet, and Citigroup will receive the income stream generated by the assets and any future capital gains.

In December 2009, Citigroup and the Treasury reached an agreement to repay the outstanding $20 billion in preferred securities and to cancel the asset guarantee. As part of this agreement, Citigroup paid a termination fee of $50 million and Treasury agreed to cancel $1.8 billion worth of the trust preferred securities originally paid as a fee for the guarantee. While the asset guarantee was in place, no losses were claimed and no federal funds paid out.

Table 2. Summary of Outstanding Assistance to AIG

Program	Federal Government					Terms and Conditions			
	Outstanding Amount End of CY2009	Outstanding Amount at Peak	Total Income CY2009	Expected Gain(+) /Loss(-)	Dividend/ Interest Rate	Warrants/ Equity Interests	Subsequent Conversion	Expiration Date
Federal Reserve Loan to AIG	$22.2 billion loan	$87.3 billion loan (Oct. 29, 2008)	$4.0 billion	-$2 billion (CBO)	3 month LIBOR+3%[a]	warrants for 79.9% (later reduced to 77.9%) of Common shares	Reduced balance by $25 billion in exchange for equity in life insurance subsidiaries; $989 million provision for loan restructuring	September 2013
TARP Preferred Share Purchase	$45.3 billion preferred shares	$45.3 billion Preferred shares	$0	-$36 billion (CBO); -$45.2 billion (Treasury)	10% (dividends paid at AIG's discretion)	warrants for 2% of common shares	$1.6 billion balance outstanding[b]	Preferred Shares outstanding until repaid. No new contracts/modifications to program after Oct. 3, 2010.
Fed Loan for Troubled Asset Purchases	$34.5 billion in loans to purchase assets	$43.9 billion loans to purchase assets (Dec. 31, 2008)	$769 million	$0	LIBOR+1%[a]	none	n/a	Securities held long-term.
Commercial Paper Funding Facility	$0	$16.7 billion (Dec 31, 2008)	n/a	$0	Overnight index swap (OIS) rate+1%; OIS+3%	none	n/a	February 2010

Source: December 2009 TARP 105(a) Report; Federal Reserve, Monthly Report on Credit and Liquidity Programs and the Balance Sheet, January 2009; Congressional Budget Office, *The Budgetary Impact of Subsidy Costs of the Federal Reserve's Actions During the Financial Crisis*, May 2010; Congressional Budget Office, *Report on the Troubled Asset Relief Program*, March 2010; U.S. Treasury, *Summary Tables of Trouble Asset Relief Program (TARP) Investments as of March 31, 2010*.

a. LIBOR = London Inter-bank Offered Rate.

b. In return for conversion of shares paying a mandatory dividend to shares paying an optional dividend, AIG took on an obligation of $1.6 billion due to the outstanding dividend balance.

In the cases of Bear Stearns and AIG, management was replaced and shareholders equity was diluted to limit moral hazard problems associated with receiving government assistance.[73] Similar steps were not taken in the case of Citigroup.

Guarantee of Bank of America's Assets

On January 16, 2009, the federal government and the Federal Reserve announced that that they would purchase an additional $20 billion of Bank of America preferred shares through TARP and guarantee a pool of up to $37 billion of Bank of America's assets and derivatives with maximum potential future losses of up to $81 billion. The guarantee would remain in place for 10 years for residential mortgage-related assets and five years for all other assets. Bank of America will bear up to the first $10 billion of losses on the assets, with any subsequent losses split 90% by the government and 10% by Bank of America. The government's share of the next $10 billion of losses will be borne jointly by the FDIC and the Treasury, and any further losses will be borne by the Fed. It was announced that the assets being guaranteed were largely acquired during Bank of America's acquisition of Merrill Lynch. Bank of America will pay the federal government a fee for the guarantee in the form of $4 billion in preferred stock with an 8% dividend rate and warrants to purchase common stock worth $2.4 billion at the time of the agreement. As part of the agreement, Bank of America was prohibited from paying dividends on common stock for three years.

The assets will remain on Bank of America's balance sheet, and Bank of America will receive the income stream generated by the assets and any future capital gains. Bank of America can further limit its cost and the benefit to the government by opting out of the guarantee early at its discretion.

In the cases of Bear Stearns and AIG, management was replaced and shareholders equity was diluted to limit moral hazard problems associated with receiving government assistance.[74] Similar steps were not taken in the case of Bank of America. On the other hand, the government has tried to encourage healthy financial firms to merge with troubled firms, and it may have felt that harsh terms on an agreement to guarantee assets that were in part acquired from Bank of America's takeover of Merrill Lynch would have discouraged future mergers. It has been reported that the asset guarantees to Bank of America were motivated by a desire to prevent them from withdrawing from their uncompleted merger agreement with Merrill Lynch.[75]

The agreement to guarantee Bank of America's assets was never finalized, and on September 22, 2009, it was announced that Bank of America would pay $425 million to exit the agreement. Although Bank of America never formally received government protection of its assets, an exit fee could be justified on the grounds that Bank of America benefited from the implicit support that the negotiations provided.

POLICY ISSUES

Cost to the Treasury

Unlike all other institutions, currency (Federal Reserve notes) is the Fed's primary liability. Along with its holdings of Treasury securities, its assets are the loans it makes (through the discount window and the new programs detailed above) and the private assets it buys directly or holds through LLCs (e.g., for AIG and the Bear Stearns takeover). It earns profits on its assets that are largely remitted to the Treasury. Its loans and asset purchases are financed by increasing its liabilities (Federal Reserve notes), and the financing does not necessarily result in any inherent cost for the Treasury. Indeed, if the loans are repaid, they would increase the profits of the Fed, which in turn would increase the Fed's remittances to the Treasury.[76] Even if the loans are not repaid, most are fully collateralized (usually over-collateralized), so the Fed would not suffer losses unless the collateral had lost value. In addition, most of its loans are made with recourse, which means that borrowers are still liable if the collateral loses value.

The Fed had net income of $38.8 billion and remitted $34.9 billion to the Treasury in 2008. Net income increased to $52.1 billion and remittances to the Treasury rose to $46.1 billion in 2009. In the past, most of the Fed's net income has derived from the interest on its Treasury securities holdings, not its loans. By the end of 2008, its loans and private assets holdings were much larger than its Treasury holdings (see **Table 4**). The earnings and any losses the Fed took on its loans would increase or reduce its net income, respectively. If loan losses caused an overall net loss, the Fed's capital (the excess of its assets compared with its liabilities) would be reduced. The Fed had capital equal to about $52 billion at end of 2009, half of which was paid-in capital of member banks and the other half of which was surplus. The Fed has not had an annual net operating loss since 1915. However, the Fed's balance sheet became more risky in 2008, due to the shift in composition of its assets from U.S. Treasuries to direct loans and private securities and due to the increase in its liabilities relative to its capital. For example, at the end of 2008, the Fed's capital would be depleted if its realized net losses were equal in value to 1.9% of its holdings of financial assets (U.S. Treasuries, loans, and other private securities).

Thus, any potential losses on loans to the Fed would not involve taxpayer dollars flowing to the Fed unless the losses exceeded the sum of its other earnings and its capital and the Treasury decided it did not want the Fed to operate as technically insolvent. However, even if the losses did not result in insolvency, any losses could result in a smaller remittance of earnings to the Treasury than would have occurred had the Fed not made the loans. Therefore, the ultimate cost to the government is the same whether loans to the financial sector are made through the Fed or the Treasury. The Fed has reported to Congress that it does not expect there to be losses on any of the actions it has undertaken under its emergency authorities (including the Maiden Lane LLCs, two of which had unrealized capital losses at the end of 2009), but it has not provided details as to how it reached that conclusion. Some analysts are concerned that a future increase in interest rates could result in losses on the Fed's asset holdings, but these losses would be realized only if the Fed were forced to sell those assets.[77]

To date, all of the Fed's lending programs have earned income for the Fed, except for Maiden Lanes I and II, whose assets have accrued unrealized capital losses.[78] In 2009, the

Fed's loan programs earned $5.5 billion, the Maiden Lane assets had fallen in value by a combined $2.3 billion, and the Fed's other assets had earned $48.8 billion, as seen in **Table 3**. (The Maiden Lane losses will not be realized until the assets are sold, and the Fed has stated that it intends to hold the assets long term.) In the aggregate, the Fed earned higher profits and increased its remittances to the Treasury.

The Fed could generate positive income from its programs but still operate those programs at a subsidy to the recipients. Subsidies would occur when the interest rates charged for loans or prices paid for assets are not high enough to fully compensate for the risks borne by the Fed in undertaking those transactions. In other words, the subsidy is equal to the difference between the price or interest rate the Fed received and what could have been received if the transaction had been made privately. CBO has estimated subsidies for each of the Fed's emergency programs, presented in **Table 3**.[79] In evaluating the program, that subsidy would need to be compared with the benefits to the broader economy from the program, which CBO does not attempt to do. CBO estimated that lending programs with high collateral requirements and done on a recourse basis (Term Auction Facility, repurchase agreements, central bank currency swaps, Primary Dealer Credit Facility, Term Securities Lending Facility) generated no subsidies. CBO also concluded that all asset purchases involved no subsidy, either because the purchases were made in the open market (e.g., purchases of Treasury and GSE-related securities) or because the Fed reported that purchases were made at market value (e.g., the Maiden Lane assets). The assumption that Maiden Lane assets were bought at prevailing market prices can be questioned because the rationale for the Fed's purchase was that these assets could not be sold in private markets at the time. CBO finds subsidies for loan facilities without recourse (the two commercial paper facilities and TALF) and for special assistance to systemically significant firms (AIG, Citigroup, and Bank of America). In total, CBO estimates that the Fed's emergency actions were done at a subsidy of $21 billion. This estimate would likely be smaller if re-estimated today, based on current information. For example, CBO finds a subsidy of $13 billion for TALF because TALF was expected to make loans of $200 billion; in reality, loans peaked at $48 billion. CBO also estimates subsidies on the asset guarantees to Citigroup and Bank of America, although those programs were ended with payments to the government and no payouts by the government.

Table 3. Estimated Subsidies and Earnings by Program (billions of Dollars).

Program/Transaction	Estimated Subsidy at Inception	2009 Earnings	2009 Capital Gains or Losses
Treasury Securities	0	22.9	0
GSE Debt/MBS	0	22.5	0.9
Central Bank Liquidity Swaps	Negative subsidy	2.2	0
Discount Window	0	0.2	n/a
Term Auction Facility	0	0.8	n/a
Primary Dealer Credit Facility	0	<0.1	n/a
TALF	13	0.4	n/a
Commercial Paper	4	4.3	4.7
Loan to AIG	2	4.0	n/a
Maiden Lane I (Bear Stearns)	0	1.3	-2.2

Table 3. (Continued)

Program/Transaction	Estimated Subsidy at Inception	2009 Earnings	2009 Capital Gains or Losses
Maiden Lane II (AIG)	0	0.4	-0.1
Maiden Lane III (AIG)	0	0.3	0
Citigroup asset guarantee	2	0.3	n/a
Bank of America asset guarantee	1	0.1	n/a
Total	21	52.1[a]	n/a

Source: Estimated subsidies from Congressional Budget Office, *The Budgetary Impact and Subsidy Costs of the Federal Reserve's Actions During the Financial Crisis*, May 2010. Earnings from Federal Reserve, *Monthly Report on Credit and Liquidity Programs and the Balance Sheet*, Tables 27-29, April 2010.

Notes: Maiden Lane capital gains or losses are those attributable to Fed, not overall. For Maiden Lanes, interest on loans from Fed are added back to earnings when Federal Reserve System's balance sheet is consolidated. CBO subsidies were calculated based on economic conditions and projections of program use at the time of inception. Negative subsidy for central bank liquidity swaps means that the Fed, according to CBO, offered the swaps on less favorable terms than foreign central banks could have received in the marketplace.

a. Net income.

Although the Fed has taken steps to minimize the risk that recent activities will result in losses, Members of Congress have raised the question of whether taxpayers should be exposed to additional fiscal risks without congressional approval, particularly because some of the Fed's actions have similarities to those authorized under TARP. H.R. 4173 requires the Fed to issue policies and procedures for emergency lending that, among other things,

- ensure that "the security for emergency loans is sufficient to protect taxpayers from losses" by assigning a lendable value to collateral that is "consistent with sound risk management practices;"[80] and
- prohibit lending to borrowers that are insolvent or establishing a lending program or facility for the purpose of helping a single and specific company to avoid bankruptcy.

How Much Can the Fed's Balance Sheet Expand? Will the Fed Run Out of Money?

As a result of the Fed's new facilities and activities, its balance sheet has increased significantly, from $874 billion on August 1, 2007, a date shortly before the financial system first experienced turmoil, to $2,312 billion at its peak on December 17, 2008, an increase of 165%. **Table 4** shows the increase in the balance sheet by category over that period. Since the size of the balance sheet peaked in December 2008, the overall size of the balance sheet has remained relatively steady, but there have been large changes in the composition of the balance sheet. For example, there has been a significant increase in the Fed's holdings of mortgage backed securities and GSE debt, and a significant decrease in lending to primary dealers, holdings of commercial paper, and swaps with central banks. The Fed also began lending through the TALF in March 2009.

When the Fed makes loans or purchases assets, the asset side of its balance sheet expands; this must be matched by an increase in its liabilities. As direct loans from the Fed multiplied, some observers questioned at what point the Fed's lending power will be exhausted. The Fed cannot "run out of money" to buy assets and extend loans because it controls its liabilities, the monetary base (federal reserve notes and bank reserves), through which it expands or contracts the amount of money outstanding. There are no statutory limits on the size of the money supply or currency outstanding and, thus, how much it can loan; the ultimate constraint on the Fed's willingness to expand the monetary base in order to expand its activities comes from the part of its congressional mandate requiring stable prices (i.e., a low and stable rate of price inflation.) If the Fed allows the money supply to grow too rapidly, then price inflation will become uncomfortably high (discussed in the section below on "Stagflation?").

Sterilization of Lending before September 2008

Earlier in the financial crisis, the Fed was concerned about inflation rising. For example, in the 12 months ending in August 2008, inflation (as measured by the consumer price index) had risen to 5.4%—significantly higher than the Fed's self-identified "comfort zone." To address that concern, the Fed initially sought to keep its balance sheet from growing in order to offset the effects of its activities on the money supply. One way to keep its balance sheet from growing would be by reducing its other assets. For example, it could "sterilize" its new loans or asset purchases through contractionary open market operations, namely, the sale of Treasury securities. In practice, before September 2008, the Fed kept the monetary base relatively constant by selling enough Treasury securities to offset the additional loans it made. (When the Fed sells Treasury securities, it removes the money it receives in the sale from circulation.) Thus, as loans outstanding rose, the Fed's holdings of Treasury securities initially declined, by $340 billion through December 17, 2008. In September 2007, 88% of its assets were Treasury securities held outright and less than 1% were loans to the financial system. On December 17, 2008, 28% of its assets were Treasury securities, 32% were loans, 17% were private securities (mostly commercial paper), and 25% were currency swaps with foreign central banks.

If sterilization through the sale of Treasury securities had continued, the Fed would eventually have held too few Treasury securities to be able to conduct open market operations.[81] As seen in **Table 4**, the overall increase in the Fed's balance sheet at its peak was $1.4 trillion, more than the Treasury securities it held before the crisis started ($816 billion) or in September 2008 ($475 billion).

The Treasury announced the Supplementary Financing Program on September 17, 2008 as an alternative method for the Fed to increase its assistance to the financial sector without increasing the amount of money in circulation.[82] Under this program, the Treasury has temporarily auctioned more new securities than it needs to finance government operations and deposited the proceeds at the Fed. (The increase in the money supply does not affect inflation because the money received by the Treasury is held at the Fed and not allowed to circulate in the economy.) Ultimately, the program will not affect the Treasury's fiscal position, however, because it will increase the profits of the Fed, which are then remitted to the Treasury. By December 17, 2008, the Treasury had borrowed and increased its deposits at the Fed by $475 billion. From January to September 2009, Treasury deposits were between $200 billion and $300 billion, and were no longer large enough to offset the growth in the asset side of the

Fed's balance sheet. Congress authorized this borrowing only indirectly by raising the statutory debt limit, in P.L. 110-343 and other subsequent legislation. In late 2009, Treasury withdrew its supplementary deposits at the Fed in order to finance government spending as the debt approached the statutory limit. Once the debt limit was increased, the Treasury increased its deposits back to around $200 billion.

The fact that the Fed has been "sterilizing" the stimulative effects of its loans on the money supply (entirely until September 2008, and partially after then) limits the effects of those loans on financial conditions. In essence, the Fed has two methods for providing the financial system with liquidity—open market operations or direct loans. The Fed increased the role of direct loans to directly meet individual financial institutions' liquidity needs. But the Fed was offsetting the effects of the direct loans on the money supply to meet its goals for inflation. Thus, the loans did not provide additional overall monetary stimulus to the economy when sterilized. Since the Fed was sterilizing the loans because of its concerns with inflation, the utility of sterilization was fundamentally a question of whether the Fed had achieved the proper balance between stabilizing the financial sector and providing price stability, two topics that are discussed below.

Quantitative Easing and Balance Sheet Growth since September 2008

As commodity prices fell later in 2008, the inflation rate also fell. The Fed became less concerned about inflation rising, and more concerned about the further deterioration in financial and economic conditions. After September 2008, the Fed further increased its direct assistance to the financial system, but no longer fully sterilized those activities. As a result, the Fed's balance sheet and the monetary base have expanded rapidly, as demonstrated in **Table 4**. The monetary base doubled from August to December 2008—an unprecedented rise.[83] Because this increase went beyond what was needed to target the federal funds rate, it has been referred to as "quantitative easing." Normally, this would trigger a rapid increase in inflation. The main force preventing such an increase is the rapid increase in excess bank reserves held at the Fed during that period. Bank reserves increased from $44 billion in August 2008 to $802 billion on December 17, 2008, as banks preferred to hold the additional reserves created by the Fed's actions in order to shore up their balance sheets to avoid runs.

In normal financial conditions, banks would lend out money they received from the Fed, and through a process referred to by economists as the "money multiplier," a $1 increase in the monetary base would lead to a much larger increase in the overall money supply. But if banks hold the money received from the Fed in bank reserves instead of lending it out, the money multiplier process will not occur, so the growth in the overall money supply will be smaller. Data from the Fed show that almost all of the increase in reserves has been through excess reserves, rather than required reserves, which is consistent with banks holding most of the increase in reserves instead of lending them out. Thus, the large increase in the monetary base since September 2008 has not been matched by a corresponding increase in the overall money supply.

Initially, the balance sheet grew because of high private demand for borrowing from the Fed, and asset purchases were not needed. But between the weeks of December 17, 2008, and March 25, 2009, the Fed's direct lending to the financial sector decreased from a weekly average of $976 billion to $848 billion. The pattern of decline was steady over that period, and presumably stemmed from the fact that as financial conditions improved, there was less financial sector demand for Fed lending. With declining loan balances, the balance sheet would have shrunk, unless other assets were added to offset the fall in direct lending.

Table 4. Changes in the Fed's Balance Sheet from August 1, 2007, to Peak on December 17, 2008 Billions of Dollars.

Assets		Liabilities and Capital	
Treasury Securities[a]	-$340	Federal Reserve Notes	+$64
MBS/GSE Debt	+$18[b]	Bank Reserves at Fed	+$785
Lending to Banks	+$538	Treasury Cash Deposits at Fed	+$475
Lending to Primary Dealers	+$47[b]	Other	+$103
Lending to/Assets Purchased for AIG	+$82[b]		
Lending for/Purchase of Commercial Paper	+$346[b]		
Assets Purchased from Bear Stearns	+$27[b]		
Swaps with Foreign Central Banks	+$572[b]	Total Liabilities	+$1,427
Other	+$148	Capital	+$11
Total Assets	**+$1,438**	**Total Liabilities and Capital**	**+$1,438**

Source: CRS calculations based on Federal Reserve Board of Governors, "Factors Affecting Reserve Balances," Data Release H.4.1, Tables 1 and 7, various dates.

Notes: GSE = government sponsored enterprise, MBS = mortgage-backed securities, ABS = asset backed securities, AIG = American International Group. See text for details.

a. Includes +$176 billion of Treasury securities temporarily swapped for private securities with Primary Dealers.

b. Item equaled zero in August 2007.

Table 5. Federal Reserve Balance Sheet, June 30, 2010 Billions of Dollars.

Assets		Liabilities and Capital	
Treasury Securities[a]	777	Federal Reserve Notes	904
MBS/GSE Debt[a]	1,283	Bank Reserves at Fed	973
Lending to Banks	1	Treasury Cash Deposits at Fed	288
Lending to Primary Dealers	0	Other	113
Lending to/Assets Purchased for AIG	90		
Lending for/Purchase of Commercial Paper	0		
Lending for/Purchase of ABS (TALF)	43		
Assets Purchased from Bear Stearns	28		
Swaps with Foreign Central Banks	1	Total Liabilities	2,278
Other	111	Capital	56
Total Assets	**2,334**	**Total Liabilities and Capital**	**2,334**

Source: CRS calculations based on Federal Reserve Board of Governors, "Factors Affecting Reserve Balances," Data Release H.4.1, Tables 1 and 7, July 1, 2010.

Notes: GSE = government sponsored enterprise, MBS = mortgage-backed securities, ABS = asset backed securities, AIG = American International Group, TALF = Term Asset-Backed Securities Lending Facility. Amounts may not add due to rounding. See text for details.

a. Includes a $14 billion of securities temporarily swapped for private securities with Primary Dealers.

On March 18, 2009, the Fed announced a commitment to purchase $300 billion of Treasury securities, $200 billion of Agency debt (later revised to $175 billion), and $1.25 trillion of Agency mortgage-backed securities. Since then, direct lending has continued to gradually decline, while the Fed's holdings of Treasury and Agency securities have steadily increased, as seen in Table 5. The Fed's planned purchases of Treasury securities were completed by the fall of 2009 and planned Agency purchases were completed by the spring of 2010. By April 2010, direct lending outside of TALF and AIG was modest. Because other assets on the Fed's balance sheet (most notably, liquidity swaps with foreign central banks) have also declined over that period, the net result of these purchases has been to keep the overall size of the balance sheet relatively constant. Thus, the Fed's asset purchases have prevented liquidity from being removed from the financial system as Fed lending fell.[84] But since the fall in lending was spurred by less demand among financial institutions, critics question if the level of liquidity needed in the crisis is still needed today.

Purchases of Treasury securities could also stimulate the economy if private interest rates fall in response; a similar effect could occur with purchases of MBS, although those purchases should also more directly stimulate residential investment by reducing mortgage rates. Whether these purchases were more stimulative than the direct lending they replaced depends on their relative effects on financial conditions and interest rates.

Future Concerns

Once the financial outlook improves, banks may decide to use their reserve holdings to rapidly increase their lending. At that point, if the Fed found itself fighting inflationary pressures, it would have to find a way to prevent banks from lending those reserves in order to prevent a rapid increase in the money supply.[85] The most straightforward method to achieve this would be to withdraw those reserves from the banking system, which would require the Fed to reduce both its assets and liabilities through asset sales. Some of the Fed's outstanding assets can be sold relatively quickly in theory, although there could be political resistance in reality. By April 2010, the Fed's balance sheet consisted predominantly of securities that could be sold in secondary markets. But the Fed has pledged to hold these assets long term. Given the Fed's concerns about the fragility of housing markets, it is not clear how these holdings could be reduced quickly if the Fed became concerned about rising inflation. (About $100 billion to $200 billion per year could be reduced by not replacing maturing assets, according to Chairman Bernanke.[86])

Another option would be to give banks incentives not to lend out reserves by raising the interest rate that the Fed pays on reserves, although it remains to be seen how interest-sensitive bank reserves are.[87] To better prevent these reserves from being lent out if necessary, the Fed began offering "term deposits" with a one to six month maturity for bank reserves. The interest rate on these term deposits would be set through auction; banks would presumably be willing to bid for term deposits only if the interest rate exceeded the rate paid by the Fed on normal reserves.

The Fed could also attempt to reduce liquidity by lending its assets out through "reverse repos." This would change the composition of liabilities on the Fed's balance sheet, replacing Federal Reserve notes or bank reserves with reverse repos. It is unlikely that reverse repos operations could be large enough to remove most of the new liquidity, however.[88]

Cash balances held at the Fed through the Treasury Supplemental Financing Program could also be used to tie up liquidity, but the size of this program is constrained by the statutory debt limit (since Treasury needs to borrow to acquire cash), and would be insufficient to significantly reduce liquidity without a large increase in the debt limit.

With an eye to the potential long-run inflationary effects of the growth in the Fed's balance sheet, the Fed and Treasury announced in March 2009 that they would seek "legislative action to provide additional tools the Federal Reserve can use to sterilize the effects of its lending or securities purchases on the supply of bank reserves." Many analysts interpreted this statement to express the desire for the Fed to gain authority to issue its own bonds. Returning to the balance sheet in **Table 4**, the Fed must match an increase in assets with an increase in liabilities. The only liability it can currently issue are federal reserve notes that increase the monetary base. If the Fed were granted new authority to issue bonds, they could then expand their liabilities without increasing the monetary base and increasing inflationary pressures.[89] Then, there would no longer be any statutory limit or check on the Fed's ability to directly allocate credit, provided it met the broad guidelines of Section 13(3). To date, legislation to allow the Fed to do so has not been considered.

With a federal funds rate of zero, unsterilized purchases of long-term assets could help further stimulate the economy by adding needed liquidity to the financial system reducing long-term interest rates (flattening the yield curve). But once the Fed decides to start raising rates, economic theory casts some doubt on the economic usefulness of maintaining a large balance sheet, but sterilizing its effects on the economy by paying interest on reserves, reverse repos, the Treasury Supplemental Program, or issuing Fed bonds. The large balance sheet has no positive effect on liquidity if it is offset by any of these actions that drain liquidity from the economy. And if investors have rational expectations, it is not clear how a large balance sheet could flatten the yield curve in the face of sterilization since the long end of the yield curve should be determined primarily by expectations of future interest rates, and sterilized purchases of assets in the present should not change those expectations, all else equal. Previous experience suggests that sterilized attempts to flatten the yield curve have failed to stimulate the economy. For example, a study by Ben Bernanke (before he was Fed Chairman) and other economists concluded that a similar policy in the 1960s called "Operation Twist" is "widely viewed today as having been a failure."[90]

Is the Fed Monetizing the Budget Deficit?

Some commentators have interpreted the Fed's decision to make large scale purchases of Treasury securities as a signal that the Fed intends to "monetize the federal deficit," which is projected this fiscal year to reach its highest share of GDP since World War II. Monetizing the deficit occurs when the budget deficit is financed by money creation rather than by selling bonds to private investors. Hyperinflation in foreign countries has consistently resulted from governments' decisions to monetize large deficits.

According to this definition, the deficit has not been monetized. Section 14 of the Federal Reserve Act legally forbids the Fed from buying newly issued securities directly from the Treasury, and all Treasury securities purchased by the Fed to date have been purchased on the secondary market, from private investors.[91] Moreover, the size of the Fed's purchases of Treasury securities thus far is small relative to the overall deficit, which was $1.4 trillion in 2009. The Fed has announced and completed purchases of $300 billion thus far, although that amount can be altered at its discretion.

Nonetheless, the effect of the Fed's purchase of Treasury securities on the federal budget is similar regardless of whether the Fed buys the securities on the secondary market or directly from Treasury. When the Fed holds Treasury securities, Treasury must pay interest to the Fed, just as it would pay interest to a private investor. These interest payments, after expenses, become profits to the Fed. The Fed, in turn, remits about 95% of its profits to the Treasury, where they are added to general revenues.[92] In essence, the Fed has made an interest-free loan to the Treasury, because almost all of the interest paid by Treasury to the Fed is subsequently sent back to Treasury.

The Fed could increase its profits and remittances to Treasury by printing more money to purchase more Treasury bonds (or any other asset). The Fed's profits are the incidental side effect of its open market operations in pursuit of its statutory mandate (to keep prices stable and unemployment low). If the Fed chose instead to buy assets with a goal of increasing its profits and remittances, it would be unlikely to meet its statutory mandate.

Limits on the Fed's Ability to Address Problems in the Financial Sector

The Fed's actions since 2007 have been primarily focused on restoring liquidity to the financial system—lending to financial firms to convert their illiquid assets into cash or U.S. Treasury securities. But as financial conditions deteriorated in spite of increasing Fed intervention, it became apparent that the problems facing financial firms were not exclusively related to liquidity.

The crux of the firms' problem in the fall of 2008 stemmed from the large losses on some of their assets, particularly mortgage-related assets.[93] This caused a number of problems for the firms related to *capital adequacy*, which is the difference between the value of their assets and the value of their liabilities. First, losses and write-downs associated with those assets have reduced the firms' existing capital. Second, in the current environment, investors and creditors are demanding that firms hold more capital relative to assets than before so that firms can better withstand any future losses.

Third, at the peak of the crisis, firms were unable to raise enough new capital. Firms can raise new capital through retained earnings, which had been greatly reduced for many firms by the poor performance of their assets, or by issuing new capital (equity) and selling it to new investors. But during the crisis, investors were reluctant to inject new capital into struggling firms. Part of the explanation for this is that losses made the firms less profitable. But another part of the reason was that investors feared that there would be further losses in the future that would reduce the value of their investment, and perhaps even cause the firm to become insolvent. Uncertainty about future losses was partly caused by the opacity surrounding the assets that have been declining in value, which makes it hard for investors to determine which assets remain overvalued and which are undervalued. The result for companies such as Bear Stearns, Lehman Brothers, AIG, Washington Mutual, and Wachovia was a downward spiral in their stock price, which had two self-reinforcing characteristics. First, there was little demand for existing stock since its worth would either have been diluted by new capital (raised privately or through government intervention) or lost in insolvency. Second, new capital could not be attracted because the fall in stock value had left the market capitalization of the firms so low. If a firm's capital is completely depleted, there is no longer a buffer between its assets and liabilities, and it becomes insolvent. In 2009, financial firms were again able to issue capital to private investors, and many did so successfully.

Many large financial firms, including the firms that have failed, are heavily dependent on short-term borrowing to meet their current obligations. As financial conditions worsened, some of the firms that had the problems described above had problems accessing short-term borrowing markets that in normal conditions could be taken for granted. In an atmosphere where creditors cannot perceive which firms have insufficient capital, they become unwilling to lend for even short intervals. This is the essence of the *liquidity* problem—although the firms' assets may exceed their liabilities, without access to short-term borrowing, the firm cannot meet its current obligations because it cannot convert its assets into cash quickly enough (at least not if it wishes to avoid "fire sale" prices).

The Fed has always been the "lender of last resort" in order for banks to avoid liquidity problems during financial turmoil. To borrow from the Fed, a financial firm must post collateral. In essence, this allows the firm to temporarily convert its illiquid assets into cash, enabling the firm to meet its short-term obligations without sacrificing its assets. The Fed has always lent to commercial banks (depository institutions) through the discount window. As discussed above, it has extended liquidity to non-bank financial firms since 2008 through new lending facilities.

Borrowing from the Fed increases liquidity but it does not change a firm's capital buffer since it now has a liability outstanding to the Fed. So borrowing from the Fed cannot solve the problems of undercapitalization that some firms faced. Indeed, the Fed will generally not lend to firms that are not creditworthy because it wants to provide liquidity only to firms that are solvent, and thus able to repay.[94]

H.R. 1424, which was signed into law on October 3, 2008 (P.L. 110-343), created the Troubled Asset Relief Program. The Treasury initially used TARP funds to address the capital adequacy problem directly by providing $250 billion in capital to banks directly through preferred share purchases by TARP.[95]

Some have asked whether there is any way the Fed could have addressed the financial firms' capital adequacy problems. All of the Fed's standing lending facilities involve collateralized lending, and as discussed above, any program involving collateralized lending would not change a firm's capital position. According to one legal analysis, there is no express statutory authority for the Fed to purchase corporate bonds, mortgages, or equity.[96] But the Fed's assistance through the three Maiden Lane LLCs it has created has some similarities to TARP. In the case of Bear Stearns, the Fed created a limited liability corporation called Maiden Lane I, and lent Maiden Lane $28.82 billion. Maiden Lane I used the proceeds of that loan and another loan from JPMorgan Chase to purchase mortgage-related assets from Bear Stearns. (A similar arrangement with AIG led to the creation of Maiden Lane II and Maiden Lane III.) Thus, although the Fed created and controlled the Maiden Lanes, the assets were purchased and held by the Maiden Lanes, not the Fed. The Fed plans to hold the Maiden Lane assets until markets recover, and then sell the assets to repay its loans. The Maiden Lanes were created under the Fed's Section 13(3) emergency authority.[97] H.R. 4173 forbids "a program or facility that is structured to remove assets from the balance sheet of a single and specific company."

The Fed was presumably granted broad emergency powers under Section 13(3) so that it had the flexibility to deal with unforeseen circumstances. Nonetheless, too broad of a reading of its powers could provoke displeasure in Congress or legal challenges. Creating TARP within the Treasury through legislation rather than the Fed through emergency powers avoided the argument of whether such a program extended beyond the Fed's intended role.

Lender of Last Resort, Systemic Risk, and Moral Hazard

Since its early days, one of the Fed's main roles has been to act as a lender of last resort to the banking system when private sources of credit become unavailable. It does so by lending through the discount window and its new lending facilities. The lender of last resort function can be seen from the perspective of an individual institution or the financial system as a whole. From the perspective of the individual institution, discount window lending is meant to provide funds to institutions that are illiquid (cannot meet current obligations out of current cash flow) but still solvent (assets exceed liabilities) when they cannot access funds from the private market. Discount window lending was unable to end bank runs, however—bank runs did not cease until the creation of federal deposit insurance. The experience of the Great Depression suggested that bank runs placed intolerably high costs on the financial system as a whole, as they led to widespread bank failures.[98] Fed lending is not meant to help insolvent institutions, with one exception explained below.

Access to Fed lending facilities and deposit insurance creates *moral hazard* for financial institutions—they can take on more risk than the market would otherwise permit because of the government safety net. To limit moral hazard, institutions with depository insurance and access to the discount window are subject to a safety and soundness regulatory regime that includes capital requirements, reserve requirements, bank examinations, and so on.

The exception to the rule that insolvent institutions cannot access Fed lending facilities is when the institution is deemed "too big to fail." Institutions that are too big to fail are ones that are deemed to be big enough that their failure could create *systemic risk*, the risk that the financial system as a whole would cease to function smoothly.[99] For example, failure could lead to systemic instability through "contagion" effects where the losses to creditors and counterparties imposed by the bankruptcy system drove those creditors and counterparties into insolvency. A systemic risk episode could impose heavy costs on the overall economy, as the bank panics of the Great Depression demonstrated. Although too big to fail institutions are not offered explicit guarantees, it can be argued that they have implicit guarantees since the government would not be willing to allow a systemic risk episode. This accentuates the moral hazard problem described above. There is no official governmental classification of which financial institutions are too big to fail, presumably since maintaining uncertainty over which institutions are too big to fail could help reduce the moral hazard problem. But the lack of official designation arguably creates a vacuum in terms of policy preparedness. (Making the problem more complex, as one report described the situation, "Officials grimly concluded that while Bear Stearns isn't too big to fail, it was too interconnected to be allowed to fail in just one day." It is unclear how to judge which institutions are too interconnected to fail.)[100]

As the cases of Bear Stearns, Fannie Mae and Freddie Mac, and AIG illustrate, some of the modern-day financial institutions that are too big to fail are not depository institutions that fall under the strict regulatory umbrella that accompanies membership in the Federal Reserve system. Nevertheless, all received direct or indirect assistance from the Fed. This highlights the shift in financial activity from a bank-dominated financial system at the time of the Fed's creation to a system whose health now depends on many types of institutions. The Fed was set up to be a lender of last resort to only the banking system. In the current crisis, it has been able to extend its lender of last resort functions to non-bank financial institutions only because of its Section 13(3) emergency powers. A policy issue going forward is whether the extension of these functions should be made permanent, and if so, what types of regulatory safeguards should accompany it. Because Section 13(3) of the Federal Reserve Act is intended for responding to unanticipated emergencies, it grants authority that is broader and more open-ended than the Fed's normal authority.

It is possible that part of the reason these institutions failed is because they took on excessive risks in the belief that they were too big to fail. Although that theory can be debated, it is clearer that the precedent of the Fed's role in the Bear Stearns acquisition may strengthen the perception of other institutions and investors that any financial firm, regardless of whether it is a depository institution, will be bailed out in the future if it is too big to fail, or merely too interconnected to fail. If so, it could be argued that the Bear Stearns episode may have increased moral hazard going forward. The government's decision not to intervene to prevent the failure of the investment bank Lehman Brothers in September 2008, but to subsequently assist AIG, Citigroup, and Bank of America may have created further market uncertainty regarding which institutions the government views as too big to fail. Lehman Brothers was larger than Bear Stearns and involved in similar business activities. Others have argued that the failure of Lehman Brothers set off a wave of unrest in money markets (see above), interbank lending markets, and the market for credit default swaps that would make the government unlikely to allow any large institution to fail in the future.[101]

The government assistance to Bear Stearns, Fannie Mae and Freddie Mac, and AIG all include clauses that significantly reduced the value of existing shareholder equity. This was partly justified in terms of reducing moral hazard—investors would be reluctant to buy equity in too big to fail companies that were taking excessive risks if the government demanded a reduction in existing shareholder value. But government assistance in all of these cases made creditors and other counterparties whole. In these cases, the moral hazard problem manifests itself in a willingness of creditors to lend to, and counterparties to transact with, a firm they know to be taking excessive risks, thereby potentially allowing the firm to take more risks. More recent government assistance to Citigroup and Bank of America was provided without similar measures to replace management or dilute shareholders. (Warrants to purchase some common stock were issued but have not yet been exercised.) Market participants may view this decision as a signal that the government is no longer placing emphasis on avoiding moral hazard.

The current situation raises three broad points about systemic risk. First, risk is at the foundation of all financial intermediation. Policymakers may wish to curb excessive risk taking when it leads to systemic risk, but too little financial risk would also be counterproductive for the economy. (Indeed, some would argue that part of the underlying problem for the financial system as a whole at present is that investors are currently too risk averse.) Second, many analysts have argued that part of the reason that so much financial intermediation has left the commercial banking system is to avoid the costs of regulation.[102] This point applies to future regulatory changes as well. An attempt to increase regulation on banks could lead more business to move to hedge funds, for example. Third, financial markets have become significantly more complex and fast-moving in recent years. Many of the financial instruments with which Bear Stearns, Lehman Brothers, and AIG were involved did not exist until recently. For regulation to be effective in this environment, it faces the challenge of trying to keep up with innovation. If used prudently, many of these innovations can reduce risk for individual investors. Yet the Bear Stearns example implies that innovation may also lead to more interconnectivity, which increases systemic risk.

Going forward, policymakers must determine whether new regulation is needed to limit moral hazard because there may be no credible way to maintain a policy that prohibits the rescue of future institutions that are too big to fail even if such a policy were desired.

The financial crisis has led to the passage of comprehensive regulatory reform in the House and Senate that address the "too big to fail" problem and the Fed's role as a regulator and lender of last resort.

Oversight, Transparency, and Disclosure of Emergency Programs

Because profits and losses borne by the Fed ultimately get passed on to taxpayers (see "Cost to the Treasury"), some Members of Congress have argued that more information about the Fed's emergency activities should be made available to the public. The Fed has not been subject to many of the oversight and reporting requirements applied to the TARP, although the amount of direct assistance outstanding from the Fed at its peak exceeded the authorized size of TARP.

Nonetheless, the Fed has publicly released a significant amount of information on its emergency actions. The Fed's financial statements are published weekly and audited by private sector auditors, with the results published in the Fed's annual report. The Fed has provided detailed information to the public on the general terms and eligibility of its borrowers and collateral by class for each crisis-response program.[103] It has also provided a rationale for why each crisis program has been created, and an explanation of the goals the program is meant to accomplish. The Emergency Economic Stabilization Act (P.L. 110-343) requires the Fed to report to the House Financial Services Committee and the Senate Banking, Housing, and Urban Affairs Committee on its justification for exercising Section 13(3), the terms of the assistance provided, and regular updates on the status of the loan. Beginning in June 2009, the Fed began releasing a monthly report that listed the number of and concentration among borrowers by type, the value and creditworthiness of collateral held by type, and the interest income earned for each of its facilities.[104] Contracts with private vendors to purchase or manage assets are also posted on the New York Fed's website.

But the Fed has kept confidential the identity of the borrowers from its facilities, the collateral posted in specific transactions, the terms of specific transactions, and the results of specific transactions (i.e., whether they resulted in profits or losses).[105] As historical precedent, the Fed has had a longstanding policy of keeping the identity of banks that borrow from its discount window confidential. Those calling for more disclosure note that the new Fed programs place the Fed in a more expansive role and are potentially riskier than the discount window, and, unlike the discount window, were not explicitly endorsed by legislation (many were authorized under its emergency authority).

The Fed has argued that allowing the public to know which firms are accessing its facilities could undermine investor confidence in the institutions receiving aid because of a perception that recipients were weak or unsound. A loss of investor confidence could potentially lead to destabilizing runs on the institution's deposits, debt, or equity. If institutions feared that this would occur, the Fed argues, then the institutions would be wary of participating in the Fed's programs, which, in the aggregate, would retard economic recovery. A historical example supporting the Fed's argument would be the Reconstruction Finance Corporation (RFC) in the Great Depression. When the RFC publicized to which banks it had given loans, those banks typically experienced depositor runs.[106] A more recent example provides mixed evidence—disclosure of TARP fund recipients. At first, TARP funds were widely disbursed, and recipients included all the major banks. At that point, there was no perceived stigma to TARP participation. More recently, many banks have repaid TARP shares at the first opportunity, and remaining participants have expressed concern that if they did not repay soon, investors would perceive them as weak. Arguments about investor confidence are arguably less compelling when applied to publicly disclosing collateral held by the Fed.

There are several different approaches to expanding disclosure or oversight:

- Congress could remove the Government Accountability Office's (GAO's) restrictions on conducting investigations of the Fed for Congress. While GAO has had longstanding authority to audit the Fed's non-monetary policy functions,[107] the Federal Banking Agency Audit Act of 1978 (31 USC 714(b)) restricts GAO from auditing certain Fed activities: (1) transactions with foreign central banks or governments; (2) "deliberations, decisions, or actions on monetary matters, including discount window operations, reserves of member banks, securities credit, interest on deposits, and open market operations;" and (3) "transactions made under the direction of the Federal Open Market Committee."[108] While the act does not specifically mention activities taken under the Fed's emergency authority, those activities have been interpreted as falling under the restrictions. Also included in the Federal Banking Audit Act of 1978 are restrictions on GAO disclosure of confidential information about the financial firms subject to the Fed's policies. Thus, if audit restrictions were removed but these disclosure restrictions remained in place, GAO audits would not necessarily accomplish some policymakers' goal of disclosing the identities of borrowers from Fed lending facilities. S. 896, which was signed into law on May 20, 2009 (P.L. 111-22), allows GAO audits of "any action taken by the Board under ... Section 13(3) of the Federal Reserve Act with respect to a single and specific partnership or corporation." This would allow GAO audits of the Maiden Lane facilities and the asset guarantees of Citigroup and Bank of America, but would maintain audit restrictions on non-emergency activities and broadly-accessed emergency lending facilities, such as the Primary Dealer Credit Facility or the commercial paper facilities. In performing the audit under S. 896, GAO must maintain the confidentiality of the private documents it accesses, but cannot withhold any information requested by Members of Congress on the committees of jurisdiction. H.R. 4173 allows GAO to audit emergency actions, discount window lending, and open market operations for operational integrity, accounting financial reporting, internal controls, collateral policies, favoritism, and third-party contracting policies. With the exception of the Maiden Lane facilities, GAO would be prohibited from releasing confidential information to Congress or the public about the transactions until the information was released by the Fed. H.R. 4173 also requires a GAO audit, according to the criteria listed above, of all lending between December 2007 and the date of enactment. It also requires a separate GAO audit to determine whether the selection of Federal Reserve regional bank presidents meets the criteria under Section 4 of the Federal Reserve Act, whether there are actual or potential conflicts of interest created by member banks choosing Fed regional bank directors, to examine the role regional banks played in the Fed's response to the crisis, and to propose reforms to regional bank governance.

- Congress could require the Fed to disclose more information on the identities of borrowers, the collateral accepted, or the terms and results of transactions. Congress requires the Fed to make some general policy reports, but does not typically require the Fed to disclose this type of specific information. Indeed, much of the information about monetary policy that the Fed currently makes public is done so on a voluntarily basis. H.R. 4173 requires the Fed to disclose the identities of borrowers and terms of borrowing to the committees of jurisdiction within seven days of a loan and allows for the information to be kept confidential if desired. It requires that the identities of borrowers and terms of borrowing be released to the public with up to a two year delay for the discount window and a one year delay after a facility has been terminated for other lending. It requires that the identities of counterparties and terms of sale be released to the public with up to a two year delay for open market operations. It requires that the identities of borrowers and borrowing terms be released to the public by December 1, 2010, for actions taken during the financial crisis.
- Congress could create specific oversight boards or committees that focus on the Federal Reserve. Currently, regular congressional oversight of the Fed is done at a general level through semi-annual hearings with the House Financial Services Committee and the Senate Banking, Housing, and Urban Affairs Committee, as well as ad hoc hearings on more focused topics. There is no routine, specific oversight of the Fed's crisis-response actions, and no group with monetary policy expertise tasked with evaluating the Fed's actions for Congress.

Greater disclosure and outside evaluation could potentially help Congress perform its oversight duties more effectively. The main argument against increasing Fed oversight would be that it could be perceived to reduce the Fed's operational independence from Congress. Chairman Bernanke has argued that "The general repeal of (the audit) exemption would serve only to increase the perceived influence of Congress on monetary policy decisions, which would undermine the confidence the public and the markets have in the Fed."[109] Most economists believe that the Fed's independence to carry out day-to-day decisions about monetary policy without congressional input strengthens the Fed's credibility in the eyes of the private sector that it will follow policies that maximize price and economic stability. Greater credibility is perceived to strengthen the effectiveness of monetary policy on the economy. This independence is seen as consistent with the democratic process because the Fed's mandate to pursue price and economic stability has been given to it by Congress, and choosing the interest rate policies best able to achieve these goals is viewed as relatively technocratic and non-political in nature.[110] The Fed's unprecedented response to the financial crisis moves it into new policy areas involving decisions that are arguably more political in nature, such as deciding which financial actors should be eligible to access Fed credit. While few policymakers argue for total independence or total disclosure and oversight, the policy challenge is to strike the right balance between the two. In February 2010 testimony, Chairman Bernanke has also advocated striking such a balance:

> we understand that the unusual nature of (the emergency credit and liquidity) facilities creates a special obligation to assure the Congress and the public of the integrity of their operation. Accordingly, we would welcome a review by the GAO of the Federal Reserve's management of all facilities created under emergency authorities. In particular, we would support legislation authorizing the GAO to audit the operational integrity, collateral policies, use of third-party contractors, accounting, financial reporting, and internal controls of these special credit and liquidity facilities.... We are also prepared to support legislation that would require the release of the identities of the firms that participated in each special facility after an appropriate delay. It is important that the release occur after a lag that is sufficiently long that investors will not view an institution's use of one of the facilities as a possible indication of ongoing financial problems, thereby undermining market confidence in the institution or discouraging use of any future facility that might become necessary to protect the U.S. economy.[111]

Effects on the Allocation of Capital

In normal conditions, the Fed primarily influences economic conditions through the purchase and sale of U.S. Treasury securities on the secondary market. This enables the Fed to influence overall economic conditions without favoring any particular financial firm or asset, thus minimizing its effect on the market allocation of capital.

As the Fed has shifted to an increasing reliance on more direct intervention in the financial system since 2008, its actions have had growing consequences for the allocation of private capital. Its actions can affect the allocation of capital by favoring certain classes or types of assets over others or by favoring certain financial firms or types of firms over others.

As discussed above, assisting Bear Stearns and AIG after their mistakes may encourage inefficiently high risk taking by other firms that are deemed "too big to fail." Punitive conditions attached to the assistance mitigate but do not eliminate these effects.[112] Allowing primary dealers to temporarily swap their illiquid assets for Treasuries protects those who invested poorly. The Fed has attempted to push down yields on certain assets that it feels have become inefficiently high (e.g., through the Term Asset Backed Securities Lending Facility), but it may be that at the height of the boom yields on these assets had become inefficiently low because investors underestimated their riskiness. The Fed's efforts could eventually reintroduce inefficient underpricing of risk. By purchasing commercial paper, the Fed has increased the relative demand for those assets, which confers an advantage to those firms that can access that market, which are generally large and have high credit ratings. Likewise, the Fed is purchasing GSE obligations and GSE-guaranteed MBS, but not similar securities issued by private firms. This increases the GSEs' funding advantage over private competitors.[113]

In a time when liquidity is scarce, access to Fed borrowing confers an advantage on banks and primary dealers over other types of institutions. It may also arguably retard the process of weeding out bad institutions, since reputation is needed to access private liquidity, but not Fed liquidity. On the other hand, during a panic both good and bad firms can be shut out of credit markets. Liquidity has positive externalities that means it would be underprovided by the private sector if it were not provided by the government. When financial markets are not functioning, credit allocation is an incidental but unavoidable side effect of liquidity provision. But some of the Fed's efforts, such as paying interest on bank reserves or possibly seeking to issue its own bonds, could be interpreted as signaling that the Fed intends to go beyond allocating credit for the sole purpose of providing liquidity because these initiatives allow the Fed to extend more credit than is needed for liquidity purposes.

The Fed's short-term goal is to avoid the downward spiral in conditions that could lead to a panic, causing serious disruptions to the credit intermediation process for all firms, prudent or otherwise. But in the long run, once financial stability has been restored, these distortions to the market allocation of capital could result in economic inefficiencies. There is also a risk that the Fed's activities could "crowd out" private lenders and investors in specific markets, such as the markets for bank reserves, private-label MBS, and commercial paper, leading to less robust private markets. This risk seems greater since the Fed has suggested methods to keep its balance sheet large (such as paying interest on bank reserves or issuing "Fed bonds") even after the economy has returned to normal. As demand for Fed lending facilities has fallen as financial conditions have improved, the Fed has already decided to purchase more GSE debt and MBS, rather than scale back its balance sheet. Even if some of the Fed's current programs are allowed to expire, if investors believed that they would be revived during the next downturn, capital allocation and incentives would remain altered.

Is the Economy Stuck in a Liquidity Trap? The Use of Quantitative Easing at Zero Interest Rates

Although monetary policy is credited with having contributed to an unusual degree of economic stability since at least the mid-1980s, some economists argue that it has been rendered ineffective by the current outlook. The argument is that lower interest rates will not boost spending because the economy is stuck in a credit crunch in which financial institutions are unwilling to lend to creditworthy borrowers because of balance sheet concerns. Borrower demand may increase in response to lower rates, but as long as institutions are trying to rebuild their balance sheets, they will remain reluctant to extend credit. Following September 2008, banks greatly increased their holdings of excess reserves, which could potentially be a troubling sign that banks currently prefer extremely safe, liquid assets over lending. Further, the Fed has already reduced the federal funds rate to near zero, and cannot reduce it further. By some measures, the recession was deep enough that zero interest rates are not stimulative enough to move the economy back to full employment quickly.[114]

A scenario where monetary stimulus has no effect on the economy is sometimes referred to as a "liquidity trap." Liquidity traps are rare in modern times, but the decade of economic stagnation suffered by Japan in the 1990s after the bursting of its financial bubble is cited as an example. Interest rates were lowered to almost zero in Japan, and the economy still did not recover quickly.[115]

There are some problems with this line of reasoning at present. First, liquidity traps are most likely to occur when overall prices of goods and services are falling (called *deflation*). When prices are falling, real interest rates are higher than nominal interest rates, so it is more likely that a very low nominal interest rate would still be too high in real terms to stimulate economic activity. Although prices fell at the end of 2008, they have been rising modestly since.[116] Inflation would not be expected to be steady the economy were in a liquidity trap. Second, monetary policy always suffers lags between a reduction in interest rates and corresponding increases in economic activity.

Most importantly, it would be wrong to conclude that the Fed has had no further policy options available to stimulate the economy since December 2008, when the Fed reduced the federal funds rate target to a range of 0% to 0.25%. At this point, the potential for further stimulus via traditional monetary policy channels had been exhausted, since the federal funds rate cannot be reduced below zero. But in a 2004 study, Ben Bernanke (a Fed governor at the time) and coauthors laid out policy options for how the Fed could further stimulate the economy once interest rates reached zero. In that study, the authors note that "nothing prevents the central bank from adding liquidity to the system beyond what is needed to achieve a policy rate of zero, a policy that is known as quantitative easing."[117] By that definition, the Fed has engaged in "quantitative easing" since September 2008—instead of adjusting the monetary base to meet the interest rate target, the Fed has adjusted the monetary base to meet the financial sector's liquidity needs.[118] But many different levels of Fed direct lending (and of the corresponding monetary base) are compatible with a zero federal funds rate. Once the federal funds rate hits zero, there is nothing stopping the Fed from further increases in lending that would have further expansionary effects on the economy. It could also engage in quantitative easing without direct lending by purchasing securities. From March 2009 to March 2010, the Fed purchased about $300 billion of longer-term Treasury securities, $1.25 trillion in MBS, and $175 billion of GSE obligations. Fed Vice Chairman Donald Kohn, while acknowledging great uncertainties, estimated that quantitative easing could increase nominal GDP by as much as $1 trillion over the next several years relative to a baseline forecast.[119]

The large increase in excess bank reserves casts doubt on the effectiveness of quantitative easing. Since the Fed has increased its balance sheet, excess reserves have averaged between $643 billion and $1,162 billion per month, compared with less than $2 billion before August 2007. The Fed can supply banks with unlimited liquidity, but if banks hold that liquidity at the Fed, the added liquidity will not stimulate economic activity.[120]

Even so, the Fed's actions may help bring down other interest rates in the economy, but this will be stimulative only if interest-sensitive spending is responsive to lower interest rates. This would occur through a flattening of the yield curve (i.e., pushing down long interest rates relative to short rates). Some economists argue that reductions in long-term rates are more stimulative than equivalent reductions in short-term rates.[121] But past experience with the efficacy of this method is mixed. Research by the New York Fed concludes that the recent purchases were effective in lowering interest rates based on the immediate response of rates to official announcements about the purchases, although this research could be questioned on the grounds that the rate reductions must be long-lasting to be stimulative, and for some of the maturities in question, interest rates over the entire period rose, on balance. Interpreting the overall effect on interest rates during the life of the asset purchase program is clouded by the fact that other changes in economic conditions also influence interest rates. The authors also use time-series evidence to estimate that the purchase program reduced the yield on ten-year securities relative to short-term securities by 0.38 to 0.82 percentage points. This evidence may be suffer from omitted variable bias, however—namely, the change in the risk-premium associated with MBS over the period in question, given the uncertainty prior to the purchase program caused by GSE conservatorship and the financial crisis. Another study by outside economists found small effects of the Fed's MBS purchases on interest rates after adjusting for prepayment and default risk, with the effect mainly occurring at the time the program was announced—before purchases had begun.[122]

Although a liquidity trap cannot be ruled out, it is premature to conclude the economy is stuck in one at this point in time. Liquidity traps are a threat when monetary policy has been kept too tight, but the Fed has eased monetary policy aggressively since the crisis began.

Stagflation?

Other critics have argued that the Fed has created the opposite problem of a liquidity trap—rising inflation due to excessive liquidity. They argue that the economy will enter a period of stagflation, where falling or negative economic growth is accompanied by high or rising inflation.[123]

Typically, one would expect an economic slowdown to be accompanied by a decline in the inflation rate. Excess capacity in the capital stock and rising unemployment would force firms and workers to lower their prices and wage demands, respectively. But critics believe the economy is in a situation where a modest but persistent increase in inflation in recent years has led individuals to come to expect higher inflation, and factor that expectation into their price and wage demands. Further driving up inflationary expectations, critics believe that individuals will observe the large increase in the budget deficit and monetary base and conclude that the government will inflate its way out of the crisis. Couple those higher inflation expectations with rising commodity prices, and critics argue that inflation will rise even if the economy slows. They point to the experience of the 1970s, when inflationary expectations became so ingrained that inflation continued to rise despite a fairly deep recession, as a potential parallel to the current situation.[124]

Data suggest that the fear of stagflation is premature—inflation remains relatively low at present. There is a consensus among economists that in the long run inflation is primarily a monetary phenomenon, and if the Fed's recent monetary stance were maintained for too long, it would not be consistent with stable inflation. But in the near term, a large amount of unemployment and excess capacity has removed most inflationary pressure. This can be seen in the example of Japan, where the Bank of Japan allowed the monetary base to increase by more than 10% per year after 2001, without inflation ever reaching high levels because of economic sluggishness. Furthermore, commodity prices fell in the second half of 2008, leading to a brief period of falling prices. Since then, inflation has been stable.

Ironically, if the Fed's actions succeed in reviving the economy, then the probability that its actions would boost inflation would increase. Under normal conditions, the doubling of the monetary base between August and December 2008 would have led to a sharp increase in inflation, but this did not occur because of the even greater increase in bank reserves held at the Fed that led to only a moderate increase in broader measures of the money supply. If banks responded to improved economic conditions by lending out the reserves they are now holding, the money supply and inflation would rise rapidly. The key to maintaining a stable inflation rate is finding the proper balance between the disinflationary pressures of the slowdown and the inflationary pressures of quantitative easing. The large amounts of liquidity that the Fed has added to the system must be removed soon enough that inflation does not rise, but not so soon that a nascent economic recovery is stubbed out. Removing all of the liquidity is complicated by the fact that the Fed has created some of it by buying assets it has pledged to hold long term. Given the uncertainty facing policymakers at present, finding the proper balance is extremely difficult.[125]

Concluding Thoughts

While turmoil plagues financial markets periodically, the current episode is notable for its breadth, depth, and persistence. It is difficult to make the case that the Fed has not responded to the current turmoil with alacrity and creativity. The slow financial and economic recovery is not necessarily a sign that the Fed's policy decisions have been wrongheaded—the Fed has provided the financial sector with unprecedented liquidity, but it cannot force institutions to use that liquidity to expand their lending or investing.

The Fed's response has raised statutory issues that Congress may wish to consider in its oversight capacity. Namely, the Fed's role in the Bear Stearns acquisition, the assistance to AIG, Citigroup, and Bank of America, the creation of the Primary Dealer Credit Facility (a sort of discount window for a group of non-member banks), and its intervention in the commercial paper market involved emergency authorities that had not been used in more than 70 years. This authority was needed because the actions involved financial institutions that were not member banks of the Federal Reserve System (i.e., depository institutions). But because the authority is broad and open-ended, the Fed's actions under this authority are subject to few legal parameters. The authority allows lending to non-member banks, but some of the loans in the Bear Stearns and AIG agreements were to LLCs that the Fed created and controls, and have been used to purchase Bear Stearns' and AIG's assets. These actions raise an important issue—if financial institutions can receive some of the benefits of Fed protection, in some cases because they are "too big to fail," should they also be subject to the costs that member banks bear in terms of safety and soundness regulations, imposed to limit the moral hazard that results from Fed and FDIC protections? H.R. 4173 attempts to limit future emergency lending to broadly available, collateralized facilities to avoid assistance to failing firms.

Some policymakers have questioned whether an institution largely independent from the elected branches of government should be able to (indirectly) place significant taxpayer funds at risk by providing the financial sector with hundreds of billions of dollars of assistance through use of its emergency powers. This raises the policy issue of how to balance the needs for congressional transparency and oversight against the economic benefits of Fed independence. H.R. 4173 removes most GAO audit restrictions and requires disclosure of the identities of borrowers with a delay. Furthermore, without congressional input, hundreds of billions of dollars of borrowing by the Treasury (through the Treasury Supplementary Financing Program) has allowed the Fed to increase its lending capacity without detrimental effects on inflation.

But as long as there is no government program to systematically manage financial difficulties at too big to fail institutions, the Fed is the only institution that can step in quickly enough to cope with problems on a case-by-case basis. While some had believed TARP provided the type of systemic approach that would allow the Fed to return to a more traditional role, the Fed's subsequent creation of lending facilities to support the commercial paper market, mortgage market, and asset-backed securities market suggests that TARP cannot cover all unforeseen contingencies. Furthermore, TARP is scheduled to expire in October 2010 and is limited in size, although Fed and TARP money have been coupled in order for TARP to have an impact beyond the $700 billion authorized by Congress.

The Fed's actions have resulted in an unprecedented expansion in its balance sheet and the portion of the money supply it controls. Normally, this would be highly inflationary, but inflation has remained low because of the financial crisis. As the economy improves, the Fed will need to contain this monetary expansion to prevent inflation from rising, but not so fast that it causes the financial system to destabilize again. The increase in the balance sheet could have already been automatically reversed by the decline in the Fed's direct lending, but the Fed has chosen to offset it through large-scale purchases of assets to maintain a high level of liquidity in the economy. The Fed views paying interest on bank reserves (authorized by P.L. 110-343) as an effective way to prevent inflation from rising.

End Notes

[1] For more information see CRS Report RL34182, *Financial Crisis? The Liquidity Crunch of August 2007*, by Darryl E. Getter et al.

[2] Current amounts of Fed lending outstanding can be found at Federal Reserve, "Factors Affecting Reserve Balances of Depository Institutions," statistical release H.4.1, updated weekly.

[3] Many of the loans and new programs described below are operated through the Federal Reserve Bank of New York, under the authorization of the Board of Governors. This report uses the term Federal Reserve, and does not distinguish between actions taken by the Board and actions taken by the Federal Reserve Bank of New York. The Federal Reserve System is composed of the Board of Governors and twelve regional banks (one of which is the New York Fed).

[4] Federal Reserve Bank of New York, "The Discount Window," *Fedpoint*, August 2007.

[5] Proposals for GAO to audit the Fed are discussed below in the section entitled "Oversight, Transparency, and Disclosure of Emergency Programs".

[6] Some of the Fed's purchase and sale of Treasury securities are made outright, but most are made through repurchase agreements, which can be thought of as short-term transactions that are automatically reversed at the end of a predetermined period, typically lasting a few days. Since the Fed must constantly adjust the amount of bank reserves available to keep the federal funds rate near its target, repurchase agreements give the Fed more flexibility to make these adjustments.

[7] For more information, see CRS Report RL30354, *Monetary Policy and the Federal Reserve: Current Policy and Conditions*, by Marc Labonte. For information on the federal funds market during the crisis, see Gara Afonso, Anna Kovner, and Antoinette Schoar, *Stressed, Not Frozen: The Federal Funds Market in the Financial Crisis*, Federal Reserve Bank of New York, Staff Report no. 437, March 2010.

[8] For more information, see the section below, "Is the Economy Stuck in a Liquidity Trap? The Use of Quantitative Easing at Zero Interest Rates."

[9] This occurred because financial firms were meeting their liquidity needs directly from the Fed, there was no longer adequate demand to borrow reserves in the private federal funds market, and the federal funds rate fell close to zero.

[10] For these purposes, the Fed defines Fannie Mae, Freddie Mac, the Federal Home Loan Banks, and Ginnie Mae as Agencies. For more information, see the section below entitled "Mortgage-Backed Securities Purchase Program and Purchase of GSE Obligations".

[11] Joseph Gagnon et al, *Large-Scale Asset Purchases by the Federal Reserve*, Federal Reserve Bank of New York, Staff Reports 441, March 2010.

[12] For more background, see James Clouse, "Recent Developments in Discount Window Policy," *Federal Reserve Bulletin*, November 1994, p. 965.

[13] Current data on the number of borrowers, loan concentration among borrowers, types of collateral posted, credit rating of collateral posted, and size of loans as a share of posted collateral for the Term Auction Facility and

discount window can be found in the Fed's *Federal Reserve System Monthly Report on Credit and Liquidity Programs and the Balance Sheet.*

[14] The Fed has centralized information on the purpose, terms, and conditions of the facilities described in this section at the following Fed website at http://www.federalreserve.gov/monetarypolicy/bst.htm.

[15] The Fed made about 7,500 loans to non-banks each year under Section 13B of the Federal Reserve Act until that section of the act was repealed in 1959.

[16] For more information, see Olivier Armantier et al, "The Federal Reserve's Term Auction Facility," Federal Reserve Bank of New York, *Current Issues in Economics and Finance,* vol. 14, no. 5, July 2008; Charles Carlstrom and Sarah Wakefield, "The Funds Rate, Liquidity, and the Term Auction Facility," Federal Reserve Bank of Cleveland, *Economic Trends,* December 14, 2007.

[17] The dates, terms, and amounts of future TAF auctions can be accessed at http://www.federalreserve.gov/monetarypolicy/tafschedule.htm.

[18] Current data on the number of borrowers, loan concentration among borrowers, types of collateral posted, credit rating of collateral posted, and size of loans as a share of posted collateral for the TAF and discount window can be found in the Fed's *Federal Reserve System Monthly Report on Credit and Liquidity Programs and the Balance Sheet.*

[19] See James McAndrews et al, *The Effect of the Term Auction Facility on the London Inter-bank Offered Rate,* Federal Reserve Bank of New York, Staff Report no. 335, July 2008; John Taylor and John Williams, *A Black Swan in the Money Market,* Federal Reserve Bank of San Francisco, Working Paper 2008-04, April 2008; Asani Sarkar and Jeffrey Shrader, *Financial Amplification Mechanisms and the Federal Reserve's Supply of Liquidity During the Financial Crisis,* Federal Reserve Bank of New York, Staff Reports 431, February 2010.

[20] As of June 2009, Treasury securities, Agency securities, and Agency-guaranteed mortgage-backed securities were no longer accepted as collateral for the TSLF because the Fed deemed these assets to no longer be illiquid. Few of these assets were posted as collateral when the Fed discontinued their use.

[21] Current data on the number of borrowers, concentration of loans among borrowers, types of collateral, and credit rating of collateral can be found in the Fed's *Federal Reserve System Monthly Report on Credit and Liquidity Programs and the Balance Sheet.*

[22] Board of Governors of the Federal Reserve System, press release, March 11, 2008.

[23] Michael Fleming, Warren Hrung, and Frank Keane, "The Term Securities Lending Facility," Federal Reserve Bank of New York, *Current Issues in Economics and Finance,* vol. 15, no. 2 (February 2009). See also Michael Fleming, Warren Hrung, and Frank Keane, *Repo Market Effects of the Term Securities Lending Facility,* Federal Reserve Bank of New York, Staff Reports 426, January 2010. The failure of Bear Stearns set off a period of market turbulence; the decline in spreads cited in these studies may have been driven by the abatement of this turbulence.

[24] For more information, see Tobias Adrian, Christopher Burke, and James McAndrews, *The Federal Reserve's Primary Dealer Credit Facility,* Federal Reserve Bank of New York, Current Issues in Economics and Finance, vol. 15, no. 4, New York, NY, August 2009.

[25] Board of Governors of the Federal Reserve System, press release, November 25, 2008.

[26] Current data on the types of loans and names of issuers whose ABS have been used for collateral can be found in the Fed's *Federal Reserve System Monthly Report on Credit and Liquidity Programs and the Balance Sheet.*

[27] Special Inspector General for TARP, *Quarterly Report to Congress,* Washington, DC, April 29, 2009, p. 227.

[28] For more information, see CRS Report RL34730, *Troubled Asset Relief Program: Legislation and Treasury Implementation,* by Baird Webel and Edward V. Murphy.

[29] Kenneth Robinson, *TALF: Jump-Starting the Securitization Markets,* Federal Reserve Bank of Dallas Economic Letter, vol. 4, no. 6, August 2009.

[30] For more information, see Richard Anderson and Charles Gascon, "The Commercial Paper Market, the Fed, and the 2007-2009 Financial Crisis," *Federal Reserve Bank of St. Louis Review,* vol. 91, no. 6 (November/December 2009), p. 589.

[31] Figure cited in Chairman Ben Bernanke, "Financial Reform to Address Systemic Risk," speech at the Council on Foreign Relations, March 10, 2009.

[32] Current data on the number of borrowers and credit rating of collateral can be found in the Fed's *Federal Reserve System Monthly Report on Credit and Liquidity Programs and the Balance Sheet.*

[33] Current data on the number of borrowers, loan concentration among borrowers, types of borrowers, and credit rating of the commercial paper can be found in the Fed's *Federal Reserve System Monthly Report on Credit and Liquidity Programs and the Balance Sheet.* See also, Tobias Adrian, Karin Kimbrough, and Dina Marchioni, "The Federal Reserve's Commercial Paper Funding Facility," Federal Reserve Bank of New York, *Economic Policy Review,* forthcoming.

[34] Andrew Tilton, "Fed Nursing the Money Markets Back to Health," Goldman Sachs U.S. Daily newsletter, January 8, 2009.

[35] The arrangement is similar to the Fed's creation of Maiden Lane limited liability corporations to purchase Bear Stearns' and AIG's assets (discussed below), but those involved one-time purchases.

[36] See David Fettig, "Lender of More Than Last Resort," Federal Reserve Bank of Minneapolis, *The Region*, December 2002.
[37] Although much of the commercial paper bought by the CPFF was issued by financial firms, most financial firms experiencing any disruption to their liquidity needs in the commercial paper market were already eligible to borrow directly from the Fed on a collateralized basis.
[38] Brian Madigan, "Bagehot's Dictum in Practice," Speech at the Federal Reserve Bank of Kansas City's Annual Economic Symposium, August 21, 2009.
[39] See CRS Report RS22950, *Fannie Mae and Freddie Mac in Conservatorship*, by Mark Jickling.
[40] In the years before the crisis, the Fed had no GSE holdings, but the Fed had purchased GSE assets in the past. According to a New York Fed report, "Agency purchases were introduced in 1971 in order to 'widen the base for System open market operations and to add breadth to the market for agency securities.' New purchases were stopped in 1981, although some maturing funds from agency holdings were reinvested in newly issued agency securities. Beginning in 1997, all holdings of agency securities were allowed to mature without replacement. The last agency holding acquired under these programs matured in December 2003." Joseph Gagnon et al, *Large-Scale Asset Purchases by the Federal Reserve*, Federal Reserve Bank of New York, Staff Reports 441, March 2010.
[41] Federal Reserve, press release, November 25, 2008.
[42] For more information on the Treasury programs, see CRS Report RS22950, *Fannie Mae and Freddie Mac in Conservatorship*, by Mark Jickling.
[43] For more information, see Linda Goldberg, Craig Kennedy, and Jason Miu, *Central Bank Dollar Swap Lines and Overseas Dollar Funding Costs*, Federal Reserve Bank of New York, Staff Reports No. 429, Feb. 2010.
[44] Current data on swaps outstanding by central bank can be found in the Fed's *Federal Reserve System Monthly Report on Credit and Liquidity Programs and the Balance Sheet*.
[45] For more information, see CRS Report R41167, *Greece's Debt Crisis: Overview, Policy Responses, and Implications*, coordinated by Rebecca M. Nelson.
[46] This authority was originally allowed beginning in 2011 in the Financial Services Regulatory Relief Act of 2006 (P.L. 109-351). The Emergency Economic Stabilization Act of 2008 granted immediate authority.
[47] See Todd Keister et al, "Divorcing Money From Monetary Policy, Federal Reserve Bank of New York, *Economic Policy Review*, September 2008.
[48] One theory as to why the interest rate paid on bank reserves did not act as an effective floor on the federal funds rate is because the GSEs participate in the federal funds market but are not paid interest on their reserves at the Fed.
[49] See the section below entitled "Future Concerns."
[50] This section discusses the special assistance that the troubled firms received from the Fed. The same firms may also have subsequently accessed Fed resources through its normal lending facilities. All lending through facilities is confidential, so knowledge of such activity is limited to self-reporting by the firms. For example, the CEO of JPMorgan Chase testified to Congress that Bear Stearns had borrowed an additional $25 billion from the Fed. (Source: Kara Scannell and Sudeep Reddy, "Officials Say They Sought to Avoid Bear Bailout," *Wall Street Journal*, April 4, 2008, p. A1.) Similarly, AIG announced that it had accessed the Commercial Paper Funding Facility. (Source: "U.S. Treasury, Federal Reserve and AIG Establish Comprehensive Solution for AIG," AIG press release, November 10, 2008.)
[51] Federal Reserve and U.S. Treasury Department, "The Role of the Federal Reserve in Preserving Financial and Monetary Stability," joint press release, March 23, 2009.
[52] For more information, see CRS Report RL34420, *Bear Stearns: Crisis and "Rescue" for a Major Provider of Mortgage-Related Products*, by Gary Shorter.
[53] Federal Reserve Bank of New York, "New York Fed Completes Financing Arrangement Related to JPMorgan Chase's Acquisition of Bear Stearns," press release, June 26, 2008. A subordinate loan is one where the principal and interest are not repaid until after the primary loan is repaid. The originally announced terms of the loans were for up to $29 billion from the New York Fed and $1 billion from JPMorgan Chase. After more thoroughly reviewing the assets the LLC would receive, the Fed changed the terms of the loan.
[54] Federal Reserve Bank of New York, "Summary of Terms and Conditions Regarding the JPMorgan Chase Facility," press release, March 24, 2008. Many of the details of the loan, including the size, were not announced on March 16.
[55] Jamie Dimon, *Testimony Before the Senate Committee on Banking, Housing, and Urban Affairs*, April 3, 2008.
[56] Federal Reserve Bank of New York, "Summary of Terms and Conditions Regarding the JPMorgan Chase Facility," press release, March 24, 2008.
[57] Timothy Geithner, "Testimony Before the Senate Committee for Banking, Housing and Urban Affairs," April 3, 2008, p. 17.
[58] Federal Reserve Bank of New York, "Statement on Financing Arrangement of JPMorgan Chase's Acquisition of Bear Stearns," press release, March 24, 2008.
[59] Federal Reserve, *Factors Affecting Reserve Balances of Depository Institutions*, press release H.4.1, September 11, 2008. Information on the portfolio will be updated quarterly and announced through this press release.

[60] Jamie Dimon, *Testimony Before the Senate Committee on Banking, Housing, and Urban Affairs*, April 3, 2008.
[61] Timothy Geithner, "Testimony Before the Senate Committee for Banking, Housing and Urban Affairs," April 3, 2008, p. 13.
[62] This section was prepared with Baird Webel, specialist in Financial Economics. For more information, see CRS Report R40438, *Ongoing Government Assistance for American International Group (AIG)*, by Baird Webel.
[63] See, for example, "U.S. to Take Over AIG in $85 Billion Bailout; Central Banks Inject Cash as Credit Dries Up," *Wall Street Journal*, September 17, 2008, pp. A1-A6.
[64] Federal Reserve, "Factors Affecting Reserve Balances," press release H.4.1, September 18, 2008.
[65] Liam Pleven et al, "AIG Bailout Hit By New Cash Woes," *Wall Street Journal*, October 9, 2008, p. A1.
[66] N.Y. Ins. Law, Sec. 1410.
[67] Full details of the preferred shares can be found on the Treasury website at http://ustreas.gov/press/ releases/ reports/ 111008aigtermsheet.pdf.
[68] See, for example, "A.I.G. Reports Loss of $61.7 Billion as U.S. Gives More Aid," New York Times, March 2, 2009, p. A1.
[69] U.S. Treasury, "U.S. Treasury and Federal Reserve Board Announce Participation in AIG Restructuring Plan," Press Release dated March 2, 2009.
[70] U.S. Department of Treasury, *Troubled Asset Relief Program Monthly 105(a) Report to Congress*, November 10, 2009.
[71] See http://www.aig.com/aigweb/internet/en/files/Counterparties_tcm385-153017.pdf/.
[72] Citigroup, "Citigroup and U.S. Government Reach Definitive Agreement on Loss Sharing Program," press release, January 16, 2009.
[73] For a full discussion, see the section below entitled "Lender of Last Resort, Systemic Risk, and Moral Hazard."
[74] For a full discussion, see the section below entitled "Lender of Last Resort, Systemic Risk, and Moral Hazard."
[75] See, for example, Deborah Solomon, "Bailout Man Turns the Screws," *Wall Street Journal*, April 7, 2009, p. A1.
[76] Assuming that the interest rate on the loans exceeded the rate of return on the Treasuries that the Fed would have purchased if the loans had not occurred.
[77] See, for example, Peter Stella, *The Federal Reserve System Balance Sheet: What Happened and Why It Matters*, International Monetary Fund, Working Paper 09/120, May 2009.
[78] Current data on the income earned and change in asset value by Fed facility can be found in the Fed's *Monthly Report on Credit and Liquidity Programs and the Balance Sheet*.
[79] Congressional Budget Office, *The Budgetary Impact and Subsidy Costs of the Federal Reserve's Actions During the Financial Crisis*, May 2010. CBO generally estimates the rate or price needed to fully compensate for risk based on what rate or price would be charged in private markets; this became difficult to estimate during the financial crisis because private markets stopped functioning smoothly. CBO estimated the subsidy of each crisis program based on market conditions at the time the programs were started. Since market conditions have improved considerably since then, ex-post profits are not a sign that there was no subsidy; rates or prices had to reflect the risk that conditions might get much worse at the time the transaction was made.
[80] Previously, Section 13(3) required that the loan be "secured to the satisfaction of the Federal Reserve bank."
[81] It should be noted that a portfolio of Treasury securities is only needed to tighten monetary policy. Expansionary monetary policy involves the purchase of Treasury securities.
[82] The program also supplies more Treasuries to investors when there is excess demand because of a "flight to quality." The Treasuries issued under the program are indistinguishable to investors from regularly-issued securities.
[83] By comparison, the monetary base rose 2% over the four previous months.
[84] Another stated rationale for these purchases is to push down interest rates throughout the economy. It is difficult to assess whether the program has succeeded in this goal since many other factors also influence interest rates. For example, interest rates on these securities have generally trended upward since the Fed's purchases began, presumably because economic conditions have improved.
[85] The Fed's views on the issues outlined in this section can be read in Ben Bernanke, "The Fed's Exit Strategy," *Wall Street Journal*, July 21, 2009, p. A15. See also Claudio Borio and Piti Disyatat, *Unconventional Monetary Policies: An Appraisal*," Bank for International Settlements, Working Paper 292, Nov. 2009.
[86] Chairman Ben Bernanke, "The Federal Reserve's Balance Sheet: An Update," Speech at the Federal Reserve Board Conference on Key Developments in Monetary Policy, October 8, 2009.
[87] One paper looks at international experience with paying interest on bank reserves to answer this question. There is very limited experience with raising short-term interest rates while maintaining excess reserve balances, however. Japan in the 1990s is the best-known case of quantitative easing, and it removed excess balances before raising rates. The authors found that Norway had successfully raised rates while maintaining excess reserves from 2005 to 2008, although they did reduce reserves by half during that period. David Bowman, Etienne Gagnon, Mike Leahy, "Interest on Excess Reserves as a Monetary Policy Instrument: The Experience of Foreign Central Banks," Federal Reserve Board, *International Finance Discussion Paper 996*, March 2010.
[88] The size of reverse repo operations are limited to the amount of securities held by the Fed available to lend and private investors' willingness to borrow them. In recent years, reverse repos outstanding have not exceeded

[89] $108 billion. Goldman Sachs reports that Fed officials have indicated that they do not believe private investors could absorb more than $100 billion in reverse repos. Ed McKelvey, "Fed Lays Groundwork to Offset Another Increase in Excess Reserves," *U.S. Daily Newsletter*, September 24, 2009.

[89] Economically, this would have the same effect as the Treasury Supplemental Financing Program, which has been unavailable since September 2009 because the federal debt has been too close to the statutory limit.

[90] Ben Bernanke, Vincent Reinhart, and Brian Sack, "Monetary Policy Alternatives at the Zero Bound," Federal Reserve Board of Governors, *Finance and Economics Discussion Series 2004-48*, 2004, p. 28.

[91] Until 1978, the Treasury had limited authority to "draw" from the Fed to finance its deficits, and used that authority sparingly. U.S. Congress, House Committee on Banking, Finance, and Urban Affairs, Domestic Monetary Policy, *Extending the Treasury-Federal Reserve Draw Authority*, committee print, 95th Cong., 2nd sess., April 5, 1978, 26-179 (Washington: GPO, 1978).

[92] The net addition to general revenues is reduced by the extra interest the Treasury must pay on debt it issued in order to deposit cash at the Fed.

[93] For more information, see CRS Report RS22963, *Financial Market Intervention*, by Edward V. Murphy and Baird Webel.

[94] In addition, the Fed faces some statutory limitations on lending to undercapitalized banks under normal circumstances. See, for example, Section 10B of the Federal Reserve Act.

[95] For more information, see CRS Report RL34730, *Troubled Asset Relief Program: Legislation and Treasury Implementation*, by Baird Webel and Edward V. Murphy.

[96] David Small and James Clouse, *The Scope of Monetary Policy Actions Authorized under the Federal Reserve Act*, Federal Reserve, FEDS Working Paper no. 2004-40, July 2004, p. 29.

[97] The Fed also created the Term Asset Backed Liquidity Facility (TALF) to lend to private investors to purchase illiquid assets of the same types that TARP was originally intended to purchase. TALF is also aimed at improving liquidity, and does not affect the capital adequacy problem directly, however.

[98] In this context, it is interesting to note that the Bear Stearns failure has been described as a non-bank run, meaning Bear Stearns was undermined because it was shunned by its counterparties and investors, analogous to a bank being shunned by its depositors. The defining characteristic of a run is that the fear of failure becomes self-fulfilling since it deprives an institution of the resources it needs to avoid failure.

[99] For more information, see CRS Report RL34412, *Containing Financial Crisis*, by Mark Jickling.

[100] Greg Ip, "Central Bank Offers Loans to Brokers, Cuts Key Rate," *Wall Street Journal*, March 17, 2008, p. A1.

[101] Chairman Bernanke argued that the Fed did not have the authority to assist Lehman Brothers because Lehman Brothers could not offer the Fed adequate collateral for a loan of the size needed, which according to Bernanke, would have been much larger than the assistance for Bear Stearns. See Ben Bernanke, "Current Economic and Financial Conditions," speech at the National Association for Business Economic Annual Meeting, October 7, 2008.

[102] This problem in relation to investment banking has to some degree been overtaken by events, as none of the five largest investment banks still exist in their original form. Lehman Brothers has entered bankruptcy, Bear Stearns and Merrill Lynch have merged with commercial banks, and Goldman Sachs and Morgan Stanley have reorganized as bank holding companies that are regulated by the Fed.

[103] All of the information outlined in this paragraph can be accessed at the Fed's website at http://www.Federalreserve.gov/monetarypolicy/bst.htm.

[104] Federal Reserve Board of Governors, *Federal Reserve System Monthly Report on Credit and Liquidity Programs and the Balance Sheet*.

[105] A federal judge ruled on August 25, 2009, that the Fed must turn information over to Bloomberg newsgroup on its emergency lending activities. The court case is Bloomberg LP v. Board of Governors of the Federal Reserve System, U.S. District Court, Southern District of New York (Manhattan), No. 08-9595.

[106] James Butkiewicz, "The Reconstruction Finance Corporation, the Gold Standard, and the Banking Panic of 1933," *Southern Economic Journal*, vol. 66, no. 2, October 1999, p. 271.

[107] A list of current GAO audits of the Fed can be found in the Fed's Annual Report.

[108] See U.S. General Accounting Office, *Federal Reserve System Audits*, GAO/T-GGD-94-44, October 27, 1993.

[109] Chairman Ben Bernanke, "Don't Strip the Fed of Supervisory Power," *Valley News*, December 1, 2009, p. A6. See also Federal Reserve Vice Chairman Donald Kohn, "Federal Reserve Independence," Testimony before the Subcommittee on Domestic Monetary Policy and Technology, House Financial Services Committee, July 9, 2009.

[110] See CRS Report RL31056, *Economics of Federal Reserve Independence*, by Marc Labonte.

[111] Chairman Ben S. Bernanke, Semiannual Monetary Policy Report to the Congress, Before the Committee on Financial Services, U.S. House of Representatives, Washington, DC, February 24, 2010.

[112] For example, the decision to make creditors whole in the case of Bear Stearns and AIG reduces incentives for creditors to curb lending to other institutions deemed "too big to fail."

[113] Some would argue that the GSE's funding advantage primarily stems from government conservatorship, and the effect of Fed's purchases are ancillary.

[114] For example, economist Glenn Rudebusch estimates that interest rates would need to reach -5% in 2009. Glenn Rudebusch, "The Fed's Monetary Policy Response to the Current Crisis," *Federal Reserve Bank of San Francisco, FRBSF Economic Letter*, no. 2009-17, May 22, 2009. See also John Williams, "Heeding Daedalus: Optimal Inflation and the Zero Lower Bound," *Brookings Papers on Economic Activity*, September 2009.

[115] While the term liquidity trap was often applied to Japan, it is theoretically defined as a situation where household demand for money becomes so great that normal sized changes in the money supply do not affect interest rates or spending. Under this strict definition, it is not clear that Japan, or any other economy, has ever experienced a liquidity trap.

[116] Asset prices have fallen, but they are not included in standard measures of inflation, which measures the prices of goods and services.

[117] Ben Bernanke, Vincent Reinhart, and Brian Sack, "Monetary Policy Alternatives at the Zero Bound: An Empirical Analysis," Federal Reserve Board, *Finance and Economic Discussion Series 2004-48*, 2004, p. 17. Other options for stimulus at zero short-term interest rates include buying longer-term assets to push down longer-term interest rates.

[118] Chairman Bernanke referred to the Fed's policies in 2008 as credit easing, rather than quantitative easing. He identifies quantitative easing as a policy where the central bank sets a growth rate for the monetary base and provides liquidity to achieve that growth rate. Under what he calls credit easing, the Fed has allowed the growth in the monetary base to be determined by the financial sector's demand for liquidity. He notes that both policies result in the growth of the central bank's balance sheet and the monetary base. See Chairman Ben S. Bernanke, *Speech at the Stamp Lecture*, London School of Economics, London, England, January 13, 2009.

[119] Donald Kohn, "Interactions Between Monetary and Fiscal Policy in the Current Situation," speech at Princeton University, Princeton, NJ, May 23, 2009.

[120] The Fed has argued that large excess reserves should not be seen as a sign that its policies have lost their effectiveness. See, for example, Todd Keister and James McAndrews, "Why Are Banks Holding So Many Excess Reserves?" *Federal Reserve Bank of New York Staff Reports*, no. 380, July 2009.

[121] Glenn Rudebusch, *The Fed's Exit Strategy for Monetary Policy*, Federal Reserve Bank of San Francisco, Economic Letter 2010-18, June 2010.

[122] Johannes Stroebel and John Taylor, "Estimated Impact of the Fed's Mortgage-Backed Securities Purchase Program," National Bureau of Economic Research, working paper 15626, Dec. 2009.

[123] See CRS Report RL34428, *Understanding Stagflation and the Risk of Its Recurrence*, by Brian W. Cashell and Marc Labonte.

[124] Rudebusch presents evidence that the growth in the Fed's balance sheet has had no effect on inflation expectations. Glenn Rudebusch, *The Fed's Exit Strategy for Monetary Policy*, Federal Reserve Bank of San Francisco, Economic Letter 2010-18, June 2010.

[125] For more information, see CRS Report RL34562, *Slow Growth or Inflation? The Federal Reserve's Dilemma*, by Brian W. Cashell and Marc Labonte.

In: Financial Alarm and Federal Reserve Response
Editors: Alexander L. Clark and Mason R. Williams
ISBN: 978-1-62100-582-7
© 2012 Nova Science Publishers, Inc.

Chapter 2

FEDERAL RESERVE SYSTEM: OPPORTUNITIES EXIST TO STRENGTHEN POLICIES AND PROCESSES FOR MANAGING EMERGENCY ASSISTANCE[*]

United States Government Accountability Office

WHY GAO DID THIS STUDY

The Dodd-Frank Wall Street Reform and Consumer Protection Act directed GAO to conduct a one-time audit of the emergency loan programs and other assistance authorized by the Board of Governors of the Federal Reserve System (Federal Reserve Board) during the recent financial crisis. This report examines the emergency actions taken by the Federal Reserve Board from December 1, 2007, through July 21, 2010. For each of these actions, where relevant, GAO's objectives included a review of (1) the basis and purpose for its authorization, as well as accounting and financial reporting internal controls; (2) the use, selection, and payment of vendors; (3) management of conflicts of interest; (4) policies in place to secure loan repayment; and (5) the treatment of program participants. To meet these objectives, GAO reviewed program documentation, analyzed program data, and interviewed officials from the Federal Reserve Board and Reserve Banks (Federal Reserve System).

WHAT GAO RECOMMENDS

GAO makes seven recommendations to the Federal Reserve Board to strengthen policies for managing noncompetitive vendor selections, conflicts of interest, risks related to emergency lending, and documentation of emergency program decisions. The Federal Reserve Board agreed that GAO's recommendations would benefit its response to future crises and agreed to strongly consider how best to respond to them.

---

[*] This is an edited, reformatted and augmented version of United States Government Accountability Office Report, GAO-11-696, dated July 2011.

WHAT GAO FOUND

On numerous occasions in 2008 and 2009, the Federal Reserve Board invoked emergency authority under the Federal Reserve Act of 1913 to authorize new broad-based programs and financial assistance to individual institutions to stabilize financial markets. Loans outstanding for the emergency programs peaked at more than $1 trillion in late 2008. The Federal Reserve Board directed the Federal Reserve Bank of New York (FRBNY) to implement most of these emergency actions. In a few cases, the Federal Reserve Board authorized a Reserve Bank to lend to a limited liability corporation (LLC) to finance the purchase of assets from a single institution. In 2009 and 2010, FRBNY also executed large-scale purchases of agency mortgage-backed securities to support the housing market. The table below provides an overview of all emergency actions covered by this report. The Reserve Banks' and LLCs' financial statements, which include the emergency programs' accounts and activities, and their related financial reporting internal controls, are audited annually by an independent auditing firm. These independent financial statement audits, as well as other audits and reviews conducted by the Federal Reserve Board, its Inspector General, and the Reserve Banks' internal audit function, did not report any significant accounting or financial reporting internal control issues concerning the emergency programs.

The Reserve Banks, primarily FRBNY, awarded 103 contracts worth $659.4 million from 2008 through 2010 to help carry out their emergency activities. A few contracts accounted for most of the spending on vendor services. For a significant portion of the fees, program recipients reimbursed the Reserve Banks or the fees were paid from program income. The Reserve Banks relied more extensively on vendors for programs that assisted a single institution than for broad-based programs. Most of the contracts, including 8 of the 10 highest-value contracts, were awarded noncompetitively, primarily due to exigent circumstances. These contract awards were consistent with FRBNY's acquisition policies, but the policies could be improved by providing additional guidance on the use of competition exceptions, such as seeking as much competition as practicable and limiting the duration of noncompetitive contracts to the exigency period. To better ensure that Reserve Banks do not miss opportunities to obtain competition and receive the most favorable terms for services acquired, GAO recommends that they revise their acquisition policies to provide such guidance.

FRBNY took steps to manage conflicts of interest for its employees, directors, and program vendors, but opportunities exist to strengthen its conflict policies. In particular, FRBNY expanded its guidance and monitoring for employee conflicts, but new roles assumed by FRBNY and its employees during the crisis gave rise to potential conflicts that were not specifically addressed in the Code of Conduct or other FRBNY policies. For example, FRBNY's existing restrictions on its employees' financial interests did not specifically prohibit investments in certain nonbank institutions that received emergency assistance. To manage potential conflicts related to employees' holdings of such investments, FRBNY relied on provisions in its code that incorporate requirements of a federal criminal conflict of interest statute and its regulations. Given the magnitude of the assistance and the public's heightened attention to the appearance of conflicts related to Reserve Banks' emergency actions, existing standards for managing employee conflicts may not be sufficient to avoid the appearance of a conflict in all situations. As the Federal Reserve System considers revising its conflict policies given its new authorit\y to regulate certain nonbank institutions, GAO recommends it consider how potential conflicts from emergency lending could inform any changes. FRBNY managed vendor conflict issues through contract protections and actions to help ensure compliance with relevant contract provisions, but these efforts had limitations. For example, while FRBNY negotiated important contract protections, such as requirements for ethical walls, it lacked written guidance on protections that should be included to help ensure vendors fully identify and remediate conflicts. Further, FRBNY's on-site reviews of vendor compliance in some instances occurred as far as 12 months into a contract. FRBNY implemented a new vendor management policy but has not yet finalized another new policy with comprehensive guidance on vendor conflict issues. GAO recommends FRBNY finalize this new policy to reduce the risk that vendors may not be required to take steps to fully identify and mitigate all conflicts.

While the Federal Reserve System took steps to mitigate risk of losses on its emergency loans, opportunities exist to strengthen risk management practices for future crisis lending. The Federal Reserve Board approved program terms and conditions designed to mitigate risk of losses and one or more Reserve Banks were responsible for managing such risk for each program. Reserve Banks required borrowers under several programs to post collateral in excess of the loan amount. For programs that did not have this requirement, Reserve Banks required borrowers to pledge assets with high credit ratings as collateral. For loans to specific institutions, Reserve Banks negotiated loss protections with the private sector and hired vendors to help oversee the portfolios that collateralized loans. The emergency programs that have closed have not incurred losses and FRBNY does not project any losses on its outstanding loans. To manage risks posed by these new lending activities, Reserve Banks implemented new controls and FRBNY strengthened its risk management function. In mid-2009, FRBNY created a new risk management division and enhanced its risk analytics capabilities. But neither FRBNY nor the Federal Reserve Board tracked total exposure and stressed losses that could occur in adverse economic scenarios across all emergency programs. Further, the Federal Reserve System's procedures for managing borrower risks did not provide comprehensive guidance for how Reserve Banks should exercise discretion to restrict program access for higher-risk borrowers that were otherwise eligible for the Term Auction Facility (TAF) and emergency programs for primary dealers. To strengthen practices for managing risk of losses in the event of a future crisis, GAO recommends that the Federal Reserve System document a plan for more comprehensive risk tracking and strengthen procedures to manage program access for higher-risk borrowers.

While the Federal Reserve System took steps to promote consistent treatment of eligible program participants, it did not always document processes and decisions related to restricting access for some institutions. Reserve Banks generally offered assistance on the same terms to institutions that met announced eligibility requirements. For example, all eligible borrowers generally could borrow at the same interest rate and against the same types of eligible collateral. Reserve Banks retained and exercised discretion to restrict or deny program access for institutions based on supervisory or other concerns. For example, due to concerns about their financial condition, Reserve Banks restricted TAF access for at least 30 institutions. Further, in a few programs, FRBNY placed special restrictions, such as borrowing limits, on eligible institutions that posed higher risk of loss. Because Reserve Banks lacked specific procedures that staff should follow to exercise discretion and document actions to restrict higher-risk eligible borrowers for a few programs, the Federal Reserve System lacked assurance that Reserve Banks applied such restrictions consistently. Also, the Federal Reserve Board did not fully document its justification for extending credit on terms similar to the Primary Dealer Credit Facility (PDCF) to affiliates of a few PDCF-eligible institutions and did not provide written guidance to Reserve Banks on types of program decisions that would benefit from consultation with the Federal Reserve Board. In 2009, FRBNY allowed one entity to continue to issue to the Commercial Paper Funding Facility, even though a change in program terms by the Federal Reserve Board likely would have made it ineligible. FRBNY staff said they consulted the Federal Reserve Board regarding this situation, but did not document this consultation and did not have any formal guidance as to whether such continued use required approval by the Federal Reserve Board. To better ensure an appropriate level of transparency and accountability for decisions to extend or restrict access to emergency assistance, GAO recommends that the Federal Reserve Board set forth its process for documenting its rationale for emergency authorizations and document its guidance to Reserve Banks on program decisions that require consultation with the Federal Reserve Board.

List of Federal Reserve Emergency Programs and Assistance Covered by this GAO Review

Dollars in billions

Programs and Assistance	Peak dollar amount outstanding	Balance as of 6/29/11	Description
Broad-based programs			
TAF - Term Auction Facility (Dec. 12, 2007–Mar. 8, 2010)	$493	$0	Auctioned one-month and three-month discount window loans to eligible depository institutions
Dollar Swap Lines (Dec. 12, 2007–Feb. 1, 2010[a])	586	0	Exchanged dollars with foreign central banks for foreign currency to help address disruptions in dollar funding markets abroad
TSLF - Term Securities Lending Facility (Mar. 11, 2008–Feb. 1, 2010)	236	0	Auctioned loans of U.S. Treasury securities to primary dealers against eligible collateral
PDCF - Primary Dealer Credit Facility (Mar. 16, 2008–Feb. 1, 2010)	130	0	Provided overnight cash loans to primary dealers against eligible collateral
AMLF - Asset-Backed Commercial Paper Money Market Mutual Fund Liquidity Facility (Sept. 19, 2008–Feb. 1, 2010)	152	0	Provided loans to depository institutions and their affiliates to finance purchases of eligible asset-backed commercial paper from money market mutual funds
CPFF - Commercial Paper Funding Facility (Oct. 7, 2008–Feb. 1, 2010)	348	0	Provided loans to a special purpose vehicle to finance purchases of new issues of asset-backed commercial paper and unsecured commercial paper from eligible issuers

Federal Reserve System

Dollars in billions			
Programs and Assistance	**Peak dollar amount outstanding**	**Balance as of 6/29/11**	**Description**
MMIFF - Money Market Investor Funding Facility (Oct. 21, 2008 but never used)	No loans provided	0	Created to finance the purchase of eligible short-term debt obligations held by money market mutual funds
TALF - Term Asset-Backed Securities Loan Facility (Nov. 25, 2008–June 30, 2010)	48	13	Provided loans to eligible investors to finance purchases of eligible asset-backed securities
Assistance to Individual Institutions			
Bear Stearns Companies, Inc. acquisition by JP Morgan Chase & Co. (JPMC)			
Bridge Loan (Mar. 14, 2008–Mar. 17, 2008)	13	0	Overnight loan provided to JPMC subsidiary, with which this subsidiary made a direct loan to Bear Stearns Companies, Inc.
Maiden Lane (Mar. 16, 2008)	29	22	Special purpose vehicle created to purchase approximately $30 billion of Bear Stearns's mortgage-related assets
AIG Assistance			
Revolving Credit Facility (Sept. 16, 2008–Jan. 14, 2011)	72	0	Revolving loan for the general corporate purposes of AIG and its subsidiaries, and to pay obligations as they came due
Securities Borrowing Facility (Oct. 8, 2008–Dec. 12, 2008)	21	0	Provided collateralized cash loans to reduce pressure on AIG to liquidate residential mortgage-backed securities (RMBS) in its securities lending portfolio
Maiden Lane II (Nov. 10, 2008)	20	9	Special purpose vehicle created to purchase RMBS from securities lending portfolio of AIG subsidiaries
Maiden Lane III (Nov. 10, 2008)	24	12	Special purpose vehicle created to purchase collateralized debt obligations on which AIG Financial Products had written credit default swaps
Life Insurance Securitization (March 2, 2009 but never implemented)	Not used	0	Authorized to provide credit to AIG that would be repaid with cash flows from its life insurance businesses

(Continued)

Dollars in billions			
Programs and Assistance	**Peak dollar amount outstanding**	**Balance as of 6/29/11**	**Description**
Loans to affiliates of some primary dealers (Sept. 21, 2008–Feb. 1, 2010)	41	0	Loans provided to broker-dealer affiliates of four primary dealers on terms similar to those for PDCF
Citigroup Inc. lending commitment (Nov. 23, 2008–Dec. 2009)	No loans provided	0	Commitment to provide non-recourse loan to Citigroup against ring-fence assets if losses on asset pool reached $56.2 billion
Bank of America Corporation lending commitment (Jan. 16, 2009–Sept. 2009)	No loans provided	0	Commitment to provide non-recourse loan facility to Bank of America if losses on ring fence assets exceeded $18 billion (agreement never finalized)
Open Market Operations			
Agency Mortgage-Backed Securities Purchase Program (Nov. 25, 2008–Mar. 31, 2010)	$1,250 total purchases	$909 (remaining principal balance)	Purchased agency mortgage-backed securities to provide support to mortgage and housing markets and to foster improved conditions in the financial markets more generally

Source: Federal Reserve Board Statistical Release H.4.1 and Federal Reserve Board documents.

Note: Dates in parentheses are the program announcement dates, and where relevant, the date the program or assistance was closed or terminated. On October 3, 2008, the Federal Reserve Board authorized the Direct Money Market Mutual Fund Lending Facility (DMLF) and rescinded this authorization one week later. DMLF was not implemented.

[a] Some dollar swap lines reopened in May 2010.

ABBREVIATIONS

ABCP	asset-backed commercial paper
Agency MBS program	Agency Mortgage-Backed Securities Purchase Program
AIG	American International Group, Inc.
AIGFP	AIG Financial Products Corp.
AMLF	Asset-Backed Commercial Paper Money Market Mutual Fund Liquidity Facility
Bank of America	Bank of America Corporation
Bear Stearns	Bear Stearns Companies, Inc.
Citigroup	Citigroup Inc.
CDO	collateralized debt obligation
COSO	Committee of Sponsoring Organizations of the Treadway Commission
CPFF	Commercial Paper Funding Facility

CRM	Credit Risk Management group
Deloitte	Deloitte & Touche LLP
DENTS	Dollars at risk in Event of Need to Terminate under Stress
DMLF	Direct Money Market Mutual Fund Lending Facility
Dodd-Frank Act	Dodd-Frank Wall Street Reform and Consumer Protection Act
FAR	Federal Acquisition Regulation
FDIC	Federal Deposit Insurance Corporation
Federal Reserve Board	Board of Governors of the Federal Reserve System
FOMC	Federal Open Market Committee
FRBB	Federal Reserve Bank of Boston
FRBNY	Federal Reserve Bank of New York
FRBR	Federal Reserve Bank of Richmond
GAAP	U.S. generally accepted accounting principles
GE	General Electric Company
Goldman Sachs	Goldman Sachs Group Inc.
JPMC	JP Morgan Chase & Co.
KPMG	KPMG LLP
Lehman Brothers	Lehman Brothers Holdings Inc.
LLC	limited liability corporation
MBS	mortgage-backed securities
Merrill Lynch	Merrill Lynch & Co.
MMIFF	Money Market Investor Funding Facility
MMMF	money market mutual fund
NRSRO	Nationally Recognized Statistical Rating Organization
OIG	Federal Reserve Board Office of the Inspector General
PDCF	Primary Dealer Credit Facility
PIMCO	Pacific Investment Management Company LLC
RCF	revolving credit facility
RFP	request-for-proposal
RBOPS	Reserve Bank Operations and Payment Systems
SBF	securities borrowing facility
SPV	special purpose vehicle
TAF	Term Auction Facility
TALF	Term Asset-Backed Securities Loan Facility
TARP	Troubled Asset Relief Program
TLGP	Temporary Liquidity Guarantee Program
TSLF	Term Securities Lending Facility
Treasury	Department of the Treasury

July 21, 2011

Congressional Addressees

The Federal Reserve System, which consists of the Board of Governors of the Federal Reserve System (Federal Reserve Board)—a federal agency—and 12 regional Reserve

Banks, played a key role in the U.S. government's policy responses to the financial crisis that began in summer 2007.[1] From late 2007 through mid-2010, Reserve Banks provided more than a trillion dollars in emergency loans to the financial sector to address strains in credit markets and to avert failures of individual institutions believed to be a threat to the stability of the financial system. The scale and nature of this assistance amounted to an unprecedented expansion of the Federal Reserve System's traditional role as lender-of-last-resort to depository institutions. In March 2008, the Federal Reserve Board cited "unusual and exigent circumstances" in invoking its emergency authority under section 13(3) of the Federal Reserve Act of 1913 to authorize a Reserve Bank to extend credit to nondepository institutions and for the first time since the Great Depression, a Reserve Bank extended credit under this authority. The Federal Reserve Board would invoke this authority on three other occasions within that month, including in connection with facilitating the sale of Bear Stearns Companies, Inc. (Bear Stearns), and on several occasions in late 2008 when the failure of Lehman Brothers Holdings Inc. (Lehman Brothers) triggered a severe intensification of the financial crisis.[2] Many of the emergency programs established under this authority were intended to address unprecedented disruptions in key nonbank funding markets that together had come to rival the banking sector in facilitating loans to consumers and businesses. The Federal Reserve Bank of New York (FRBNY), which operated most of these programs under authorization from the Federal Reserve Board, faced a number of unique operational challenges related to implementation and oversight for numerous emergency programs, many of which required large vendor procurements to fill gaps in Federal Reserve System expertise. To date, most of the Reserve Banks' emergency loans have been repaid, and FRBNY projects repayment on all outstanding loans.

During and after the crisis, some members of Congress and others expressed concern that certain details of the Federal Reserve System's emergency lending activities, including the names of borrowers receiving loans, were kept confidential.[3] In addition, certain ties between Reserve Banks and financial institutions, such as those with a director on a Reserve Bank's board of directors, raised questions about whether the Federal Reserve System took appropriate steps to prevent favoritism and mitigate conflicts of interest. Title XI of the Dodd-Frank Wall Street Reform and Consumer Protection Act (Dodd-Frank Act) contains provisions intended to enhance transparency and accountability related to the Federal Reserve System's emergency lending activities.[4] The Dodd-Frank Act granted us new authority to audit certain Federal Reserve System lending activities and required us to conduct a one-time audit of emergency loans and other assistance provided by the Federal Reserve System from December 1, 2007, through July 21, 2010, the enactment date of the act. Specifically, the Dodd-Frank Act directed us to review all programs created as a result of section 13(3) of the Federal Reserve Act as well as specified programs authorized under other Federal Reserve Act provisions. It did not grant us authority to review discount window loans made before enactment. Accordingly, this report does not cover the Federal Reserve System's discount window lending during the recent financial crisis.[5] Table 1 lists all programs covered by our review, including the broad-based programs and assistance extended to individual institutions.

Accordingly, for each of the emergency programs or actions, where relevant, the objectives of this report are to: (1) describe the basis and purpose for the establishment of the program; (2) assess the Reserve Banks' controls over financial reporting and accounting; (3) evaluate the Reserve Banks' policies and practices for the use, selection, and payment of vendors; (4) evaluate the effectiveness of policies and practices for identifying and managing conflicts of interest for Reserve Bank employees, Reserve Bank vendors, and members of Reserve Banks' boards of directors; (5) assess the effectiveness of security and collateral policies in place to mitigate risk of losses; and (6) examine the extent to which program implementation resulted in consistent and equitable treatment of eligible participants.

Table 1. List of Federal Reserve Emergency Programs and Assistance Covered by Our Review

Programs and assistance	Status	Description
Broad-based programs		
Term Auction Facility (Dec. 12, 2007)	Closed on March 8, 2010	Auctioned one-month and three-month discount window loans to eligible depository institutions
Dollar Swap Lines (Dec. 12, 2007)	Closed on February 1, 2010 (some reopened in May 2010)	Exchanged dollars with foreign central banks for foreign currency to help address disruptions in dollar funding markets abroad
Term Securities Lending Facility (Mar. 11, 2008)	Closed on February 1, 2010	Auctioned loans of U.S. Treasury securities to primary dealers against eligible collateral
Primary Dealer Credit Facility (Mar. 16, 2008)	Closed on February 1, 2010	Provided overnight cash loans to primary dealers against eligible collateral
Asset-Backed Commercial Paper Money Market Mutual Fund Liquidity Facility (Sept. 19, 2008)	Closed on February 1, 2010	Provided loans to depository institutions and their affiliates to finance purchases of eligible asset-backed commercial paper from money market mutual funds
Commercial Paper Funding Facility (Oct. 7, 2008)	Closed on February 1, 2010	Provided loans to a special purpose vehicle to finance purchases of new issues of asset-backed commercial paper and unsecured commercial paper from eligible issuers
Money Market Investor Funding Facility (Oct. 21, 2008, but never used)	Closed on October 30, 2009	Created to finance the purchase of eligible short-term debt obligations held by money market mutual funds
Term Asset-Backed Securities Loan Facility (Nov. 25, 2008)	Closed; $13 billion outstanding	Provided loans to eligible investors to finance purchases of eligible asset-backed securities
Assistance to individual institutions		
Bear Stearns Companies, Inc. acquisition by JP Morgan Chase & Co.		
Bridge Loan (Mar. 14, 2008)	Repaid on March 17, 2008	Overnight loan provided to JP Morgan Chase & Co. bank subsidiary, with which this subsidiary made a direct loan to Bear Stearns Companies, Inc.
Maiden Lane (Mar. 16, 2008)	$22 billion outstanding	Special purpose vehicle created to purchase approximately $30 billion of Bear Stearns's mortgage-related assets

Table 1. (Continued)

Programs and assistance	Status	Description
American International Group, Inc. (AIG)		
Revolving Credit Facility *(Sept. 16, 2008)*	Repaid on January 14, 2011	Revolving loan for the general corporate purposes of AIG and its subsidiaries, and to pay obligations as they came due
Securities Borrowing Facility *(Oct. 8, 2008)*	Closed on December 12, 2008	Provided collateralized cash loans to reduce pressure on AIG to liquidate residential mortgage-backed securities (RMBS) in its securities lending portfolio
Maiden Lane II *(Nov.10, 2008)*	$9 billion outstanding	Special purpose vehicle created to purchase RMBS from the securities lending portfolio of AIG subsidiaries
Maiden Lane III *(Nov.10, 2008)*	$12 billion outstanding	Special purpose vehicle created to purchase collateralized debt obligations on which AIG Financial Products had written credit default swaps
Life Insurance Securitization *(March 2, 2009, but never used)*	Never used	Authorized to provide credit to AIG that would be repaid with cash flows from its life insurance businesses
Credit extensions to affiliates of some primary dealers *(Sept. 21, 2008)*	Closed on February 1, 2010	Loans provided to broker-dealer affiliates of four primary dealers on terms similar to those for Primary Dealer Credit Facility
Citigroup lending commitment *(Nov. 23, 2008)*	Terminated in December 2009	Commitment to provide nonrecourse loan to Citigroup against ring-fence assets if losses on asset pool reached $56.2 billion
Bank of America lending commitment *(Jan. 16, 2009)*	Terminated in September 2009	Commitment to provide nonrecourse loan facility to Bank of America if losses on ring-fence assets exceeded $18 billion (agreement never finalized)
Open market operations		
Agency Mortgage-Backed Securities Purchase Program *(Nov. 25, 2008)*	Closed; $909 billion (remaining principal balance)	Purchased agency mortgage-backed securities to provide support to mortgage and housing markets and to foster improved conditions in the financial markets more generally

Source: Federal Reserve Board Statistical Release H.4.1 and Federal Reserve Board documents.

Note: Dates in parentheses are the dates the programs were announced. The outstanding balances for TALF, Maiden Lane, Maiden Lane II, Maiden Lane III, and the Agency Mortgage-Back Security purchase program are as reported in the Federal Reserve Board Statistical Release H.4.1 as of June 29, 2011. Outstanding balances for the Maiden Lanes include outstanding principal and accrued interest. On October 3, 2008, the Federal Reserve Board authorized the Direct Money Market Mutual Fund Lending Facility and rescinded this authorization 1 week later. This program was not implemented.

SCOPE AND METHODOLOGY

To describe the basis and purpose for the establishment of the programs, we reviewed documentation supporting the Federal Reserve Board's authorizations for the emergency programs, Federal Reserve System documents and press releases describing the purpose of the programs, and other relevant program documentation, including announced terms and conditions. We interviewed Federal Reserve System officials and staff to obtain their perspectives on the basis and purpose for each program. To illustrate financial and economic conditions at the time these programs were authorized, we reviewed our work on the financial crisis and reports and studies by the Federal Reserve System, the Congressional Budget Office, the Congressional Research Service, and others.

To assess Reserve Banks' controls over financial reporting and accounting, we developed an audit strategy designed to leverage, to the extent possible, the audit work performed by the Federal Reserve System's external and internal auditors specific to the emergency programs. To understand the audit coverage, including audit requirements and audit oversight, of the accounting and financial reporting internal controls over the emergency programs, we reviewed relevant legislation and Federal Reserve System documentation. We also interviewed Federal Reserve System officials, the Federal Reserve Board's Office of the Inspector General (OIG), and internal and external audit staff. To determine the extent of the audit coverage over these programs, we evaluated the internal and external auditors' scope of work. We reviewed relevant external audit reports, including those issued by the Reserve Banks' independent external auditor, Deloitte & Touche LLP (Deloitte), and GAO. We also reviewed relevant reports issued by the Federal Reserve Board, Reserve Bank internal audit functions, and OIG. To determine whether Deloitte's audit conclusions pertaining to the accounting and financial reporting internal controls over the emergency programs were appropriately supported, we reviewed Deloitte's key audit documentation, including audit strategy, planning, and accounting memoranda; internal control and account balance testing audit procedures and results; and summary memorandums. We evaluated the quality of this documentation against relevant auditing standards. Our review was specific to the audit documentation pertaining to the accounting and financial reporting internal controls related to the emergency programs. We also reviewed independent service auditors' reports on the internal controls over the vendor organizations that provided custodial, administrative, or accounting services to FRBNY for certain of its emergency programs and determined whether FRBNY and Deloitte considered the results of the independent service auditors' reports in planning and conducting their audits and reviews.

To evaluate the Reserve Banks' policies and practices for the use, selection, and payment of vendors, we analyzed acquisition policies and guidance for FRBNY, the Federal Reserve Bank of Boston (FRBB), and the Federal Reserve Bank of Richmond (FRBR) to understand how the Reserve Banks used, selected, and paid vendors for the emergency programs. We obtained and analyzed contract and vendor payment information and interviewed Reserve Bank staff to determine the extent to which the Reserve Banks used vendors for each program and the services provided. We excluded some contracts for routine data subscriptions and registration fees. We determined, based on discussions with Reserve Bank staff and comparisons to other information sources, that the data were sufficiently reliable for the purposes of our review. To determine the processes and criteria for selecting vendors, we interviewed bank staff and obtained and analyzed source selection documents for significant contracts—defined as contracts of more than $500,000 or that included work significant to the creation or operation of each program. Finally, we obtained and reviewed significant contracts and vendor payment information for all contracts to determine the total amount and structure of vendor payments and the source of funds used to pay vendors.

To evaluate the effectiveness of Reserve Bank polices and practices for managing conflicts of interest, we reviewed information about the roles played by Reserve Bank management and employees, vendors, and Reserve Bank directors to identify relevant types of conflicts of interest created by the establishment and operation of the emergency programs. We reviewed relevant statutory prohibitions on conflicts of interest that apply to federal government and Federal Reserve System employees and federal government guidance for agencies' management of employee conflicts of interest. Our review of conflict issues for Reserve Bank employees and vendors focused on FRBNY, which implemented most of the emergency actions. To determine how FRBNY mitigated conflicts for its management and staff, we obtained and reviewed its relevant policies, including its Code of Conduct, and steps it took to help ensure compliance with these policies. Specifically, we reviewed the extent to which FRBNY implemented additional guidance, training, or other new practices to help ensure identification and management of conflicts arising from its employees' involvement in the emergency programs. We also obtained and reviewed documentation of the basis for decisions on any waiver requests to allow FRBNY officials, staff, or vendors to participate in decisions related to the programs that might otherwise present a conflict of interest. We did not review documentation related to employees' decisions to recuse themselves from matters due to conflicts because such documentation is not required by law or regulation. To determine steps taken by FRBNY to ensure that its vendors identified and mitigated conflicts related to their roles in helping to administer the emergency assistance, we reviewed relevant vendor contract provisions, written vendor plans documenting steps to identify and manage relevant conflicts, documentation of on-site reviews of vendor firms to help ensure compliance with conflict policies, and other relevant documentation. We compared FRBNY's management of vendor conflicts issues to actions taken by the Department of the Treasury (Treasury) to manage risks related to vendor conflicts for its largest financial stability program, the Troubled Asset Relief Program. We reviewed FRBNY's conflict of interest policies to determine the extent to which these policies have been revised to address any lessons learned from the crisis. We also interviewed FRBNY's Ethics Officer and other staff on the application of conflict of interest policies.

To assess the effectiveness of security and collateral policies in place to mitigate risk of losses, we reviewed relevant documentation and interviewed Federal Reserve System officials to identify key features of security and collateral policies and determine how these policies were designed to mitigate risk of losses for each emergency program. We obtained and analyzed financial data to describe the level of income and losses from the programs. We reviewed and corroborated internal and external audit findings related to the effectiveness of operational controls related to security and collateral policies and reviewed the steps taken by the Reserve Banks to address any recommendations based on these findings. For two programs, the Term Auction Facility (TAF) and the Primary Dealer Credit Facility (PDCF), we obtained and analyzed detailed collateral data to determine compliance with program requirements for collateral. For example, we examined the consistency of prices and haircuts applied to TAF and PDCF collateral. For PDCF collateral data, the lack of sufficiently detailed data documentation for some key pricing variables made it difficult to draw reliable conclusions about whether assets pledged to the PDCF as collateral were priced consistently. More broadly, we obtained and analyzed documentation of steps taken by the Reserve Banks to develop risk governance structures and practices needed to manage the risks associated with the emergency programs and assistance. For example, we reviewed relevant documentation and interviewed Federal Reserve System officials to determine the extent to which the Federal Reserve System estimated and monitored potential losses from the emergency lending activities and documented its procedures for managing program access for higher-risk borrowers. Finally, given the impact of these activities on excess earnings that the Federal Reserve Board remits to Treasury from its emergency programs, we obtained and reviewed relevant documentation and interviewed Federal Reserve Board staff. In addition, to determine the broader implications of the Federal Reserve Board's practices for projecting future excess earnings, we interviewed Treasury staff who project the Federal Reserve Board's excess earnings. The scope of our review of the security and collateral policies included the broad-based programs and the loans provided to avert the failures of specific institutions determined to be systemically significant. Our scope for this objective did not include the Agency Mortgage-Backed Securities Purchase Program (Agency MBS program), which did not provide loans, and therefore required no collateral.

To examine the extent to which program implementation resulted in consistent and equitable treatment of eligible participants, we reviewed and analyzed documentation of the basis for the Federal Reserve Board's decisions about which types of institutions would be eligible to participate in the emergency programs. To determine the extent to which the Reserve Banks offered the same terms and conditions to all participants, which for some programs included financial institutions affiliated with Reserve Bank directors, we reviewed documentation of program terms and conditions and obtained and analyzed program transaction data. Specifically, we reviewed Reserve Banks' documentation of restrictions put in place for specific institutions and analyzed program transaction data to determine the extent to which other borrowing institutions received loans on terms that deviated from the announced terms and conditions. For example, we reviewed Reserve Bank documentation of the processes and basis for exercising discretion about whether to restrict or deny program access for some institutions to determine what steps were taken to help ensure this discretion was exercised consistently. To assess whether program use was consistent with the Federal Reserve Board's announced policy objectives, we analyzed program transaction data to identify significant trends in the use of the programs and reviewed relevant studies by the Federal Reserve System and others to identify factors that likely contributed to these trends. To understand factors contributing to such trends, we also interviewed Federal Reserve System staff and industry associations representing types of institutions that were eligible to participate in the programs. To identify the largest participants across the emergency programs, we aggregated dollar transaction amounts for borrowing entities at the parent company level. To account for differences in the terms over which loans were outstanding, we multiplied each loan amount by the number of days the loan was outstanding and divided this amount by the number of days in a year (365). Our scope for this objective included the broad-based programs and did not include the special assistance provided to avert the failures of specific individual institutions.

For parts of our methodology that involved the analysis of computer-processed data, we assessed the reliability of these data and determined that they were sufficiently reliable for our purposes. Data sets for which we conducted data reliability assessments include Federal Reserve Board transaction data for the emergency programs and assistance, data from releases of the Federal Reserve Board's weekly statistical release H.4.1, FRBB data on the Asset-Backed Commercial Paper Money Market Mutual Fund Liquidity Facility (AMLF), and FRBNY data on other programs and assistance. To assess the reliability of these data, we obtained written responses from the Reserve Banks to questions about how they collected and maintained the integrity of these data. For some program data, we interviewed Federal Reserve System staff about steps they took to maintain the integrity and reliability of program data. We believe that these data are sufficiently reliable for the purpose of our analysis.

We conducted this performance audit from August 2010 to July 2011 in accordance with generally accepted government auditing standards. Those standards require that we plan and perform the audit to obtain sufficient, appropriate evidence to provide a reasonable basis for our findings and conclusions based on our audit objectives. We believe that the evidence obtained provides a reasonable basis for our findings and conclusions based on our audit objectives.

BACKGROUND

Overview of the Federal Reserve System

The Federal Reserve Act of 1913 established the Federal Reserve System as the country's central bank. The Federal Reserve Act made the Federal Reserve System an independent, decentralized bank to better ensure that monetary policy would be based on a broad economic perspective from all regions of the country. The Federal Reserve Board has defined the term "monetary policy" as the actions undertaken by a central bank, such as the Federal Reserve System, to influence the availability and cost of money and credit to help promote national economic goals. The Federal Reserve Act of 1913, as amended, gave the Federal Reserve System responsibility for setting monetary policy. The Federal Reserve System consists of the Federal Reserve Board located in Washington, D.C.; 12 Reserve Banks, which have 24 branches located throughout the nation; and the Federal Open Market Committee (FOMC), which is composed of the Board of Governors, as well as five Reserve Bank presidents, serving on a rotating basis.

The Federal Reserve Board is a federal agency that is responsible for maintaining the stability of financial markets; supervising financial and bank holding companies, state-chartered banks that are members of the Federal Reserve System, and the U.S. operations of foreign banking organizations; and supervising the operations of the Reserve Banks.[6] The top officials of the Federal Reserve Board are the seven members of the Board of Governors who are appointed by the President and confirmed by the U.S. Senate. Although the Federal Reserve Board is required to report to Congress on its activities, its decisions do not have to be approved by either the President or Congress.

Unlike the Federal Reserve Board, the Reserve Banks are not federal agencies. Each Reserve Bank is a federally chartered corporation with a board of directors. The membership of each Reserve Bank board of directors is determined by a process intended to ensure that each bank board represents the public and member banks in its district.[7] Under the Federal

Reserve Act, Reserve Banks are subject to the general supervision of the Federal Reserve Board. The Federal Reserve Board has delegated some of its responsibilities such as supervision and regulation to the Reserve Banks. The Federal Reserve Act authorizes the Reserve Banks to make discount window loans, execute monetary policy operations at the direction of the FOMC, and examine bank holding companies and member banks under rules and regulations prescribed by the Federal Reserve Board. The Reserve Banks also provide payment services, such as check clearing and wire transfers, to depository institutions, Treasury, and government agencies.

The FOMC plays a central role in the execution of the Federal Reserve System's monetary policy mandate to promote price stability and maximum employment. The FOMC consists of the seven members of the Board of Governors, the President of FRBNY, and four other Reserve Bank presidents who serve on a rotating basis. The FOMC is responsible for directing open market operations to influence the total amount of money and credit available in the economy. FRBNY carries out FOMC directives on open market operations by engaging in purchases or sales of certain securities, typically U.S. government securities, in the secondary market. FRBNY conducts these transactions through primary dealers, a designated group of broker-dealers and banks that transact with FRBNY in its conduct of open market operations. For example, FRBNY purchases of U.S. government securities from a primary dealer increase the supply of reserves in the banking system, which can lower the federal funds rate—the interest rate that depository institutions pay when they borrow unsecured loans of reserve balances overnight from each other. FRBNY's sales of U.S. government securities to primary dealers reduce the supply of reserves and can increase the federal funds rate. Changes in the federal funds rate can have a strong impact on other short-term interest rates.

Unlike federal agencies funded through congressional appropriations, the Federal Reserve Board and the Reserve Banks are self-funded entities that deduct their expenses from their revenue and transfer the remaining amount to Treasury.[8] Although the Federal Reserve Board's primary mission is to support a stable economy, not to maximize the amount transferred to Treasury, the Federal Reserve System revenues contribute to total U.S. revenues, and deductions from System revenues thus represent an indirect cost to U.S. taxpayers. As discussed later in this report, the Federal Reserve System revenues transferred to Treasury have increased substantially in recent years, chiefly as a result of interest income earned from the Federal Reserve System's large-scale emergency programs. To the extent that Reserve Banks suffer losses on emergency loans, these losses would be deducted from the excess earnings transferred to Treasury. If such losses were to exceed a Reserve Bank's earnings, a Reserve Bank could reduce its remittances to Treasury to zero. According to Federal Reserve System officials, under an extreme scenario under which a Reserve Bank's losses eroded all of its capital, a Reserve Bank could, in its financial accounting, claim reductions in future remittances to Treasury as an addition to current capital.[9] Another option for a Reserve Bank to replenish capital would be to request that its member banks purchase additional stock in the Reserve Bank beyond the amount required for membership in the Federal Reserve System under the Federal Reserve Act.

Financial Crisis

The recent financial crisis was the most severe that the United States has experienced since the Great Depression. The dramatic decline in the U.S. housing market that began in 2006 precipitated a decline in the price of financial assets around mid-2007 that were associated with housing, particularly mortgage-related assets based on subprime loans. Some institutions found themselves so exposed that they were threatened with failure—and some failed—because they were unable to raise the necessary capital as the value of their portfolios declined. Other institutions, ranging from government-sponsored enterprises such as Fannie Mae and Freddie Mac to large securities firms, were left holding "toxic" mortgages or mortgage-related assets that became increasingly difficult to value, were illiquid, and potentially had little worth. Moreover, investors not only stopped buying securities backed by mortgages but also became reluctant to buy securities backed by many other types of assets. Because of uncertainty about the financial condition and solvency of financial entities, the prices banks charged each other for funds rose dramatically, and interbank lending effectively came to a halt. The resulting liquidity and credit crisis made the financing on which businesses and individuals depend increasingly difficult to obtain as cash-strapped banks held on to their assets. By late summer of 2008, the potential ramifications of the financial crisis included the continued failure of financial institutions, increased losses of individual wealth, reduced corporate investments, and further tightening of credit that would exacerbate the emerging global economic slowdown that was beginning to take shape.

During the crisis, Congress, the President, federal regulators, and others undertook a number of steps to facilitate financial intermediation by banks and the securities markets. In addition to the Federal Reserve Board's emergency programs, significant policy interventions led by others included, but were not limited to, the following:

- *Troubled Asset Relief Program.* On October 3, 2008, Congress passed and the President signed the Emergency Economic Stabilization Act of 2008, which authorized Treasury to establish the Troubled Asset Relief Program (TARP). Treasury's Capital Purchase Program was the primary initiative under TARP for stabilizing the financial markets and banking system. Treasury created the program in October 2008 to stabilize the financial system by providing capital to qualifying regulated financial institutions through the purchase of senior preferred shares and subordinated debt.[10] On October 14, 2008, Treasury allocated $250 billion of the $700 billion in overall TARP funds for the Capital Purchase Program but adjusted its allocation to $218 billion in March 2009 to reflect lower estimated funding needs based on actual participation and the expectation that institutions would repay their investments. The program was closed to new investments on December 31, 2009, and, in total, Treasury invested $205 billion in 707 financial institutions over the life of the program.
- *Temporary Liquidity Guarantee Program.* In October 2008, the Federal Deposit Insurance Corporation (FDIC) created the Temporary Liquidity Guarantee Program (TLGP) to complement the Capital Purchase Program and the Federal Reserve Board's Commercial Paper Funding Facility (CPFF) and other liquidity programs in restoring confidence in financial institutions and repairing their capacity to meet the credit needs of American households and businesses.[11] TLGP's Debt Guarantee

Program was designed to improve liquidity in term-funding markets by guaranteeing certain newly issued senior unsecured debt of financial institutions and their holding companies. Under the Debt Guarantee Program, FDIC guaranteed more than $600 billion of newly issued senior unsecured debt for insured depository institutions, their holding companies, and qualified affiliates and provided temporary unlimited coverage for certain non-interest-bearing transaction accounts at insured institutions. TLGP's debt guarantee program ceased issuing new guarantees on October 31, 2009.

THE FEDERAL RESERVE BOARD USED EMERGENCY AND OTHER AUTHORITIES TO AUTHORIZE LIQUIDITY PROGRAMS TO STABILIZE MARKETS AND INSTITUTIONS

Between late 2007 and early 2009, the Federal Reserve Board created more than a dozen new emergency programs to stabilize financial markets and provided financial assistance to avert the failures of a few individual institutions. The Federal Reserve Board authorized most of this emergency assistance under emergency authority contained in section 13(3) of the Federal Reserve Act.[12] Three of the programs covered by this review—TAF, dollar swap lines with foreign central banks, and the Agency MBS program—were authorized under other provisions of the Federal Reserve Act that do not require a determination that emergency conditions exist, although the swap lines and the Agency MBS program did require authorization by the FOMC. In many cases, the decisions by the Federal Reserve Board, the FOMC, and the Reserve Banks about the authorization, initial terms of, and implementation of the Federal Reserve System's emergency assistance were made over the course of only days or weeks as the Federal Reserve Board sought to act quickly to address rapidly deteriorating market conditions. FRBNY implemented most of these emergency activities under authorization from the Federal Reserve Board. In 2009, FRBNY, at the direction of the FOMC, began large-scale purchases of mortgage-backed securities (MBS) issued by the housing government-sponsored enterprises, Fannie Mae and Freddie Mac, or guaranteed by Ginnie Mae.[13] Purchases of these agency MBS were intended to provide support to the mortgage and housing markets and to foster improved conditions in financial markets more generally. Most of the Federal Reserve Board's broad-based emergency programs closed on February 1, 2010. Figure 1 provides a timeline for the establishment, modification, and termination of Federal Reserve System emergency programs subject to this review.

In December 2007, the Federal Reserve Board Created TAF and Opened Swap Lines under Nonemergency Authorities to Address Global Strains in Interbank Lending Markets

In the months before the authorization of TAF and new swap line arrangements, which were the first of the emergency programs subject to this review, the Federal Reserve Board took steps to ease emerging strains in credit markets through its traditional monetary policy tools. In late summer 2007, sudden strains in term interbank lending markets emerged primarily due to intensifying investor concerns about commercial banks' actual exposures to various mortgage-related securities. The cost of term funding (loans provided at terms of 1 month or longer) spiked suddenly in August 2007, and commercial banks increasingly had to borrow overnight to meet their funding needs.[14] The Federal Reserve Board feared that the disorderly functioning of interbank lending markets would impair the ability of commercial banks to provide credit to households and businesses. To ease stresses in these markets, on August 17, 2007, the Federal Reserve Board made two temporary changes to the terms at which Reserve Banks extended loans through the discount window. First, it approved the reduction of the discount rate—the interest rate at which the Reserve Banks extended collateralized loans at the discount window—by 50 basis points.[15] Second, to address specific strains in term-funding markets, the Federal Reserve Board approved extending the discount window lending term from overnight to up to 30 days, with the possibility of renewal. According to a Federal Reserve Board study, this change initially resulted in little additional borrowing from the discount window.[16] In addition to the discount window changes, starting in September 2007, the FOMC announced a series of reductions in the target federal funds rate—the FOMC-established target interest rate that banks charge each other for loans. In October 2007, tension in term funding subsided temporarily. However, issues reappeared in late November and early December, possibly driven in part by a seasonal contraction in the supply of year-end funding.

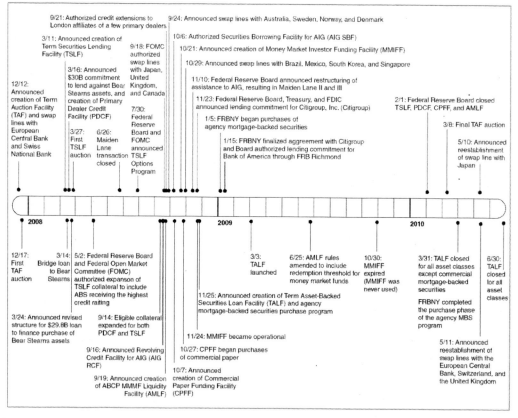

Source: Federal Reserve System documents and press releases.

Figure 1. Timeline of Federal Reserve Emergency Actions, December 2007–June 2010.

Term Auction Facility

On December 12, 2007, the Federal Reserve Board announced the creation of TAF to address continuing disruptions in U.S. term interbank lending markets. The Federal Reserve Board authorized Reserve Banks to extend credit through TAF by revising the regulations governing Reserve Bank discount window lending. TAF was intended to help provide term funding to depository institutions eligible to borrow from the discount window.[17] In contrast to the traditional discount window program, which loaned funds to individual institutions at the discount rate, TAF was designed to auction loans to many eligible institutions at once at a market-determined interest rate (for a more detailed explanation of TAF, see app. XIII). Federal Reserve Board officials noted that one important advantage of this auction approach was that it could address concerns among eligible borrowers about the perceived stigma of discount window borrowing.[18] Federal Reserve Board officials noted that an institution might be reluctant to borrow from the discount window out of concern that its creditors and other counterparties might become aware of its discount window use and perceive it as a sign of distress. The auction format allowed banks to approach the Reserve Banks collectively rather than individually and obtain funds at an interest rate set by auction rather than at a premium set by the Federal Reserve Board.[19] Additionally, whereas discount window loan funds could be obtained immediately by an institution facing severe funding pressures, TAF borrowers did not receive loan funds until 3 days after the auction. For these reasons, TAF-eligible borrowers may have attached less of a stigma to auctions than to traditional discount window borrowing. The first TAF auction was held on December 17, 2007, with subsequent auctions occurring approximately every 2 weeks until the final TAF auction on March 8, 2010.

Dollar Swap Lines

Concurrent with the announcement of TAF, the FOMC announced the establishment of dollar swap arrangements with two foreign central banks to address similar disruptions in dollar funding markets abroad. In a typical swap line transaction, FRBNY exchanged dollars for the foreign central bank's currency at the prevailing exchange rate, and the foreign central bank agreed to buy back its currency (to "unwind" the exchange) at this same exchange rate at an agreed upon future date (for a more detailed explanation, see app. IX).[20] The market for interbank funding in U.S. dollars is global, and many foreign banks hold U.S.-dollar-denominated assets and fund these assets by borrowing in U.S. dollars. In contrast to U.S. commercial banks, foreign banks did not hold significant U.S.-dollar deposits, and as a result, dollar funding disruptions were particularly acute for many foreign banks during the recent crisis. In December 2007, the European Central Bank and Swiss National Bank requested dollar swap arrangements with the Federal Reserve System to increase their ability to provide U.S. dollar loans to banks in their jurisdictions. Federal Reserve Board staff memoranda recommending that the FOMC approve these swap arrangements noted that continuing tension in dollar funding markets abroad could further exacerbate tensions in U.S. funding markets.[21] On December 6, 2007, the FOMC approved requests from the European Central Bank and Swiss National Bank and authorized FRBNY to establish temporary swap lines under section 14 of the Federal Reserve Act.[22] During 2008, the FOMC approved temporary swap lines with 12 other foreign central banks.[23] FRBNY's swap lines with the 14 central banks closed on February 1, 2010. In May 2010, to address the re-emergence of strains in dollar funding markets, FRBNY reopened swap lines with the Bank of Canada, the Bank of England, the European Central Bank, the Bank of Japan, and the Swiss National Bank through January 2011. On December 21, 2010, the FOMC announced an extension of these lines through August 1, 2011. On June 29, 2011, the Federal Reserve Board announced an extension of these swap lines through August 1, 2012.

In March 2008, the Federal Reserve Board Invoked Emergency Authority to Facilitate Sale of Bear Stearns and Expansion of Liquidity Support to Primary Dealers

In early March 2008, the Federal Reserve Board observed growing tension in the repurchase agreement markets—large, short-term collateralized funding markets—that many financial institutions rely on to finance a wide range of securities. Under a repurchase agreement, a borrowing institution generally acquires funds by selling securities to a lending institution and agreeing to repurchase the securities after a specified time at a given price. The securities, in effect, are collateral provided by the borrower to the lender. In the event of a borrower's default on the repurchase transaction, the lender would be able to take (and sell) the collateral provided by the borrower. Lenders typically will not provide a loan for the full market value of the posted securities, and the difference between the values of the securities and the loan is called a margin or haircut. This deduction is intended to protect the lenders against a decline in the price of the securities provided as collateral.[24] In early March, the Federal Reserve Board found that repurchase agreement lenders were requiring higher haircuts for loans against a range of securities and were becoming reluctant to lend against mortgage-related securities. As a result, many financial institutions increasingly had to rely on higher-quality collateral, such as U.S. Treasury securities, to obtain cash in these markets, and a shortage of such high-quality collateral emerged.[25] In March 2008, the Federal Reserve Board cited "unusual and exigent circumstances" in invoking section 13(3) of the Federal Reserve Act to authorize FRBNY to implement four emergency actions to address deteriorating conditions in these markets: (1) TSLF, (2) a bridge loan to Bear Stearns, (3) a commitment to lend up to $30 billion against Bear Stearns assets that resulted in the creation of Maiden Lane LLC, and (4) PDCF.

Term Securities Lending Facility

On March 11, 2008, the Federal Reserve Board announced the creation of the Term Securities Lending Facility (TSLF) to auction 28-day loans of U.S. Treasury securities to primary dealers to increase the amount of high-quality collateral available for these dealers to borrow against in the repurchase agreement markets. Through competitive auctions that allowed dealers to bid a fee to exchange harder-to-finance collateral for easier-to-finance Treasury securities, TSLF was intended to promote confidence among lenders and to reduce the need for dealers to sell illiquid assets into the markets, which could have further depressed the prices of these assets and contributed to a downward price spiral.[26] TSLF auctioned loans of Treasury securities against two schedules of collateral. Schedule 1 collateral included Treasury securities, agency debt, and agency MBS collateral that FRBNY accepted in repurchase agreements for traditional open market operations with primary dealers.[27] Schedule 2 included schedule 1 collateral as well as a broader range of assets, including highly rated mortgage-backed securities.[28] The Federal Reserve Board determined that providing funding support for private mortgage-backed securities through the schedule 2 auctions fell outside the scope of FRBNY's authority to conduct its securities lending program under section 14 of the Federal Reserve Act. Accordingly, for the first time during this crisis, the Federal Reserve Board invoked section 13(3) of the Federal Reserve Act to authorize the extension of credit, in this case in the form of Treasury securities, to nondepository institutions—in this case, the primary dealers. As discussed later in this section, the Federal Reserve Board later expanded the range of collateral eligible for TSLF as the crisis intensified. TSLF closed on February 1, 2010. See appendix XIV for a more detailed explanation of this program.

Bridge Loan to Bear Stearns

Shortly following the announcement of TSLF, the Federal Reserve Board invoked its emergency authority for a second time to authorize an emergency loan to avert a disorderly failure of Bear Stearns.[29] TSLF was announced on March 11, 2008, and the first TSLF auction was held on March 27, 2008. Federal Reserve Board officials noted that although TSLF was announced to address market tensions impacting many firms, some market participants concluded that its establishment was driven by specific concerns about Bear Stearns. Over a few days, Bear Stearns experienced a run on its liquidity as many of its lenders grew concerned that the firm would suffer greater losses in the future and stopped providing funding to the firm, even on a fully secured basis with high-quality assets provided as collateral.[30] Late on Thursday, March 13, 2008, the senior management of Bear Stearns notified FRBNY that it would likely have to file for bankruptcy protection the following day unless the Federal Reserve Board provided the firm with an emergency loan. The Federal Reserve Board feared that the sudden failure of Bear Stearns could have serious adverse impacts on markets in which Bear Stearns was a significant participant, including the repurchase agreements market. In particular, a Bear Stearns failure may have threatened the liquidity and solvency of other large institutions that relied heavily on short-term secured funding markets. On Friday, March 14, 2008, the Federal Reserve Board voted to authorize FRBNY to provide a $12.9 billion loan to Bear Stearns through JP Morgan Chase Bank, National Association, the largest bank subsidiary of JP Morgan Chase & Co. (JPMC), and to accept $13.8 billion of Bear Stearns's assets as collateral.[31] Appendix IV includes more information about this back-to-back loan transaction, which was repaid on Monday, March 17, 2008, with almost $4 million of interest. This emergency loan enabled Bear Stearns to avoid bankruptcy and continue to operate through the weekend. This provided time for potential acquirers, including JPMC, to assess Bear Stearns's financial condition and for FRBNY to prepare a new liquidity program, PDCF, to address strains that could emerge from a possible Bear Stearns bankruptcy announcement the following Monday. Federal Reserve Board and FRBNY officials hoped that bankruptcy could be averted by the announcement that a private sector firm would acquire Bear Stearns and stand behind its liabilities when the markets reopened on the following Monday.

Maiden Lane LLC

On Sunday, March 16, 2008, the Federal Reserve Board announced that FRBNY would lend up to $30 billion against certain Bear Stearns's assets to facilitate JPMC's acquisition of Bear Stearns. Over the weekend, JPMC had emerged as the only viable acquirer of Bear

Stearns. In congressional testimony, Timothy Geithner, who was the President of FRBNY in March 2008, provided the following account:

> Bear approached several major financial institutions, beginning on March 13. Those discussions intensified on Friday and Saturday. Bear's management provided us with periodic progress reports about a possible merger. Although several different institutions expressed interest in acquiring all or part of Bear, it was clear that the size of Bear, the apparent risk in its balance sheet, and the limited amount of time available for a possible acquirer to conduct due diligence compounded the difficulty. Ultimately, only JPMorgan Chase was willing to consider an offer of a binding commitment to acquire the firm and to stand behind Bear's substantial short-term obligations.[32]

According to FRBNY officials, on the morning of Sunday, March 16, 2008, JPMC's Chief Executive Officer told FRBNY that the merger would only be possible if certain mortgage-related assets were taken off Bear Stearns's balance sheet. Negotiations between JPMC and FRBNY senior management resulted in a preliminary agreement under which FRBNY would make a $30 billion nonrecourse loan to JPMC collateralized by these Bear Stearns assets. A March 16, 2008, letter from then-FRBNY President Geithner to JPMC's Chief Executive Officer documented the terms of the preliminary agreement.[33]

Significant issues that threatened to unravel the merger agreement emerged soon after the announcement. Bear Stearns board members and shareholders thought JPMC's offer to purchase the firm at $2 per share was too low and threatened to vote against the merger. Perceived ambiguity in the terms of the merger agreement raised further concerns that JPMC could be forced to stand behind Bear Stearns's obligations even in the event that the merger was rejected. Moreover, some Bear Stearns counterparties stopped trading with Bear Stearns because of uncertainty about whether JPMC would honor certain Bear Stearns obligations. FRBNY also had concerns with the level of protection provided under the preliminary lending agreement, under which FRBNY had agreed to lend on a nonrecourse basis against risky collateral. The risks of an unraveled merger agreement included a possible Bear Stearns bankruptcy and losses for JPMC, which might have been legally required to stand behind the obligations of a failed institution. Recognizing the risk that an unraveled merger posed to JPMC and the broader financial markets, FRBNY officials sought to renegotiate the lending agreement.

During the following week, the terms of this agreement were renegotiated, resulting in the creation of a new lending structure in the form of Maiden Lane LLC. From March 17 to March 24, 2008, FRBNY, JPMC, and Bear Stearns engaged in dual track negotiations to address each party's concerns with the preliminary merger and lending agreements. On March 24, 2008, FRBNY and JPMC agreed to a new lending structure that incorporated greater loss protections for FRBNY. Specifically, FRBNY created a special purpose vehicle (SPV), Maiden Lane LLC, that used proceeds from a $28.82 billion FRBNY senior loan and a $1.15 billion JPMC subordinated loan to purchase Bear Stearns's assets. A more detailed discussion of the security and collateral policies for Maiden Lane LLC appears later in this report and appendix IV includes more details about the Maiden Lane LLC transaction.

Primary Dealer Credit Facility

While one team of Federal Reserve Board and FRBNY staff worked on options to avert a Bear Stearns failure, another team worked to ready PDCF for launch by Monday, March 17, 2008, when Federal Reserve Board officials feared a Bear Stearns bankruptcy announcement might trigger runs on the liquidity of other primary dealers. As noted previously, the liquidity support from TSLF would not become available until the first TSLF auction later in the month. On March 16, 2008, the Federal Reserve Board announced the creation of PDCF to provide overnight collateralized cash loans to the primary dealers. FRBNY quickly implemented PDCF by leveraging its existing legal and operational infrastructure for its existing repurchase agreement relationships with the primary dealers.[34] Although the Bear Stearns bankruptcy was averted, PDCF commenced operation on March 17, 2008, and in its first week extended loans to 10 primary dealers. Bear Stearns was consistently the largest PDCF borrower until June 2008. Eligible PDCF collateral initially included collateral eligible for open-market operations as well as investment-grade corporate securities, municipal securities, and asset-backed securities, including mortgage-backed securities. As discussed later, the Federal Reserve Board authorized an expansion of collateral types eligible for PDCF loans later in the crisis. This program was terminated on February 1, 2010. See appendix XI for additional details about this program.

In Fall 2008, the Federal Reserve Board Modified Existing Programs and Launched Additional Programs to Support other Key Markets

In September 2008, the bankruptcy of Lehman Brothers triggered an intensification of the financial crisis, and the Federal Reserve Board modified the terms for its existing liquidity programs to address worsening conditions. On September 14, 2008, shortly before Lehman Brothers announced it would file for bankruptcy, the Federal Reserve Board announced changes to TSLF and PDCF to provide expanded liquidity support to primary dealers. Specifically, the Federal Reserve Board announced that TSLF-eligible collateral would be expanded to include all investment-grade debt securities and PDCF-eligible collateral would be expanded to include all securities eligible to be pledged in the tri-party repurchase agreements system, including noninvestment grade securities and equities.[35] In addition, TSLF schedule 2 auctions would take place weekly rather than only bi-weekly. On September 21, 2008, the Federal Reserve Board announced that it would extend credit—on terms similar to those applicable for PDCF loans—to the U.S. and London broker-dealer subsidiaries of Merrill Lynch & Co. (Merrill Lynch), Goldman Sachs Group Inc. (Goldman Sachs), and Morgan Stanley to provide support to these subsidiaries as they became part of bank holding companies that would be regulated by the Federal Reserve System.[36] On September 29, 2008, the Federal Reserve Board also announced expanded support through TAF and the dollar swap lines. Specifically, the Federal Reserve Board doubled the amount of funds that would be available in each TAF auction cycle from $150 billion to $300 billion, and the FOMC authorized a $330 billion expansion of the swap line arrangements with foreign central banks.

In the months following Lehman's bankruptcy, the Federal Reserve Board authorized several new liquidity programs under section 13(3) of the Federal Reserve Act to provide support to other key funding markets, such as the commercial paper and the asset-backed security markets. In contrast to earlier emergency programs that represented relatively modest extensions of established Federal Reserve System lending or open market operation activities, these newer programs incorporated more novel design features and targeted new market participants with which the Reserve Banks had not historically transacted. As was the case with the earlier programs, many of these newer programs were designed and launched under extraordinary time constraints as the Federal Reserve Board sought to address rapidly deteriorating market conditions. In order of their announcement, these programs included: (1) AMLF to provide liquidity support to money market mutual funds (MMMF) in meeting redemption demands from investors and to foster liquidity in the asset-backed commercial paper (ABCP) markets, (2) CPFF to provide a liquidity backstop to eligible issuers of commercial paper, (3) the Money Market Investor Funding Facility (MMIFF) to serve as an additional backstop for MMMFs, and (4) the Term Asset-Backed Securities Loan Facility (TALF) to assist certain securitization markets that supported the flow of credit to households and businesses.

Asset-backed Commercial Paper Money Market Mutual Fund Liquidity Facility

On September 19, 2008, the Federal Reserve Board authorized FRBB to establish AMLF to provide liquidity support to MMMFs facing redemption pressures.[37] According to FRBB staff, the processes and procedures to implement AMLF were designed over the weekend before FRBB commenced operation of AMLF on September 22, 2008. MMMFs were a major source of short-term credit for financial institutions, including through MMMFs' purchases and holdings of ABCP. ABCP continued to be an important source of funding for many businesses.[38] Following the announcement that a large MMMF had "broken the buck"—net asset value fell below $1 per share—as a result of losses on Lehman's commercial paper, other MMMFs faced a large wave of redemption requests as investors sought to limit their potential exposures to the financial sector. The Federal Reserve Board was concerned that attempts by MMMFs to raise cash through forced sales of ABCP and other assets into illiquid markets could further depress the prices of these assets and exacerbate strains in short-term funding markets. AMLF's design, which relied on intermediary borrowers to use Reserve Bank loans to fund the same-day purchase of eligible ABCP from MMMFs, reflected the need to overcome practical constraints in lending to MMMFs directly. According to Federal Reserve System officials, MMMFs would have had limited capacity to borrow directly from the Reserve Banks in amounts that would be sufficient to meet redemption requests because of statutory and fund-specific limitations on fund borrowing. To quickly support the MMMF market, the Federal Reserve Board authorized loans to entities that conduct funding and custodial activities with MMMFs to fund the purchase of ABCP from MMMFs. Eligible borrowers were identified as discount-window-eligible depository institutions (U.S. depository institutions and U.S. branches and agencies of foreign banks) and U.S. bank holding companies and their U.S. broker-dealer affiliates.[39] The interest rate on AMLF loans was lower than the returns on eligible ABCP, providing incentives for eligible intermediary borrowers to participate. AMLF closed on February 1, 2010. See appendix II for more detail on AMLF.

Commercial Paper Funding Facility

On October 7, 2008, the Federal Reserve Board announced the creation of CPFF to provide a liquidity backstop to U.S. issuers of commercial paper. Commercial paper is an important source of short-term funding for U.S. financial and nonfinancial businesses.[40] CPFF became operational on October 27, 2008, and was operated by FRBNY. In establishing CPFF, FRBNY created an SPV that was to directly purchase new issues of eligible ABCP and unsecured commercial paper with the proceeds of loans it received from FRBNY for that purpose.[41] In the weeks leading up to CPFF's announcement, the commercial paper markets showed clear signs of strain: the volume of commercial paper outstanding declined, interest rates on longer-term commercial paper increased significantly, and increasing amounts of commercial paper were issued on an overnight basis as money-market funds and other investors became reluctant to purchase commercial paper at longer-dated maturities.[42] As discussed previously, during this time, MMMFs faced a surge of redemption demands from investors concerned about losses on presumably safe instruments. The Federal Reserve Board concluded that disruptions in the commercial paper markets, combined with tension in other credit markets, threatened the broader economy as many large commercial paper issuers promoted the flow of credit to households and businesses. By standing ready to purchase eligible commercial paper, CPFF was intended to eliminate much of the risk that commercial paper issuers would be unable to issue new commercial paper to replace their maturing commercial paper obligations. By reducing this risk, CPFF was expected to encourage investors to continue or resume their purchases of commercial paper at longer maturities. CPFF closed on February 1, 2010. For more detail on CPFF, see appendix VII.

Money Market Investor Funding Facility

On October 21, 2008, the Federal Reserve Board authorized FRBNY to work with the private sector to create MMIFF to serve as an additional backstop for MMMFs. MMIFF complemented AMLF by standing ready to purchase a broader range of short-term debt instruments held by MMMFs, including certificates of deposit and bank notes. MMIFF's design featured a complex lending structure through which five SPVs would purchase eligible instruments from eligible funds. In contrast to other Federal Reserve Board programs that created SPVs, MMIFF SPVs were set up and managed by private sector entities. According to FRBNY staff, JPMC, in collaboration with other firms that sponsored large MMMFs, brought the idea for an MMIFF-like facility to FRBNY in early October 2008. For reasons discussed later in this report's section on FRBNY's use of vendors, FRBNY worked with JPMC to set up the MMIFF SPVs but did not contract directly with JPMC or the firm that managed the MMIFF program. While MMIFF became operational in late November 2008, it was never used. For more detail on MMIFF, see appendix X.

Term Asset-Backed Securities Loan Facility

In November 2008, the Federal Reserve Board authorized FRBNY to create TALF to reopen the securitization markets in an effort to improve access to credit for consumers and businesses.[43] During the recent financial crisis, the value of many asset-backed securities (ABS) dropped precipitously, bringing originations in the securitization markets to a virtual halt. Problems in the securitization markets threatened to make it more difficult for households and small businesses to access the credit that they needed to, among other things, buy cars and homes and expand inventories and operations.[44] TALF provided nonrecourse loans to eligible U.S. companies and individuals in return for collateral in the form of securities that could be forfeited if the loans were not repaid.[45] TALF was one of the more operationally complex programs, and the first TALF subscription was not held until March

2009. In contrast to other programs that had been launched in days or weeks, TALF required several months of preparation to refine program terms and conditions and consider how to leverage vendor firms to best achieve TALF policy objectives. TALF closed on June 30, 2010. For more detail on TALF, see appendix XII.

In Late 2008 and Early 2009, the Federal Reserve Board Announced Its Participation in Government Assistance to Individual Institutions

In late 2008 and early 2009, the Federal Reserve Board again invoked its authority under section 13(3) of the Federal Reserve Act to authorize assistance to avert the failures of three institutions that it determined to be systemically significant: (1) American International Group, Inc. (AIG); (2) Citigroup, Inc. (Citigroup); and (3) Bank of America Corporation (Bank of America).

AIG

In September 2008, the Federal Reserve Board and the Treasury determined through analysis of information provided by AIG and insurance regulators, as well as publicly available information, that market events could have caused AIG to fail, which would have posed systemic risk to financial markets. The Federal Reserve Board and subsequently Treasury took steps to ensure that AIG obtained sufficient liquidity and could complete an orderly sale of its operating assets and continue to meet its obligations. On September 16, 2008, one day after the Lehman Brothers bankruptcy announcement, the Federal Reserve Board authorized FRBNY to provide a revolving credit facility (RCF) of up to $85 billion to help AIG meet its obligations. The AIG RCF was created to provide AIG with a revolving loan that AIG and its subsidiaries could use to address strains on their liquidity. The announcement of this assistance followed a downgrade of the firm's credit rating, which had prompted collateral calls by its counterparties and raised concerns that a rapid failure of the company would further destabilize financial markets. Two key sources of AIG's difficulties were AIG Financial Products Corp. (AIGFP) and a securities lending program operated by certain insurance subsidiaries of AIG.[46] AIGFP faced growing collateral calls on credit default swaps it had written on collateralized debt obligations (CDO).[47] Meanwhile, AIG faced demands on its liquidity from securities lending counterparties who were returning borrowed securities and demanding that AIG return their cash collateral. Despite the announcement of the AIG RCF, AIG's condition continued to decline rapidly in fall 2008.

On subsequent occasions, the Federal Reserve Board invoked section 13(3) of Federal Reserve Act to authorize either new assistance or a restructuring of existing assistance to AIG.

- First, in October 2008, the Federal Reserve Board authorized the creation of the securities borrowing facility (SBF) to provide up to $37.8 billion of direct funding support to a securities lending program operated by certain AIG domestic insurance companies. From October 8, 2008, through December 11, 2008, FRBNY provided cash loans to certain AIG domestic life insurance companies, collateralized by investment grade debt obligations.

- In November 2008, as part of plans to restructure the assistance to AIG to further strengthen its financial condition, and once again avert the failure of the company, the Federal Reserve Board and Treasury restructured AIG's debt. Under the restructured terms, Treasury purchased $40 billion in shares of AIG preferred stock and the cash from the sale was used to pay down a portion of AIG's outstanding balance from the AIG RCF. The limit on the facility also was reduced to $60 billion, and other changes were made.
- Also in November 2008, the Federal Reserve Board authorized the creation of two SPVs—Maiden Lane II LLC and Maiden Lane III LLC—to purchase certain AIG-related assets. Similar to Maiden Lane LLC, these SPVs funded most of these asset purchases with a senior loan from FRBNY.[48] Maiden Lane II replaced the AIG SBF and served as a longer-term solution to the liquidity problems facing AIG's securities lending program. Maiden Lane III purchased the underlying CDOs from AIG counterparties in connection with the termination of credit default swap contracts issued by AIGFP and thus the elimination of the liquidity drain from collateral calls on the credit default swaps sold by AIGFP.
- In March 2009, the Federal Reserve Board and Treasury announced plans to further restructure AIG's assistance. According to the Federal Reserve Board, debt owed by AIG on the AIG RCF would be reduced by $25 billion in exchange for FRBNY's receipt of preferred equity interests totaling $25 billion in two SPVs. AIG created both SPVs to hold the outstanding common stock of two life insurance company subsidiaries—American Life Insurance Company and AIA Group Limited.[49]
- Also in March 2009, the Federal Reserve Board authorized FRBNY to provide additional liquidity to AIG by extending credit by purchasing a contemplated securitization of income from certain AIG life insurance operations. FRBNY staff said this life insurance securitization option was abandoned for a number of reasons, including that it would have required FRBNY to manage a long-term exposure to life insurance businesses with which it had little experience.

For more detail on the assistance to AIG, see appendix III.[50]

Citigroup

On November 23, 2008, the Federal Reserve Board authorized FRBNY to provide a lending commitment to Citigroup as part of a package of coordinated actions by Treasury, FDIC, and the Federal Reserve Board to avert a disorderly failure of the company.[51] As discussed in our April 2010 report on Treasury's use of the systemic risk determination, Treasury, FDIC, and the Federal Reserve Board said they provided emergency assistance to Citigroup because they were concerned that the failure of a firm of Citigroup's size and interconnectedness would have had systemic implications.[52] FRBNY agreed to lend against the residual value of approximately $300 billion of Citigroup assets if losses on these assets exceeded certain thresholds. Based on analyses by the various parties and an outside vendor, FRBNY determined that it would be unlikely that losses on the Citigroup "ring-fence" assets would reach the amount at which FRBNY would be obligated to provide a loan.[53] At Citigroup's request, Treasury, FDIC, and FRBNY agreed to terminate this loss-sharing agreement in December 2009. As part of the termination agreement, Citigroup agreed to pay a

$50 million termination fee to FRBNY. FRBNY never provided a loan to Citigroup under this lending commitment.[54] See appendix VI for more detail.

Bank of America

On January 15, 2009, the Federal Reserve Board authorized FRBR to provide a lending commitment to Bank of America. As with Citigroup, the Federal Reserve Board authorized this assistance as part of a coordinated effort with Treasury and FDIC to assist an institution that the agencies determined to be systemically important. The circumstances surrounding the agencies' decision to provide this arrangement for Bank of America, however, were somewhat different and were the subject of congressional hearings.[55] While the Citigroup loss-sharing agreement emerged during a weekend over which the agencies attempted to avert an impending failure of the firm, the agencies' discussions with Bank of America about a possible similar arrangement occurred over several weeks during which Bank of America was not facing imminent failure. According to Federal Reserve Board officials, possible assistance for Bank of America was first discussed in late December 2008 when Bank of America management raised concerns about the financial impact of completing the merger with Merrill Lynch, which was expected at the time to announce larger-than-anticipated losses (and did in fact announce these losses the following month). Following the January 1, 2009, completion of Bank of America's acquisition of Merrill Lynch, the Federal Reserve Board and the other agencies agreed to provide a loss-sharing agreement on selected Merrill Lynch and Bank of America assets to assure markets that unusually large losses on these assets would not destabilize Bank of America. On September 21, 2009, the agencies and FRBR terminated the agreement in principle to enter into a loss-sharing agreement with Bank of America. The agreement was never finalized, and FRBR never provided a loan to Bank of America under this lending commitment. As part of the agreement to terminate the agreement in principle, Bank of America paid a $57 million to FRBR in compensation for out-of-pocket expenses incurred by FRBR and an amount equal to the commitment fees required by the agreement. See appendix V for more detail.

In 2009 and 2010, FRBNY Executed Large-Scale Purchases of Agency MBS to Provide Broader Support to the Economy

On November 25, 2008, the FOMC announced that FRBNY would purchase up to $500 billion of agency mortgage-backed securities to support the housing market and the broader economy.[56] The FOMC authorized the Agency MBS program under its authority to direct open market operations under section 14 of Federal Reserve Act. By purchasing MBS securities with longer maturities, the Agency MBS program was intended to lower long-term interest rates and to improve conditions in mortgage and other financial markets. The Agency MBS program commenced purchases on January 5, 2009, a little more than a month after the initial announcement. FRBNY staff noted that a key operational challenge for the program was its size. As discussed later in this report, FRBNY hired external investment managers to provide execution support and advisory services needed to help execute purchases on such a large scale. In March 2009, the FOMC increased the total amount of planned purchases from

$500 billion to up to $1.25 trillion. The program executed its final purchases in March 2010 and settlement was completed in August 2010. See appendix I for more detail.

Table 2. Summary of Extensions for Broad-Based Emergency Programs

Programs extended	Date extension announced	Term of extension	
AMLF, PDCF, and TSLF	December 2, 2008	Original expiration:	January 30, 2009
		New expiration:	April 30, 2009
AMLF, CPFF, MMIFF, PDCF, TSLF, and swap lines with foreign central banks	February 3, 2009	Planned expiration:	April 30, 2009
		New expiration:	October 30, 2009
AMLF, CPFF, PDCF, TSLF, and swap lines with foreign central banks	June 25, 2009	Planned expiration:	October 30, 2009
		New expiration:	February 1, 2010

Source: GAO analysis of Federal Reserve Board press releases and program terms and conditions.
Note: MMIFF was never used and the Federal Reserve Board allowed it to expire on October 30, 2009. In November 2008, TALF was authorized to make new loans until December 31, 2009, and the Federal Reserve Board later authorized an extension for new loans against most eligible collateral until March 31, 2010, and against one eligible collateral type until June 30, 2010. Other extensions of swap line arrangements were announced on May 2, 2008 and September 29, 2008. As noted earlier in this section, in May 2010, FRBNY reopened swap lines with the Bank of Canada, the Bank of England, the European Central Bank, the Bank of Japan, and the Swiss National Bank. These swap lines were initially set to expire on August 1, 2011. On June 29, 2011, the Federal Reserve Board announced an extension of these swap lines through August 1, 2012.

Most Programs Were Extended a Few Times before Closing in Early 2010

On several occasions, the Federal Reserve Board authorized extensions of its emergency loan programs, and most of these programs closed on February 1, 2010. For example, AMLF, PDCF, and TSLF were extended three times. The Federal Reserve Board cited continuing disruptions in financial markets in announcing each of these extensions. Table 2 provides a summary of the extensions for the emergency programs.

THE FEDERAL RESERVE SYSTEM AND ITS EMERGENCY ACTIVITIES WERE SUBJECT TO MULTIPLE AUDITS AND REVIEWS

The Emergency Programs Have All been Subject to Audits and Reviews

The Federal Reserve Act requires the Federal Reserve Board to order an annual independent audit of the financial statements of each of the 12 Reserve Banks.[57] Each Reserve Bank prepares annual financial statements that reflect its financial position as of the end of the calendar year and its related income and expenses for the year. The Federal Reserve Board also prepares combined financial statements of the Reserve Banks, which include the accounts and results of operations of the 12 Reserve Banks. As shown in figure 2, the loans and other financial assistance provided through the Federal Reserve's emergency programs are recorded in the Reserve Banks' publicly reported financial statements. Most of the activity pertaining to the emergency programs is recorded exclusively in FRBNY's financial statements, including several SPVs that have been consolidated in FRBNY, including Maiden Lane LLC, Maiden Lane II LLC, Maiden Lane III LLC, CPFF LLC, and TALF LLC (LLCs).[58] The emergency programs that are not recorded exclusively in FRBNY's financial statements include:

- financial transactions of AMLF, which are reported in FRBB's financial statements;
- financial transactions of TSLF, the dollar swap lines, and the Agency MBS program which are allocated on a percentage basis to each Reserve Bank;
- financial transactions of TAF, which are reported in the financial statements of each Reserve Bank that made a TAF loan; and
- financial transaction of the Bank of America program, which was reported in FRBR's financial statements.[59]

The Reserve Banks have voluntarily adopted the internal control reporting requirements of the Sarbanes-Oxley Act of 2002[60] and provide an assessment of the effectiveness of their internal control over financial reporting annually to their boards of directors.[61] Internal control over financial reporting includes those policies and procedures that (1) pertain to the maintenance of records that, in reasonable detail, accurately and fairly reflect the transactions and dispositions of the assets of the entity; (2) provide reasonable assurance that transactions are recorded as necessary to permit preparation of financial statements in accordance with accounting principles, and that receipts and expenditures of the entity are being made only in accordance with authorizations of management and directors; and (3) provide reasonable assurance regarding prevention or timely detection of unauthorized acquisition, use, or disposition of the entity's assets that could have a material effect on the financial statements.

The management of each Reserve Bank assesses its internal control over financial reporting as it relates to the financial statements based upon the criteria established in the *Internal Control-Integrated Framework* issued by the Committee of Sponsoring Organizations of the Treadway Commission (COSO) (see table 3).[62] Similarly, in 2009, the LLCs began providing an assessment of their internal controls over financial reporting annually to the Board of Directors of FRBNY using the COSO framework and criteria.

Since 2007, Deloitte has been the independent external auditor for the Federal Reserve System. Accordingly, Deloitte performs the audits of the individual and combined financial statements of the Reserve Banks and those of the consolidated LLCs. Deloitte also provides opinions on the effectiveness of each Reserve Bank's internal control over financial reporting. In 2009, Deloitte began providing opinions on the effectiveness of each LLC's internal control over financial reporting.[63] To help ensure auditor independence, the Federal Reserve Board requires that its external auditor be independent in all matters relating to the audits. Specifically, Deloitte may not perform services for the Reserve Banks or others that would place it in a position of auditing its own work, making management decisions on behalf of the Reserve Banks, or in any other way impairing its audit independence.

Federal Reserve System

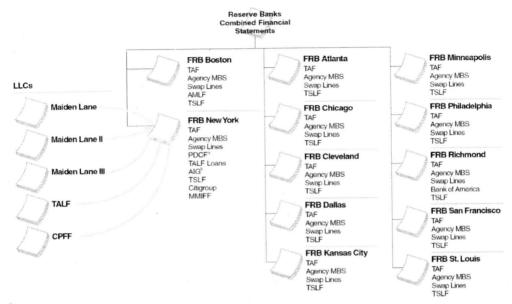

Represents financial statements
Source: GAO analysis of Reserve Banks annual reports.
[a] Includes the credit extensions to affiliates of some primary dealers.
[b] Includes the AIG RCF, AIG SBF, and Life Insurance Securitization.

Figure 2. Financial Reporting of the Federal Reserve's Emergency Programs.

Table 3. COSO's Internal Control Framework

Component	Description
Control environment	Sets the tone of the organization, influencing the control consciousness of its people. It is the foundation for all other components of internal control, providing discipline and structure. Control environment factors include the integrity, ethical values, and competence of the entity's people; management's philosophy and operating style; the way management assigns authority and responsibility, and organizes and develops its people; and the attention and direction provided by the board of directors.
Risk assessment	Refers to the organization's identification and analysis of risks relevant to achieving its objectives, forming a basis for determining how the risks should be managed. Because economic, industry, regulatory and operating conditions will continue to change, mechanisms are needed to identify and deal with the special risks associated with change.
Control activities	The policies and procedures that help ensure that management's directives are carried out. They help ensure that necessary actions are taken to address risks to achievement of the entity's objectives. Control activities occur throughout the organization, at all levels and in all functions. They include a range of activities as diverse as approvals, authorizations, verifications, reconciliations, reviews of operating performance, security of assets and segregations of duties.
Information and communication	The identification, capture, and communication of information in a form and time frame that enable people to carry out their responsibilities.
Monitoring	A process that assesses the quality of internal control performance over time. This is accomplished through ongoing monitoring of activities, separate evaluations or a combination of the two.

Source: COSO's Internal Control-Integrated Framework.

FRBNY management also engaged external firms to review certain aspects of the emergency programs. For example, FRBNY engaged the auditing firm KPMG LLP (KPMG) to assist FRBNY in developing a conflict of interest inspection and fraud-review program for certain programs created in response to the financial crisis. In 2009 and 2010, KPMG executed reviews of vendors and agents supporting the Agency MBS program, Maiden Lane LLC, Maiden Lane II LLC, Maiden Lane III LLC, TALF, and CPFF. The scope of this work covered an evaluation of the vendors' and agents' adherence to their own conflict of interest policies and more program-specific provisions contained within their engagement agreement with FRBNY. These reviews are discussed in greater detail later in this report. In 2009, FRBNY contracted with a management consulting firm, Oliver Wyman, to conduct an independent review of the governance and management infrastructure surrounding its new market facilities and emergency programs created throughout 2008. This review was specifically focused on the three Maiden Lane LLCs, CPFF, and MMIFF and included an examination of internal reporting and management updates, business and strategic plans for relevant Reserve Bank functions, internal risk assessments, Reserve Bank policies and procedures, committee charters, and organizational summaries.

In addition to external audits and reviews, the Federal Reserve System has a number of internal entities that conduct audits and reviews of the Reserve Banks, including the emergency programs. For example, each Reserve Bank has an internal audit function that conducts audits and other reviews to evaluate the adequacy of the Reserve Bank's internal controls, the extent of compliance with established procedures and regulations, and the effectiveness of the Reserve Bank's operations. The internal audit function conducts audits in accordance with the *International Standards for the Professional Practice of Internal Auditing* and maintains organizational independence from management by reporting directly to the audit committee of the Reserve Bank's board of directors.[64] During the period from 2008 through 2010, FRBNY's internal audit function conducted audits pertaining to the Agency MBS program, TSLF, Swap Lines, TAF, CPFF, TALF, and PDCF, as well as the three Maiden Lane LLCs. In 2008 and 2009, the FRBB's internal audit function performed an audit of AMLF. The objectives and scope of these audits varied, but included such areas as the adequacy and effectiveness of internal controls, vendor management, governance, lending and collateral processes, and information technology. The FRBNY and FRBB internal audit functions provided recommendations to Reserve Bank management to address any findings.

Also, the Reserve Banks and emergency programs, including the LLCs, are subject to oversight by the Federal Reserve Board. The Federal Reserve Board's Division of Reserve Bank Operations and Payment Systems (RBOPS) performs annual Reserve Bank examinations that include a wide range of oversight activities. RBOPS monitors the activities of each Reserve Bank and LLC on an ongoing basis, and conducts a comprehensive on-site review of each Reserve Bank at least once every 3 years. The reviews also include an assessment of each Reserve Bank's internal audit function's efficiency and conformance to the *International Standards for the Professional Practice of Internal Auditing* and applicable policies and procedures. In addition, RBOPS formed special program-related review teams and conducted risk-based reviews of most of the Federal Reserve's emergency programs. RBOPS uses the COSO framework as criteria in reviewing Reserve Banks, including emergency programs and LLC operations. RBOPS also assesses compliance with FOMC policies by annually reviewing the accounts and holdings of the Reserve Banks' domestic and foreign currency open market accounts, which include transactions executed as part of the Agency MBS and swap line programs.

During 2009 and 2010, RBOPS conducted reviews of the following emergency programs: TSLF, PDCF, CPFF, AIG RCF, dollar swap lines, Maiden Lane, Maiden Lane II, Maiden Lane III, TALF, and the Agency MBS program. The scope of these reviews varied but primarily focused on the programs' implementation and administration, including evaluating the effectiveness of controls and determining whether the operations of the programs were consistent with Federal Reserve Board authorizations. RBOPS reported the results of these reviews along with any recommendations to improve operations to FRBNY's management. In follow-up reviews, RBOPS officials found that FRBNY had satisfactorily addressed the issues found during the initial reviews; therefore, RBOPS closed many of the recommendations.

The OIG also conducts audits, reviews, and investigations related to the Federal Reserve Board's programs and operations, including those programs and operations that have been delegated to the Reserve Banks by the Federal Reserve Board. The OIG is required to submit a semiannual report to the Chairman of the Federal Reserve Board and to Congress. In November 2010, the OIG reported on its review of six of the emergency programs: TSLF, PDCF, MMIFF, TALF, CPFF, and AMLF. The OIG stated that the purpose of its review was to determine the function and status of these programs and to identify risks in each of the programs to assist the Federal Reserve Board in its general supervision and oversight of the Reserve Banks.[65]

Figure 3 provides an overview of audit and review coverage of the emergency programs since 2008.

Audits and Reviews Have Not Identified Significant Accounting or Financial Reporting Internal Control Issues Concerning the Emergency Programs

The Reserve Banks and LLCs Received "Clean" Opinions on their Financial Statements

Deloitte rendered unqualified (clean) opinions on the individual and combined Reserve Banks' financial statements for the years 2007, 2008, 2009, and 2010. As described earlier in this report, the Reserve Banks' financial statements include the activity pertaining to the emergency programs, including the accounts and operations of the LLCs, which are consolidated into FRBNY's financial statements. Deloitte also has rendered clean opinions on the financial statements of each LLC beginning with the creation of Maiden Lane LLC in 2008. A clean opinion indicates that the financial statements prepared by management are free of material misstatements and are presented fairly in accordance with U.S. generally accepted accounting principles (GAAP) or, in the case of the Reserve Banks, accounting principles established by the Federal Reserve Board, which is a comprehensive basis of accounting other than GAAP.[66]

Program	External auditor[a]	Internal audit function	Reserve Bank Operations and Payment Systems	Office of Inspector General
Agency MBS	✓	✓		
AIG[b]	✓		✓	
AMLF	✓	✓		✓
Bank of America Corporation	✓			
Citigroup, Inc.	✓			
CPFF	✓	✓	✓	✓
Swap Lines	✓	✓	✓	
Maiden Lane LLC	✓	✓		
Maiden Lane II LLC	✓	✓		
Maiden Lane III LLC	✓	✓	✓	
MMIFF	✓			✓
PDCF[c]	✓	✓	✓	✓
TAF	✓	✓		
TALF	✓	✓	✓	✓
TSLF	✓	✓	✓	✓

Source: GAO analysis of audit reports and reviews.

Note: This figure does not include the Bear Stearns bridge loan, which was a one-time loan and was not a program.

[a] Audit coverage was provided as a part of the overall audit of the Reserve Bank or LLC financial statements.

[b] Includes the AIG RCF, AIG SBF, and Life Insurance Securitization.

[c] Includes the credit extensions to affiliates of some primary dealers.

Figure 3. Audit and Review Coverage of the Emergency Programs.

The independent external auditor conducted its financial statement audits of the Reserve Banks and LLCs in accordance with U.S. generally accepted auditing standards as established by the Auditing Standards Board and in accordance with the auditing standards of the Public Company Accounting Oversight Board.[67] These standards require that the auditor plan and perform the audit to obtain reasonable assurance about whether the financial statements are free of material misstatement and whether effective internal control over financial reporting was maintained in all material respects. The audits of the Reserve Banks' and LLCs' financial statements included examining, on a test basis, evidence supporting the amounts and disclosures in the financial statements, assessing the accounting principles used and significant estimates made by management, and evaluating the overall financial statement presentation.

Audits and Reviews Did Not Identify Any Significant Issues Related to the Reserve Banks' or LLCs' Internal Control over Financial Reporting

Since the development and implementation of the emergency programs, the independent external auditor's internal control opinions related to the Reserve Banks and LLCs have all been clean, indicating that these entities have maintained, in all material respects, effective internal control over financial reporting. As noted previously, FRBNY is responsible for administering each of the emergency programs, except for AMLF, which was administered by FRBB; TAF, which was administered by each Reserve Bank that issued TAF loans; and the Bank of America program, which was administered by FRBR. As administrator of the programs, management at each Reserve Bank is responsible for establishing and maintaining effective internal control over financial reporting as it relates to the preparation of the financial statements, which include the activities of the emergency programs. A clean opinion on internal control is not a guarantee that internal controls are effective because of the possibility of collusion or improper management override of controls; however, it does provide reasonable assurance with respect to financial reporting.

Deloitte conducted its audits of each Reserve Bank's and LLC's internal control over financial reporting in accordance with auditing standards of the Public Company Accounting Oversight Board. Those standards require that the auditor obtain an understanding of internal control over financial reporting, assess the risk that a material weakness exists, and test and evaluate the design and operating effectiveness of internal control based on the assessed risk.[68] Deloitte assessed the Reserve Banks' and LLCs' internal control over financial reporting against criteria established by COSO, which, as discussed earlier, are the same criteria Reserve Bank management used for its assessment of internal control.

In the course of conducting its audits of the Reserve Banks and LLCs, the independent external auditor identified internal control deficiencies affecting financial reporting; however, these deficiencies were not considered significant deficiencies or material weaknesses, and therefore would not likely lead to a material misstatement in financial reporting.[69] Nonetheless, the external auditor communicated these control deficiencies, along with any observations and recommendations for improving operational or administrative efficiency and for improving internal control, to the management of the Reserve Banks and LLCs.

As mentioned in the previous section, in addition to the independent external auditor, the Reserve Banks' internal audit function, RBOPS, and the OIG performed audits and reviews of the emergency programs. Similar to the external audits, the audits and reviews conducted by these other groups did not report any significant accounting or financial reporting internal control issues.

The Federal Reserve System's External Auditor Revised the Approach and Scope of Its Audits to Address the Emergency Programs

Since the beginning of the financial market turmoil in 2007 and the implementation of the emergency programs, the Federal Reserve System's balance sheet has grown in size and has changed in composition. For example, total combined assets of the Reserve Banks have increased significantly from more than $914 billion as of December 31, 2007, to more than $2.4 trillion as of December 31, 2010. From 2007 through 2008, assets increased to more than $2.2 trillion. This increase in assets was, in part, the result of a large increase in loans to depository institutions including TAF loans and other loans made through TSLF, AMLF, PDCF, and AIG RCF; a large increase in the use of the Swap Lines program; and the inclusion of investments held by the consolidated LLCs. As of December 31, 2010, although many of the emergency programs were winding down activities, Reserve Bank assets were more than $2.4 trillion. The assets remained elevated from pre-emergency program levels, in part because of the increased holdings of agency MBS.

The size and complexity of these emergency programs and their rapid implementation increased the external auditor's risks for the audit of the Reserve Banks' and LLCs' financial statements. For example, the emergency programs, including the LLCs, created accounting risks because of the complexities of using different accounting principles for FRBNY's consolidated financial statements (which, as described earlier in this report, are prepared in accordance with accounting principles established by the Federal Reserve Board) and for the LLCs' financial statements (which are prepared in accordance with GAAP). Accounting complexities also existed in determining the proper method of accounting for loans under AMLF and the proper treatment of the loan restructuring pertaining to the AIG RCF.

The economic environment at the time of the creation of these new emergency programs also increased audit risk concerning asset valuation and the establishment of an allowance for loan losses for some of these programs. Furthermore, attention to these new programs also increased audit risk associated with determining the adequacy of financial statement disclosures, both in terms of required disclosures and disclosures to provide transparency over the emergency programs' financial transactions.

In addition, the financial stability measures implemented by the Federal Reserve Board also increased the audit risk pertaining to assessing the design and effectiveness of internal controls that were established for the new programs. Specifically, while many of the transactions associated with the emergency programs were executed under existing internal control processes, some of the programs required the Reserve Banks to develop new policies and procedures and design specific financial reporting internal control processes for the transactions. However, the rapid implementation of the new programs also required the Reserve Banks to execute these transactions at the same time they were developing and documenting accounting policies and control processes for these transactions, thereby increasing the risk that transactions related to these programs may not be processed properly. Audit risk pertaining to internal controls was further increased because of the Reserve Banks' and LLCs' significant use of third-party vendors, also referred to as service organizations, for custodial, administrative, or accounting services pertaining to the investment portfolios of certain emergency programs The service organizations perform these services under their own internal control policies and procedures, which introduce an additional element of risk to the Reserve Banks' internal control systems.

In response to the development and implementation of the emergency programs and the risks associated with these programs, for its 2008 audits of the Reserve Banks and LLCs, the external auditor revised its audit approach and scope to (1) address the accounting complexities and other accounting issues resulting from these new emergency programs, (2) provide additional audit coverage of the Reserve Banks' and LLCs' financial reporting internal controls, and (3) provide testing of the financial transactions of the new emergency programs. Beginning with the 2008 audits, a key area of focus for the external auditor was FRBNY's monitoring controls over the service organizations and the results of the independent service auditors' reports provided on the service organizations' internal controls.[70] For its 2009 and 2010 audits, the external auditor continued to consider the audit risks associated with the emergency programs when developing its audit approach. For example, for the 2009 audits, the external auditor adjusted its audit scope to include testing of TALF, which was created late in 2008 and, as anticipated, had a full year of transactions in 2009. For its 2010 audits of the Reserve Banks and LLCs, the external auditor's audit plan took into consideration the changes in the level of transactions pertaining to some of the emergency programs, such as the lower level of activity in TALF and the effect of the discontinuance of TAF on loans to depository institutions.

In addition, to the extent possible, the external auditor leveraged relevant internal control work performed by the Reserve Banks' management and internal audit function in forming an opinion on the effectiveness of internal control over financial reporting. Specifically, the external auditor

- reviewed management's documentation of the internal control processes and the results of management's testing and monitoring of internal controls,
- assessed the competence and objectivity of the internal auditors and reviewed the internal auditors' audit documentation and results,
- reperformed management's tests of internal controls on a sample basis or accepted management's results in cases where internal controls were not considered to be key or high risk,
- performed its own independent audit tests in cases where the internal control was considered to be key or high risk to financial reporting objectives, and
- considered the results of the Reserve Bank reviews performed by RBOPS to determine whether the results of these reviews had an impact on the Reserve Banks' financial statements.

RESERVE BANKS WOULD BENEFIT FROM STRENGTHENING GUIDANCE FOR NONCOMPETITIVE CONTRACTS AWARDED IN EXIGENT CIRCUMSTANCES

The Reserve Banks, primarily FRBNY, awarded 103 contracts worth $659.4 million from 2008 through 2010 to help carry out their emergency lending activities. A few contracts accounted for most of the spending on vendor services. The Reserve Banks relied more on vendors more extensively for programs that provided assistance to single institutions than for broad-based programs. Most of the contracts, including 8 of the 10 highest-value contracts, were awarded noncompetitively due to exigent circumstances as permitted under FRBNY's acquisition policies. FRBNY is not subject to the Federal Acquisition Regulation (FAR) and its acquisition policies lack some of the details found in that regulation. For example, FRBNY's policies lack guidance on the use of competition exceptions, such as seeking as much competition as is practicable or limiting the duration of noncompetitive contracts to the period of the exigency. Without such guidance, FRBNY may be missing opportunities to obtain competition and help ensure that it receives the most favorable terms for the goods and services it acquires. The vast majority of the vendor fees were paid directly from program income, or program recipients reimbursed the Reserve Banks for vendor fees.

Reserve Banks Relied Extensively on Vendors to Establish and Operate the Emergency Programs, Particularly Those Designed to Assist Single Institutions

From 2008 through 2010, vendors were paid $659.4 million across 103 contracts to help establish and operate the Reserve Banks' emergency programs. The 10 largest contracts accounted for 74 percent of the total amount paid to all vendors.[71] When the Reserve Banks used vendors, most of the spending on services for each emergency program or assistance was for one or two vendors. For example, FRBNY used 19 vendors for the AIG RCF at a cost of $212.9 million, yet two contracts accounted for $175.3 million (82 percent) of that total.[72] Similarly, the Pacific Investment Management Company LLC (PIMCO) CPFF investment management contract accounted for $33.6 million (77 percent) of the $43.4 million that all five CPFF vendors were paid. The Agency MBS program was one notable exception to this pattern. Under the Agency MBS program, FRBNY used four separate investment managers with identical responsibilities and compensation and no single vendor dominated the program. FRBNY was responsible for creating and operating all but two emergency programs and assistance and therefore awarded nearly all of the contracts.[73] See table 4 for the total number and value of contracts for the emergency programs and assistance.

As shown in table 4, the Reserve Banks relied on vendors more extensively for programs that assisted single institutions than for broad-based emergency programs. The six programs that provided assistance to single institutions accounted for more than 75 percent of both the number and value of emergency program contracts. Vendors were paid more for services related to both the AIG RCF and the first Maiden Lane than for all of the broad-based programs combined. The types of services that the Reserve Banks acquired for the single-institution programs were distinctly different than the services acquired for the broad-based programs.

Assistance to Single Institutions

The Reserve Banks relied on vendors to help assess and manage the diverse and complex pools of assets that secured assistance to single institutions. Under section 13(3) of the Federal Reserve Act, the loans Reserve Banks made pursuant to Federal Reserve Board authorizations of the various emergency programs and assistance were to be secured to the Reserve Banks' satisfaction. The assistance provided to individual institutions was generally secured by existing assets that either belonged to or were purchased from the institution, its subsidiaries, or counterparties.[74] The Reserve Banks did not have sufficient expertise available to evaluate these assets and therefore used vendors to do so. For example, loans FRBNY agreed to extend to AIG under the AIG RCF were secured by a range of assets, including the equity of AIG's regulated and nonregulated subsidiaries and secured guarantees of many of AIG's primary nonregulated subsidiaries. FRBNY hired Morgan Stanley to evaluate various divestiture scenarios. The Reserve Banks also relied extensively on vendors to manage the assets for the three Maiden Lane LLCs. FRBNY selected BlackRock as the investment manager for these programs and the company was paid $181.8 million for a variety of services including valuing assets, disposing of securities, and negotiating with counterparties.

Broad-Based Emergency Programs

For the broad-based emergency programs, FRBNY hired vendors primarily for transaction-based services and collateral monitoring. Under these programs, the Reserve Banks purchased assets or extended loans in accordance with each program's terms and conditions. Because of this, the services that vendors provided for these programs were focused more on providing liquidity (purchasing assets or extending loans) than analyzing and managing securities, as was the case for the single institution assistance. FRBNY hired investment managers for the Agency MBS and CPFF programs, but the vendors were primarily tasked with purchasing assets and their role was fundamentally different than the investment manager services provided under the single institution assistance.

Table 4. Number of Contracts and Fees Paid, By Emergency Program, Calendar Years 2008–2010

Dollars in millions	Program	Number of contracts[a]	Total fees paid
Broad-based programs	Agency MBS program	6	$81.4
	AMLF	1	0.025
	CPFF	5	43.4
	MMIFF	1	0.4
	TALF	18	29.2
Programs that assisted a single institution	AIG Revolving Credit Facility	19	$212.9
	Bank of America lending commitment	3	22.8
	Citigroup lending commitment	3	21.4
	Maiden Lane (Bear Stearns)	42	158.4
	Maiden Lane II (AIG)	9	27.9
	Maiden Lane III (AIG)	12	57.0
	General[b]	4	4.5
Total		103	$659.4

Source: GAO analysis of Reserve Bank data.

Note: Reserve Bank programs and assistance listed include only those for which the Reserve Banks used vendors.

[a] Because some contracts included work on multiple programs, the sum of the contracts for each program is greater than the 103 total contracts identified in the table. Also, 36 subvendors were paid $3.3 million for the three Maiden Lane programs, CPFF, and TALF. The table does not include fees for subcontracts.

[b] Of the four general contracts, two were for advisory services related to how FRBNY managed the emergency programs overall. The other two included work on multiple programs, but FRBNY could not separate out what proportion of the total fees was assigned to each program.

For TALF, vendors primarily provided collateral monitoring, custodial, and administrative services. The Reserve Banks did not use vendors, or used only a single vendor for TAF, TSLF, PDCF, the dollar swap lines, and AMLF. These programs were primarily short-term emergency lending programs against traditional collateral and were thus similar to the Reserve Banks' traditional open market operations.

Nonvendors Working on Emergency Programs

FRBNY did not have contracts with the firms that helped operate PDCF, TSLF, TALF, and MMIFF. PDCF and TSLF relied on two clearing banks, JPMC and Bank of New York Mellon, to execute transactions between FRBNY and program recipients (primary dealers).[75] Agreements between the clearing banks and FRBNY identified eligible collateral and other program terms, but the clearing banks were paid by program participants and Reserve Bank officials did not know what fees the clearing banks were paid. Similarly, TALF relied on TALF agents that represented program participants rather than FRBNY. Program participants had to go through a TALF agent to participate in the program and the agents were responsible for conducting due diligence on potential borrowers and identifying and mitigating conflicts of interest. However, the TALF agents were not FRBNY vendors.

A group of private companies led by JPMC designed the MMIFF program and presented it to FRBNY as a backstop for MMMFs. Under the proposal, FRBNY was to extend loans to five LLCs that would purchase short-term debt instruments. The program was created and operated by service providers that did not have contracts with FRBNY. For example, the private companies determined that JPMC should be responsible for setting up the program, registering eligible participants, soliciting sellers, and ensuring that purchases were within program investment limits. JPMC and all other MMIFF vendors had contracts with each of the five LLCs rather than with FRBNY, although FRBNY officials noted that the loan agreements between FRBNY and the LLCs gave FRBNY many contractual rights, including the ability to remove vendors and review fees.[76] FRBNY never extended loans under MMIFF, however, because no recipients signed up for the program.

Reserve Banks Awarded Largest Contracts Noncompetitvely and Would Benefit From Additional Guidance on Seeking Competition

Although FRBNY awarded contracts both competitively and noncompetitively for the emergency programs, the highest-value contracts were awarded noncompetitively due to exigent circumstances. FRBNY awarded almost two-thirds of its contracts noncompetitively, which accounted for 79 percent of all vendor compensation (see figure 4). Eight of the 10 largest contracts were awarded noncompetitively. The largest noncompetitive contract was valued at more than $108.4 million, while the largest competitive contract was valued at $26.6 million.

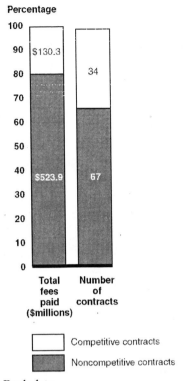

Source: GAO analysis of Reserve Bank data.

Notes:
1. Total fees paid does not add to $659.4 million as shown in table 4 because we excluded two contracts for which competition was not applicable. For example, Deloitte provided audit services for the emergency programs, but the work was performed under an existing contract with the Federal Reserve Board rather than contracts with individual Reserve Banks.
2. FRBNY entered into 25 contracts that were valued under the small purchase threshold of $100,000 set in Operating Bulletin 10. As small purchases, FRBNY was not required to engage in full competition for these contracts. FRBNY competitively awarded three contracts and noncompetitively awarded 22 contracts. Small purchases are included in the graph.

Figure 4. Number of Contracts and Fees Paid, by Procurement Method, 2008–2010.

Vendor Selection Process

FRBNY awarded contracts in accordance with its acquisition policy, which applied to all services associated with the emergency programs and single-institution assistance. FRBNY is a private corporation created by statute and is not subject to the FAR. Instead, FRBNY developed its own acquisition policy, called Operating Bulletin 10.[77] FRBNY relies on decentralized acquisition processes in which individual business areas, such as the Capital Markets Group or the Financial Risk Management Group, are responsible for acquiring goods and services but may draw on the knowledge and experience of other business areas such as the legal, credit, or accounting groups. Operating Bulletin 10 does not address how or when to use vendors but provides detailed guidance on awarding contracts competitively and on special circumstances permitting noncompetitive awards. Under the competitive request-for-proposal (RFP) process, Operating Bulletin 10 provides guidance on how to create and maintain potential vendor lists for competitive procurements. FRBNY distributes RFPs to as many prospective vendors as practical. The number of vendors that receive an RFP varies depending on the good or service being procured. For example, FRBNY solicited proposals from 62 vendors when selecting the TALF collateral monitors and 6 vendors when selecting a Maiden Lane custodian. In some cases, in order to meet policy objectives, FRBNY expedited the RFP process to award competitive contracts quickly. To do so, FRBNY shortened the amount of time potential vendors had to submit proposals. FRBNY also conducted initial assessments of the received proposals to reduce the number of vendors that were invited for further evaluation. For the Agency MBS program, FRBNY completed the RFP process and awarded contracts in as few as 4 weeks.

Operating Bulletin 10 states that business areas may use noncompetitive processes in special circumstances, such as when a service is available from only one vendor or in exigent circumstances. FRBNY cited exigent circumstances for the majority of the noncompetitive contract awards.[78] In their justification memorandum, FRBNY officials stated that they did not believe there was adequate time to award contracts competitively and had to use the exigent circumstances exception. FRBNY officials said that the success of a program was often dependent on having vendors in place quickly to begin setting up the operating framework for the program.

For example, FRBNY noncompetitively selected PIMCO as the CPFF investment manager 1 day after announcing the program. Though PIMCO's final contract was not signed until 3 weeks later, the company immediately began working to set up CPFF infrastructure and registering program participants so that the program would be fully operational when it began.

A guiding principle of the FAR, which applies to all executive agencies, not to the Reserve Banks, is to ensure that agencies are able to deliver the best value product or service in a timely manner while fulfilling agencies' policy objectives. Similarly, Operating Bulletin 10 provides a framework for acquiring goods and services at the most favorable terms. However, while the FAR requires certain activities for noncompetitive awards and identifies specific steps to take, Operating Bulletin 10 does not. Without similar guidance, FRBNY could be missing opportunities to enhance competition and provide the best value service in noncompetitive awards. Examples of activities required or restricted by the FAR include the following:

- *Soliciting multiple bids.* The FAR requires contracting officers to solicit as many offers as is practicable in the absence of full and open competition.[79] FRBNY officials stated that in noncompetitive circumstances business areas are encouraged to collect a reasonable number of competitive quotations and noted that, in at least some cases, staff members contacted multiple vendors before awarding contracts noncompetitively. However, FRBNY did not contact multiple vendors before awarding some of the largest noncompetitive emergency program and assistance contracts.[80]
- *Restrictions on contract duration and scope.* Operating Bulletin 10 does not place any limits or restrictions on the duration of a noncompetitive contract, nor does it require subsequent competition. In contrast, the FAR generally limits the duration of contracts awarded under "exigent circumstances" to the time necessary to meet the unusual and compelling requirements and award a new contract using competitive procedures, and such contracts may generally not exceed 1 year.[81] FRBNY's longest

and most expensive contracts were awarded noncompetitively and lasted more than 2 years and, in some cases, could potentially last as long as 10 years.[82] Some of these contracts included distinct services that, while related, were needed at different times and with different degrees of urgency. FRBNY officials said that in some cases they think there would be limited benefits to opening noncompetitive contracts to competition. FRBNY held subsequent competitions for competitively awarded Agency MBS program and TALF contracts when the terms of the programs changed.

- *Justifying noncompetitive procedures.* Operating Bulletin 10 requires business areas to draft a memorandum that includes sufficient documentation to justify the noncompetitive acquisition. However, Operating Bulletin 10 does not provide guidance on what information should be included in the memorandum. FRBNY justification memoranda typically included background information on the emergency program, vendor scope of work, vendor selection factors, and an explanation of the special circumstances necessitating noncompetitive awards. The memoranda did not typically identify efforts made to promote competition, which the FAR requires.

Vendor Selection Criteria

FRBNY considered a number of factors when selecting vendors for both competitive and noncompetitive contract awards, including a vendor's knowledge and expertise and ability to meet program requirements. FRBNY also considered a vendor's previous working relationship with FRBNY or program participants as part of the selection criteria for competitively and noncompetitively awarded contracts. FRBNY selected vendors that had previous working relationships with FRBNY and the program recipients so that it could leverage that familiarity to shorten the vendor's learning curve or ramp-up time. For example, FRBNY noncompetitively selected BlackRock as the investment manager for Maiden Lanes II and III because BlackRock had already evaluated the underlying assets pursuant to an engagement with AIG prior to the extension of credit by FRBNY. FRBNY also was more likely to award subsequent competitive and noncompetitive contracts to vendors that were already providing services for a different emergency program or individual-institution assistance because of the vendor's familiarity and positive performance. For example, Ernst & Young was awarded a $10.7 million noncompetitive contract to conduct due diligence for Maiden Lane. Later, Ernst & Young received another noncompetitive contract ultimately worth $70.9 million to provide similar services for the AIG programs and Maiden Lane II and III. Ernst & Young also received two competitive contracts worth $1.4 million to provide services for TALF and Maiden Lane.

The Reserve Banks also considered potential conflicts of interest, institutional capacity, and expertise when selecting vendors both competitively and noncompetitively and weighted each factor differently depending on their requirements. In addition, FRBNY reviewed cost in some competitive procurements that it was responsible for, but cost generally was not the determining factor. FRBNY considered low cost as an additional benefit but selected vendors based on consideration of a number of the above-mentioned factors.

- *Conflicts of interest.* The Reserve Banks reduced their potential vendor pool, in some cases, by removing vendors that may have had perceived or actual conflicts of interest for both competitive and noncompetitive contracts. For example, FRBR did

not consider BlackRock as a service provider for the Bank of America lending commitment because Bank of America owned a significant stake in BlackRock.
- *Institutional capacity.* FRBNY determined a vendor's institutional capacity by evaluating the size of the firm and its ability to devote resources, both personnel and financial, to the program. FRBNY sought vendors that had sufficiently large businesses, as determined by assets under management or market share, to support the needs of the emergency programs and individual-institution assistance. FRBNY also was sensitive to the amount of work that a vendor was performing for it and was cautious about exceeding a vendor's operational capacity.
- *Expertise.* FRBNY sought to hire the most expert firms both competitively and noncompetitively. FRBNY sought to hire vendors that had extensive experience and were well respected in the industry. For example, FRBNY competitively selected TREPP LLC, a leading provider of commercial mortgage-backed securities analytics, as the collateral monitor for commercial mortgage-backed securities for TALF.

Vendor Fees Generally Came from Program Income or Participants

From 2008 through 2010, vendors were paid $659.4 million through a variety of fee structures. The Reserve Banks generally used traditional market conventions when determining fee structures. For example, investment managers were generally paid a percentage of the portfolio value and law firms were generally paid an hourly rate. Fees for these contracts were subject to negotiation between the Reserve Banks and vendors. For some of the large contracts that were awarded noncompetitively, FRBNY offered vendors a series of counterproposals and was able to negotiate lower fees than initially proposed. FRBNY staff assessed fee proposals for several of these larger contracts that were awarded noncompetitively. Reserve Bank staff compared vendors' fee proposals to fees that other institutions paid for similar services. However, Reserve Bank staff could not always find comparable portfolios on which to evaluate fee proposals. When determining fees, the Reserve Banks did not always know how much work a vendor would perform under a contract because of uncertainty about the size and duration of the emergency programs, so it used varying fee structures to address this uncertainty. For example, FRBNY officials said that they were not certain how extensively CPFF would be used. Compensation based solely on basis points could have resulted in low fees if the program was not widely used or high fees if it was used extensively. After considering various scenarios, FRBNY and PIMCO, the CPFF investment manager, negotiated a fixed quarterly fee of $3 million plus a variable fee of 0.25 basis points on the outstanding amount of commercial paper.[83] Participation in CPFF peaked in January 2009 at nearly $350 billion and then fell rapidly so PIMCO's compensation came primarily from the variable portion of its fee early in the program and from the fixed portion of its fee later in the program.

The Reserve Banks used different funding sources to pay vendor fees. The Reserve Banks generally paid vendor fees one of three ways depending on program terms:[84]

- *Reserve Banks paid vendors directly and were not reimbursed.* For the Agency MBS program, AMLF, and TALF, the Reserve Banks paid vendors directly and were not

reimbursed. However, as of May 31, 2011, income to date from each of these programs has exceeded vendor fees.
- *Reserve Banks paid vendors and were reimbursed.* Under the terms of the AIG, Citigroup, and Bank of America assistance, the companies were required to reimburse the Reserve Banks for the $257.2 million in vendor fees that the Reserve Banks paid vendors for services related to those programs.[85]
- *Vendors were paid according to a financial structure known as a "waterfall."* For five programs—CPFF, TALF, and the three Maiden Lane programs—vendors were paid according to a "waterfall" structure in which program cash flows were used to pay vendors before FRBNY and its counterparties were repaid.[86] Vendor fees reduced the income that FRBNY received from these programs. According to the waterfall structure, FRBNY received all or most of residual income from the programs after expenses, loans, and interest were repaid.

WHILE FRBNY TOOK STEPS TO MANAGE CONFLICTS OF INTEREST FOR EMPLOYEES, DIRECTORS, AND PROGRAM VENDORS, OPPORTUNITIES EXIST TO STRENGTHEN CONFLICT POLICIES

During the crisis, FRBNY took steps to manage conflicts of interest related to the emergency programs for its employees, program vendors, and members of its Board of Directors, but opportunities exist to strengthen its conflicts policies. FRBNY expanded its guidance and monitoring for employee conflicts of interest based on existing provisions in its Code of Conduct that incorporate the requirements of a federal criminal conflict of interest statute and its regulations. The code also includes a general prohibition on employee ownership of certain debt or equity interests. However, additional provisions concerning prohibited financial interests could help to ensure that conflicts are appropriately identified and managed for employees involved in decisions relating to emergency assistance. In addition, FRBNY managed vendor conflict issues through contract protections, established practices to perform onsite reviews and request conflict remediation plans, and implemented a new vendor management policy. However, the new policy does not provide comprehensive guidance on managing vendor conflict issues. FRBNY staff stated they are developing an additional vendor management policy that formalizes practices used during the crisis. FRBNY could use this opportunity to provide detailed guidance on steps FRBNY staff should take to manage vendor conflicts. Finally, while Reserve Bank directors did not have responsibility for authorizing the emergency assistance, some directors had a limited role in overseeing how the Reserve Banks managed the assistance and programs once they were established. Like employees, all directors were subject to statutory requirements governing conflicts of interest.

During the Crisis, FRBNY Expanded Its Efforts to Manage Employee Conflicts

Historically, FRBNY has managed potential and actual conflicts of interest for its employees primarily through enforcement of its Code of Conduct, which outlines broad principles for ethical behavior and specific restrictions on financial interests and other activities, such as restrictions on employees' investments in depository institutions and bank holding companies. A personal conflict of interest can result from an employee having financial or other interests that conflict with the interests of the Reserve Bank. During the crisis, new roles and responsibilities assumed by FRBNY and its employees and interaction with nonbank entities gave rise to potential conflicts of interest that were not specifically addressed, as they were for investments in depository institutions. However, according to FRBNY officials, the Code of Conduct, which incorporates the requirements of a federal criminal statute and its regulations, along with the statute itself, generally prohibits any FRBNY employee from working on a matter related to an institution in which the employee has financial interests, such as investments in the institution.

During the crisis, FRBNY expanded its efforts to address personal conflicts for its employees by (1) providing additional training and guidance on existing policies governing conflicts of interest, including the Code of Conduct; (2) implementing program-specific information barriers and ethical guidelines to limit sharing of sensitive program information within and outside FRBNY; and (3) expanding guidance on prohibited financial interests and increasing the monitoring of compliance with these restrictions for some employees.

Expanded Training and Guidance on Existing Conflict Policies

During the crisis, FRBNY provided its employees with additional training and guidance on its existing conflict of interest policies. FRBNY's Code of Conduct outlines ethical standards that broadly require employees to avoid any situation that might give rise to an actual conflict of interest or the appearance of a conflict of interest. In addition, to prevent the occurrence of certain actual conflicts of interest, the Code of Conduct includes specific restrictions on employees' financial holdings and other activities. Moreover, FRBNY employees are subject to the criminal conflict of interest restrictions in section 208 of title 18 of the U.S. Code, which FRBNY has incorporated into its Code of Conduct. Section 208 generally prohibits employees from participating personally and substantially in their official capacities in any matter in which, to their knowledge, they have a financial interest, if the particular matter will have a direct and predictable effect on that interest.[87] According to FRBNY's Code of Conduct, it is the responsibility of employees to use their judgment to inform FRBNY's Ethics Office in the event that a potential or actual conflict of interest might impact their ability to participate in a particular matter. The financial crisis resulted in an increased volume of ethics-related inquiries, particularly at FRBNY, which led FRBNY to strengthen its training and communication systems related to its Code of Conduct. On its intranet, FRBNY launched an ethics Web site featuring a Web-based version of its Code of Conduct and special guidance for employees. Special guidance included investment guidance bulletins issued in response to the crisis and guidance for staff members in Bank Supervision and those with access to monetary policy information.

FRBNY also took additional steps to limit access to nonpublic information—such as program-specific information or information received as a result of market outreach—to employees on a need-to-know basis. The Ethics Office issued general guidance to all Bank staff on the handling of material nonpublic information. This guidance was supplemental to FRBNY's existing Code of Conduct and a policy designed to protect the handling, custody, and release of supervisory information. FRBNY also introduced a quarterly lunch session to introduce its new staff, many of whom were hired to implement the emergency programs, to its ethics rules.

Program-Specific Information Barriers and Ethical Guidelines

In addition to promoting awareness of existing conflict policies, FRBNY issued new ethical guidance and information barrier policies to address specific conflicts that could arise in some of its emergency programs. Before the crisis, FRBNY policies were in place to limit access to sensitive information, such as supervisory information about the financial condition of depository institutions. These policies served to reduce the possibility that an employee could share sensitive information with others who could profit by trading on this information. As a result of their involvement in FRBNY's emergency activities, many employees required access to new types of sensitive information that were not explicitly covered by FRBNY's information access and disclosure policies. For CPFF and MMIFF, FRBNY staff responsible for managing the risks of the programs needed access to confidential information about the financial condition of eligible issuers of commercial paper and their related borrowing amounts and the types and amounts of an eligible seller's money market instruments sold into the program, respectively. In addition, TALF and the Agency MBS program presented additional ethics issues arising from overall program activity that could influence the value of an employee's financial assets whose ownership was not already prohibited by FRBNY's Code of Conduct.

FRBNY implemented program-specific information barriers for CPFF and MMIFF and ethical guidelines for TALF and the Agency MBS program. Information barriers for CPFF and MMIFF restricted access to nonpublic information about program registrants and sellers to FRBNY program staff on a need-to-know basis and required these employees to remove the identity of program participants in written materials providing program updates and metrics to FRBNY management and other staff. Furthermore, these information barriers restricted staff over the wall responsible for conducting monetary policy from receiving information about how the program's asset manager could invest program cash flows in U.S. government securities, which could impact monetary policy. The information barrier policy required assigned FRBNY program staff to disclose their financial holdings related to each borrower and seller and restricted staff from transacting in securities of the borrower and seller for the duration of the program and 90 days thereafter. For TALF and the Agency MBS program, FRBNY set forth ethical guidelines that specified prohibited financial interests for assigned program staff. Specifically, FRBNY staff were advised to avoid having financial interests in program-eligible securities such as ABS, agency MBS, commercial MBS, any investment fund concentrated in any one of these securities, and any debt or equity interest in any of the government-sponsored enterprises. Lastly, FRBNY staff working on these programs were advised to discuss potential exemptions of existing investments with FRBNY's Ethics Office and to avoid new purchases or sales of related investments for the duration of the program and 90 days thereafter.

Expanded Guidance for Prohibited Financial Interests and Management of Conflicts

FRBNY's Code of Conduct included restrictions on financial interests that were intended to prevent personal conflicts that could arise in the conduct of FRBNY's traditional activities, which included supervising and making discount window loans to depository institutions and conducting monetary policy operations with primary dealers. For example, the existing Code of Conduct includes a provision that specifically prohibits FRBNY employees from holding certain debt or equity interests in depository institutions or their affiliates. However, the Code of Conduct was not written to include specific restrictions on employees' holdings of certain financial interests that could potentially be affected by an employee's participation in matters concerning FRBNY's recent emergency activities. These financial interests include the debt or equity of some nondepository institutions that received emergency assistance, or certain types of securities actively traded or purchased through an emergency program. FRBNY staff said that the Code of Conduct and 18 U.S.C. § 208 broadly prohibit employees who worked on the emergency programs from holding investments that could have been affected by their participation in matters concerning those programs. According to FRBNY staff, absent a waiver, employees were prohibited from working on an emergency program while holding investments that would be affected by their participation in matters concerning those programs.

During the crisis, FRBNY took steps to help identify and manage new potential personal conflicts that could arise from employees' new roles with respect to the emergency programs. FRBNY used its financial disclosure requirements to help identify potential conflicts. According to FRBNY officials, the ethical guidelines discussed previously gave rise to employee self-disclosures of program-eligible securities. Furthermore, according to FRBNY officials, employees working on TALF, the Agency MBS program, and other programs including CPFF and MMIFF were required to disclose their financial holdings with greater frequency outside of FRBNY's annual disclosure process. In addition, effective fall 2008, FRBNY prohibited all employees from making new investments in certain nonbank holding companies, while employees in the Capital Markets Group were already prohibited from holding investments related to primary dealers.

For matters where FRBNY identified the possibility of a conflict related to an employee's financial interests, according to FRBNY staff, its Ethics Office made a determination as to whether a conflict existed. In cases where a conflict was determined to exist, FRBNY's Ethics Office generally advised divestiture or recusal or granted a waiver allowing the employee to continue to hold the relevant investment.[88] FRBNY staff said that out of 12 self-disclosures of related program-eligible securities sent to the Ethics Office, 4 disclosures resulted in the employee being required to divest related assets. According to FRBNY staff, some FRBNY employees recused themselves from involvement in discussions in cases where they believed their participation would have been in violation of section 208.

According to FRBNY staff, in cases where FRBNY did not require an employee to divest or recuse, its Ethics Office determined either that no conflict of interest existed based on statutory standards or that a waiver was appropriate. According to FRBNY staff, in determining whether to recommend a waiver, the Ethics Office followed the regulations and guidance issued by the Office of Government Ethics. FRBNY waiver recommendations cited the following reasons for granting waivers: (1) the criticality of the employee's services; (2) the insubstantial value of the employees' stock interest, which generally represented less than 2 to 5 percent of their investment portfolio or net worth; (3) the limited role designated to the employee for their responsibilities relating to the personal financial interest; (4) a determination that forced divestiture would lead to an appearance of a conflict; and (5) a determination that the investments did not exceed a *de minimis* threshold of $15,000 as set forth in the Office of Government Ethics regulations, and in the Code, as an exemption for interests in securities.[89]

Our review of several recommendations for waivers granted from September 19, 2008, through March 31, 2010, indicated that FRBNY employees who requested waivers were generally allowed to continue to retain their related personal financial investments. Most of the financial interests were in institutions receiving emergency assistance, including AIG, Bank of America, Citigroup, General Electric Company (GE), and JPMC. For example, on September 19, 2008—3 days after the Federal Reserve Board authorized FRBNY to assist AIG—the then-FRBNY President granted, under authority delegated by the FRBNY Board of Directors, a waiver to a senior management official with financial interests in AIG and GE who was involved in decision making related to these two companies.[90] Similar to criteria noted previously, the waiver recommendation from FRBNY's Chief Ethics Officer cited reasons based on (1) the criticality of the official's responsibilities, (2) the combined value of the official's interests comprising less than 5 percent of the official's total financial holdings, and (3) the *de minimis* nature of the official's investment in AIG. Specifically, the waiver recommendation from FRBNY's Chief Ethics Officer noted that the official's participation in decisions related to AIG and GE was critical to the official's senior-level responsibilities. In addition, in this recommendation, the Chief Ethics Officer expressed concern that the official's divestiture of the holdings could violate securities laws because of the official's access to material, nonpublic information. Furthermore, the waiver recommendation noted that should FRBNY's actions impact the equity of either company, divestiture by the official could have created the appearance of a conflict. The waiver recommendation further noted that while this official would be permitted to provide advice on decisions about assistance to AIG and GE, FRBNY's president would make final decisions on these issues. We did not assess the appropriateness of FRBNY's decisions to grant waivers and recognize that these decisions are case-specific and necessarily require subjective judgments. The challenge of applying such judgments is highlighted by guidance from the Office of Government Ethics, which notes that while a waiver analysis usually requires the consideration of several competing factors, appearance concerns will always play an important role in the decision whether to grant a waiver.

FRBNY Has Not Revised Its Code of Conduct to Reflect Expanded Role

While the crisis highlighted the potential for Reserve Banks to provide emergency assistance to a broad range of institutions, FRBNY has not revised its conflict policies and procedures to more fully reflect potential conflicts that could arise with this expanded role. For example, specific investment restrictions in FRBNY's Code of Conduct continue to focus on traditional Reserve Bank counterparties—depository institutions or their affiliates and the primary dealers—and have not been expanded to further restrict employees' financial interests in certain nonbank institutions that have participated in FRBNY emergency programs and could become eligible for future ones, if warranted.

As discussed earlier in this report, the management of each Reserve Bank assesses their internal controls based upon the criteria established in the *Internal Control–Integrated Framework* issued by COSO.[91] These standards state that because economic, industry, regulatory, and operating conditions will continue to change, mechanisms are needed to identify and deal with the special risks associated with change. Circumstances for which an internal control system originally was designed also may change, causing the system to be less able to warn of the risks brought by new conditions. Accordingly, management needs to determine whether the internal control system continues to be relevant and able to address new risks. Federal Reserve Board and FRBNY staff told us that the Federal Reserve System plans to review and update the Reserve Banks' Codes of Conduct as needed given the Federal Reserve System's recently expanded role in regulating systemically significant financial institutions. These reviews present an opportunity to also consider how FRBNY's experience managing employee conflicts of interest related to its emergency programs could inform efforts to update the Reserve Banks' conflict of interest policies.

FRBNY staff told us that although FRBNY's Code of Conduct did not include specific restrictions that would have addressed all potential conflicts for employees that arose during the crisis, they believe the Code of Conduct and 18 U.S.C. § 208 provided the flexibility needed to address such conflicts. Furthermore, Federal Reserve Board staff said that expanding the list of restricted investments to address all potential conflicts would be difficult because anticipating which nondepository entities would participate in an emergency program during a crisis is not possible. However, given the public's heightened attention to conflicts of interest related to the Federal Reserve System's emergency programs, Reserve Banks' continued reliance on their existing standards for managing employee conflicts of interest may not be sufficient to avoid situations in which significant appearance concerns must be weighed against—and possibly judged to be outweighed by—other factors, such as the criticality of an official's services. Office of Government Ethics regulations state that one of many factors to weigh in determining whether a disqualifying financial interest is sufficiently substantial to be deemed likely to affect the integrity of the employee's services to the government is the sensitivity of the matter. Office of Government Ethics guidance notes that where the particular matter is controversial or sensitive, the wisdom of granting a waiver can be questionable.[92] The case of a senior Reserve Bank official holding investments in an institution receiving substantial emergency assistance highlights the potential for appearance concerns even in cases when the employee's investments come under a regulatory *de minimis* exemption or comprise a small percentage of the employee's total investments. While we recognize that the current codes of conduct provide flexibility to address unanticipated conflicts, a crisis situation may not provide time for formal review of a potential conflict before key decisions must be made. Without additional provisions in conflicts policies and procedures, the Reserve Banks risk being exposed to the appearance of conflicts and to questions about the integrity of their decisions and actions.

FRBNY Primarily Used Contract Protections to Manage Risks Related to Vendor Conflicts, and the Lack of a Comprehensive Policy Created Certain Limitations

FRBNY managed risks related to vendor conflicts of interest primarily through contract protections and oversight of vendor compliance with these contracts. However, FRBNY's efforts to manage these risks had some limitations. In implementing the emergency programs, FRBNY used vendors on a scale unprecedented for a Reserve Bank. When the crisis began,

FRBNY's policies for managing vendor relationships did not include comprehensive guidance on steps FRBNY staff should take to help ensure that vendor conflicts were identified and mitigated. During the crisis, FRBNY established practices for managing vendor relationships and vendor conflicts. While not part of a formal policy, FRBNY's Legal Division negotiated contract provisions intended to help ensure that vendors took appropriate steps to mitigate conflicts of interest related to the services they provided for FRBNY. In addition, FRBNY's Compliance Division identified higher-risk vendors and provided greater attention to potential conflicts related to these vendors' activities. However, FRBNY continues to lack a policy to guide communication efforts between its Legal and Compliance divisions.

Although we did not identify any instances in which a conflict compromised achievement of policy goals, we found that in some cases FRBNY could have taken additional steps to provide greater assurance that vendor conflicts were identified and mitigated. First, FRBNY generally did not contractually require vendors to demonstrate they had taken action to help ensure that they identified and took steps to manage conflicts on an ongoing basis. FRBNY staff said they had regular conversations with vendors about steps the vendors were taking to identify and mitigate conflicts, but FRBNY required few vendors to provide a written conflict mitigation plan. Second, FRBNY performed on-site reviews to check for vendor compliance with contract provisions related to conflicts mitigation, but some of these reviews occurred 12 months into a contract or later. As discussed below, although FRBNY is taking steps, it has not yet finalized a comprehensive conflict policy to help ensure that its future management of risks related to vendor conflicts incorporates both best practices and lessons learned from the recent crisis.

FRBNY's Legal Division negotiated provisions in its vendor contracts that were intended to help ensure that vendors took steps to mitigate conflicts of interest related to the services they provided to FRBNY. Similar to the potential for personal conflicts for FRBNY employees, a personal conflict for a vendor employee could arise if an employee's personal financial interests or activities conflicted with the vendor employee's responsibilities in connection with the services provided to FRBNY. In addition, FRBNY recognized that organizational conflicts of interest could arise to the extent that a vendor firm's financial interest in providing services to its other clients could conflict with its duties to FRBNY. FRBNY staff noted that some types of vendor services, such as asset management services, presented greater risks related to conflicts of interest than other types of services, such as legal or administrative services. For example, conflicts of interest are inherent in asset management because firms may manage similar assets for different clients with competing interests. Specifically, BlackRock and PIMCO managed similar assets for both FRBNY and other clients that may have had competing interests. In addition, the potential for conflicts existed for vendor firms and employees of these firms that had access to nonpublic FRBNY program information that could be used for vendor or vendor employee gain. Examples of contract provisions FRBNY applied to help ensure these conflicts were mitigated included, but were not limited to, provisions that required the vendor firm to

- enforce confidentiality and nondisclosure agreements that imposed additional requirements on the vendor firm regarding the handling of confidential information received in connection with the vendor's duties to FRBNY;

- limit access to confidential information on a "need to know" basis by identifying a list of "restricted" employees with access to confidential information relevant to FRBNY program-specific operations;
- implement an ethical "wall" to physically separate FRBNY program-specific team members from non-FRBNY operations, including moving these members to another floor or building with electronic access restrictions;
- monitor e-mails for improper communication of trading activity, ideas, and the sharing of nonpublic information;
- impose restrictions on personal financial transactions to restrict employees from participating in or conducting trading for program-specific related assets;
- engage in discussions with individuals in the vendor's Legal and Compliance divisions prior to accepting new assignments in connection with services provided for FRBNY; and
- establish incident reporting procedures to disclose any potential or actual conflicts and request waivers from FRBNY, if necessary.

FRBNY staff said that attorneys from FRBNY's Legal and Compliance divisions advised on the inclusion of these types of contract protections based on the nature of the vendors' services. During the crisis, while FRBNY developed certain contractual provisions that it used repeatedly in its vendor contracts for mitigation of conflicts of interest, it did not create new comprehensive guidelines on the types of conflict mitigation protections that should be included in vendor contracts. In contrast, Treasury, which also employed a number of vendors as it implemented TARP, issued new interim guidelines for its management of TARP vendor conflicts of interest in January 2009, following our December 2008 recommendation that Treasury develop a comprehensive system to ensure that vendor conflicts would be fully identified and appropriately addressed. In our recommendation to Treasury we noted that without a comprehensive system to monitor conflicts of interest, the potential exists for gaps in internal controls as a result of the need to begin program activities before policies and procedures have been fully developed and implemented. Treasury's interim guidelines provided for the inclusion of some types of conflict protections that FRBNY did not always include in its contracts but generally included for some high-risk vendors. These included requiring the vendor firm to

- provide Treasury with sufficient information to evaluate any organizational and personal conflicts of interest, including a detailed, written plan to mitigate organizational conflicts of interest;
- certify that information provided to Treasury related to the conflict mitigation plan was complete and accurate in all material respects; and
- subsequently notify Treasury of any new conflicts that emerged during the term of the contract and to periodically recertify the completeness and accuracy of information provided related to conflicts.

Rather than requiring written conflict remediation plans that were specific to the services provided for FRBNY, FRBNY generally reviewed and allowed its vendors to rely on their existing enterprisewide policies for identifying conflicts of interest. However, in some situations, FRBNY requested that additional program-specific controls be developed. Without program-specific remediation plans from its vendors, FRBNY lacked assurance that vendor conflicts would be fully identified and appropriately addressed.

FRBNY's Chief Ethics Officer told us that FRBNY reviewed our 2008 recommendation on Treasury's management of vendor conflicts and took steps to implement this recommendation in part by requesting conflict remediation plans from some of its vendors. In December 2008, FRBNY sent a letter to thirteen vendors requesting in writing that they (1) disclose any actual or potential conflicts of interest related to their services for FRBNY and (2) for any such conflicts, provide a comprehensive conflict mitigation plan. FRBNY received written responses from five of these vendors and only a few of these responses were accompanied by a detailed conflict mitigation plan. Two of the responding vendors identified potential or actual conflicts and said that they would rely on their firm's existing conflict mitigation policies and seek waivers, as needed, to mitigate these conflicts. The other three vendor responses indicated that these firms were not aware of any potential or actual conflicts. One of these vendors, which provided custodial services for multiple FRBNY programs, submitted an identical response for its engagement in two of the programs. Although this firm represented that it was not aware of any potential conflicts for itself or its affiliates, one of its affiliates later borrowed from one of the programs beginning in December 2008. FRBNY's Ethics Officer did not become aware of the vendor's affiliate's use of the program until he reviewed the Federal Reserve Board's public disclosure of the borrowers' names on December 1, 2010. FRBNY staff noted that the vendor firm had information barriers in place to prevent sharing of sensitive program information with this borrowing affiliate. An FRBNY official told us that due to the nature of the vendor's responsibilities, which were primarily administrative, FRBNY considered the engagement of this vendor to present a low risk of a material conflict of interest.

For vendors posing greater risks related to conflicts of interest, FRBNY staff told us that they had early and ongoing conversations and reviewed the vendor's conflict policies and procedures. For example, FRBNY staff noted that they had early and ongoing discussions with BlackRock that helped assure them that BlackRock had implemented ethical walls and taken other steps to mitigate potential conflicts of interest. For BlackRock and other vendors with which FRBNY had frequent communications about conflict mitigation, FRBNY staff said they did not require additional program-specific conflict remediation plans because they considered the policies and procedures put in place by the vendors to be sufficient. Nevertheless, as discussed below, during KPMG's on-site conflict of interest reviews of some FRBNY vendors, KPMG recommended that FRBNY require a few of these vendors consider implementing program-specific mitigation plans.

FRBNY completed on-site reviews of many significant program vendors in 2009 and 2010, and in some cases, these reviews were not timely. In early 2009, FRBNY drafted a schedule for both high-level and in-depth reviews to be performed primarily for investment managers across the emergency programs to assess their performance and compliance with contract obligations. In June 2009, FRBNY sent a request for proposal to several audit firms to assist it in developing a conflict of interest inspection and fraud review program for its critical vendors given FRBNY's limited internal capacity. KPMG, the winning bidder, performed its reviews as the utilization of the programs was generally slowing down. Generally these reviews were designed to help ensure conflict of interest policies and procedures including ethical walls and information barriers met FRBNY's requirements for vendors, to determine whether the emergency program included testing over existing controls and to complete a risk-based assessment of the vendor's compliance control environment as it related to contractual provisions, among other things. The reviews were conducted across three categories of vendors—investment managers, collateral monitors, and transaction agents—and generally excluded reviews of less critical vendors who performed custodial and administrative services. FRBNY relied on its own resources to oversee compliance of custodial and administrative service vendors while focusing additional on-site reviews on operational, financial, and information security risks to the Reserve Bank.

These reviews of vendor performance and contract compliance were, in some instances, performed 12 to 14 months into a vendor's contract with FRBNY. The reviews generally indicated that the vendors had adopted and implemented comprehensive, enterprisewide compliance programs. During the reviews, KPMG made critical risk observations for FRBNY's consideration in conducting future vendor contract negotiations. In several cases, because of the timing of KPMG's review, critical findings of noncompliance with relevant contract provisions were left undetected until late in the operation of the emergency programs. For some vendors, these reviews found that

- vendors relied on existing information barriers to mitigate conflicts of interest as opposed to implementing FRBNY program-specific "ethical wall" barriers to help manage organizational conflicts of interest,
- opportunities existed for vendors to improve access restrictions for information systems and to conduct periodic reviews to limit the sharing of nonpublic information, and
- opportunities existed for vendors to review restrictions on employee personal trading activities related to the eligible assets of the emergency programs to better ensure there was no improper trading activity.

At the conclusion of these reviews, FRBNY held meetings with vendor senior management to share the results and in certain cases received follow-up documentation on how the vendor planned to remediate critical findings. Before engaging KPMG, FRBNY's Compliance Division began to develop internal capacity to conduct its own vendor reviews. In January 2010, the Assurance and Advisory Services unit, a newly formed team within FRBNY's compliance function, assumed responsibility for conducting vendor and third-party reviews, including reviews of vendor and third-party compliance with conflict mitigation plans they submitted to FRBNY.

In May 2010, FRBNY implemented a new vendor management policy to serve as a framework to minimize reputational, operational, credit, and market risks associated with its use of vendors. The policy requires the business manager assigned to a particular program to provide a risk assessment for that program's service providers, taking into consideration the nature, scope, and cost of the vendors' services. The risk level assigned determines the frequency at which FRBNY staff managing vendors should report and review the vendors' performance, perform on-site reviews, and escalate and communicate respective risk events to FRBNY. Furthermore, the policy provides that a plan be developed and documented for all of the steps for its high risk vendors. This new policy immediately began covering high risk vendor relationships that resulted from FRBNY's emergency programs. Before May 2010, according to FRBNY staff, some FRBNY business areas, such as the Investment Support

Office with respect to the Maiden Lane facilities and the Markets Group with respect to broad-based programs, had implemented vendor oversight programs that included procedures for performing risk-based reviews of vendors' significant processes, walkthroughs and testing of key internal controls, and assessments of contract compliance.

While FRBNY's vendor management policy incorporates some lessons learned from the crisis, it does not provide detailed guidance on steps FRBNY staff should take to ensure that vendors mitigate conflicts, such as types of protections that should be included in vendor contracts to help ensure that vendors provide information needed by FRBNY to evaluate potential and actual conflicts of interest. FRBNY staff told us that they are developing a vendor conflict policy that formalizes the practices it used during the financial crisis. A more comprehensive policy that formalizes practices FRBNY had in place and incorporates additional protections, as appropriate, could enable FRBNY to more fully identify and appropriately manage vendor conflicts of interest.

Reserve Bank Directors Are Generally Subject to the Same Conflict Rules as Federal Employees and a Few Directors Played a Limited Role in Risk Oversight of the Programs

Individuals serving on the boards of directors of the Reserve Banks are generally subject to the same conflict of interest statute and regulations as federal employees. As with other employees, 18 U.S.C. § 208 generally prohibits Reserve Bank directors from participating personally and substantially in their official capacities in any matter in which, to their knowledge, they have a financial interest, if the particular matter will have a direct and predictable effect on that interest.[93] In addition, all Reserve Bank boards of directors are subject to a Federal Reserve Board policy on conflicts of interest for which they receive annual training. There are three classes of Reserve Bank directors: Class A directors are elected by banks that are members of the Federal Reserve System in their respective regions and represent these banks, Class B directors are elected by banks to represent the public, and Class C directors are appointed by the Federal Reserve Board to represent the public with due consideration to the interests of agriculture, commerce, industry, services, labor, and consumers. Class B and C directors are not allowed to be officers, directors, or employees of any bank. Class C directors are prohibited from owning shares of a bank.

A number of Reserve Bank directors were affiliated with institutions that borrowed from the emergency programs, but Reserve Bank directors did not participate directly in making decisions about authorizing, setting the terms, or approving a borrower's participation in the emergency programs. As noted previously, the Federal Reserve Board, and in some cases, the FOMC, authorized the creation and modification of most of the emergency programs under authorities granted by the Federal Reserve Act. FRBNY's Board of Directors assisted the Reserve Bank in helping ensure risks were managed through FRBNY's Audit and Operational Risk Committee.[94] During the crisis, at least one Class A director served on the Audit and Operational Risk Committee at any given time. According to FRBNY officials, FRBNY's Reserve Bank Directors' limited role in assessing the effectiveness of the Bank's management of operational risk for the emergency programs gave rise to limited waiver requests or recusals. We plan to explore these relationships in greater detail in our study on Reserve Bank governance.[95]

In their role as market participants, Reserve Bank directors engaged in consultations with FRBNY management and staff. According to FRBNY officials, a director providing information to FRBNY management and staff in his or her role as chief executive officer of an institution does not equate to "participating personally and substantially"—as defined by 18 U.S.C. § 208—because the director is not playing a direct role with respect to approving a program or providing a recommendation. According to FRBNY officials, FRBNY's Capital Markets Group contacted representatives from primary dealers, and commercial paper issuers, and other institutions to gain a sense of how to design and calibrate some of its emergency programs. FRBNY contacted institutions for this purpose irrespective of whether one of FRBNY's directors was affiliated with an institution. Some of these institutions that borrowed from the emergency programs also had senior executives that served on FRBNY's board of directors. For example, JPMC was extensively involved in the emergency programs as both a borrower and a vendor at the same time its Chief Executive Officer served as a Class A FRBNY director. According to the Federal Reserve Board officials, the Federal Reserve Board allowed borrowers to access its emergency programs only if they satisfied publicly announced eligibility criteria. Thus, Reserve Banks granted access to borrowing institutions affiliated with Reserve Bank directors only if these institutions satisfied the proper criteria, regardless of potential director-affiliated outreach or whether the institution was affiliated with a director. Similarly, Lehman Brothers' Chief Executive Officer served on the FRBNY board and while Lehman Brothers' primary dealer participated in PDCF, the firm was not provided individual assistance to avert its failure.

As discussed later in this report, our review of the implementation of several program requirements did not find evidence that appeared to indicate a systemic bias towards favoring one or more eligible institutions. While some institutions that borrowed from these programs were affiliated with a Class A director, these institutions were subject to the same terms and conditions as those that were not affiliated with Reserve Bank directors. According to our review of minutes from meetings of FRBNY and FRBB boards of directors, discussions of emergency programs during board meetings generally occurred after the programs were publicly announced and generally covered explanations of the related emergency lending authority, administration of the program, and descriptive information about the programs' operations and risks, and the impact on the Reserve Banks' balance sheets. In addition, all Reserve Bank directors are prohibited from disclosing nonpublic information related to the programs and such disclosures may risk violating insider trading laws. Effective December 16, 2010, FRBNY revised its bylaws and committee charters governing the activities of its Board of Directors. Specifically, FRBNY implemented Dodd-Frank Act amendments to the Federal Reserve Act concerning Reserve Bank governance while imposing additional controls to enhance its corporate governance policies.[96] One of these revisions permits only two out of five Audit and Operational Risk Committee members to be Class A directors.[97] These enhanced standards by FRBNY, although implemented after the unwinding of many of the emergency programs, helped mitigate the appearance of actual and potential director conflicts. As noted earlier, a forthcoming report on Reserve Bank governance issues will include additional discussion of conflicts of interest for Reserve Bank directors.

OPPORTUNITIES EXIST TO STRENGTHEN RISK MANAGEMENT POLICIES AND PRACTICES FOR FUTURE EMERGENCY PROGRAMS

The Federal Reserve Board approved key program terms and conditions that served to mitigate risk of losses and delegated responsibility to one or more Reserve Banks for executing each emergency lending program and managing its risk of losses. For several programs, the Federal Reserve Board required borrowers to post collateral in excess of the loan amount. For programs that did not have this requirement, Reserve Banks required borrowers to pledge highly-rated assets as collateral. Also, for assistance to specific institutions, the Reserve Banks negotiated loss protections with the institutions and hired vendors to help oversee the portfolios collateralizing loans. As of July 2011, most of the Federal Reserve Board's emergency loan programs have closed and all of those that have closed have closed without losses. Moreover, currently, the Federal Reserve Board does not project any losses on FRBNY's outstanding loans to TALF borrowers and the Maiden Lane SPVs. To manage risks posed by the emergency programs, Reserve Banks developed new controls and FRBNY strengthened its risk management practices over time. For example, FRBNY expanded its risk management function and enhanced its risk reporting and risk analytics capabilities. Although FRBNY has improved its ability to monitor and manage risks from its emergency lending, opportunities exist for FRBNY and the Federal Reserve System as a whole to strengthen risk management procedures and practices for any future emergency lending. Specifically, neither FRBNY nor the Federal Reserve Board tracked total potential exposures in adverse economic scenarios across all emergency programs. Moreover, the Federal Reserve System's existing procedures lack specific guidance on how Reserve Banks should exercise discretion to restrict or deny program access to higher-risk borrowers that otherwise met program eligibility requirements. Without enhanced risk tracking and risk management procedures, the Federal Reserve System could lack important tools needed to comprehensively manage risk exposure in the event of a future crisis.

Programs Contained Multiple Loss Protection Features Aimed at Balancing Loss Protections with Financial Stability Goals

The Federal Reserve System sought to balance loss protections with its financial stability goals in designing security and collateral policies to help mitigate the risk of losses for its emergency lending programs.[98] The context for the Federal Reserve System's management of risk of losses on its loans differed from that for private sector institutions. In contrast to private banks that seek to maximize profits on their lending activities, the Federal Reserve System stood ready to accept risks that the market participants were not willing to accept to help stabilize markets. When authorizing each program, the Federal Reserve Board generally established the key program terms and conditions according to which a Reserve Bank could make emergency loans. The Reserve Bank was responsible for developing and implementing procedures and practices to execute and manage the risks of the program subject to the Federal Reserve Board's program design. As noted earlier in this report, section 13(3) of the Federal Reserve Act establishes a broad criterion that emergency loans must be secured to the satisfaction of the individual Reserve Bank making the loans. In setting program terms and conditions, the Federal Reserve Board sought to make loans available on terms that would be effective in addressing market strains during crisis conditions but onerous compared to terms available during normal market conditions.

For the purpose of considering the Federal Reserve System's security and collateral policies, its emergency lending activities can be grouped into three broad categories:

- overcollateralized loans to institutions facing liquidity challenges—that is, loans that were backed by collateral in excess of the loan value;[99]
- broad-based liquidity programs that made loans to intermediary entities (eligible financial institutions or newly-created LLCs) to finance purchases of debt instruments in key credit markets; and
- Loans and commitments to provide loans collateralized by asset portfolios of specific institutions.

Overcollateralized Loan Programs and Loans to Specific Institutions

The Federal Reserve Board's early broad-based lending programs—TAF, TSLF, and PDCF—made overcollateralized loans to institutions facing liquidity pressures and contained similar sets of features intended to mitigate risk of losses:

- *Borrower eligibility requirements.* The Federal Reserve Board generally limited access to these programs to U.S. institutions that were regulated by U.S. federal financial regulators and met certain regulatory standards for financial soundness. For example, TAF eligibility was limited to U.S. depository institutions (which include U.S. branches and agencies of foreign banks) that were eligible for primary credit at the discount window and expected by their local Reserve Bank to remain primary-credit-eligible during the term the TAF loan would be outstanding.[100] Moreover, primary dealers were the only eligible participants for TSLF and PDCF. According to FRBNY staff, a firm's continued designation as a primary dealer depended, among other things, on its continuing to meet minimum capital and other requirements set forth by FRBNY. The next section of this report discusses the borrower eligibility requirements for these lending programs in greater detail.
- *Collateral eligibility and haircut requirements.* The Federal Reserve Board defined types of assets that would be eligible as collateral and required loans under these programs to be overcollateralized. In the event that a borrower defaulted on a loan, the Reserve Bank would have had rights to seize the assets posted as collateral. To help ensure that the value recovered from the collateral would be sufficient to avoid losses on the loan, the Federal Reserve Board placed limits on the types of assets eligible as collateral and required borrowers to overcollateralize by pledging collateral with a total market value greater than the loan amount. The difference between the market value of an asset pledged as collateral and the amount that could be borrowed against this asset is called the margin or haircut. The Reserve Banks applied schedules of haircuts that were designed to apply higher haircuts to higher-risk asset types. For example, the programs applied higher haircuts to MBS collateral (approximately 7 percent) than to short-term U.S. Treasury collateral (approximately 1 percent). As discussed in the next section, some asset types were required to have

certain minimum credit ratings from at least two Nationally Recognized Statistical Rating Organizations (NRSROs, or rating agencies).

CREDIT RATINGS AND THE RATING AGENCIES

A credit rating is an assessment of the creditworthiness of an obligor as an entity or with respect to specific securities or investment instruments. In the past few decades, credit ratings have assumed increased importance in the financial markets, in large part due to their use in law and regulation. In 1975, the Securities and Exchange Commission (SEC) first used NRSRO to describe those rating agencies whose ratings could be relied upon to determine capital charges for different types of securities broker-dealers held that are registered with SEC. Since then, SEC has used the NRSRO designation in a number of regulations, and the term has been widely embedded in numerous federal and state laws and regulations as well as in investment guidelines and private contracts. The ratings produced by the NRSROs generally are letter-based symbols intended to reflect assessments of credit risk for entities issuing securities in public markets. Typically, credit rating agencies designate issuers or securities considered investment-grade, or lower risk, with higher letter ratings, and issuers or securities considered speculative-grade, or higher risk, with lower letter ratings. For example, Standard & Poor's and Fitch Ratings designate investment-grade, long-term debt with ratings of AAA, AA, A, and BBB, and speculative-grade, long-term debt with ratings of BB, B, CCC, CC, and C. The rating scale that a ratings agency uses to assign short-term obligations may differ from the scale it uses for long-term obligations. For example, the highest rating assigned to short-term commercial paper obligations is A-1, P-1, or F-1, depending on the NRSRO assigning the rating.

Source: Based on GAO-10-782.

- *Recourse to borrower's assets.* Loans under some programs were made with recourse to the borrowing institution's assets. In the event of a default on a recourse loan, the Reserve Bank would have a claim on the borrower's assets that could allow it to recover all or part of any shortfall arising from the liquidation of the collateral pledged by the borrower.
- *Monitoring program use and financial condition for eligible borrowers.* Reserve Banks had discretion to restrict access to otherwise eligible institutions that they determined to pose greater risk of loss. For TAF, Federal Reserve System staff said that they recognized that supervisory ratings, which were a factor considered in determining primary credit and TAF eligibility, might not reflect recent adverse changes in an institution's financial condition.[101] Accordingly, FRBNY staff told us that FRBNY and the other Reserve Banks coordinated with bank examiners and monitored market-based indicators to gain additional insights into the soundness of TAF borrowers. Similarly, for PDCF and TSLF, FRBNY staff told us that FRBNY closely monitored the financial condition of primary dealers as part of its efforts to manage the risks of PDCF and TSLF lending.

Table 5 provides an overview of the key loss protection features for the Federal Reserve Board's overcollateralized lending programs.

The collateral eligibility and haircut requirements for TAF were based on discount window requirements. The Federal Reserve Board approved adjustments to the collateral requirements for TSLF and PDCF over time to address changing conditions in the repurchase agreements markets. Federal Reserve System staff said that haircuts for eligible collateral were generally set to be higher than haircuts that private lenders would require under normal market conditions and lower than prevailing haircuts during crisis conditions.

- *TAF.* TAF loan terms of 28 and 84 days increased risk of loss relative to the traditional discount window program, through which Reserve Banks extended overnight loans. Although market practice generally entails applying higher haircuts for longer loan terms, the Federal Reserve Board did not increase discount window haircuts for TAF to account for potential changes in collateral value or the borrower's financial condition. FRBNY staff said that the Reserve Banks' practice of repricing collateral daily mitigated the risk that deterioration of collateral value over longer loan terms would increase the risk of loss. This is because if on any particular day the collateral value fell below the amount needed to secure a loan based on haircut requirements, the Reserve Bank could require a borrower to pledge more collateral. Moreover, for 84-day TAF loans, the Federal Reserve Board directed Reserve Banks to require borrowing institutions to have additional collateral pledged to the discount window beyond the collateral needed based on the discount window haircut schedule.[102]
- *TSLF and PDCF.* TSLF, which extended term loans of Treasury securities against eligible collateral, initially accepted only collateral eligible for open market operations and private MBS receiving the highest rating from at least two rating agencies. PDCF, which made overnight cash loans against eligible collateral (in the form of a repurchase agreement transaction), accepted all collateral eligible for TSLF as well as a range of investment-grade securities. The initial haircut schedules for TSLF and PDCF were generally based on FRBNY's existing open market operations practices.[103] According to FRBNY staff, haircuts for assets that were not eligible for open market operations were calculated based in part on discount window margins. Similar to TAF, TSLF also had daily repricing practices to help mitigate risk. PDCF was an overnight operation and to the extent a primary dealer requested a new loan on the day that an old loan matured, the collateral was priced and haircuts were applied on the day of the new loan. In September 2008, the Federal Reserve Board expanded the collateral eligibility requirements for TSLF to include investment-grade securities and for PDCF to include all assets eligible for borrowing in the tri-party repurchase agreement system. The collateral eligibility expansion for PDCF allowed FRBNY to lend to primary dealers in exchange for riskier forms of collateral, including stocks and noninvestment grade bonds.

Some of the emergency assistance FRBNY provided to avert the failures of Bear Stearns and AIG also took the form of overcollateralized loans:

- *Bridge loan to Bear Stearns.* FRBNY's $12.9 billion bridge loan to Bear Stearns (through a JPMC bank subsidiary) was an overnight loan collateralized by $13.8 billion of Bear Stearns collateral. According to FRBNY staff, JPMC's bank subsidiary applied haircuts to the Bear Stearns collateral to determine the amount that could be loaned against the collateral (known as "lendable value") and FRBNY's Financial Institution Supervision Group reviewed these haircuts. According to an FRBNY document, types of collateral pledged by Bear Stearns included, but were not limited to, common stock, convertible bonds, and municipal bonds. FRBNY's loan to the JPMC subsidiary was made without recourse to this subsidiary's assets as its role was to serve as a conduit for lending to Bear Stearns. In the event of default, FRBNY would have had recourse to Bear Stearns.

Table 5. Summary of Terms and Conditions for TAF, TSLF, and PDCF

Category	TAF	TSLF	PDCF
Eligible borrowers	Discount window primary-credit eligible institutions	Primary dealers	Primary dealers
Collateral eligibility	Discount window collateral	• Schedule 1: Collateral eligible for open market operations with FRBNY (U.S. Treasury securities, agency debt securities, and agency MBS) • Schedule 2: Initially included all Schedule 1 collateral, and highly rated MBS; over time, expanded to include other highly rated ABS and investment grade securities	Initially included investment grade securities and was expanded to include all assets eligible for triparty repurchase agreements with the two major clearing banks, including noninvestment grade securities and stocks
Haircuts	Yes	Yes	Yes
Recourse to borrower's assets	Yes	Yes	Yes
Term	28 or 84 days	28 days	Overnight

Source: GAO analysis based on Federal Reserve Board terms and conditions for TAF, TSLF, and PDCF.

- *AIG SBF.* Through the AIG SBF, FRBNY provided loans to AIG that were collateralized by investment grade debt obligations. These loans were made with recourse to AIG's assets beyond the assets pledged as collateral and FRBNY generally applied higher haircuts than it required for these collateral types in PDCF.
- *AIG RCF.* Under FRBNY's credit agreement with AIG (and related security agreement), amounts borrowed by AIG under the AIG RCF were secured by a substantial portion of the assets of AIG and its primary nonregulated subsidiaries, including AIG's ownership interest in its regulated U.S. and foreign subsidiaries. This credit agreement included provisions intended to help ensure that the proceeds AIG received from planned AIG assets sales would be used to permanently repay outstanding balances under the AIG RCF. In addition, the security agreement provided for AIG's borrowings under this facility to be guaranteed by each of AIG's domestic, nonregulated subsidiaries that had more than $50 million in assets. As a

condition of providing this loan, FRBNY also created a trust to receive AIG preferred stock for the benefit of the U.S. Treasury. On January 14, 2011, as part of the recapitalization, the trust exchanged these preferred shares for about 562.9 million shares of AIG common stock, which was transferred subsequently to Treasury.

Broad-Based Liquidity Programs that Made Loans to Intermediary Entities

The Federal Reserve Board's broad-based programs launched in late 2008 and early 2009 employed more novel lending structures to provide liquidity support to a broader range of key credit markets. These broad-based liquidity programs included AMLF, CPFF, MMIFF, and TALF. Through these programs, the Reserve Banks generally extended loans to an intermediary entity—a financial institution or an SPV—to fund the entity's purchases of assets from eligible sellers in strained funding markets. In contrast to earlier programs, the Reserve Banks provided loans to these intermediary entities to help channel support to strained funding markets rather than to address the entities' liquidity needs. The assets purchased by the intermediary entity served as collateral for the loan from the Reserve Bank. These liquidity programs, with the exception of TALF, did not overcollateralize loans through haircuts. In addition, if a Reserve Bank could not recover the full value of a loan from collateral seized in the event of a default, except as noted below, the Reserve Bank generally would not have had recourse to other assets of a borrowing institution under these programs. To help mitigate the risk of losses, TALF, as well as the programs that did not require overcollateralization, accepted only highly-rated assets as collateral. In addition, CPFF, MMIFF, and TALF incorporated various security features, such as the accumulation of excess interest and fee income to absorb losses, to provide additional loss protection. Table 6 provides an overview of the security and collateral features for these broad-based liquidity programs.

AMLF. Through AMLF, the Federal Reserve Board authorized FRBB to make loans to intermediary borrowers that were secured by highly-rated ABCP purchased from money market funds. If an AMLF borrower defaulted, FRBB would have attempted to recover losses through its claim on the assets collateralizing the ABCP. As discussed earlier, AMLF was created to provide liquidity support to MMMFs and its less traditional lending structure reflected practical constraints in lending directly to these funds and the need to encourage participation by intermediary borrowers. AMLF did not apply haircuts and accepted only highly-rated ABCP as collateral.[104] Federal Reserve System staff said that requiring overcollateralization for AMLF loans would have been inconsistent with policy objectives to effectively provide liquidity support to MMMFs. If MMMFs sold assets to the intermediary borrowers through AMLF at less than book value to fund redemption requests from MMMF shareholders, they would have incurred losses to the detriment of remaining MMMF shareholders, creating further incentives for MMMF shareholders to redeem shares, which would have further exacerbated strains on their liquidity. Accordingly, the Federal Reserve Board sought to help fund purchases of MMMF assets at book value. Therefore, it authorized loans to intermediary borrowers that were equal to the book value of the ABCP to provide adequate incentives to these borrowers to participate. Upon providing an AMLF loan, FRBB accepted the risk of credit loss on the ABCP securing the loan. Applying haircuts to AMLF loans would have reduced the economic incentives for eligible borrowers to participate as they would have had to fund part of the ABCP purchases on their own.[105] Furthermore, the

Federal Reserve Board authorized nonrecourse lending to increase incentives for intermediary borrowers to participate. In the event of losses on the ABCP collateral, the borrower could surrender the ABCP to FRBB and choose not to repay its loan. However, under the terms of the AMLF program lending agreement, the nonrecourse provisions of the loan could be voided, giving FRBB full recourse to recover any losses from a borrower's assets, if the borrower was found to have misrepresented compliance with AMLF requirements.

CPFF. Through CPFF, FRBNY extended loans to a newly created SPV that purchased (and held as collateral) new issues of eligible ABCP and unsecured commercial paper, which then served as collateral for the FRBNY loan.[106] The Federal Reserve Board restricted the SPV to purchases of ABCP and unsecured commercial paper that received the highest rating from at least one major credit rating agency and, if rated by multiple major credit rating agencies, received the highest rating by two or more of them. FRBNY conducted additional monitoring of the financial condition of participating ABCP conduits and corporate issuers to manage the risks posed by issuers at higher risk of default. The loans to the SPV were collateralized by the assets of the SPV. The assets of the SPV consisted of (1) the purchased ABCP, which was itself secured by the assets backing such ABCP; (2) the purchased unsecured commercial paper; (3) program fees, including registration fees and surcharges on unsecured commercial paper issuers that wanted to participate in the program; and (4) other assets, such as income from the SPV's investment of the fees. To secure purchases of commercial paper that were not backed by collateral, the Federal Reserve Board required issuers of unsecured paper to pay surcharges on the face value of the commercial paper that collectively would serve as an insurance fund to absorb potential losses. The Federal Reserve Board set the level of this surcharge at 100 basis points per annum to the face value of the commercial paper based on an analysis of historical loss rates on unsecured paper. Unsecured commercial paper issues that were guaranteed by the FDIC's TLGP were exempt from the surcharge requirement. All CPFF borrowers were required to pay a one-time registration fee.[107] The CPFF SPV accumulated surcharges on unsecured paper, registration fees, and interest earned in excess of the target Federal Funds rate the SPV paid on loans from FRBNY. At FRBNY's direction, this "excess income" was invested in permitted investments as these investments and any return they generated also served as collateral for the loans extended by FRBNY to the SPV. The amount of these investments provided a cushion against potential losses. Finally, the Federal Reserve Board generally limited each participant's CPFF borrowings to the maximum amount of paper it had outstanding between January and August 2008.[108] This participation limit served to prevent excessive program use and to limit FRBNY's possible exposure to a single institution.

MMIFF. MMIFF employed a relatively complex lending structure intended to facilitate additional liquidity support for MMMFs while building in additional loss protection through a new subordinated note feature. Unlike AMLF, which made loans to intermediary borrowers to finance purchases of highly-rated ABCP, MMIFF created five SPVs that would use FRBNY loans to help finance purchases of a broader range of eligible assets from MMMFs. MMIFF-eligible assets included short-term debt obligations of 50 financial institutions that were determined to be broadly held by many MMMFs. FRBNY would have funded 90 percent of each SPV's purchases of eligible MMIFF assets with a senior loan.

Table 6. Summary of Terms and Conditions for AMLF, MMIFF, CPFF, and TALF

Category	AMLF	MMIFF	CPFF	TALF[a]
Eligible borrowers	U.S. depository institutions and their broker-dealer affiliates and holding companies	MMIFF SPVs	CPFF LLC, which used FRBNY loans to purchase new issues of ABCP and commercial paper from U.S. issuers of highly rated commercial paper	U.S. companies without foreign government control
Collateral eligibility	Selected U.S. dollar-denominated ABCP rated not lower than A-1/P-1/F-1	U.S. dollar-denominated Certificates of deposit, bank notes, and commercial paper issued by selected institutions with a short-term debt rating not lower than A-1/P-1/F-1	3-month U.S. dollar-denominated commercial paper (including ABCP) rated not lower than A-1/P-1/F-1	Selected triple-A ABS
Haircuts[b]	No	No	No	Yes
Recourse to borrower's assets[c]	No	Recourse to SPVs only	Recourse to CPFF LLC only	No
Interest rate	Primary credit rate	Primary credit rate	Overnight indexed swap rate + 300 basis points for ABCP; overnight indexed swap rate + 100 basis points for unsecured commercial paper	Interest rates vary by collateral types and the terms of the loans
Other (fees or surcharges)	None	None	Registration fee; for unsecured commercial paper issues, surcharge of 100 basis points[d]	Administrative fee of 10 basis points for non-mortgage-related MBS and 20 basis points for commercial MBS
Term	Up to 120 days or 270 days	7 to 90 days	90 days	3 or 5 years

Source: GAO analysis based on Federal Reserve Board terms and conditions for AMLF, MMIFF, CPFF, and TALF.

[a]The administrative fee for TALF nonmortgage-related ABS was initially 5 basis points and was later increased to 10 basis points for nonmortgage-related MBS and 20 basis points for commercial MBS. TALF 5-year loans were available only on commercial MBS and ABS backed by student loans and Small Business Administration loans.

[b]The MMIFF was designed to achieve overcollateralization by requiring participating MMFs to fund 10 percent of the purchase price of eligible assets in the form of a subordinated note.

[c]If an AMLF or TALF borrower was found to have materially misrepresented its compliance with program requirements, the relevant Reserve Bank may have had recourse to its assets to recover any losses under the terms of the borrowing agreement. According to FRBNY staff, depending on the particular commercial paper in question, the CPFF SPV may have had various levels of recourse against the issuer of the commercial paper.

[d]Unsecured commercial paper issues that were guaranteed by the FDIC's TLGP were exempt from the surcharge requirement. According to FRBNY, the fees and surcharges also constituted collateral.

The remaining 10 percent of MMIFF purchases would have been funded by a subordinated note issued by the MMIFF SPV to the selling MMMF. The first 10 percent of any losses on assets held by a MMIFF SPV would have been absorbed by the subordinated note holders. This would have provided for overcollateralization of FRBNY's loans to the SPV. MMIFF was never used. Feedback FRBNY received from MMMFs indicated that they viewed MMIFF as a backstop that they would access only as a last resort.[109]

TALF. TALF borrowers served as intermediaries that used TALF loans from FRBNY to finance the purchase ABS, which served as collateral for the TALF loans. Borrowers requested TALF loans through primary dealers and a few other firms that served as TALF agents. To increase the support that TALF borrowers could provide to the securitization markets, the Federal Reserve Board set borrower eligibility requirements to permit broad participation by U.S. entities. TALF loans were made without recourse to borrowers' assets beyond the ABS collateral. TALF contained multiple layers of loss protection:

- First, the Federal Reserve Board required TALF collateral to be rated AAA or its equivalent by two of the rating agencies that it deemed eligible to provide credit ratings for TALF.[110] The rating requirement helped to ensure that the securities TALF accepted as collateral presented minimal credit risks. Due diligence performed on securities to be purchased served as another pillar of loss protection. FRBNY, with the support of vendors, reviewed the credit risks related to individual ABS that FRBNY might consider accepting as TALF collateral.[111]
- Second, the Federal Reserve Board required TALF loans to be overcollateralized through haircut requirements. FRBNY officials said that TALF haircuts were designed to approximate multiples of stressed historical impairment rates for ABS. These haircut requirements determined the amount of a TALF borrower's equity in the ABS collateral. This equity represented the amount of money that a TALF borrower would lose by surrendering the collateral and not repaying the loan.
- Third, an SPV created by FRBNY—TALF LLC—received a portion of the interest income earned by FRBNY on TALF loans and if a TALF borrower chose to not repay its loan, this accumulated excess interest income could be used by TALF LLC to purchase collateral surrendered by the borrower from FRBNY.
- Finally, if the excess interest income accumulated in TALF LLC was insufficient to purchase the surrendered collateral, Treasury initially committed to lend up to $20 billion of TARP funds to TALF LLC for any such purchases. The Federal Reserve Board authorized FRBNY to lend up to $180 billion for any purchases exceeding this maximum TARP commitment.[112] Both loans would be secured by the assets of TALF LLC, and FRBNY's loan, if made, would be senior to Treasury's loan.

Maiden Lane Portfolios and Lending Commitments for Citigroup and Bank of America

FRBNY took similar steps to mitigate its risk of losses from its loan to Maiden Lane, the SPV created to purchase and hold Bear Stearns's assets; and its loans to Maiden Lanes II and III, the SPVs created to purchase and hold certain assets related to AIG. In each case, FRBNY extended a senior loan to the SPV and this loan was collateralized by the portfolio of assets held by the SPV. Figure 5 illustrates the lending structures and certain aspects of the loss protection features for the Maiden Lane transactions. These features included:

- *First loss positions for JPMC and AIG.* For Maiden Lane, JPMC agreed to take a first loss position by making a $1.15 billion subordinated loan to help finance the SPV's $30 billion purchase of the Bear Stearns asset portfolio. JPMC would begin to receive payments on this subordinated loan only after FRBNY received the full principal and interest on its $28.8 billion senior loan to the SPV. This lending structure protects FRBNY from up to $1.15 billion in losses on the portfolio. AIG agreed to assume a similar first loss position for Maiden Lanes II and III. For Maiden Lane II, AIG's insurance subsidiaries agreed to sell residential mortgage-backed securities valued at $20.5 billion to the SPV for $19.5 billion, accepting the $1 billion discount as a fixed deferred purchase price. The AIG subsidiaries would receive payments on this fixed deferred purchase price, plus interest, only after full repayment of the interest and principal on FRBNY's loan. Finally, for Maiden Lane III, AIG agreed to take a $5 billion equity interest in the SPV to help fund Maiden Lane III's $29.3 billion purchase of CDOs.
- *Asset selection and filters.* The broad categories of assets selected for inclusion in these portfolios were based on the policy objectives of the transaction, but FRBNY specified certain asset filters, or criteria, that were intended to exclude certain higher-risk assets. For example, FRBNY accepted only U.S. dollar denominated assets into the three portfolios to avoid the complexities of managing currency exposures from foreign currency assets. In addition, for Maiden Lane, FRBNY agreed to accept only commercial and residential loans that were "performing," or no more than 30 days past due, as of March 14, 2008, the date of the bridge loan to Bear Stearns. For Maiden Lane III, FRBNY did not accept synthetic CDO exposures that were derivative instruments rather than cash securities.[113]
- *Valuation and due diligence.* FRBNY hired vendors to help verify the value of the assets in these portfolios and to conduct due diligence to exclude assets that were proposed for inclusion but did not meet the specified asset filters or lacked documentation. The purchase price for the Maiden Lane assets was based on Bear Stearns's recorded values for these assets as of March 14, 2008. FRBNY hired an external audit firm, Ernst & Young, to conduct due diligence for all three portfolios and to help ensure the accuracy of settlement amounts for Maiden Lanes II and III.
- *Portfolio management.* For each portfolio, FRBNY retained sole discretion over the decisions about how to manage the assets to maximize the value recovered on FRBNY's senior loan. FRBNY hired BlackRock to manage these portfolios and to advise on a strategy for investing and disposing of the assets. For Maiden Lane, FRBNY agreed to a 2-year reinvestment period during which all cash income from the portfolio (net of expenses) would be reinvested in relatively low-risk investments, and FRBNY would not be permitted to receive repayment on its loan prior to the ending of the reinvestment period unless the JPMC loan was repaid in full. According to FRBNY staff, JPMC requested this reinvestment period out of concern that FRBNY could sell portfolio assets at prices that would recover value for FRBNY but incur losses for JPMC. FRBNY staff said FRBNY agreed to this reinvestment strategy because it would not increase risk of loss on its senior loan.

FRBNY hired other vendors to help oversee and manage the risks of specific asset classes included in the Maiden Lane portfolio. For example, FRBNY hired vendors to advise on the risks posed by commercial real estate loans.

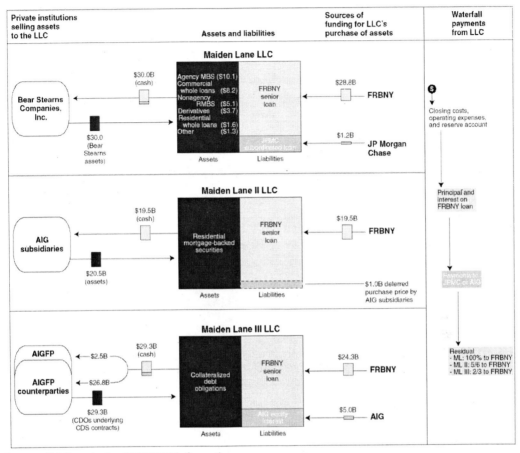

Source: GAO analysis of FRBNY information.

Figure 5. Comparison of the Transaction Structures for Maiden Lane LLC, Maiden Lane II LLC, and Maiden Lane III LLC.

For the assistance provided to Citigroup and Bank of America, FRBNY and FRBR, respectively, coordinated with Treasury and FDIC to negotiate similar types of loss protections. In contrast to the Maiden Lane transactions, FRBNY and FRBR agreed to provide loans under certain circumstances but did not anticipate having to lend—and ultimately did not lend—to these institutions under these agreements. Specifically, in each case, as part of a loss-sharing agreement on a designated portfolio of assets, the Reserve Bank agreed to provide a loan to be collateralized by assets remaining in the portfolio if cash losses on these assets exceeded certain thresholds. Citigroup and Bank of America agreed to a first-loss position, and Treasury and FDIC agreed to share losses in second- and third-loss positions, respectively. The FRBNY loan would have been a one-time, all or nothing loan secured by a first priority perfected security interest in all of the remaining assets at the time that the loan was triggered.[114] Based on analysis conducted by BlackRock, FRBNY concluded that losses on the Citigroup assets reaching the point at which FRBNY could be required to lend were unlikely. FRBR staff said that they reached a similar conclusion on Bank of America based on analysis performed by PIMCO. In both cases, the Reserve Banks hired external audit firms to conduct due diligence on the asset portfolios. FRBNY did not complete its due diligence before signing a final lending agreement with Citigroup in January 2009 but incorporated protections into this agreement that allowed FRBNY to reject specific assets based on additional due diligence. Following approximately 11 months of due diligence by FRBNY's vendor, FRBNY, Treasury, FDIC, and Citigroup agreed to a final set of assets to be included in the portfolio. As discussed earlier, Bank of America requested a termination of the term sheet before a final agreement was executed among the parties.

Emergency Programs That Have Closed Have Not Incurred Losses and the Federal Reserve Board Expects No Losses on Those with Outstanding Balances

The Federal Reserve System earned $19.9 billion in revenue from the broad-based programs and did not incur losses on any of the programs that have closed. As noted earlier, financial stability—rather than profit maximization—was the Federal Reserve Board's primary objective when designing these programs. TALF, under which FRBNY made $71.1 billion of loans for terms of 3 or 5 years, is the only broad-based program with loans outstanding. As of April 27, 2011, the Federal Reserve Board reported that no TALF borrowers had chosen to surrender their collateral instead of repaying their loans. As of June 29, 2011, approximately $13 billion of TALF loans remained outstanding out of $71.1 billion in total TALF lending. The Federal Reserve Board does not project any losses from TALF.

FRBNY loans to the Maiden Lanes remain outstanding and FRBNY projects full repayment of these loans. For the three portfolios, figure 6 illustrates the coverage ratio, or the ratio of the value of the assets in the portfolios to the amount outstanding on FRBNY's senior loan, over time. In the months following these transactions, each portfolio experienced declines that brought the portfolio value below the amount owed to FRBNY. However, as market conditions improved in late 2009 and 2010, the value of these portfolios increased and as of June 29, 2011, all three had a positive coverage ratio. Until the assets in these portfolios mature or are sold, FRBNY remains exposed to the risk of losses. The Federal Reserve Board does not project any losses on FRBNY's loans to the Maiden Lanes.

In March 2011, FRBNY announced that it had declined a $15.7 billion conditional offer from AIG to purchase the Maiden Lane II assets. On March 30, 2011, FRBNY announced that it would sell these assets individually and in segments over time through a competitive process. The Federal Reserve Board has reported that as of June 9, 2011, FRBNY had sold approximately $10 billion of these assets in competitive auctions. According to FRBNY, it continues to evaluate market conditions to assess the appropriate timing and method of asset dispositions out of Maiden Lane and Maiden Lane III. While no large scale disposition has been announced to date, FRBNY noted that some opportunistic sales have occurred in these portfolios.

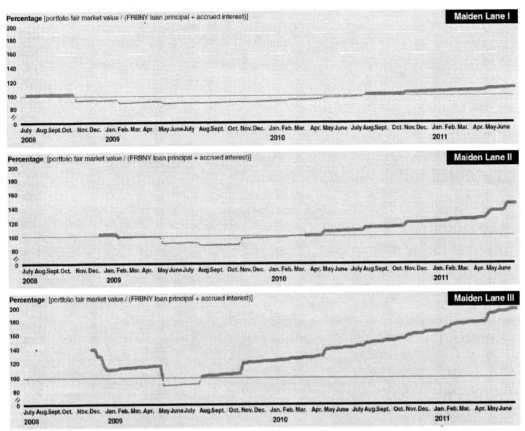

———Period of time where portfolio fair value was more than FRBNY's loan principal balance and accrued interest

------Period of time where portfolio fair value was less than FRBNY's loan principal balance and accrued interest

Source: GAO analysis of Federal Reserve Board statistical release H.4.1.

Figure 6. Coverage Ratios for Maiden Lane, Maiden Lane II, and Maiden Lane III, July 2008–June 29, 2011.

While Reserve Banks Strengthened Controls and Risk Management over Time, Opportunities Exist to Further Strengthen Policies for Future Emergency Programs

In deploying large new emergency programs, often under severe time constraints, the Reserve Banks faced challenges in establishing controls and risk governance structures to keep pace with the associated risks. FRBNY, which implemented most of the programs, took steps to enhance controls over time, in many cases in response to recommendations from external and internal auditors. Although some control weaknesses were not remediated until late in a program's life, these weaknesses generally do not appear to have impacted loan performance. In addition, FRBNY took steps during the crisis to enhance its risk management, including by expanding its capabilities to perform risk analytics and reporting needed to support risk management decisions for its emergency programs. However, the

Federal Reserve System's existing policies for operating a few programs continue to lack specific guidance that would help ensure Reserve Bank management and staff take appropriate steps to manage and mitigate risks posed by higher-risk depository institutions and primary dealers in the event of a future crisis.

Internal Controls over Compliance with Program Requirements Improved over Time

To help ensure compliance with program rules and requirements established to mitigate risk of losses, the Reserve Banks leveraged existing control processes and developed new controls for new activities. According to Reserve Bank staff, to the extent possible, the Reserve Banks relied on existing discount window systems and procedures to monitor compliance with program requirements. For example, for TAF, which functioned as an extension of the discount window, Reserve Banks relied on existing discount window systems for processing TAF loans and monitoring compliance with requirements related to collateralization and minimum supervisory ratings. For both TAF and TSLF, FRBNY staff implemented new procedures to help ensure compliance with auction rules and requirements. For several other broad-based programs, FRBNY and FRBB staff said they used existing systems to monitor compliance with some program requirements but had to develop new procedures and practices to monitor data and activities not captured by these systems. For example, FRBB staff explained that while they used the Federal Reserve System's existing loan-processing application to process AMLF loans and track AMLF loan data, they had to create a new database to track data fields not tracked by this application, including the amortized cost of the ABCP. In addition, over time, FRBNY developed procedures to help ensure that vendors and other third parties implemented key program requirements correctly.[115] For PDCF and TSLF, for example, FRBNY staff conducted checks of clearing bank data from the preceding day's loan activity (ex-post) to provide assurance that clearing banks were correctly implementing collateral requirements. Similarly, for CPFF and TALF, FRBNY developed new procedures and guidance to help ensure that vendors and other third parties complied with program rules and requirements.

Our review identified weaknesses in controls over security and collateral policies for some programs, and these weaknesses were also identified by the external auditor, Reserve Bank internal audit, or RBOPS. The Reserve Banks generally remediated these weaknesses within a year of their identification, and these weaknesses do not appear to have impacted loan performance. Examples of control weaknesses include the following:

- *PDCF and TSLF collateral-management processes.* FRBNY initially lacked processes to help ensure that primary dealers did not pledge "close-linked" collateral—that is, assets whose returns were closely linked with the financial performance of the borrowing dealer. The initial bilateral agreements with primary dealers did not prohibit primary dealers from pledging close-linked collateral. The bilateral agreements were later amended to prohibit such collateral from being pledged. In addition, FRBNY did not initially monitor whether the clearing banks allowed primary dealers to provide their own prices for assets pledged as collateral. For TSLF, the tri-party agreements among FRBNY, each primary dealer, and its clearing bank expressly prohibited the clearing bank from using a primary dealer's prices for collateral provided by that primary dealer. For PDCF, which used the legacy tri-party agreements in place for traditional open market operations, there was no such express prohibition. FRBNY later agreed with each clearing bank that the clearing bank would not use a dealer's prices for collateral pledged by that dealer.

- *Validating vendor and clearing bank valuations of collateral.* During much of the crisis, FRBNY did not take certain steps to validate collateral valuation and pricing performed by vendors for some programs until late in the program's operation. For example, FRBNY did not begin validating BlackRock's valuations of the Maiden Lane portfolio until the second quarter of 2009. In addition, FRBNY staff told us that while they did ex-post checks of the clearing banks' application of haircut and collateral-eligibility requirements for PDCF and TSLF, they did not systematically check the reasonableness of the prices clearing banks applied to the primary dealers' collateral. According to FRBNY staff, for TSLF, they implemented a program to check the clearing banks' pricing for collateral towards the end of the TSLF program. As discussed in the next section, in summer 2009, FRBNY enhanced its in-house capabilities to perform financial analytics needed to validate valuation analyses performed by vendors and clearing banks.
- *TALF agent due diligence.* In January 2010, FRBNY issued revised guidance to TALF agents to address concerns that two primary dealers had not conducted appropriately thorough reviews of certain borrowers. In addition, FRBNY performed on-site reviews of selected TALF agents and required TALF agents to provide due diligence files on all borrowers.
- *Oversight of vendor compliance with program requirements.* As discussed earlier, FRBNY did not always conduct timely on-site reviews of vendor processes and controls. For example, although PIMCO played a key role in administering CPFF program requirements starting in October 2008, FRBNY did not conduct an on-site review of PIMCO's controls until March 2009. As discussed earlier, in May 2010, FRBNY issued new policy guidance on vendor oversight.

Our review of the implementation of selected program requirements revealed relatively infrequent instances of incorrect application of these requirements. Specifically, our review of the detailed collateral data for PDCF found that the correct haircuts were applied in the vast majority of cases. Specifically, we found only about 2 percent of cases where the haircut applied was either above or below that prescribed by the haircut schedules. For PDCF, we identified some instances of apparent discrepancies between prices that clearing banks applied to the same types of assets. However, we were unable to determine the source of these differences. As a result, we were unable to determine the extent to which these discrepancies may have impacted the level of undercollateralization. FRBNY staff noted that these differences may have been due in part to differences in the pricing sources and pricing algorithms used by the two clearing banks. In the vast majority of the cases, the haircut setting for the TAF collateral was consistent with published discount window haircut rates. There were not pricing discrepancies between the same collateral pledged by different borrowers, and TAF loans were covered by the value of the collateral after application of TAF haircut rates.

FRBNY Took Several Steps to Enhance Its Risk Management

During the crisis, FRBNY took steps to strengthen its financial risk-management function by expanding and clarifying its risk management structure and enhancing its risk analytics capabilities and risk reporting for its emergency programs. However, according to FRBNY officials, some of the significant organizational changes and staff additions to enhance risk management did not occur until summer 2009, when use of many programs was winding down.

When the crisis began, FRBNY's risk management group did not have the staffing resources and expertise needed to adequately oversee the risks of FRBNY's new, large-scale emergency programs. FRBNY's Credit Risk Management group (CRM) was housed within its Financial Institution Supervision Group and had a small staff of around 10 employees. According to FRBNY, this staff size was commensurate with the much more limited level of credit risk FRBNY had traditionally assumed through its vendor relationships, discount window lending, and open market operations. According to FRBNY's Chief Risk Officer, FRBNY management moved CRM outside of the Financial Institution Supervision Group to make it part of an independent group shortly following the Bear Stearns assistance and creation of PDCF. FRBNY's Chief Risk Officer said that CRM's responsibilities in 2008 and early 2009 focused on tracking and reporting FRBNY's risk exposures from its emergency lending and collaborating with FRBNY program staff to assess specific risks.

Outside of CRM, FRBNY assigned special teams to manage risks related to certain emergency lending activities. For example, in summer 2008, FRBNY management created an Investment Support Office to oversee the day-to-day vendor oversight and portfolio management for the Maiden Lane portfolio. FRBNY created an Investment Committee, composed of FRBNY officers from a range of functions, to serve as the oversight body for the Maiden Lane portfolio. FRBNY also assigned oversight responsibilities to the Investment Support Office and Investment Committee for the Maiden Lane II and III portfolios. As discussed later, FRBNY modified this management structure for the Maiden Lane portfolios in June 2010. In fall 2008, FRBNY also assembled an AIG monitoring team to manage the risks of its lending to AIG. For TALF, FRBNY created a TALF project team to establish and implement the program.

In January 2009, FRBNY hired an outside consulting firm to conduct an independent review of its management infrastructure surrounding its emergency programs. In response to specific recommendations made by the vendor's March 2009 report and as part of its ongoing efforts to enhance its risk management function, FRBNY made the following changes: (1) the creation of a Financial Risk Management Division to be headed by the Chief Risk Officer, (2) enhancements to its risk analytics capabilities and risk reporting, (3) reorganization and clarification of its management structure for making key risk decisions for the Maiden Lane portfolios, and (4) the creation of a new policy to establish a process for the early review and monitoring of new activities that could expose FRBNY to increased or additional risks.

Creation of the Financial Risk Management Division. In the second quarter of 2009, following the report of the outside consulting firm, FRBNY formally established the role of Chief Risk Officer and appointed the head of the Credit Payments Risk Group, which included the CRM function, to that role. In summer 2009, FRBNY expanded its risk management capabilities, adding expertise that would come to be organized as two new functions, Structured Products and Risk Analytics. Currently, these two functions and the classic credit risk management function comprise the Financial Risk Management Division. Figure 7 illustrates the organizational structure for FRM as of January 2011. Staff within this division were assigned to be risk liaisons to the AIG monitoring team and selected members of the TALF business team. According to FRBNY staff, FRBNY significantly expanded FRM's resources in summer 2009. FRBNY staff estimated that by October 2009 FRM had about 24 employees.

Enhanced risk reporting and analytics. In summer 2009, FRBNY made improvements to its risk reporting and risk analytics for its emergency programs and assistance to individual institutions. In June 2009, FRM staff made two significant enhancements to the risk reports provided to senior FRBNY management. First, FRM created a set of risk indicators that provided summary metrics and information for FRBNY's emergency lending activities. Second, FRBNY began reporting its aggregate credit exposures to the institutions that were the largest borrowers across FRBNY's emergency programs. Previously, FRBNY had produced management-level reports that showed the largest credit exposures within each emergency program and aggregate credit exposures of primary dealers—TSLF, PDCF, and other dealer exposures—and banks—TAF and regular discount window exposures. According to FRBNY staff, during the second quarter of 2009, FRBNY began staffing the new Risk Analytics group within FRM. According to FRBNY officials, this group's responsibilities include performing modeling and other analytics to validate work performed by FRBNY vendors.

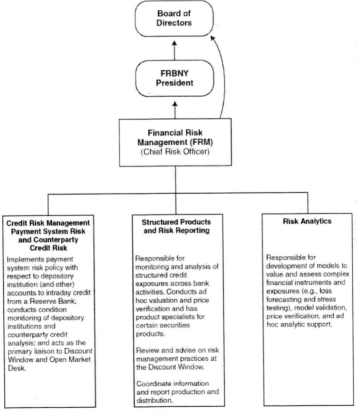

Source: GAO presentation of FRBNY information.

Figure 7. Organizational Structure of FRBNY's Financial Risk Management Division, as of January 2011.

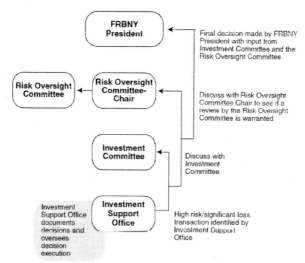

Source: GAO presentation of FRBNY information.

Figure 8. Risk Escalation Protocols for Oversight of Maiden Lane Portfolios, as of June 2010.

Risk management for the Maiden Lane portfolios. In June 2010, FRBNY formally reorganized its management structure for the Maiden Lane portfolios. Previously, the Investment Committee had been the oversight and decision-making body for the Maiden Lane portfolios. FRBNY assigned the newly formed Risk Oversight Committee with membership of senior officers from across the organization to provide an additional layer of oversight for higher-risk decisions. As illustrated in figure 8, FRBNY set forth risk escalation procedures by which the Investment Support Office would make routine day-to-day decisions and escalate higher-risk issues to the Investment Committee, the Risk Oversight Committee, and the FRBNY President, as appropriate.

Policy for reviewing new initiatives. In December 2009, FRBNY implemented a new policy that established a process for the early review and monitoring of new programs or activities that could expose FRBNY to increased or additional risks. This policy outlines high-level protocols to better ensure proper review, consultation, and consideration of risks for significant new initiatives. For example, for major new lending programs or changes to such programs, the policy directs FRBNY to assign responsibilities for documenting a high-level implementation plan and sharing this plan with relevant stakeholders within FRBNY to help ensure proper consideration of the expected outcomes, risks, and risk controls for the program.

Opportunities Exist to Improve the Federal Reserve System's Risk Management for Any Future Emergency Activities

While FRBNY's policy for reviewing new initiatives provides guidance that would be useful in the event of future deployment of emergency programs, opportunities exist for FRBNY and the Federal Reserve System as a whole to strengthen risk management practices and procedures for future emergency lending activities. Our review identified two areas where the Federal Reserve System had less robust practices for managing the risk of losses from its emergency lending: (1) monitoring the size of losses that could occur under more adverse economic conditions within and across emergency programs and (2) documenting procedures used to guide Reserve Bank efforts to monitor and mitigate risks posed by eligible borrowers who pose higher risk of loss.

Estimation of Stress Losses for Emergency Programs. First, while for some of its programs FRBNY estimated stress losses that could occur under more adverse economic scenarios, neither FRBNY nor the Federal Reserve Board systematically estimated and tracked stress loss estimates across all emergency lending programs. FRBNY did not calculate estimates for stress losses for TAF, TSLF, and PDCF, and FRBB did not create such estimates for its AMLF lending. As a result, there was no information on the size of potential total stress losses for the Federal Reserve Board to consider as it made decisions to authorize and modify its emergency lending programs. In addition, FRBNY estimated and monitored the level of undercollateralization that could occur in stress scenarios for some TAF, TSLF, and PDCF borrowers, but these estimates did not represent potential stress losses for these borrowers or for these programs.

The Federal Reserve System has directed the largest institutions it regulates to perform stress testing to quantify the impact of adverse macroeconomic and financial market scenarios, both at the level of an individual counterparty and aggregated across counterparties. Federal Reserve Board and FRBNY staff we spoke with said calculating stress losses for some programs was appropriate. Accordingly, stress loss estimates were periodically calculated for the Maiden Lane portfolios. In addition, in January 2009, FRBNY began estimating expected and stressed losses for CPFF and for weekly CPFF reports created for senior officials, calculated the size of these estimated losses relative to its capital.[116] For that month, an FRBNY analysis estimated that CPFF losses in a stressed scenario could have reached approximately $35 billion—nearly three times the size of FRBNY's capital as of December 31, 2008.[117]

However, Federal Reserve Board and FRBNY staff we spoke with said that they did not believe it would be useful for the Federal Reserve System to calculate stress losses for all emergency programs. For areas where FRBNY did not routinely estimate and track stress losses, FRBNY staff indicated that doing so was unnecessary because the haircuts applied to the collateral built in a cushion based on an analysis of expected changes in the price of the collateral. However, while these haircuts provided some protection against historical price movements for assets pledged as collateral, they did not reflect potential price movements during a financial crisis. For example, these haircuts did not provide protection against price declines in stressed scenarios. Although FRBNY staff told us that estimating stress losses for TAF, PDCF, and TSLF was unnecessary, FRBNY did conduct analysis to help monitor its potential exposure to price declines that exceeded haircuts for its lending to some institutions through these programs.

In the second quarter of 2008, to better monitor risk for collateralized exposures to depository institutions and primary dealers, FRBNY's CRM began including a metric known as "Dollars at risk in Event of Need to Terminate under Stress" (DENTS) in its daily risk reports provided to its senior management. For a stress scenario with severe declines in collateral values, the DENTS metric represented an estimate of the potential shortfall that could occur between the collateral value and the FRBNY loan amount. CRM's risk reports reported the DENTS for depository institutions and primary dealers with loans outstanding. FRBNY staff explained that DENTS estimates were used as rough estimates of stress exposures but did not reflect the likely level of losses in a stress scenario. For example, in the event of a borrower default, FRBNY would not be forced to liquidate collateral immediately at stressed prices, as assumed by the DENTS calculation. While FRBNY's monitoring of DENTS provided useful information about potential risk exposures from the three programs, the Federal Reserve System lacked estimates of potential total losses from these programs under stressed conditions. While the Federal Reserve System's emergency programs did not suffer losses during the crisis, a more comprehensive view of the total potential risk exposures from its emergency programs under adverse economic scenarios could help the Federal Reserve Board and Reserve Banks to make more informed risk management decisions in the event of a future crisis.

Procedures for Restricting Program Access. During the crisis, existing discount window program guidance did not provide details on how Reserve Banks should exercise certain discretion to deny TAF access to otherwise eligible depository institutions that posed higher risks. In addition, FRBNY lacked documented procedures to guide Reserve Bank decisions to restrict lending to higher-risk primary dealers through TSLF and PDCF. In 2010, after TAF, PDCF, and TSLF had closed, the Federal Reserve System enhanced its guidance to Reserve Banks on monitoring higher-risk borrowers at the discount window and FRBNY created a new risk management framework for primary dealers. However, these documents do not include detailed guidance that may be needed to help ensure that Reserve Bank staff take consistent and appropriate steps to manage program access by higher-risk borrowers if these programs are deployed in the future.

For TAF, Reserve Banks relied on existing discount window procedures for monitoring the financial condition of depository institutions, but discount window guidance lacked specific protocols to guide discretion they used to deny TAF access to some institutions. A November 30, 2007, Federal Reserve System staff memo noted that "protocols could be developed to guide a Reserve Bank's response to a [TAF] bid by a depository institution about which the Reserve Bank has concerns" to address the risk that a depository institution's financial condition could deteriorate during the term of its TAF funding (generally 28 or 84 days). However, according to Federal Reserve Board and FRBNY staff with whom we spoke, such protocols were not subsequently developed during the crisis. According to the Federal Reserve Board, Reserve Banks exercised this discretion to restrict access by at least 30 institutions. The Federal Reserve Board was unable to readily verify the completeness of the list of TAF restrictions provided to us. Without specific guidance on how such restrictions should have been applied for TAF, whether each Reserve Bank considered appropriate criteria in deciding to reject TAF bidders remains unclear.

In July 2010, the Subcommittee on Credit Risk Management, a committee of credit risk management leaders from the Reserve Banks, revised its guidance on standards and practices Reserve Banks should follow to monitor and manage risks posed by higher-risk institutions borrowing from the discount window. These revisions provided more granular risk classifications of depository institutions, including a new classification ("Group A") that would include institutions at risk of losing TAF eligibility—specifically, primary-credit-eligible institutions at high risk of losing their primary-credit eligibility. While the revised guidance indicates that it may be appropriate to disallow term borrowing, which would include TAF, for Group A institutions, it does not specify criteria that could be considered for applying this discretion. For Group A institutions, the guidance notes that "if appropriate, [the Reserve Bank should] evaluate imposing a term limit on discount window credit extensions."

According to FRBNY staff, the Federal Reserve System has not formally analyzed the consistency and appropriateness of Reserve Banks' decisions to restrict TAF access. Without such an analysis, the Federal Reserve System lacks assurance that Reserve Bank staff took consistent and appropriate steps to manage these risks.

While TSLF and PDCF program terms and conditions allowed all primary dealers to participate, FRBNY monitored the financial condition of primary dealers and applied special restrictions to two primary dealers it determined to pose higher risks. FRBNY staff said they had an on-site presence at some primary dealer firms subject to Securities and Exchange Commission regulation starting in March 2008. FRBNY developed procedures to guide staff efforts to monitor and mitigate risks posed by higher-risk CPFF issuers, but FRBNY staff said such procedures were not developed for TSLF and PDCF. In June 2010, FRBNY documented a risk management framework for primary dealers. While this framework outlines steps FRBNY's CRM group should take to monitor the financial condition and level of risk posed by primary dealers, it lacks details on what steps should be taken to determine whether special restrictions are warranted in the event that serious risk concerns emerge. In such situations, the framework advises "more comprehensive reviews...to assess an appropriate level of risk" but does not specify what these reviews should include, such as specific practices followed during the crisis (for example, establishing an on-site presence). A more specific plan for consistently and appropriately applying special restrictions to primary dealers could help to ensure that FRBNY manages risk effectively during a crisis.

The recent crisis illustrated that liquidity can disappear rapidly for depository institutions and primary dealer firms and some of these firms failed or nearly failed even as they continued to qualify for these Federal Reserve System programs. Moreover, the urgent nature of a crisis limits the time available for crafting these procedures, which underscores the benefit of having taken preparatory steps beforehand. Without more specific guidance on information to monitor and the type and amount of documentation to maintain, Reserve Bank staff responsible for implementing future emergency loan programs may not take consistent and appropriate steps to mitigate the risks posed by higher-risk borrowers. If such protocols are not established in advance of a future crisis, it may be difficult for Reserve Banks to develop them in a timely manner under crisis conditions that strain staff resources.

While Emergency Programs and Assistance Impact Excess Earnings to Treasury, the Federal Reserve Board Does Not Formally Make Projections for Several Reasons

Each year, pursuant to its policy, the Federal Reserve Board remits the Federal Reserve System's "excess earnings" to Treasury. These excess earnings consist of Federal Reserve System earnings in excess of operating expenditures, capital paid out in dividends to member banks, and an amount reserved by Reserve Banks to equate surplus with capital paid-in. The Federal Reserve Board's emergency lending programs and the purchase of $1.25 trillion of agency MBS have resulted in large increases in the excess earnings remitted to Treasury in 2009 and 2010 (see figure 9). Most of the emergency programs have closed, but at the time of this report, the agency MBS remaining on the Federal Reserve System's balance sheet and income from the Maiden Lane transactions continue to contribute to elevated levels of excess earnings.

According to Federal Reserve Board staff, the Federal Reserve Board does not formally project the Reserve Banks' expected excess earnings on a regular basis, primarily because it considers excess earnings to be a by-product of monetary policy decisions. Federal Reserve Board staff said they run ad-hoc simulations, at the request of FOMC members, to analyze the potential impacts of possible future monetary policy decisions, including their impact on the size and composition of the Federal Reserve System's balance sheet and the level of excess earnings. However, they do not believe that creating a single set of formal projections for excess earnings would have significant benefits for monetary policy decision making because the conduct of monetary policy is based on the Federal Reserve's statutory mandate to foster maximum employment and stable prices, and the path of Federal Reserve earnings has very limited influence on these fundamental macroeconomic objectives. Before the recent financial crisis, the most significant factors contributing to changes in excess earnings were changes in interest rates and changes in Reserve Bank holdings of U.S. Treasuries as a result of FOMC monetary policy directives. The Federal Reserve System's emergency programs and assistance and the FOMC's Agency MBS program significantly changed the composition of income-earning assets held on Reserve Bank balance sheets. According to Federal Reserve Board staff, increased income from the Federal Reserve Board's financial stability programs did not influence how the Reserve Banks and the Federal Reserve Board budgeted operating expenses. Although the Federal Reserve System is not funded by congressional appropriations, the Federal Reserve Board annually provides Congress with a budget document that outlines its planned expenditures for the year. Furthermore, Federal Reserve Board officials noted that the Federal Reserve Board and the Reserve Banks promote transparency with respect to their expenditures by publishing audited financial statements on their Web sites.

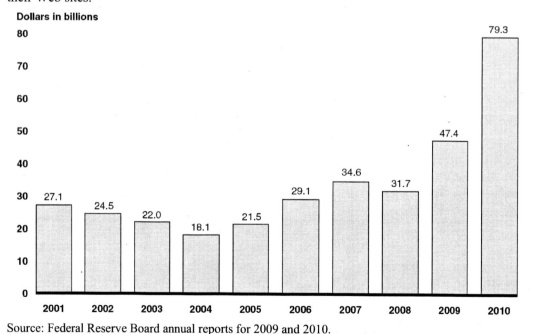

Source: Federal Reserve Board annual reports for 2009 and 2010.

Figure 9. Federal Reserve Board Excess Earnings Distributed to Treasury, 2001–2010.

For projections made as part of receipts estimation for the administrations annual *Budget of the U.S. Government*, Treasury includes a line item with projections for the amount of Federal Reserve System excess earnings that could be remitted to Treasury in the coming year. Treasury staff told us they do not receive or rely upon Federal Reserve Board forecasts. Although the Federal Reserve System's recent activities have complicated the projection exercise, Treasury staff said that the Federal Reserve Board's public disclosures provide sufficient information for them to develop projections for the administration's budget. For example, they have used the consolidated income statement for the Reserve Banks (from the Reserve Banks' public financial statements) as a starting point to project future earnings. They have also incorporated information from Federal Reserve Board press releases about monetary policy decisions. For example, Treasury adjusted its projections to reflect the November 2010 announcement that FRBNY would implement a new $600 billion program to purchase Treasury securities. In recent years, the Federal Reserve System has published detailed information about its holdings of agency MBS securities and changes in these holdings. According to Treasury staff with whom we spoke, these additional disclosures have been sufficient to help Treasury project excess earnings. Treasury relies on the administration's forecasts for future interest rates as an input to its excess earnings projections. Treasury staff are able to make projections for the administration's budget without the Federal Reserve Board formally projecting excess earnings and sharing these projections with Treasury or the public.

WHILE THE FEDERAL RESERVE BOARD TOOK STEPS TO PROMOTE CONSISTENT TREATMENT OF PARTICIPANTS, IT LACKED GUIDANCE AND DOCUMENTATION FOR SOME ACCESS DECISIONS

The Federal Reserve Board and its Reserve Banks took steps to promote consistent treatment of eligible program participants and generally offered assistance on the same terms and conditions to eligible institutions in the broad-based emergency programs. However, in a few programs, the Reserve Banks placed restrictions on some participants that presented higher risk. As discussed earlier, Reserve Banks lacked specific guidance for exercising certain discretion to restrict program access for higher-risk borrowers for a few programs; therefore, whether such restrictions were applied consistently is unclear. Furthermore, the Federal Reserve Board did not fully document its justification for authorizing credit extensions on terms similar to those available through PDCF for affiliates of a few primary dealers and did not provide guidance to Reserve Banks on the types of program decisions that required consultation with Federal Reserve Board policymakers. Taken collectively, the lack of guidance and documentation for certain decisions regarding program access may lessen the transparency and consistency of such decisions and could unintentionally lead to inconsistent treatment of participants.

The Federal Reserve Board Designed Program Eligibility Requirements to Target Assistance to Groups of Institutions Facing Liquidity Strains

The Federal Reserve Board created each broad-based emergency program to address liquidity strains in a particular funding market and designed the program eligibility requirements primarily to target significant participants in these markets. As discussed earlier in the report, the programs extended loans both directly to institutions facing liquidity strains and through intermediary borrowers. For programs that extended credit directly, the Federal Reserve Board took steps to limit program eligibility to institutions it considered to be generally sound. For programs that provided loans to intermediary borrowers, the Federal Reserve Board based eligibility requirements in part on the ability of borrowing institutions, as a group, to channel sufficient liquidity support to eligible sellers.

TAF. TAF loans were auctioned to depository institutions eligible for primary credit at the discount window and expected by their local Reserve Bank to remain primary-credit-eligible during the term the TAF loan would be outstanding. U.S. branches and agencies of foreign banks that were statutorily permitted to borrow from the discount window were also permitted to borrow from TAF. The Monetary Control Act of 1980 mandates that the Reserve Banks provide equal access to discount window credit to U.S. branches and agencies of foreign banks, and the Federal Reserve Board interpreted this requirement to apply to TAF, which was authorized under section 10B of the Federal Reserve Act, the same authority under which Reserve Banks provide traditional discount window loans.

Dollar swap lines. Under the dollar swap lines, FRBNY's counterparties were 14 foreign central banks, which each loaned dollars obtained through the swap lines to eligible institutions in their respective jurisdictions pursuant to their own lending programs.[118] The FOMC's consideration of a new swap line arrangement generally followed a request from an interested foreign central bank, but not all requests were granted. In fall 2008, the Federal Reserve Board received a number of requests for swap lines arrangements from foreign central banks in countries with emerging market economies. An October 2008 Federal Reserve Board staff memorandum outlined criteria in support of a recommendation that the FOMC approve swap lines with four emerging-market-economy central banks. FOMC approvals of swap line requests from such banks were generally based on the economic and financial mass of the country's economy, a record of sound economic management, and the probability that the swap line would make an economic difference.[119] According to Federal Reserve Board staff, the swap line arrangements were generally made with foreign central banks of important U.S. trading partners or global financial centers, such as Switzerland, Japan, and England, based on global funding needs.

TSLF and PDCF. The Federal Reserve Board limited program eligibility for TSLF and PDCF to the primary dealers, who were key participants in the repurchase agreement markets and traditional FRBNY counterparties. FRBNY officials explained that FRBNY was able to leverage its existing relationships with primary dealers and their clearing banks to quickly deploy TSLF and PDCF. For example, FRBNY already had longstanding legal agreements with these primary dealers to govern their participation in FRBNY's securities lending program and certain open market operations (repurchase agreement transactions).[120] The

Federal Reserve Board considered the primary dealers to be generally sound because primary dealers must meet certain standards set out by FRBNY in order to maintain their designation as primary dealers. For example, FRBNY requires that the primary dealer be a bank or broker-dealer supervised by SEC, the Federal Reserve Board, or one of the other bank supervisors. Although less regulated institutions, such as hedge funds, also participated in the repurchase agreement market, the Federal Reserve Board decided not to extend program eligibility beyond the primary dealers.

AMLF. The Federal Reserve Board developed program eligibility requirements for two sets of AMLF participants: (1) MMMFs that could sell eligible ABCP through the program to obtain cash to satisfy redemption demands from fund investors and (2) intermediary borrowers that could use AMLF loan proceeds to purchase ABCP from the MMMFs at book value. AMLF targeted 2a-7 MMMFs as eligible sellers because of the key economic role they played as a source of short-term credit for financial institutions and concerns about their vulnerability to rapid, large-scale redemption demands. In particular, the 2a-7 MMMFs were significant investors in highly-rated ABCP, and a policy objective of AMLF was to support the ABCP market by encouraging these MMMFs to continue to purchase and hold ABCP.[121]

The Federal Reserve Board authorized U.S. depository institutions, U.S. bank holding companies and their broker-dealer affiliates, and U.S. branches and agencies of foreign banks to participate as AMLF borrowers. Federal Reserve Board officials said that they identified the types of AMLF borrowers based on the entities' operational ability to purchase ABCP securities directly from MMMFs. MMMFs generally conducted custodial and funding activities with institutions that were eligible as AMLF borrowers and FRBB officials said that they anticipated institutions that provided custodian bank services, which include holding and administering the accounts with MMMF assets, to MMMFs to be the likely AMLF borrowers. Moreover, by lending to discount window-eligible institutions and entities that were affiliated with discount-window eligible institutions (U.S. bank holding companies and their broker-dealer affiliates), FRBB could deploy AMLF quickly. According to FRBB staff, lending through discount-window eligible institutions was particularly important, because MMMFs are not permitted to maintain transactional accounts with a Reserve Bank.

MMIFF. As discussed earlier, MMIFF's design featured a relatively complex lending structure through which FRBNY could make loans to five SPVs that would help to finance purchases of eligible short-term debt obligations from MMMFs and other eligible MMIFF investors.[122] Eligible MMIFF investors were initially restricted to 2a-7 MMMFs to facilitate a rapid launch and to allow time for additional analysis of the potential legal risks of including a broader set of investors. When FRBNY analyses indicated that the additional participants would not affect the ratings of the ABCP issued by the SPVs, the Federal Reserve Board expanded program eligibility to include securities lenders and investment funds that operated in a manner similar to MMMFs. Although MMIFF was never used, FRBNY staff said that the program likely benefited eligible participants through its presence as a backstop.

CPFF. Issuers of ABCP and financial and nonfinancial unsecured issuers whose paper received the top-tier ratings from one or more NRSROs were eligible to sell commercial paper through CPFF. FRBNY estimated that top-tier commercial paper eligible for CPFF represented nearly 90 percent of the commercial paper market. As a result, CPFF was expected to provide a backstop for a large part of the commercial paper market. Federal Reserve Board officials said that nonfinancial issuers were granted access to CPFF to address liquidity strains that had spread from financial markets to these issuers. Nonfinancial issuers that were significant participants in the commercial paper markets included large automobile manufacturers and restaurant chains. Eligible CPFF borrowers included U.S. subsidiaries of foreign companies who were participants in U.S. commercial paper markets.

TALF. TALF was open to any eligible U.S. company that owned eligible collateral. Eligible TALF borrowers included a broad range of institutions ranging from depository institutions to U.S. organized investment funds. Federal Reserve Board officials told us that broad participation in TALF would facilitate the program goal of encouraging the flow of credit to consumers and small businesses. To prevent participation by borrowers that might pose fraud or reputational risk, FRBNY required all prospective TALF borrowers to approach the program through one of the primary dealers or other firms that acted as TALF agents.[123] FRBNY directed TALF agents to conduct due diligence on prospective TALF borrowing institutions and "material investors" in these institutions.[124] While TALF eligibility rules allowed participation by U.S.-domiciled institutions with foreign investors, it prohibited participation by entities controlled by a foreign government.

While Reserve Banks Generally Offered the Same Terms to Eligible Participants, Some Programs Lacked Documented Procedures to Systematically Apply Special Restrictions

The Federal Reserve Board promoted consistent treatment of eligible participants in its emergency programs by generally offering assistance on the same terms and conditions to all eligible participants. As previously discussed, in a few programs, FRBNY placed special restrictions on individual borrowing institutions but procedures for a few programs did not have specific guidance to help ensure that restrictions were applied consistently to higher-risk borrowers. Moreover, for TAF, the Federal Reserve Board could not readily provide documentation of all TAF restrictions placed on individual institutions. Our review of Federal Reserve System data for selected programs found that incorrect application of certain program requirements was generally infrequent and that cases of incorrect application of criteria did not appear to indicate intentional preferential treatment of one or more program participants.[125]

The Federal Reserve Board Generally Offered Same Terms and Conditions to Eligible Participants

The Federal Reserve Board generally set the same program terms and conditions for all eligible participants within each of its emergency programs. In designing the programs to promote financial stability, the Federal Reserve Board generally did not seek to make loan terms more or less restrictive based on differences in the levels of credit risk posed by eligible borrowers. As discussed previously, for emergency programs that involved recourse loans directly to borrowers facing liquidity strains, the Federal Reserve Board designed eligibility requirements to restrict access to generally sound institutions, such as primary-credit eligible depository institutions, primary dealers, and commercial paper issuers with top-tier credit ratings. With the exception of a few cases discussed later, all institutions that met the announced eligibility requirements for a particular emergency program could borrow at the same interest rate, against the same types of collateral, and where relevant, with the same schedule of haircuts applied to their collateral. One Federal Reserve Board official explained that even if the Federal Reserve Board had sought to negotiate different terms with each borrower, it would not have had time for separate negotiations with so many borrowers.

Relatively Few Cases of Incorrect Application of Program Requirements Occurred

Our review of the implementation of selected program requirements found isolated instances where these requirements were incorrectly applied. Errors identified by our review do not appear to indicate a systematic bias towards favoring one or more eligible institutions. For example, our review of TAF collateral data found that in almost all cases, TAF loans were less than the amount of the lendable value of collateral pledged (based on application of TAF haircuts) and the pricing of the TAF collateral was generally consistent. Similarly, TAF collateral haircuts were consistent with the published collateral haircut rates. Our review of detailed collateral data for PDCF found that both clearing banks applied the contracted-for haircuts in the vast majority of cases. We found that 50 of the 1,376 PDCF loans did not post collateral in the amount required by program guidelines and the total amount of undercollateralization comprised about 0.1 percent of the total value of all PDCF loans.

Existing Procedures for a Few Programs Lacked Specific Guidance Needed to Help Ensure Consistent Decisions to Restrict Access by Certain Borrowers

As discussed earlier in this report, Reserve Banks exercised discretion to restrict program access for some borrowers in TAF, PDCF, and CPFF to limit risk exposure. For TAF and CPFF, restrictions included directing some borrowing institutions to limit or terminate their use of the program and PDCF restrictions included specific limits on a primary dealer's borrowing or higher haircuts applied to its eligible collateral. FRBNY generally based its decisions about these restrictions on supervisory and other information it obtained about the financial condition of program participants or on a perceived misuse of particular programs.

However, a few programs lacked specific procedures for processes that the lending Reserve Bank should follow to exercise discretion to restrict access for higher-risk borrowers. While FRBNY had specific documented guidance for CPFF to guide its response to higher-risk commercial paper issuers, other emergency lending programs lacked similar documented guidance for making decisions about whether to apply certain restrictions. For TAF, PDCF, TSLF, and CPFF, Table 7 summarizes the Reserve Bank guidelines and practices related to discretionary actions taken.

For TAF-related decisions, Federal Reserve Board staff told us that Reserve Banks applied general discount window guidance issued by the Reserve Banks' Subcommittee on Credit Risk Management, which they considered to be appropriate as TAF loans were made under the same broader authority and internal policies as the discount window. However, while Reserve Banks have traditionally exercised discretion in adjusting lending terms for individual institutions through the discount window program, TAF presented Reserve Banks with new risk management considerations, including how to determine that it was prudent for the Reserve Bank to extend TAF credit to an otherwise eligible institution for terms as long as

84 days. Because Reserve Banks' existing discount window procedures did not contain specific guidance on exercising discretion and documenting actions to restrict higher-risk TAF borrowers, the Federal Reserve System lacked assurance that such restrictions were applied consistently.

Table 7. Summary of Reserve Bank Practices for Applying Special Restrictions to Some Borrowers

Program	Factors Reserve Banks considered in restricting or denying program access	Restrictions applied
TAF	• An institution became ineligible for TAF if it was no longer eligible for primary credit. • Institutions qualifying for primary credit but posing heightened credit risk based on judgments made from supervisory input and other sources could be excluded from TAF at the discretion of the Reserve Banks. • Existing discount window policy provided guidance on how Reserve Banks should monitor and identify higher-risk borrowers, but lacked specific guidance on how Reserve Banks should exercise discretion to restrict access to term funding through TAF.	According to Federal Reserve Board staff, Reserve Banks restricted at least 6 institutions from participating in the 84-day TAF auctions and at least 25 institutions from participating in any TAF auction. The Reserve Banks made these restrictions based on the concern that the institutions would not remain in sound condition through the term of the loan.
PDCF and TSLF	• All primary dealers were eligible. • Dealers that posed higher risk could have been subject to additional restriction on an exception basis. • Per FOMC directive, TSLF restrictions could have been placed on the volume of securities loans to individual borrowers. • No additional written criteria for exclusion of use or restriction.	For two primary dealers in PDCF, FRBNY imposed higher haircuts on certain collateral types. For one of these dealers, FRBNY placed a specific borrowing cap.
CPFF	• Noncompliance with CPFF's credit rating criteria. • Significant probability of default in the next 3 to 6 months, even with use of the facility. • ABCP program had been inactive for an extended period of time due to difficulties in maintaining acceptance by market of business model (e.g. certain credit arbitrage vehicles). This condition may often be accompanied by lapsed compliance with program documents. • Material misrepresentation on certification of maximum amount of commercial paper it would be eligible to issue through CPFF.	Based on credit risk assessments of borrowing institutions, FRBNY took the following discretionary actions • Required stronger sponsor support or additional collateral in the case of ABCP issuers. • Required collateralization or guarantee from another entity in the case of unsecured commercial paper issuers. • Imposed a limit on issuance that is below the maximum otherwise allowed. • Disallowed or limited new issuance through CPFF to replace maturing commercial paper held by CPFF LLC. • Advised registrant not to participate.

Sources: GAO analysis of program documentation for TAF, PDCF, TSLF, and CPFF.

Moreover, the Federal Reserve Board provided us with a list of decisions by the Reserve Banks to direct depository institutions to restrict borrowings to the 28-day TAF auctions (rather than allowing access to 84-day TAF credit as well) or to exclude them from TAF auctions altogether by directing them to borrow under the discount window program. However, Federal Reserve Board staff noted that this list may be incomplete as TAF restrictions may not always have been formally recorded by all Reserve Banks. According to FRBNY staff, the Federal Reserve System has not formally analyzed the consistency and appropriateness of Reserve Banks' decisions to restrict TAF access. Complete documentation of these decisions would be needed for the Federal Reserve System to fully assess the consistency of Reserve Banks' decisions to restrict TAF access.

For PDCF and TSLF, FRBNY generally lacked criteria during the life of the programs for applying restrictions to help ensure that restrictions were applied consistently across the primary dealers. FRBNY staff said that decisions to place restrictions on 2 of the 20 primary dealers were made on an ad-hoc basis. As discussed earlier in this report, in June 2010, after both PDCF and TSLF had closed, FRBNY created a credit risk management framework for primary dealers that codified FRBNY's practice of applying borrowing limits or special haircuts on an exception basis to higher-risk primary dealers. This documented framework outlines FRBNY's general approach for reviewing and monitoring risks related to primary dealers' role as counterparties in open market operations and notes that more comprehensive reviews of primary dealers may be needed in the event that concerns are raised from the monitoring process. However, the framework does not specify the steps that would be included in a more comprehensive review, such as what communication should take place with the institution and its regulator.

Without clear, documented guidance to direct Reserve Banks' efforts to monitor and restrict access by higher-risk borrowers, there is little assurance that Reserve Bank decisions to restrict certain institutions under any future deployment of such emergency lending programs will be consistent within a centralized program or programs operated across Reserve Banks. FRBNY staff commented that the range of activities that may trigger restrictions may not be captured even if a guideline was established. However, by having written procedures to guide decision-making for restrictions and suggestions for documentation of the rationale for such decisions, the Federal Reserve Board may more be able to review such decisions and ensure that future implementation of emergency lending programs will result in consistent treatment of higher-risk borrowers.

The Federal Reserve Board Did Not Fully Document the Basis for Extending Credit to a Few Affiliates of Primary Dealers

The Federal Reserve Board did not fully document the basis for its decisions to extend credit on terms similar to those available at PDCF to certain broker-dealer affiliates of four of the primary dealers. In September and November of 2008, the Federal Reserve Board invoked section 13(3) of the Federal Reserve Act to authorize FRBNY to extend credit to the London-based broker-dealer subsidiaries of Merrill Lynch, Goldman Sachs, Morgan Stanley, and Citigroup, as well as the U.S. broker-dealer subsidiaries of Merrill Lynch, Goldman Sachs, and Morgan Stanley. Federal Reserve Board officials told us that the Federal Reserve Board did not consider the extension of credit to these subsidiaries to be a legal extension of PDCF but separate actions to specifically assist these four primary dealers by using PDCF as an operational tool.

However, to fulfill its statutory requirement under the Emergency Economic Stabilization Act of 2008 to publicly report on the justification of each action taken under section 13(3) of the Federal Reserve Act, the Federal Reserve Board included short descriptions of these exceptional credit extensions in its report on the basis for authorizing PDCF and in its April 2009 report providing an update on the emergency programs. But the Emergency Economic Stabilization Act of 2008 reports, other public disclosures and submitted documents we reviewed did not provide complete explanations of how these exceptional credit extensions satisfied section 13(3) criteria. In a September 21, 2008, press release, for example, the Federal Reserve Board explained only that "transitional credit" for the U.S. broker-dealer subsidiaries of Goldman Sachs and Morgan Stanley was intended to increase liquidity support to these firms as they transitioned to managing their funding within a bank holding company structure and noted that a similar arrangement would be provided for the broker-dealer subsidiary of Merrill Lynch. In explaining the basis for these exceptional credit extensions, Federal Reserve Board officials cited the continuing strains in financial markets and concerns about the possible failures of these dealers at the time. However, the Federal Reserve Board could not provide documentation explaining why these extensions were provided specifically to affiliates of these four primary dealers.

Federal Reserve Board officials told us that the Federal Reserve Board did not draft detailed memoranda to document the rationale for all uses of section 13(3) authority but that unusual and exigent circumstances existed in each of these cases as critical funding markets were in crisis. However, without more complete documentation, how assistance to these broker-dealer subsidiaries satisfied the statutory requirements for using this authority remains unclear. Moreover, without more complete public disclosure of the basis for these actions, these decisions may not be subject to an appropriate level of transparency and accountability.

The Dodd-Frank Act includes new requirements for the Federal Reserve Board to report to Congress on any loan or financial assistance authorized under section 13(3), including the justification for the exercise of authority; the identity of the recipient; the date, amount, and form of the assistance; and the material terms of the assistance. To address these new reporting requirements, the Federal Reserve Board will have to take steps to further enhance its reporting requirements to more consistently and comprehensively document its analysis and recommendations to carryout its section 13(3) authority going forward.[126] Without improved documentation requirements, the Federal Reserve Board risks making disclosures that are not consistent with these new reporting requirements.

The Federal Reserve Board Generally Has Not Provided Documented Guidance to Reserve Banks on Types of Program Decisions That Require Consultation with the Federal Reserve Board

In authorizing the Reserve Banks to operate its emergency programs, the Federal Reserve Board has not provided documented guidance on the types of program policy decisions—including allowing atypical uses of broad-based assistance—that should be reviewed by the Federal Reserve Board. Standards for internal control for federal government agencies provide that transactions and other significant events should be authorized and executed only by persons acting within the scope of their authority. An FRBNY official said that FRBNY recognized the importance of distinguishing between "policy-level" decisions that required consultation with the Federal Reserve Board and "execution" decisions that did not. A Federal Reserve Board official described execution decisions as those that fell within the program design parameters authorized by the Federal Reserve Board. Outside of the established protocols for the discount window, FRBNY staff said that the Federal Reserve Board generally did not provide written guidance on expectations for types of decisions or events requiring formal Federal Reserve Board review, although program decisions that deviated from policy set by the Federal Reserve Board were generally understood to require Board staff consultation.[127]

In December 2009, FRBNY's Capital Markets Group revised its risk escalation protocols to help ensure that risk events were brought to the attention of the appropriate set of FRBNY decision makers based on their level of risk, but the Federal Reserve Board was unable to readily provide a similar set of documented protocols for consultation that should have taken place related to the emergency programs. FRBNY's policy defines examples of such risk events, which include unplanned, nonroutine occurrences that increase the Markets Group's operational or reputational risk exposure. We identified two atypical uses of broad-based programs to support an institution determined to be systemically significant. According to Federal Reserve Board officials, FRBNY generally consulted Federal Reserve Board officials on such matters. However, our review found that FRBNY staff were not directed to do so by documented guidance and, furthermore, Federal Reserve Board staff could not provide documentation of its consideration of these atypical uses.

- FRBNY allowed an AIG-sponsored conduit to continue to use the CPFF following a January 2009 Federal Reserve Board rule change that likely would have made the conduit ineligible for the program if it had been a new applicant. Specifically, in January 2009, the Federal Reserve Board changed CPFF rules to prohibit ABCP conduits that had been inactive before the CPFF's creation from using the program. According to FRBNY staff, FRBNY identified three conduits using the CPFF at the time of the rule change that were likely to have been inactive before the creation of the program. FRBNY staff said they interpreted the revised eligibility requirements as applying prospectively to new applicants but that they nonetheless, and in accordance with their general understanding with Federal Reserve Board staff, encouraged existing conduits that would not have met the revised criteria to decrease their usage. Of the three conduits, two exited the program within a few months. However, the third conduit, which was sponsored by AIG, was permitted to continue to borrow from CPFF at similar levels until a week before CPFF closed. According to FRBNY staff, the decision to allow continued access by this AIG-sponsored conduit was part of FRBNY's overall management of its assistance to AIG, which included scheduled reductions in other more significant AIG-related CPFF exposures beginning in 2009. While the Federal Reserve Board documented the basis for the January 2009 change to CPFF terms and conditions to prohibit access by inactive conduits, neither the Federal Reserve Board nor FRBNY staff could readily provide documentation supporting the decision to allow the AIG conduit to continue its borrowing. However, FRBNY staff said that they kept the Federal Reserve Board staff apprised of FRBNY's efforts to achieve an orderly repayment of the AIG-related commercial paper holdings in CPFF. Whether FRBNY consulted the appropriate set of Federal Reserve Board policymakers before making this decision is unclear.

- In October 2008, according to Federal Reserve Board staff, the Federal Reserve Board allowed the Swiss National Bank to use dollars under its swap line agreement to provide special assistance to UBS, a large Swiss banking organization. Specifically, on October 16, 2008, the Swiss National Bank announced that it would use dollars obtained through its swap line with FRBNY to help fund an SPV it would create to purchase up to $60 billion of illiquid assets from UBS. According to FRBNY data, from December 11, 2008, through June 2009, Swiss National Bank drew dollar amounts generally not exceeding about $13 billion to help fund this SPV that served a function similar to that of the Maiden Lane SPVs. Federal Reserve Board staff acknowledged that this was an atypical use of swap line dollars as the swap line agreements were initially designed to help foreign central banks provide dollar loans broadly to institutions facing dollar funding strains. Although the FOMC had delegated approval authority to FRBNY for each swap line draw by the Swiss National Bank, Federal Reserve Board staff said that this proposed use by Swiss National Bank was informally brought to the attention of the FOMC Foreign Currency Subcommittee members for their consideration before the Swiss National Bank's announcement. Federal Reserve Board staff said that Foreign Currency Subcommittee members believed that this use was consistent with the broader policy objective of stabilizing dollar funding markets and that the Swiss National Bank was a very reliable counterparty. Federal Reserve Board staff said that this consultation was not required by the policies and procedures established for the swap lines program. According to FRBNY staff, this use of swap line dollars was permitted under FRBNY's amended agreement with the Swiss National Bank.

Without documented guidance for Reserve Banks on types of program decisions that require consultation with the Federal Reserve Board, Reserve Bank staff and officials may fail to escalate significant policy decisions to the appropriate set of policymakers at the Federal Reserve Board. This uncertainty may increase the risk that a Reserve Bank may permit an exceptional use of emergency assistance that is inconsistent with the Federal Reserve Board's policy goals or exposes the Federal Reserve System to increased reputational risk. For example, although required approvals of swap line draws generally were routine in nature, going forward additional requirements for special approval and documentation for exceptional uses could help to ensure the proper level of transparency and accountability for any such uses in the future.

The Federal Reserve Board Took Steps to Prevent Use that Would be Inconsistent with Its Policy Objectives

To assess whether program use was consistent with the Federal Reserve Board's announced policy objectives, we analyzed program transaction data to identify significant trends in borrowers' use of the programs. According to Federal Reserve Board staff, they designed program terms and conditions to discourage use that would have been inconsistent with program policy objectives. As discussed earlier, program terms—such as the interest charged and haircuts applied—generally were designed to be favorable only for institutions facing liquidity strains. Within and across the programs, certain participants used the programs more frequently and were slower to exit than others. Reserve Bank officials noted that market conditions and the speed with which the participant recovered affected use of the program by individual institutions. As a result of its monitoring of program usage, the Federal Reserve Board modified terms and conditions of several programs to reinforce policy objectives and program goals.

Large Global Institutions Were among the Largest Users of Several Programs

Several of the programs saw greater use by large global institutions that were significant participants in the funding markets targeted by the Federal Reserve Board. Tables 8 and 9 rank the largest borrowing institutions according to aggregate borrowing (irrespective of differences in term to maturity) and total borrowing after adjusting for differences in loan terms. For both tables, we show transaction amounts for AMLF and TALF, but do not factor these amounts into the rankings as entities participating in these programs served as intermediary borrowers whose purchases provided liquidity support to other market participants. We aggregated dollar transaction amounts for borrowing entities at the parent company level. For each parent company, total amounts borrowed include amounts borrowed by the parent company, its subsidiaries, branches or agencies, and in the case of CPFF, dollar amounts of ABCP issued by entities sponsored by the holding company or one of its subsidiaries. In cases where we identified an acquisition that took place during the operation of a program, we consolidated transaction amounts following the completion of the acquisition. Table 8 aggregates total dollar transaction amounts by adding the total dollar amount of all loans but does not adjust these amounts to reflect differences across programs in the term over which loans were outstanding. For example, an overnight PDCF loan of $10 billion that was renewed daily at the same level for 30 business days would result in an aggregate amount borrowed of $300 billion although the institution, in effect, borrowed only $10 billion over 30 days. In contrast, a TAF loan of $10 billion extended over a 1-month period would appear as $10 billion. As a result, the total transaction amounts shown in table 8 for PDCF are not directly comparable to the total transaction amounts shown for TAF and other programs that made loans for periods longer than overnight.

To account for differences in the terms for loans that were outstanding, we multiplied each loan amount by the number of days the loan was outstanding and divided this amount by the number of days in a year (365). Table 9 shows the top 20 borrowing institutions in terms of term-adjusted total transaction amount for emergency programs and other assistance provided directly to institutions facing liquidity strains.

U.S. branches and agencies of foreign banks and U.S. subsidiaries of foreign institutions received over half of the total dollar amount of TAF and CPFF loans made (see figure 10). As noted previously, such institutions were permitted to borrow under the terms and conditions of the lending programs. For both programs, FRBNY staff explained that as long as participating institutions were eligible to use the program, monitoring whether certain types of institutions accessed a program more than others was not relevant to the programs' objectives. Federal Reserve Board officials told us the programs sought to support funding markets that were global, and agencies and branches of foreign firms were significant participants in lending to U.S. households and businesses.

Table 8. Institutions with Largest Total Transaction Amounts (Not Term-Adjusted) across Broad-Based Emergency Programs (Borrowing Aggregated by Parent Company and Includes Sponsored ABCP Conduits), December 1, 2007 through July 21, 2010

Dollar in billions

Borrowing Parent Company	TAF	PDCF	TSLF	CPFF	Subtotal	AMLF	TALF	Total loans
Citigroup Inc.	$110	$2,020	$348	$33	$2,511	$1	-	$ 2,513
Morgan Stanley	-	1,913	115	4	2,032	-	9	2,041
Merrill Lynch & Co.	0	1,775	166	8	1,949	-	-	1,949
Bank of America Corporation	280	947	101	15	1,342	2	-	1,344
Barclays PLC (United Kingdom)	232	410	187	39	868	-	-	868
Bear Stearns Companies, Inc.	-	851	2	-	853	-	-	853
Goldman Sachs Group Inc.	-	589	225	0	814	-	-	814
Royal Bank of Scotland Group PLC (United Kingdom)	212	-	291	39	541	-	-	541
Deutsche Bank AG (Germany)	77	1	277	-	354	-	-	354
UBS AG (Switzerland)	56	35	122	75	287	-	-	287
JP Morgan Chase & Co.	99	112	68	-	279	111	-	391
Credit Suisse Group AG (Switzerland)	0	2	261	-	262	0	-	262
Lehman Brothers Holdings Inc.	-	83	99	-	183	-	-	183
Bank of Scotla-nd PLC (United Kingdom)	181	-	-	-	181	-	-	181
BNP Paribas SA (France)	64	66	41	3	175	-	-	175
Wells Fargo & Co.	159	-	-	-	159	-	-	159
Dexia SA (Belgium)	105	-	-	53	159	-	-	159
Wachovia Corporation	142	-	-	-	142	-	-	142

Table 8. (continued)

Dollar in billions Borrowing Parent Company	TAF	PDCF	TSLF	CPFF	Subtotal	AMLF	TALF	Total loans
Dresdner Bank AG (Germany)	123	0	1	10	135	-	-	135
Societe Generale SA (France)	124	-	-	-	124	-	-	124
All other borrowers	1,854	146	14	460	2,475	103	62	2,639
Total	$3,818	$8,951	$2,319	$738	$15,826	$217	$71	$16,115

Source: GAO analysis of Federal Reserve System data.

Note: The total dollar amounts borrowed represent the sum of all loans and have not been adjusted to reflect differences in terms to maturity for the loans. Total borrowing is aggregated at the parent company level and generally includes borrowing by branches, agencies, subsidiaries, and sponsored ABCP conduits that we could identify. Total borrowing for each parent company consolidates amounts borrowed by acquired institutions following the completion of acquisitions. PDCF totals include credit extensions to affiliates of some primary dealers and TSLF totals include loans under the TSLF Options Program (TOP).

Table 9. Institutions with Largest Total Term-Adjusted Borrowing across Broad-Based Emergency Programs, December 1, 2007 through July 21, 2010

Dollars in billions Borrowing Parent Company	TAF	PDCF	TSLF	CPFF	Subtotal	AMLF	TALF	Total loans	Percent of total
Bank of America Corporation	$48	$6	$8	$6	$67	$0	-	$67	6%
Citigroup Inc.	15	8	27	8	58	0	-	58	5
Royal Bank of Scotland Group PLC (United Kingdom)	25	-	23	10	58	-	-	58	5
Barclays Group PLC (United Kingdom)	24	2	15	10	50	-	-	50	4
UBS AG (Switzerland)	7	0	9	18	35	-	-	35	3
Deutsche Bank AG (Germany)	9	0	22	-	30	-	-	30	3
Wells Fargo & Co.	25	-	-	-	25	-	-	25	2
Dexia SA (Belgium)	10	-	-	13	23	-	-	23	2
Credit Suisse Group AG (Switzerland)	0	0	21	-	21	0	-	21	2
Bank of Scotland PLC (United Kingdom)	20	-	-	-	20	-	-	20	2
Commerzbank AG (Germany)	16	-	-	4	20	-	-	20	2

Table 9. (continued)

Dollars in billions									
Borrowing Parent Company	TAF	PDCF	TSLF	CPFF	Subtotal	AMLF	TALF	Total loans	Percent of total
Goldman Sachs Group Inc.	-	2	17	0	20	-	-	20	2
Merrill Lynch & Co.	0	5	14	-	19	-	-	19	2
BNP Paribas SA(France)	11	0	3	4	19	-	-	19	2
Societe Generale SA (France)	17	-	-	-	17	-	-	17	1
Morgan Stanley	-	8	8	1	17	-	28	45	4
Wachovia Corporation	16	-	-	-	16	-	-	16	1
JP Morgan Chase & Co.	13	0	3	-	16	15	-	31	3
AIG	-	-	-	15	15	-	-	15	1
Norinchukin Bank (Japan)	15	-	-	-	15	-	-	15	1
All other borrowers	204	4	11	94	313	13	211	537	47
Total	**$474**	**$35**	**$179**	**$183**	**$870**	**$ 29**	**$ 240**	**$1,139**	**100%**

Source: GAO analysis of Federal Reserve System data.

Note: The dollar amounts borrowed for each loan were term-adjusted by multiplying the loan amount by the term to maturity for the loan and dividing by 365 days. Term to maturity is calculated as the difference between the original loan maturity date and the trade date and does not reflect repayments of loans that occurred before the original loan maturity date. Total borrowing is aggregated at the parent company level and generally includes borrowing by branches, agencies, subsidiaries, and sponsored ABCP conduits that we could identify. Total borrowing for each parent company consolidates amounts borrowed by acquired institutions following the completion of acquisitions. PDCF totals include credit extensions to affiliates of some primary dealers and TSLF totals include loans under the TSLF Options Program (TOP).

Under TAF, approximately 65 percent of the loans were made to U.S. branches, agencies, and subsidiaries of foreign institutions. Federal Reserve Board officials told us that the use of the program by U.S. branches and agencies of foreign banks was expected because these institutions were facing liquidity strains in dollar funding markets. FRBNY staff identified a few possible reasons for high use by U.S. branches and agencies of foreign banks. First, many of them faced liquidity strains arising from the need to bring certain illiquid U.S. dollar assets back onto their balance sheets and could not finance these assets elsewhere.[128] In addition, many of these institutions held U.S.-dollar dominated collateral that could be pledged to TAF but not in their home country. A FRBNY memorandum noted that U.S. banks generally bid for smaller loan amounts and could not bid as aggressively as their foreign counterparts, because they did not have enough collateral pledged at the discount window.

Under CPFF, approximately 60 percent of the commercial paper was issued by U.S. subsidiaries of foreign institutions over the life of the program. At the time CPFF was created, U.S. companies owned by foreign institutions were among the most significant participants in the U.S. commercial paper market.

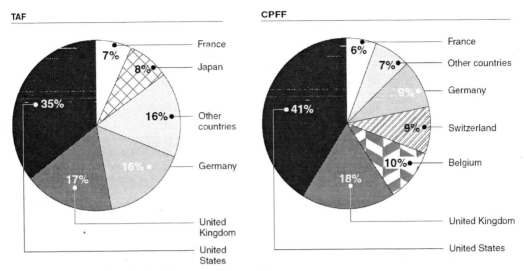

Source: GAO analysis of Federal Reserve System data.
Note: For TAF, the total dollar amount of TAF loans are aggregated at the level of the parent company for participating depository institutions. For CPFF, the total dollar amount of issuance through CPFF is aggregated at the parent company level and includes ABCP issuance by entities sponsored by the parent company or one of its subsidiaries. The country of domicile for parent companies is based on SNL Financial data.

Figure 10. Total Transaction Amount by Parent Company Country of Domicile for TAF and CPFF.

The Federal Reserve Board's analysis of TALF showed that under TALF, while the majority of the U.S. companies that received loans had U.S. domiciled material investors, 36 percent had one or more non-U.S. domiciled "material investors."[129] Federal Reserve Board officials noted that the loans were made to TALF borrowers, not to the material investors in the companies that borrowed from TALF. While only U.S. companies with eligible collateral could participate in TALF, "material investors" that invested in TALF borrowers could be foreign entities. According to the Federal Reserve Board, 26 percent of "material investors" were domiciled abroad with a majority of non-U.S. domiciled material investors located in Cayman Islands, followed by Korea and Bermuda. As with TALF borrowers, primary dealers and other firms acting as TALF agents also conducted due diligence on "material investors" to help ensure that they did not present credit, fraud, or reputational risk to FRBNY. FRBNY officials commented that by requiring all TALF-eligible securities to be entirely or almost entirely backed by loans to U.S. residents or U.S. businesses, TALF benefited the intended beneficiaries, such as small businesses. Additionally, FRBNY officials commented that like many firms, some TALF borrowers were partly owned by foreign entities or had investors that were based abroad.

Use of the Programs Peaked at the Height of the Financial Crisis and Fell as Market Conditions Recovered

Use of the programs generally peaked during the height of the financial crisis and fell as market conditions recovered. Figure 11 shows how the use of broad-based programs changed over time. Federal Reserve Board officials told us that even as the market recovered, funding conditions improved for certain borrowers but not others. As a result, in PDCF, TSLF, and CPFF, several participants remained in the programs even as others exited. However, all activities wound down before the programs were terminated, and in the case of TSLF and PDCF, several months before program termination. Federal Reserve Board officials told us as market conditions improved and use of CPPF declined, they were in active discussions with firms that remained in CPFF to confirm they were going to be able to leave CPFF in an orderly manner.

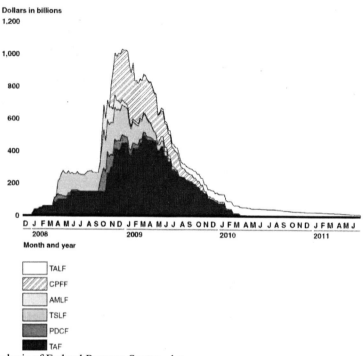

Source: GAO analysis of Federal Reserve System data.
Note: PDCF loans outstanding includes loans to affiliates of primary dealers. TSLF loans outstanding includes TOP loans.

Figure 11. Total Loans Outstanding for Broad-Based Programs, December 1, 2007–June 29, 2011.

For some programs, the Federal Reserve Board actively managed program terms to help ensure that usage decreased as markets returned to normal. In TAF and TSLF, the Federal Reserve Board made active decisions to wind down the programs through actions such as lowering the amount offered through each auction or ceasing the auctions. For AMLF, FRBB staff continually weighed the pros and cons of potential changes to terms and conditions in the context of market conditions. For example, in May 2009, FRBB staff considered whether to increase the interest rate above primary credit rates to discourage ABCP issuers from using the program. However, they determined that such a change would have made the program unattractive to the borrowers and discouraged them from participating as intermediaries, which would have reduced the program's efficacy should MMMFs experience heightened redemption pressures. For CPFF, FRBNY staff held conversations with issuers about reducing their use of the program, including the firms' plans for repayment.

The Federal Reserve Board Modified Terms and Conditions of Several Programs to Reinforce Policy Objectives and Program Goals

For several programs, the Federal Reserve Board modified the terms and conditions to reinforce its policy objectives. To reinforce the principle that the programs should only act as temporary liquidity backstops and not as substitute for normal market funding, the Federal Reserve Board revised the eligibility criteria for CPFF and AMLF. As discussed earlier in this section, for CPFF, the Federal Reserve Board made ABCP issuers that were inactive prior to CPFF's creation generally ineligible. In June 2009, AMLF terms were revised such that MMMFs had to experience and demonstrate a minimum level of investor redemptions before they could sell ABCP to eligible borrowers. The Federal Reserve Board's decision to establish a redemption filter was influenced by a spike in AMLF activity in May 2009. According to FRBB staff, the May 2009 activity reflected market participant and MMMF concerns that there could be credit rating downgrades of some ABCP issuers and their sponsors, which could in turn make certain ABCP ineligible as AMLF collateral. MMMFs, fearing the potential ineligibility of such ABCP, sold the ABCP through AMLF before the downgrades would become effective. For TALF, to meet the objective of attracting a broad range of participants, the Federal Reserve Board added four additional TALF agents, comprised of three minority-owned firms and one midsized firm. Federal Reserve Board officials told us the change was made to address the concern that established customers of primary dealer-agents had an advantage in gaining access to the program. Similarly, for TAF, the Federal Reserve Board lowered the minimum bid rate from $10 million to $5 million to make the program more broadly available.

AMLF Borrowing Was Concentrated Among Large Custodian Banks

AMLF borrowing was concentrated among a few large custodian banks (and their affiliates) that held pre-existing relationships with MMMFs. Two of these banks and affiliates of these banks accounted for 85 percent of the total borrowing over the life of the program. FRBB's review of AMLF found that at the fund level, six individual funds from three groups of mutual funds commonly referred to as "fund complexes" accounted for 25 percent of the loans extended under AMLF, and seventeen individual funds of six fund complexes accounted for half of the loans. FRBB officials commented that the two largest borrowers were among the three largest providers of fund administration and account services for MMMFs and that it was not unexpected that the largest borrowers were entities that had pre-existing custodial relationships with MMMFs.

CONCLUSION

During the financial crisis that began in the summer of 2007, the Federal Reserve System took unprecedented steps to stabilize financial markets and support the liquidity needs of failing institutions that it considered to be systemically significant. Federal Reserve System staff often designed and implemented the emergency programs over the course of only days or weeks as they sought to address rapidly deteriorating market conditions. To varying degrees, these emergency actions involved the Reserve Banks in activities that went beyond their traditional responsibilities. In particular, FRBNY, which implemented most of the assistance, faced a number of operational challenges related to implementing and overseeing several broad-based emergency programs, the three Maiden Lane portfolios, and other assistance to AIG and Citigroup. FRBNY hired vendors to help manage the complexities associated with its assistance to individual institutions and its interventions in new markets, such as the markets for commercial paper and asset-backed securities. In addition, FRBNY had to create new policies, procedures, and controls to manage key risks within and across the programs.

Over time, FRBNY and the other Reserve Banks took steps to improve program management and oversight, in many cases in response to recommendations made by their external auditor, Reserve Bank internal audit functions, or the Federal Reserve Board's RBOPS. For example, FRBNY greatly expanded its risk management function in 2009, by, among other things, establishing a new risk management division and creating a Risk Analytics group within this division to validate the valuation work performed by vendors on the Maiden Lane portfolios. Expanded staff expertise in this and other areas has allowed FRBNY to be a more knowledgeable customer of vendor services. In addition, in May 2010, FRBNY issued a new vendor management policy to outline guidelines and requirements for assessing and overseeing the risks posed by vendor firms. However, the Reserve Banks have not yet fully incorporated some lessons learned from the crisis into their policies for managing use of vendors, risk of losses from emergency lending, and conflicts of interest. Such enhanced policies could offer additional insights to guide future Federal Reserve System action, should it ever be warranted.

Vendors have been a critical component of helping create and operate the emergency programs, with most of the fees concentrated among a few contracts that were awarded without competition. While the Reserve Banks followed their acquisition policies regarding vendor selection, the largest contracts were awarded under an exigency exception to the competition requirement in those policies. The acquisition policies did not provide additional guidance on awarding contracts under exigency exceptions such as seeking as many proposals as practical or limiting the duration of contracts to the period of the exigency. Given the nature of the events leading to the emergency programs, it is reasonable to expect that future emergencies could follow a similar pattern of sudden financial shocks that leave the Reserve Banks little time to develop and implement responses, including hiring vendors. Because exigent circumstances may limit the Reserve Banks' ability to follow their normal acquisition procedures, taking steps to ensure that they seek as much competition as is practicable is critical to the vendor selection process.

The emergency programs brought FRBNY into new relationships with institutions that fell outside of its traditional lending activities, and these changes created the possibility for conflicts of interest for both FRBNY employees and vendors. FRBNY recognized the importance of identifying and managing conflicts related to employees' access to sensitive information and to employees' financial interests that were not specifically prohibited in its Code of Conduct but could be affected by their participation in matters concerning these emergency programs. However, while FRBNY staff told us that they believe their existing policies and guidance are sufficient for managing employee conflicts during a crisis situation, these policies may still allow for situations to arise in which the appearance of a conflict of interest for an FRBNY official could raise questions about the integrity of FRBNY's programs and operations. This possibility is of particular concern given the extraordinary sensitivity and potential importance of emergency lending activities. While FRBNY's current standards are consistent with 18 U.S.C. § 208 and its regulations, the lack of more specific procedures for managing conflicts during emergency lending activities exposes FRBNY to the risk of the appearance of conflicts which can compromise FRBNY's effectiveness by causing observers to question its integrity. The Federal Reserve System plans to update the Reserve Banks' codes of conduct to reflect its broader role in regulating systemically important institutions. These planned efforts present an opportunity to consider how recent experiences with managing employee conflicts might inform changes to these policies. With respect to vendors, FRBNY has not yet finalized a policy for managing risks related to conflicts of interest in connection with its emergency programs. In contrast, Treasury articulated a detailed policy for managing TARP vendor conflicts of interest in January 2009. FRBNY created a new vendor-management policy in 2010, but this policy is not sufficiently detailed or comprehensive in its guidance on steps FRBNY staff should take to help ensure vendor conflicts are mitigated. FRBNY staff have said they plan to develop a documented policy that codifies practices FRBNY put in place during the crisis. The lack of a comprehensive policy for managing vendor conflicts could expose FRBNY to greater risk that it would not fully identify and appropriately manage vendor conflicts of interest in the event of future crisis situations.

While the Federal Reserve Board's emergency lending programs included multiple loss-protection features and have not incurred losses to date, opportunities exist for the Federal Reserve System to improve its risk management practices related to crisis lending. First, for TAF and the programs for the primary dealers, Reserve Banks' existing policies lacked specific guidance on how staff should exercise discretion and document their actions to restrict or deny program access for otherwise eligible institutions that posed higher risk of losses. FRBNY staff recognized the importance of monitoring and restricting higher-risk institutions for these programs because institutions could pose unacceptable risks even though they continued to meet eligibility requirements. Since these programs closed, Reserve Banks have enhanced their guidance for monitoring exposures to depository institutions and primary dealers, but revised guidance continues to lack details applicable to a crisis-driven lending situation. In addition, FRBNY staff indicated that the Federal Reserve System has not assessed the consistency of TAF restrictions across the 12 Reserve Banks. Without more detailed procedures, Reserve Bank staff responsible for implementing future emergency programs may not take consistent and appropriate steps to mitigate the risks posed by higher-risk borrowers. Furthermore, without documentation and analysis of decisions to apply restrictions to particular borrowers and the processes that led to those restrictions, the Reserve Banks lack assurance that they are applied consistently across borrowers. Second, neither the Federal Reserve Board nor FRBNY quantified stress losses across all of the emergency programs and assistance. While FRBNY tracked potential losses under stressed scenarios for some programs, including CPFF and the Maiden Lane portfolios, FRBNY staff said they did not quantify stressed losses for TAF, TSLF, or PDCF. In a future crisis, without a more comprehensive view of risk exposures within and across Reserve Banks, the Federal Reserve Board may lack critical information needed to make decisions about authorizing and modifying its emergency lending activities.

Although the Reserve Banks generally offered the same terms to program participants, the Federal Reserve Board lacked documentation and guidance to manage some atypical uses of the emergency programs. The Emergency Economic Stabilization Act of 2008 required the Federal Reserve Board to publicly report on the justification and terms for its exercises of emergency assistance pursuant to section 13(3) of the Federal Reserve Act, and the Dodd-Frank Act includes new reporting requirements for the Federal Reserve Board to expand its disclosures concerning the basis for such assistance. However, we found that the Federal Reserve Board had not fully documented the reasons for extending credit on terms similar to those of PDCF to U.S. and London-based affiliates of a few primary dealers—Goldman Sachs, Morgan Stanley, and Merrill Lynch. Without a more complete documentation process for public disclosure, the reporting on these decisions will not help ensure the appropriate level of transparency and accountability consistent with the new requirements. In addition, the Federal Reserve Board has not always provided clear guidance on the types of program decisions for which Reserve Banks should seek approval by the Federal Reserve Board. While the Federal Reserve Board approved significant program changes and Reserve Bank staff periodically consulted with Federal Reserve Board staff, the scope of authority for Reserve Banks to allow atypical uses of a broad-based program remains unclear. Without documented guidance, Reserve Banks operating future emergency programs may not escalate significant policy decisions to the appropriate officials at the Federal Reserve Board, increasing the risk that a Reserve Bank may permit an exceptional use of emergency assistance that is inconsistent with the Federal Reserve Board's policy goals or that exposes the Federal Reserve Board to increased financial or reputational risk. Moreover, more complete documentation could help the Federal Reserve Board comply with the Dodd-Frank Act's reporting requirements on its use of its section 13(3) emergency authority.

RECOMMENDATIONS FOR EXECUTIVE ACTION

While creating control systems at the same time that the emergency programs were being designed and implemented posed unique challenges, the recent crisis provided invaluable experience that the Federal Reserve System can apply in the future should the use of these authorities again become warranted. Going forward, to further strengthen policies for selecting vendors, ensuring the transparency and consistency of decision making involving the implementation of any future emergency programs, and managing risks related to these programs, we recommend that the Chairman of the Federal Reserve Board direct Federal Reserve Board and Reserve Bank staff to take the following seven actions:

- Revise Reserve Banks' formal acquisition policies and procedures to provide additional guidance on the steps staff should follow in exigent circumstances, specifically to address soliciting as much competition as possible, limiting the duration of noncompetitive contracts to the period of the exigency, and documenting efforts to promote competition.
- As part of the Federal Reserve System's planned review of the Reserve Banks' codes of conduct given their expanded statutory authority under the Dodd-Frank Act, consider how Reserve Banks' experience managing employee conflicts of interest, including those related to certain nonbank institutions that participated in the emergency programs, could inform the need for changes to the Reserve Banks' conflict policies.

- Finalize a comprehensive policy for FRBNY's management of risks related to vendor conflicts of interest that formalizes FRBNY practices and lessons learned from the crisis. This policy could include guidance on when to include contract protections that were not always found in FRBNY's vendor contracts, such as requirements for higher-risk vendor firms to provide a written conflict remediation plan and certify compliance with this plan.
- Strengthen procedures in place to guide Reserve Banks' efforts to manage emergency program access for higher-risk borrowers by providing more specific guidance on how Reserve Bank staff should exercise discretion and document decisions to restrict or deny program access for depository institutions and primary dealers that would otherwise be eligible for emergency assistance.
- Document a plan for estimating and tracking losses that could occur under more adverse economic conditions within and across all emergency lending activities and for using this information to inform policy decisions, such as decisions to limit risk exposures through program design or restrictions applied to eligible borrowing institutions.
- In drafting regulations to establish the policies and procedures governing emergency lending under section 13(3) of the Federal Reserve Act, set forth the Federal Reserve Board's process for documenting, to the extent not otherwise required by law, its justification for each use of this authority.
- Document the Federal Reserve Board's guidance to Reserve Banks on types of emergency program decisions and risk events that require approval by or consultation with the Board of Governors, the Federal Open Market Committee, or other designated groups or officials at the Federal Reserve Board.

List of Congressional Addressees

The Honorable Harry Reid
Majority Leader
United States Senate

The Honorable Mitch McConnell
Minority Leader
United States Senate

The Honorable Tim Johnson
Chairman
The Honorable Richard C. Shelby
Ranking Member
Committee on Banking, Housing, and Urban Affairs
United States Senate
The Honorable Bernie Sanders
United States Senate

The Honorable John Boehner
Speaker of the House of Representatives

The Honorable Eric Cantor
Majority Leader
House of Representatives

The Honorable Nancy Pelosi
Minority Leader
House of Representatives

The Honorable Kevin McCarthy
House Majority Whip
House of Representatives

The Honorable Steny Hoyer
House Minority Whip
House of Representatives

The Honorable Spencer Bachus
Chairman
The Honorable Barney Frank
Ranking Member
Committee on Financial Services
House of Representatives

APPENDIX I. AGENCY MORTGAGE-BACKED SECURITIES PURCHASE PROGRAM

Background

On November 25, 2008, the Federal Open Market Committee (FOMC) announced that the Federal Reserve Bank of New York (FRBNY) would purchase up to $500 billion of agency mortgage-backed securities (agency MBS) to support the housing market and the broader economy. Agency MBS include mortgage-backed securities (MBS) issued by the housing government-sponsored enterprises (enterprises), which are Fannie Mae and Freddie Mac, or guaranteed by Ginnie Mae.[130] The FOMC authorized the Agency Mortgage-Backed Securities Purchase Program (Agency MBS program) under its authority to direct open market operations under section 14 of the Federal Reserve Act of 1913. By purchasing agency MBS with longer maturities (generally 30 years), the Agency MBS program was intended to lower long-term interest rates for mortgages and thereby support the housing market and other financial markets more generally. The Agency MBS program commenced purchases on January 5, 2009, about 6 weeks after the initial announcement. In March 2009, the FOMC increased the total amount of planned purchases from $500 billion up to $1.25 trillion. The program executed its final purchases in March 2010 and settlement was completed in August 2010.

Agency MBS play a significant role in the U.S. mortgage finance system. As part of their mission to assist the U.S. secondary mortgage market and facilitate the flow of mortgage credit, the enterprises purchase mortgages, package most of them into MBS, and issue and guarantee these MBS in the secondary market. The enterprises purchase conventional mortgages that meet their underwriting standards, known as conforming mortgages, from primary mortgage lenders such as banks or thrifts. In turn, banks and thrifts use the proceeds to originate additional mortgages. The enterprises hold some of the mortgages that they purchase in their portfolios. However, most of the mortgages are packaged into MBS, which are sold to investors in the secondary mortgage market. In exchange for a fee (the guarantee fee) the enterprises guarantee the timely payment of interest and principal on MBS that they issue. Ginnie Mae, a wholly-owned government corporation, guarantees the timely payment of principal and interest on MBS issued by private institutions. Securities guaranteed by Ginnie Mae finance the vast majority of loans backed by the Federal Housing Administration and the Department of Veterans Affairs, as well as loans backed by the Rural Housing Service and the Office of Public and Indian Housing within the Department of Housing and Urban Development. Every month, cash flows from the mortgages underlying agency MBS are distributed to the investors who hold the agency MBS.

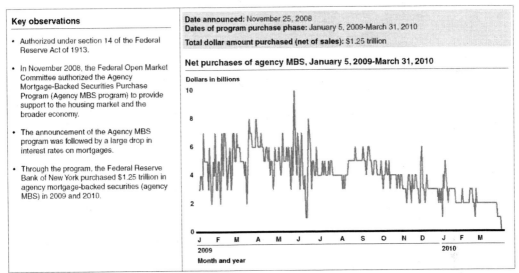

Source: GAO analysis of Board of Governors of the Federal Reserve System documents and data.
Note: The purchase phase completed on March 31, 2010, and on June 28, 2010, FRBNY announced it would purchase coupon swaps to facilitate settlement which were completed in August 2010.

Figure 12. Overview of Agency MBS Program.

Large scale purchases of agency MBS through the Agency MBS program were intended to lower yields on agency MBS and lower long-term interest rates on mortgages. For the months preceding the announcement of the Agency MBS program and for the period of the program's operation, figure 13 illustrates changes in yields for 30-year MBS guaranteed by Fannie Mae, 30-year interest rates on mortgages, and the spread between the yields that investors required to purchase 30-year Fannie Mae securities and the yields investors required for 10-year Treasury securities (a frequently-cited benchmark for interest rates). The coupon rate on MBS issued by Fannie Mae is used as an input by mortgage lenders to calculate interest rate levels that they offer to homeowners. On the day the FOMC announced the Agency MBS program, the rate required by investors to invest in 30-year Fannie Mae MBS fell by 63 basis points, which exceeded the 55-basis point decline following the announcement that the Federal Housing Finance Agency placed Fannie Mae and Freddie Mac in conservatorship.[131] Mortgage rates available to homeowners and homebuyers also dropped significantly in the week after the Agency MBS program announcement. Freddie Mac publishes a weekly average from a survey of mortgage originators it conducts. The average interest rates on 30-year fixed-rate mortgages offered by its survey respondents dropped 44 basis points to 5.53 percent in the week following the Agency MBS program announcement. For the remainder of FRBNY's purchases, mortgage rates remained at levels at least 37 basis points below their levels before the Agency MBS program announcement (see figure 13).

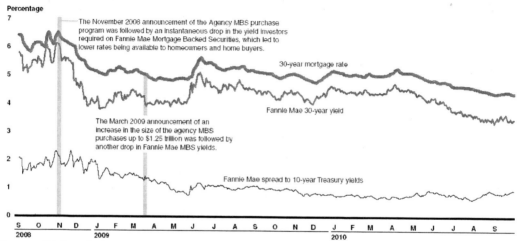

Source: GAO analysis of Freddie Mac and broker-dealer data.

Figure 13. Changes in Agency MBS Spreads (Fannie Mae) and 30-Year Mortgage Rates, September 2008–September 2010.

FRBNY staff noted that a key operational challenge for the program was its size. FRBNY hired investment managers to provide execution support and advisory services needed to help execute large-scale purchases. FRBNY did not have the systems or staff resources to operate a program of this size. FRBNY had not been active in the MBS market and needed partners with the infrastructure and the expertise needed to navigate this complex, system-intensive market. Initially, FRBNY relied on four external investment managers to conduct the purchases to minimize operational and financial risk. The initial need for four external investment managers reflected the short time frame for launching the program and the complexity of the agency MBS market. FRBNY wanted the program to be operational within 6 weeks of the November 2008 announcement. On August 17, 2009, FRBNY moved to using only one investment manager for purchases. On March 2, 2010, FRBNY began using an in-house team to execute purchases on some days. Table 10 shows the total agency MBS purchases executed by the four investment managers and FRBNY.

Because of guarantees provided by Fannie Mae, Freddie Mac, and Ginnie Mae, FRBNY and other purchasers of agency MBS are not exposed to credit risk associated with mortgage borrowers. While there has been some credit risk associated with Fannie Mae and Freddie Mac's ability to guarantee the principal and interest payments on agency MBS, the federal government has taken actions to greatly lessen such concerns by providing financial assistance to the enterprises after they were placed in conservatorship.[132] Because Ginnie Mae is wholly-owned by the federal government, MBS guaranteed by Ginnie Mae have long been viewed as similar to Treasury securities from a credit risk perspective. Agency MBS are subject to interest rate risk—the risk of possible losses and changes in value from increases or decreases in market interest rates. For example, increases in interest rates reduce the market value of agency MBS. While decreases in interest rates increase the market value of agency MBS, some of this increase can be offset by borrower prepayments on mortgages underlying the agency MBS. Prepayments can lower returns to holders of agency MBS if borrowers prepay the loans when interest rates decline.[133]

Key Vendors for the Agency MBS Program

FRBNY used a number of vendors to manage this program. As table 11 shows, while most were investment managers, it also had key contracts with others.

Table 10. Total Agency MBS Purchases by Investment Manager, January 2009–July 2010

Dollars in billions			
Investment manager	Purchases	Sales	Net
BlackRock	$275,122	$85,815	$189,307
FRBNY	57,243	41,169	16,074
Goldman Sachs Asset Management	281,667	87,694	193,973
Pacific Investment Management Company LLC	273,198	96,661	176,537
Wellington Management Company	962,914	288,806	674,108
Total	$1,850,145	$600,145	$1,249,999

Source: GAO analysis of Board of Governors of the Federal Reserve System data.

Table 11. Vendors for Agency MBS Program that Earned Fees Greater than $1 Million, 2008–2010

Vendor	Services provided	Contract date	Awarded competitively?	Total fees paid (2008–2010)
Wellington Management Company	Investment manager	12/30/2008	Yes	$26,557,427
JP Morgan Chase & Co.	Administrator, custodian	12/31/2008	Yes	16,248,051
BlackRock	Investment manager	12/30/2008	Yes	11,157,427
Goldman Sachs	Investment manager	12/30/2008	Yes	11,157,426
Pacific Investment Management Company LLC	Investment manager	12/30/2008	Yes	11,157,426
BlackRock	Risk reporting	8/17/2009	Yes	5,126,000

Source: GAO presentation of FRBNY information.

APPENDIX II. ASSET-BACKED COMMERCIAL PAPER MONEY MARKET MUTUAL FUND LIQUIDITY FACILITY

Background

On September 19, 2008, the Board of Governors of the Federal Reserve System (Federal Reserve Board) authorized the creation of the Asset-Backed Commercial Paper Money Market Mutual Fund Liquidity Facility (AMLF) under section 13(3) of the Federal Reserve Act of 1913 to provide liquidity support to money market mutual funds (MMMF) facing redemption pressures and to promote liquidity in the asset-backed commercial paper (ABCP) markets.[134] AMLF became operational on September 22, 2008, and was operated by the Federal Reserve Bank of Boston (FRBB). AMLF was initially set to expire on January 30, 2009. The Federal Reserve Board authorized three separate extensions of the program to address continuing strains in financial markets. AMLF expired on February 1, 2010.

MMMFs are mutual funds that are registered under the Investment Company Act of 1940, and regulated under rule 2a-7 under that act.[135] MMMFs invest in high-quality, short-term debt instruments such as commercial paper, treasury bills and repurchase agreements. Generally, these funds, unlike other investment companies, seek to maintain a stable net asset value per share (market value of assets minus liabilities divided by number of shares outstanding), typically $1 per share. While investments in MMMFs are not covered by federal deposit insurance, given restrictions on the types of investments MMMFs may hold, many investors have viewed MMMFs as a safe alternative to bank savings accounts.

In September 2008, following the failure of Lehman Brothers Inc. (Lehman Brothers), many MMMFs faced severe liquidity pressures as redemption requests from their investors increased significantly. Many MMMF investors became concerned about potential losses on their investments when they learned that the Reserve Primary Money Fund, a large MMMF that suffered losses on holdings of Lehman Brothers commercial paper, "broke the buck"—that is, the net asset value of the fund dropped below its target value of $1 per share. Under normal circumstances, MMMFs would have been able to meet redemption demands by drawing on their cash reserves or selling assets, including ABCP, into liquid markets. However, these markets were strained; interest rates on ABCP spiked in September 2008. The Federal Reserve Board grew concerned that stress in the ABCP market would be exacerbated should MMMFs choose to sell assets at a discount or reduce their purchases of ABCP to meet extraordinary demands on their liquidity. Such actions could have further depressed the price of these assets and potentially resulted in further losses to MMMFs and increased redemption requests as investor confidence in MMMFs weakened.

To quickly support the MMMF market, the Federal Reserve Board authorized loans to discount window eligible depository institutions and their primary dealer affiliates to purchase ABCP from MMMFs. By providing MMMFs the option to sell ABCP at amortized cost—the carrying value of the investment in the MMMF's accounting records—rather than at deeply discounted prices, AMLF was intended to help MMMFs raise cash in a way that did not exacerbate market stresses. AMLF's design reflected the need to overcome practical constraints in lending to MMMFs directly. According to Federal Reserve Board officials, MMMFs were concerned that they would have limited ability to borrow directly from the Federal Reserve System because of statutory and fund-specific limitations on fund borrowing.

Because the interest rate on the AMLF loan was lower than the returns on eligible ABCP, eligible intermediary borrowers had an incentive to participate. By fostering liquidity in the ABCP market and money markets more generally, the AMLF may have encouraged MMMFs to continue to purchase ABCP as they would have the option to later pledge the ABCP to AMLF.

If an AMLF borrower defaulted, FRBB would have attempted to recover losses through its claim on the assets collateralizing the ABCP. AMLF did not apply haircuts and accepted only highly rated ABCP as collateral. Federal Reserve System staff said that requiring overcollateralization for AMLF loans would have been inconsistent with policy objectives to quickly and effectively provide liquidity support to MMMFs. If MMMFs sold assets to the intermediary borrowers through AMLF at less than book value to fund redemption requests from MMMF shareholders, they would have incurred losses to the detriment of remaining MMMF shareholders, creating further incentives for MMMF shareholders to redeem shares. Accordingly, the Federal Reserve Board sought to help fund purchases of MMMF assets at book value. Therefore, it authorized loans to intermediary borrowers that were equal to the book value of the ABCP. Upon providing an AMLF loan, FRBB accepted the risk of credit loss on the ABCP securing the loan. Applying haircuts to AMLF loans would have reduced the economic incentives for eligible borrowers to participate as they would have had to fund part of the ABCP purchases on their own. Furthermore, the Federal Reserve Board authorized nonrecourse lending to increase incentives for intermediary borrowers to participate. In the event of losses on the ABCP collateral, the borrower could surrender the ABCP to FRBB and choose not to repay its loan. Under the terms of the AMLF program lending agreement, the nonrecourse provisions of the loan could be voided, giving FRBB full recourse to recover any losses from a borrower's assets, if the borrower was found to have misrepresented compliance with AMLF requirements. Figure 15 illustrates the structure of the AMLF.

Terms and Conditions for AMLF

Borrower Eligibility Requirements

Initially all U.S. depository institutions, U.S. bank holding companies (parent companies or their U.S. broker-dealer subsidiaries), or U.S. branches and agencies of foreign banks with eligible ABCP were eligible to participate in AMLF. All borrowers were required to execute legal borrowing agreements with FRBB representing, among other things, that the borrower met the stated requirements and would pledge only eligible collateral.

Table 12 ranks the largest AMLF borrowers at the holding company level. JP Morgan Chase & Co. and State Street Corporation, which have large bank subsidiaries that are major providers of custodial services for MMMFs, accounted for more than 92 percent of total AMLF loans.

Seller Eligibility Requirements

MMMFs registered under Securities and Exchange Commission Rule 2a-7 pursuant to the Investment Company Act of 1940 were eligible to participate in AMLF. In May 2009, prior to the release of results from the U.S. government's examination of whether the largest banking organizations had sufficient capital to withstand adverse economic scenarios, AMLF experienced a moderate increase in utilization.[136] This activity coincided with the potential for these results to have resulted in credit rating downgrades of some highly rated ABCP that would have made this ABCP ineligible for sale through AMLF. On June 25, 2009, the Federal Reserve Board responded by implementing a redemption requirement so that an MMMF would have to experience a minimum level of redemptions—defined as 5 percent of net assets in a single day or at least 10 percent of net assets within the prior 5 business days—before it could sell eligible ABCP through AMLF. This change was intended to ensure that AMLF provided liquidity support, not credit risk support, to MMMFs.

Table 12. Largest AMLF Borrowers by Total Dollar Amount of Loans

Dollars in billions			
	Parent company of AMLF borrowing institution(s)	Total AMLF loans	Percent of total
1	JP Morgan Chase & Co.	$111.4	51.3%
2	State Street Corporation	89.2	41.1
3	Bank of New York Mellon	12.9	5.9
4	Bank of America Corporation	1.6	0.7
5	Citigroup Inc.	1.4	0.7
6	SunTrust	0.5	0.2
7	Credit Suisse	0.2	0.1
	Total	**$217.3**	**100.0%**

Source: GAO analysis of Federal Reserve Board data.

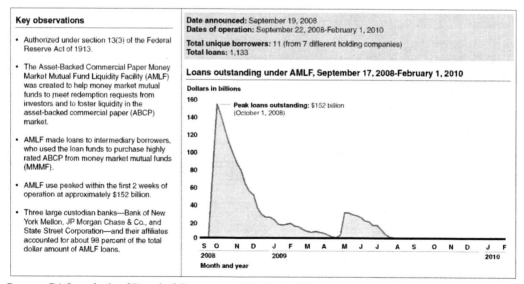

Source: GAO analysis of Board of Governors of the Federal Reserve System documents and data.

Figure 14. Overview of AMLF.

Table 13 ranks the largest sellers of ABCP through AMLF at the level of the fund family. Twenty fund managers accounted for approximately 88 percent of ABCP sold through AMLF.

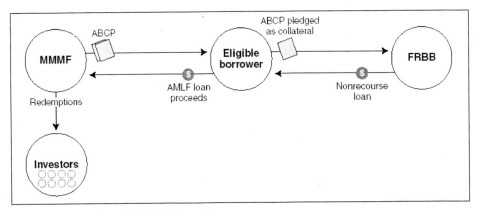

Source: GAO presentation of FRBB information.

Figure 15. Structure of the AMLF.

Collateral Eligibility Requirements

To be eligible for purchase through AMLF, ABCP was required to be U.S.-dollar denominated and to be rated not lower than A-1/P-1/F-1 by a major Nationally Recognized Statistical Rating Organization (NRSRO). If rated by multiple NRSROs, the ABCP was required to have this highest rating from at least two or more major NRSROs. On April 22, 2009, the Federal Reserve changed the asset eligibility requirements to exclude ABCP that was rated A-1/P-1/F-1 and on "negative watch." This change was intended to provide a greater level of credit risk protection for FRBB.

Term to Maturity for Loans

AMLF loan maturities matched the remaining maturity of the pledged ABCP collateral and could not exceed 120 days for borrowers that were depository institutions and 270 days for all other eligible borrowers.[137]

Table 13. Largest MMMF (Aggregated by Fund Family) Sellers of Asset-Backed Commercial Paper through AMLF

Dollars in billions			
Rank	Fund family seller	Total dollar amount of ABCP sold through AMLF	Percent of total AMLF loans
1	Reserve Funds	$19	8.9%
2	JP Morgan Chase & Co.	18	8.1
3	Dreyfus	17	7.6
4	Columbia Funds	15	6.9
5	Barclays	13	5.9
6	Wells Fargo	12	5.6
7	BlackRock	12	5.5

Table 13. (continued)

Dollars in billions

Rank	Fund family seller	Total dollar amount of ABCP sold through AMLF	Percent of total AMLF loans
8	Federated	10	4.7
9	Morgan Stanley	10	4.4
10	Short Term Investments Trust	9	4.4
11	Goldman Sachs	9	4.0
12	Evergreen	9	3.9
13	Merrill Lynch	7	3.2
14	T. Rowe Price	6	2.8
15	Fidelity	5	2.5
16	DWS Investments	5	2.4
17	UBS	5	2.3
18	Master Money LLC	4	1.8
19	General Money Market Fund	3	1.5
20	Charles Schwab	3	1.2
	All other sellers	27	12.3
Total		$217	100.0%

Source: GAO analysis of Federal Reserve Board data.

Interest Rates

The interest rate on AMLF loans was equal to the primary credit rate in effect at the time the loan was extended. The AMLF program did not include any fees or surcharges.

Recourse Status

AMLF loans were made without recourse to the intermediary borrower. However, under the AMLF lending agreement, FRBB would have had recourse to a borrower's assets in the event that the borrower had misrepresented the eligibility of the collateral pledged to the AMLF.

APPENDIX III. ASSISTANCE TO AMERICAN INTERNATIONAL GROUP, INC.

Key observations

- Authorized under section 13(3) of the Federal Reserve Act of 1913.
- American International Group, Inc. (AIG) was one of the largest recipients of federal government assistance during the recent financial crisis.
- AIG has repaid its borrowings under the revolving credit facility and the securities borrowing facility.
- The Federal Reserve Bank of New York (FRBNY) does not project losses on its loans to Maiden Lane II LLC and Maiden Lane III LLC.

Source: GAO summary of Board of Governors of the Federal Reserve System documents.

Overview

In late 2008 and early 2009, the Board of Governors of the Federal Reserve System (Federal Reserve Board) invoked section 13(3) of the Federal Reserve Act of 1913 to authorize the Federal Reserve Bank of New York (FRBNY) to take the following actions to assist American International Group, Inc. (AIG):

- providing a revolving credit facility (RCF) to lend up to $85 billion to help AIG and its subsidiaries address strains on their liquidity;
- creating a securities borrowing facility (SBF) to provide up to $37.8 billion of direct funding support to a securities lending program operated by certain regulated U.S. life insurance subsidiaries of AIG;
- creating a special purpose vehicle (SPV), Maiden Lane II LLC, and providing a $19.5 billion loan to this SPV to help finance the purchase of assets that had contributed to liquidity strains for its securities lending program;
- creating another SPV, Maiden Lane III LLC, to help resolve liquidity strains associated with certain credit default swaps (CDS) to which AIG Financial Products Corp. (AIGFP) was a party by providing a $24.3 billion loan to this SPV to finance the purchase of collateralized debt obligations (CDO) from AIG counterparties in connection with terminating CDS contracts on those CDOs; and
- purchasing a contemplated securitization of income (AIG life insurance securitization) from certain AIG life insurance companies.[138]

The AIG RCF and SBF have closed and were fully repaid and FRBNY expects full repayment on amounts outstanding on its loans to Maiden Lane II LLC and Maiden Lane III LLC. The Federal Reserve Board authorized changes to the borrowing limit and other terms for the AIG RCF over time, and AIG fully repaid amounts outstanding from the AIG RCF in January 2011. AIG's borrowing under the AIG SBF peaked at $20.6 billion before the AIG SBF was fully repaid in connection with the creation of Maiden Lane II LLC in December 2008. As of June 29, 2011, $8.6 billion and $12.3 billion in principal and accrued interest remained outstanding on FRBNY's senior loans to Maiden Lane II LLC and Maiden Lane III LLC, respectively. As discussed below, FRBNY recently began to hold auctions to sell parts of the Maiden Lane II LLC portfolio. According to FRBNY staff, the AIG life insurance securitization option was abandoned for a number of reasons, including that it would have required FRBNY to manage a long-term exposure to life insurance businesses with which it had little experience.

Background

From July 2008 through early September 2008, AIG faced increasing pressure on its liquidity following a downgrade in its credit ratings in May 2008 due in part to losses from its securities lending program. This deterioration followed liquidity strains earlier in the year, although AIG was able to raise capital in May 2008 to address its needs at that time. Two key sources of AIG's difficulties were AIGFP and a securities lending program operated by certain AIG insurance subsidiaries.[139] AIGFP faced growing collateral calls on CDS it had written on CDOs.[140] Meanwhile, AIG faced demands on its liquidity from securities lending counterparties who were returning borrowed securities and demanding that AIG return their cash collateral. Declines in its securities lending reinvestment portfolio of residential mortgage-backed securities (RMBS) and declining values of CDOs against which AIGFP had written CDS protection forced AIG to use an estimated $9.3 billion of its cash reserves in July and August 2008 to repay securities lending counterparties that terminated existing agreements and to post additional collateral required by the trading counterparties of AIGFP. AIG attempted to raise additional capital in the private market in September 2008 but was unsuccessful. On September 15, 2008, the rating agencies downgraded AIG's debt rating, which resulted in the need for an additional $20 billion to fund its added collateral demands and transaction termination payments. In addition, AIG's share price fell from $22.76 on September 8, 2008, to $4.76 per share on September 15, 2008. Following the credit rating downgrade, an increasing number of counterparties refused to transact with AIG for fear that it would fail. Also around this time, the insurance regulators decided they would no longer allow AIG's insurance subsidiaries to lend funds to the parent company under a revolving credit facility that AIG maintained. Furthermore, the insurance regulators demanded that any outstanding loans be repaid and that the facility be terminated.

The Federal Reserve Board and the Department of the Treasury (Treasury) determined through analysis of information provided by AIG and insurance regulators, as well as publicly available information, that market events in September 2008 could have caused AIG to fail, which would have posed systemic risk to financial markets given market conditions. Consequently, the Federal Reserve Board and Treasury took steps to ensure that AIG obtained sufficient liquidity and could complete an orderly sale of its operating assets, continue to meet its obligations and close its investment positions in its securities lending program and AIGFP. The Federal Reserve Board explained that a major concern was public confidence in the financial system and the economy. The Federal Reserve Board and Treasury said that financial markets and financial institutions were experiencing unprecedented strains resulting from the placement of Fannie Mae and Freddie Mac under conservatorship; the failure of financial institutions, including Lehman Brothers Holdings Inc. (Lehman Brothers); and the collapse of the housing markets. The Federal Reserve Board said that in light of these events, a disorderly failure of AIG could have contributed to higher borrowing costs, diminished availability of credit, and additional failures. They concluded that the effects of the collapse of AIG would have been much more severe than that of Lehman Brothers because of its global operations, large and varied retail and institutional customer base, and different types of financial service offerings. The Federal Reserve Board and Treasury said that a default by AIG would have placed considerable pressure on numerous counterparties and triggered serious disruptions in the commercial paper market. Moreover, counterparties of AIGFP would no longer have protection or insurance against losses if AIGFP, a major seller of CDS contracts, defaulted on its obligations and CDO values continued to decline.

The Federal Reserve Board intended the initial September 2008 assistance to enable AIG to meet these obligations to its counterparties and begin the process of selling noncore business units in order to raise cash to repay the credit facility and other liabilities. However, AIG's continuing financial deterioration and instability in the financial markets resulted in subsequent assistance by FRBNY and Treasury.

While AIG has repaid its direct assistance provided by FRBNY, FRBNY's loans to Maiden Lane II LLC and Maiden Lane III LLC remain outstanding and Treasury continues to have significant equity exposure. We have issued several reports that provide additional background on the federal government's assistance to AIG.[141]

AIG Revolving Credit Facility (AIG RCF)

Date announced: September 16, 2008

Dates of operation: September 16, 2008–January 14, 2011

Key observations

- The Federal Reserve Bank of New York (FRBNY) initially was authorized to loan AIG up to $85 billion.
- Two key sources of AIG's liquidity problems were a securities lending program operated by its subsidiaries and credit default swaps.
- AIG's use of the AIG RCF peaked at $72 billion in October 2008.
- AIG paid down its RCF balance in January 2011.

Source: GAO summary of Board of Governors of the Federal Reserve System documents and data.

Background

On September 16, 2008, one day after the Lehman Brothers Holdings Inc. bankruptcy announcement, the Federal Reserve Board invoked section 13(3) of the Federal Reserve Act to authorize FRBNY to provide loans of up to $85 billion through the AIG RCF to help AIG and its subsidiaries to address strains on their liquidity. The announcement of this assistance followed a downgrade of the firm's credit rating, which had prompted collateral calls by its counterparties and raised concerns that a rapid failure of the company would further destabilize financial markets.

Under FRBNY's credit agreement with AIG (and related security agreement), amounts borrowed by AIG under the AIG RCF were secured by a substantial portion of the assets of AIG and its primary nonregulated subsidiaries, including AIG's ownership interest in its regulated U.S. and foreign subsidiaries. This credit agreement included provisions intended to help ensure that the proceeds AIG received from planned AIG assets sales would be used to permanently repay outstanding balances under the AIG RCF. In addition, the security agreement provided for AIG's borrowings under this facility to be guaranteed by each of AIG's domestic, nonregulated subsidiaries that had more than $50 million in assets. As a condition of providing this loan, FRBNY also created a trust to receive AIG preferred stock for the benefit of the Department of the Treasury. On January 14, 2011, the trust exchanged these preferred shares for about 562.9 million shares of AIG common stock, which was then transferred to Treasury as part of the broader recapitalization of AIG.

Due to restructuring and mandatory repayments from the sale of assets, the borrowing limit on the amount of direct assistance available to AIG through the AIG RCF was lowered several times over the life of the facility, and the amount AIG owed the facility also declined. Figure 16 illustrates the AIG RCF balance owed and the total amount available from October

2008 through December 1, 2010. The AIG RCF was fully repaid by AIG and closed on January 14, 2011.

AIG RCF Terms and Conditions

Total amount available. The borrowing limit for the AIG RCF was initially $85 billion and was lowered to $60 billion in November 2008, and lowered further to $35 billion in December 2009.

Interest rate. Initially, the interest rate on funds drawn on the AIG RCF was the London Interbank Offer Rate (LIBOR) plus 8.5 percent (with a minimum floor on LIBOR set at 3.5 percent). Under the initial terms, AIG was also required to pay a one-time commitment fee of 2 percent on the aggregate amount available under the facility, or $1.7 billion, and an ongoing commitment fee each quarter equal to 8.5 percent of the average undrawn funds available during the previous quarter. In November 2008, the interest rate was lowered to LIBOR plus 3 percent and the fee on undrawn funds was reduced to 0.75 percent. On April 17, 2009, the minimum floor on LIBOR was removed.

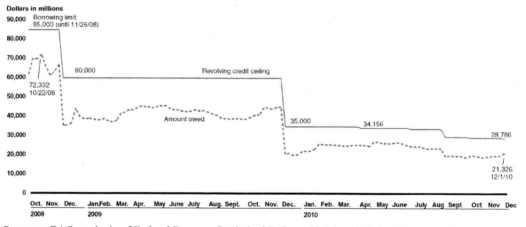

Sources: GAO analysis of Federal Reserve Statistical Release H.4.1 and Federal Reserve data.

Figure 16. FRBNY Revolving Credit Facility Balance Owed and Total Amount Available, October 2008–December 1, 2010.

Table 14. Vendors for AIG RCF that Earned Fees Greater than $1 Million, 2008–2010

Vendor	Services provided	Contract date	Awarded competitively?	Total fees paid (2008–2010)
Morgan Stanley	Investment banking advisory services	10/16/2008	No	$108,400,327
Ernst & Young	Due diligence	9/19/2008	No	$66,887,780
Davis Polk & Wardwell	Legal services	9/16/2008	No	$32,595,896
Houlihan Lokey	Valuation services	4/9/2009	Yes	$1,390,881
Sidley Austin	Legal services	4/13/2009	No	$1,312,494

Source: GAO presentation of FRBNY information.

Duration. The Federal Reserve Board initially authorized the AIG RCF for up to 2 years and in November 2008 extended the term over which it could be available to 5 years.

Key Vendors for AIG RCF

FRBNY used a number of vendors to help manage and administer the AIG RCF. Table 14 lists AIG RCF vendors that have been paid more than $1 million.

AIG Securities Borrowing Facility (SBF)

Background

On October 6, 2008, the Federal Reserve Board authorized the creation of the AIG SBF to provide up to $37.8 billion of direct funding support to a securities lending program operated by certain domestic insurance subsidiaries of AIG. The securities lending program allowed AIG's insurance subsidiaries, primarily AIG's life insurance companies, to lend securities in return for cash collateral that these AIG insurance subsidiaries then invested in investments such as RMBS. From October 8, 2008, through December 11, 2008, FRBNY provided cash loans to certain AIG domestic life insurance companies, collateralized by investment grade debt obligations.

As of October 1, 2008, AIG had drawn down approximately $62 billion on the AIG RCF. AIG used those funds, in part, to settle transactions with counterparties that were returning securities they had borrowed under AIG's securities lending program. The withdrawal of AIG's securities lending counterparties placed strains on AIG's liquidity as closing out these transactions required AIG to return cash collateral that had been pledged by these counterparties. By providing overnight loans against investment grade debt obligations, the AIG SBF was intended to reduce pressure on AIG's subsidiaries to meet demands for returning cash collateral by liquidating the portfolio of RMBS in strained markets. The size of the AIG SBF was intended to be large enough to allow AIG to replace all of its securities lending program counterparties.

Terms and Conditions for AIG SBF

Collateral. Through the AIG SBF, FRBNY provided loans to AIG that were collateralized by investment grade debt obligations. These loans were made with recourse to AIG's assets beyond the assets pledged as collateral and FRBNY generally applied higher haircuts than it required for these collateral types in the Primary Dealer Credit Facility (PDCF).

Term of loans. Overnight, although loans could be rolled over.

Interest rate. The interest rate on AIG SBF loans was 100 basis points plus the average overnight repurchase agreement rate offered by dealers for the relevant collateral type.

Program duration. The AIG SBF was authorized to provide loans until September 16, 2010, but was terminated in December 2008.

AIG's borrowing under the AIG SBF peaked at $20.6 billion before the AIG SBF was fully repaid in connection with the creation of Maiden Lane II LLC in December 2008.

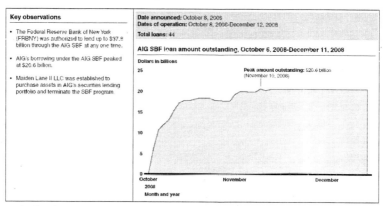

Source: GAO analysis of Board of Governors of the Federal Reserve System documents and data.

Figure 17. Overview of AIG SBF.

Maiden Lane II LLC

> **Date announced:** November 10, 2008
>
> **Dates of operation:** December 12, 2008–present
>
> **Key observations**
>
> - The Federal Reserve Bank of New York (FRBNY) established Maiden Lane II LLC to fund the purchase of RMBS from the securities lending portfolio operated by certain insurance subsidiaries of AIG.
> - FRBNY provided a senior loan of $19.5 billion and AIG's first loss position was $1 billion.
> - As of June 29, 2011, total principal and accrued interest owed to FRBNY was $8.6 billion, and as of that date, the portfolio had a fair value of $12.5 billion based on valuations as of March 31, 2011.
> - As of June 9, 2011, FRBNY had sold assets with a current face amount of approximately $10 billion through competitive auctions.

Source: GAO summary of Board of Governors of the Federal Reserve System documents and data.

Background

FRBNY created Maiden Lane II LLC to alleviate capital and liquidity pressures on AIG associated with the securities lending program operated by certain domestic insurance subsidiaries of AIG. On November 10, 2008, FRBNY announced plans to create an RMBS facility—Maiden Lane II LLC—to purchase RMBS assets from AIG's securities lending portfolio. The Federal Reserve Board authorized FRBNY to lend up to $22.5 billion to Maiden Lane II LLC; AIG also acquired a subordinated, $1 billion interest in the facility, which would absorb the first $1 billion of any losses. On December 12, 2008, FRBNY extended a $19.5 billion loan to Maiden Lane II LLC to fund its portion of the purchase price of the securities (see figure 18). The proceeds AIG's insurance subsidiaries received from the purchase of the securities by Maiden Lane II LLC were used to repay in full obligations under the AIG SBF and terminate that program. As of June 29, 2011, Maiden Lane II LLC owed $8.6 billion in principal and interest to FRBNY.

Terms and Conditions for Maiden Lane II

Assets in the Maiden Lane II LLC portfolio. The Maiden Lane II LLC portfolio included RMBS assets purchased from 11 domestic AIG insurance company subsidiaries with an estimated fair market value of $20.8 billion as of October 31, 2008. Maiden Lane II LLC purchased only U.S.-dollar-denominated RMBS held in AIG's securities lending portfolio. Foreign-currency-denominated RMBS were excluded to avoid the complexity of managing currency exposures.

Terms to maturity of FRBNY loan. FRBNY extended its senior loan for a term of up to 6 years with the option to extend at its discretion.

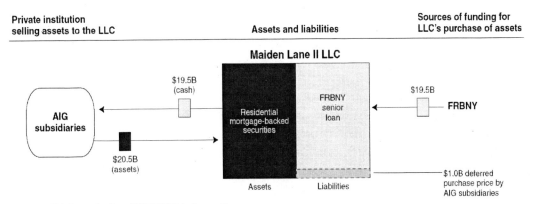

Source: GAO analysis of FRBNY information.

Figure 18. Maiden Lane II LLC Transaction.

Interest rates. The interest rate on FRBNY's senior loan is one-month LIBOR plus 100 basis points. After FRBNY's senior loan has been repaid in full plus interest, to the extent that there are remaining cash proceeds from the Maiden Lane II LLC portfolio, AIG's domestic insurance company subsidiaries would be entitled to receive from the LLC additional deferred consideration in the amount of up to $1 billion, plus interest at a rate of one-month LIBOR plus 300 basis points.

Cash flow waterfall. Repayment of FRBNY's loan was to begin immediately upon the receipt of proceeds from Maiden Lane II LLC's RMBS portfolio. Payments from the maturity or liquidation of the assets in the LLC were to occur on a monthly basis, and were to be made in the following order (each category must be fully paid before proceeding to the next lower category):

1. necessary costs and expenses of the LLC, including those incurred in managing and holding or liquidating assets, plus the funding of a cash reserve for future expenses;
2. entire $19.5 billion principal due to FRBNY;

3. all interest due to FRBNY on its senior secured loan;
4. up to $1 billion of deferred consideration to AIG's domestic insurance company subsidiaries; and
5. interest due in respect of such deferred consideration.

After payment of all of the foregoing, 1/6th of any remaining cash flows from the RMBS assets will be paid as deferred consideration to participating domestic AIG insurance company subsidiaries, and 5/6th will be paid to FRBNY as contingent interest on the senior loan.

Financial Performance

As of June 29, 2011, approximately $8.6 billion remained outstanding on FRBNY's loan to Maiden Lane II LLC. FRBNY projects full repayment of this loan. In the months following the Maiden Lane II LLC transaction, the portfolio experienced declines that brought the portfolio value below the amount owed to FRBNY. However, as market conditions improved in late 2009 and 2010, the value of the portfolio increased and as of June 29, 2011, the fair value of the portfolio (approximately $12.5 billion based on valuations as of March 31, 2011) exceeds the amount owed to FRBNY.

On March 30, 2011, FRBNY announced that it would begin a process to sell the assets in the Maiden Lane II LLC portfolio through BlackRock both individually and in segments over time as market conditions warrant through a competitive sales process. As of June 9, 2011, FRBNY had sold assets with a current face amount of approximately $10 billion through competitive auctions.

Key Vendors for Maiden Lane II

FRBNY used vendors to help manage this program. The key vendors are listed in table 15.

Maiden Lane III LLC

Date announced: November 10, 2008

Dates of operation: November 25, 2008–present

Key observations

- The Federal Reserve Bank of New York (FRBNY) created a special purpose vehicle called Maiden Lane III LLC to restructure the financial support for AIG by purchasing collateralized debt obligations (CDO) from certain AIG Financial Products Corp. (AIGFP) counterparties.
- To finance Maiden Lane III LLC's purchase of the CDOs, FRBNY provided a senior loan of $24.3 billion and AIG provided a $5 billion equity investment.
- As of June 29, 2011, total principal and interest owed to FRBNY was $12.3 billion. As of that date, the portfolio had a fair value of $24.2 billion based on valuations as of March 31, 2011.

Source: GAO summary of Board of Governors of the Federal Reserve System documents and data.

Table 15. Vendors for Maiden Lane II LLC that Earned Fees Greater than $1 Million, 2008–2010

Vendor	Services provided	Contract date	Awarded competitively?	Total fees paid (2008–2010)
BlackRock	Investment manager	12/12/2008	No	$24,102,579
Ernst & Young	Due diligence	9/19/2008	No	$1,192,888

Source: GAO presentation of FRBNY information.

Background

On November 10, 2008, FRBNY announced plans to create a separate facility—Maiden Lane III LLC—to purchase CDOs on which AIGFP had written CDS contracts. This facility was aimed at facilitating the restructuring of AIG by addressing the greatest threat to AIG's liquidity. In connection with the purchase of the CDOs, AIG's CDS counterparties agreed to terminate the CDS contracts. The Federal Reserve Board authorized FRBNY to lend up to $30 billion to Maiden Lane III LLC. On November 25, 2008, and December 18, 2008, FRBNY extended a total of $24.3 billion in loans to Maiden Lane III LLC; AIG also contributed $5 billion of equity to Maiden Lane III LLC, which would absorb the first $5 billion of any losses (see figure 19).

FRBNY's loan to Maiden Lane III LLC is expected to be repaid with the proceeds from the maturity or liquidation of the assets in the facility. As with Maiden Lane II LLC, the repayment will occur through cash flows from the underlying securities as they are paid off. Maiden Lane III LLC may hold the assets to maturity. Until this time, the government's investment remains exposed to risk of loss. In connection with the purchases of CDOs by Maiden Lane III LLC and the termination of the related credit derivative contracts, Maiden Lane III LLC paid AIGFP's counterparties $26.8 billion and AIGFP $2.5 billion.

Terms and Conditions for Maiden Lane III LLC

Assets in the Maiden Lane III portfolio. The Maiden Lane III LLC portfolio consists of U.S. dollar denominated CDOs with an estimated fair value of approximately $29.3 billion and a par value of approximately $62.1 billion as of October 31, 2008. Maiden Lane III LLC did not acquire bonds for which AIGFP could not produce certain documentation. In addition, Maiden Lane III LLC did not purchase cash CDO positions that AIG and its affiliates owned outright or synthetic CDO exposures that were derivative instruments rather than cash securities.[142]

Term to maturity of FRBNY loan. FRBNY extended its senior loan for up to 6 years with option to extend at FRBNY's discretion.

Interest rates. The interest rate on the loan from FRBNY is one-month LIBOR plus 100 basis points. AIG's equity contribution will accrue distributions at a rate of one-month LIBOR plus 300 basis points.

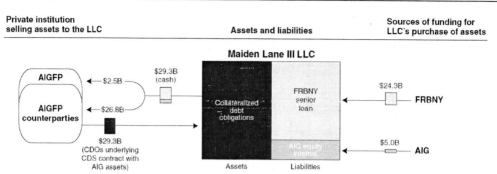

Source: GAO analysis of FRBNY information.

Figure 19. Maiden Lane III LLC Transaction.

Cash flow waterfall. Repayment of FRBNY's senior loan was to begin immediately upon the receipt of proceeds from the Maiden Lane III LLC portfolio. Payments from the portfolio holdings of Maiden Lane III LLC are to be made in the following order and each category must be fully paid before proceeding to the next category:

1. necessary costs and operating expenses of Maiden Lane III LLC, and amounts to fund a reserve account for expenses payable and other payments that may be incurred with the management of CDO defaults;
2. all principal due on FRBNY's loan;
3. all interest due on FRBNY's loan;
4. repayment of AIG's $5 billion equity contribution;
5. distributions accruing to AIG on its equity contribution; and
6. amounts due under certain currency hedging transactions to the extent the counterparty to the hedge is in default.

Any remaining funds resulting from holding or selling the assets in Maiden Lane III LLC are to be distributed between FRBNY and AIG's subsidiaries. FRBNY will receive 67 percent of the remaining proceeds, while the AIG subsidiaries will receive 33 percent of any remaining proceeds.

Financial Performance

As of June 29, 2011, approximately $12.3 billion remained outstanding on FRBNY's loan to Maiden Lane III LLC. FRBNY projects full repayment of this loan. In the months following the Maiden Lane LLC transaction, the portfolio experienced declines that brought the portfolio value below the amount owed to FRBNY. However, as market conditions improved in late 2009 and 2010, the value of the portfolio has increased and as of June 29, 2011, the fair value of the portfolio (approximately $24.2 billion based on valuations as of March 31, 2011) exceeds the amount owed to FRBNY.

Key Vendors for Maiden Lane III

FRBNY uses a number of vendors associated with Maiden Lane III. Table 16 lists the key vendors associated with this program.

Table 16. Vendors for Maiden Lane III LLC that Earned Fees Greater than $1 Million, 2008–2010

Vendor	Services provided	Contract date	Awarded competitively?	Total fees paid (2008–2010)
BlackRock	Investment manager	11/25/2008	No	$50,031,879
Ernst & Young	Due dilgence	9/19/2008	No	$2,820,172
Bank of New York Mellon	Administrator, custodian	11/25/2008	Yes	$1,390,452
Davis Polk & Wardwell	Legal services	9/16/2008	No	$1,018,815

Source: GAO presentation of FRBNY information.

APPENDIX IV. ASSISTANCE TO FACILITATE PRIVATE SECTOR ACQUISITION OF BEAR STEARNS COMPANIES, INC.

Key observations

- ·Authorized under section 13(3) of the Federal Reserve Act of 1913.
- On March 14, 2008, the Federal Reserve Bank of New York (FRBNY) extended credit to Bear Stearns Companies, Inc. (Bear Stearns) to provide additional time for a private sector solution that would avoid a disorderly failure of the firm.
- On March 16, 2008, FRBNY agreed to lend up to $30 billion against Bear Stearns's assets to facilitate JP Morgan Chase & Co.'s acquisition of the firm.
- Pursuant to a renegotiation of this lending agreement, FRBNY and JP Morgan Chase & Co. made loans to a special purpose vehicle, Maiden Lane LLC, which used the proceeds from these loans to purchase and hold Bear Stearns's assets.
- As of June 29, 2011, approximately $22 billion in principal and accrued interest remained outstanding on FRBNY's loan to Maiden Lane LLC. FRBNY projects full repayment of this loan.

Source: GAO summary of Board of Governors of the Federal Reserve System documents and data.

Background

In March 2008, the Board of Governors of the Federal Reserve System (Federal Reserve Board) invoked its emergency authority under section 13(3) of the Federal Reserve Act of 1913 to authorize the Federal Reserve Bank of New York (FRBNY) to take two actions to avert a disorderly failure of Bear Stearns Companies, Inc. (Bear Stearns): (1) a loan to help fund the firm through the weekend of March 15-16, 2008, to allow more time for a private sector solution and (2) an agreement to lend up to $30 billion against Bear Stearns's assets to facilitate an acquisition of the firm.

Bridge Loan to Bear Stearns

Shortly following the announcement of the Term Securities Lending Facility (TSLF), the Federal Reserve Board invoked its emergency authority under section 13(3) of the Federal Reserve Act to authorize an emergency loan to avert a disorderly failure of Bear Stearns. TSLF was announced on March 11, 2008, and the first TSLF auction was held on March 27, 2008. Federal Reserve Board officials noted that although TSLF was announced to address market tensions impacting many firms, some market participants concluded that its establishment was driven by specific concerns about Bear Stearns. Over a few days, Bear Stearns experienced liquidity problems as many of its lenders grew concerned that the firm would suffer greater losses in the future and stopped providing funding to the firm, even on a fully-secured basis with high-quality assets provided as collateral.[143] Late on Thursday, March 13, 2008, the senior management of Bear Stearns notified FRBNY that it would likely have to file for bankruptcy protection the following day unless the Federal Reserve Board authorized an emergency loan to the firm. The Federal Reserve Board feared that the sudden failure of Bear Stearns could have serious adverse impacts on markets in which Bear Stearns was a significant participant, including the repurchase agreements market. In particular, a Bear Stearns failure may have threatened the liquidity and solvency of other large institutions that relied heavily on short-term secured funding markets. On Friday, March 14, 2008, the Federal Reserve Board voted to authorize FRBNY to provide a $12.9 billion loan to Bear Stearns through JP Morgan Chase Bank, National Association, the largest bank subsidiary of JP Morgan Chase & Co. (JPMC), and accept $13.8 billion of Bear Stearns's assets as collateral.[144]

Figure 20 illustrates the back-to-back loan transaction, which was repaid on Monday, March 17, 2008, with almost $4 million of interest.

This emergency loan enabled Bear Stearns to avoid bankruptcy and continue to operate through the weekend. This provided time for potential acquirers, including JPMC, to assess Bear Stearns's financial condition and for FRBNY to prepare a new liquidity program, the Primary Dealer Credit Facility (PDCF), to address strains that could emerge from a possible Bear Stearns bankruptcy announcement the following Monday. Federal Reserve Board and FRBNY officials hoped that a bankruptcy could be averted by the announcement that a private sector firm would acquire Bear Stearns and stand behind its liabilities when the markets reopened on Monday.

Maiden Lane LLC

On Sunday, March 16, 2008, the Federal Reserve Board announced that FRBNY would lend up to $30 billion against certain Bear Stearns's assets to facilitate JPMC's acquisition of Bear Stearns. Over the weekend, JPMC had emerged as the only viable acquirer of Bear Stearns. In congressional testimony, Timothy Geithner, who was FRBNY's President in March 2008, provided the following account:

> Bear approached several major financial institutions, beginning on March 13. Those discussions intensified on Friday and Saturday. Bear's management provided us with periodic progress reports about a possible merger. Although several different

institutions expressed interest in acquiring all or part of Bear, it was clear that the size of Bear, the apparent risk in its balance sheet, and the limited amount of time available for a possible acquirer to conduct due diligence compounded the difficulty. Ultimately, only JP Morgan Chase was willing to consider an offer of a binding commitment to acquire the firm and to stand behind Bear's substantial short-term obligations.[145]

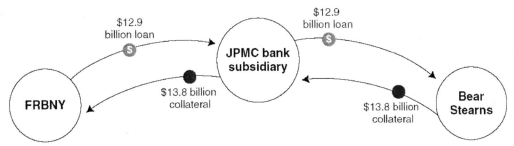

Source: GAO presentation of Federal Reserve Board information.

Figure 20. FRBNY Bridge Loan to Bear Stearns.

According to FRBNY officials, on the morning of Sunday, March 16, 2008, JPMC's Chief Executive Officer told FRBNY that the merger would only be possible if certain mortgage-related assets were removed from Bear Stearns's balance sheet. Negotiations between JPMC and FRBNY senior management resulted in a preliminary agreement under which FRBNY would make a $30 billion nonrecourse loan to JPMC collateralized by these Bear Stearns assets. A March 16, 2008, letter from then-FRBNY President Geithner to JPMC's Chief Executive Officer documented the terms of the preliminary agreement.[146]

During the following week, however, the terms of this agreement were renegotiated, resulting in the creation of a new lending structure in the form of Maiden Lane LLC. Significant issues that threatened to unravel the merger agreement emerged soon after the announcement. Bear Stearns's board members and shareholders thought JPMC's offer to purchase the firm at $2 per share was too low and threatened to vote against the merger. Perceived ambiguity in the terms of the merger agreement raised further concerns that JPMC could be forced to stand behind Bear Stearns's obligations even in the event that the merger was rejected. Moreover, some Bear Stearns's counterparties stopped trading with Bear Stearns because of uncertainty about whether certain Bear Stearns obligations would be covered by JPMC. FRBNY also had concerns with the level of protection provided under the preliminary lending agreement, under which FRBNY had agreed to lend on a nonrecourse basis against risky collateral. The risks of an unraveled merger agreement included a possible Bear Stearns bankruptcy and losses for JPMC, which might have been legally required to stand behind the obligations of a failed institution. Recognizing the risk that an unraveled merger posed to JPMC and the broader financial markets, FRBNY officials sought to renegotiate the lending agreement.

From March 17-March 24, 2008, FRBNY, JPMC, and Bear Stearns engaged in dual track negotiations to address each party's concerns with the preliminary merger and lending agreements. On March 24, 2008, FRBNY and JPMC agreed to a new lending structure that incorporated greater loss protections for FRBNY.

This new lending structure took the form of FRBNY and JPMC loans to a newly-created special purpose vehicle (SPV), Maiden Lane LLC, which used the proceeds from these loans to purchase and hold Bear Stearns's assets. FRBNY extended a senior loan to the SPV and this loan was collateralized by the portfolio of assets held by the SPV. Key loss protection features for Maiden Lane LLC included:

- *First loss position for JPMC.* JPMC agreed to take a first loss position by making a $1.15 billion subordinated loan to help finance the SPV's $30 billion purchase of the Bear Stearns asset portfolio (see figure 21). JPMC would begin to receive payments on this subordinated loan only after FRBNY received the full principal and interest on its $28.8 billion senior loan to the SPV. This lending structure protects FRBNY from up to $1.15 billion in losses on the portfolio.
- *Asset selection and filters.* The broad categories of assets selected for inclusion in the Maiden Lane portfolio were based on the policy objectives of the transaction, but FRBNY specified certain asset filters, or criteria, that were intended to exclude certain higher risk assets. For example, FRBNY accepted only U.S. dollar denominated assets to avoid the complexities of managing currency exposures from foreign currency assets. In addition, FRBNY agreed to accept only commercial and residential loans that were "performing," or no more than 30 days past due, as of March 14, 2008, the date of the bridge loan to Bear Stearns.
- *Valuation and due diligence.* FRBNY hired vendors to help value the assets in the portfolio and to conduct due diligence to exclude assets that were proposed for inclusion but did not meet the specified asset filters or lacked documentation. The purchase price for the Maiden Lane assets was based on Bear Stearns's recorded values for these assets as of March 14, 2008. FRBNY hired an external audit firm, Ernst & Young, to conduct due diligence for the portfolio.
- *Portfolio management.* For the Maiden Lane portfolio, FRBNY retained sole discretion over the decisions about how to manage the assets to maximize the value recovered on FRBNY's senior loan. FRBNY hired BlackRock to manage the portfolio and to advise on a strategy for investing and disposing of the assets. For Maiden Lane, FRBNY agreed to a 2-year reinvestment period during which all cash income from the portfolio would be reinvested in relatively low-risk investments; and FRBNY would not be permitted, without penalty, to receive repayment on its loan prior to the end of the reinvestment period unless the JPMC loan was repaid in full. According to FRBNY staff, JPMC requested this reinvestment period out of concern that FRBNY could sell portfolio assets at prices that would recover value for FRBNY but incur losses for JPMC. FRBNY staff said they agreed to this reinvestment strategy because it would not increase the risk of loss on its senior loan. FRBNY hired other vendors to help oversee and manage the risks of specific asset classes included in the Maiden Lane portfolio. For example, FRBNY hired vendors to advise on the risks posed by commercial real estate loans.

Table 17. Vendors for Maiden Lane LLC that Earned Fees Greater than $1 Million, 2008–2010

Vendor	Services provided	Contract date	Awarded competitively?	Total fees paid (2008–2010)
BlackRock	Investment manager	9/9/2008	No	$107,648,136
Ernst & Young	Due diligence	4/15/2008	No	$11,657,764
State Street Corporation	Administrator, custodian	6/26/2008	Yes	$9,182,946
EMC	Primary servicer	6/1/2008	No	$8,455,193
NationStar	Special servicer	2/5/2010	Yes	$3,456,150
Clayton	Servicer surveillance, advisory services	7/8/2009	Yes	$2,739,711
Cleary Gottlieb Stein & Hamilton	Legal services	9/13/2008	No	$2,422,169
Deloitte & Touche	Audit services	9/1/2008	N/A	$1,725,586
Axiom	Legal services	11/19/2008	No	$1,413,821
Wells Fargo	Primary servicer	6/1/2008	No	$1,300,949
Simpson Thacher & Bartlett	Legal services	3/24/2008	No	$1,147,617
Kelley Drye & Warren	Legal services	9/22/2009	No	$1,001,123

Sources: GAO presentation of FRBNY information.

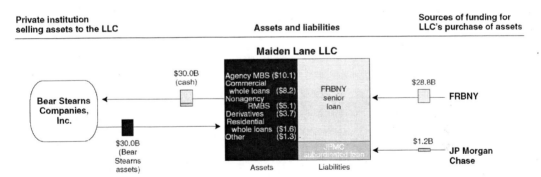

Source: GAO analysis of FRBNY information.

Figure 21. Maiden Lane LLC Transaction.

Key Vendors for Maiden Lane LLC

FRBNY used a number of vendors to help manage and administer Maiden Lane LLC. Table 17 lists Maiden Lane LLC vendors that have received more than $1 million in fees.

APPENDIX V. BANK OF AMERICA CORPORATION LENDING COMMITMENT

> **Key observations**
>
> - Authorized under section 13(3) of the Federal Reserve Act of 1913.
> - The Federal Reserve Bank of Richmond (FRBR) agreed to provide a lending commitment as part of a larger package of assistance intended to avert a disorderly failure of Bank of America Corporation (Bank of America).
> - FRBR did not finalize an agreement with Bank of America Corporation to provide this lending commitment. As part of the agreement to terminate the agreement-in-principle, Bank of America paid a $57 million fee to FRBR in compensation for out-of-pocket expenses and commitment fees.

Source: GAO summary of Board of Governors of the Federal Reserve System documents and data.

Background

On January 15, 2009, the Board of Governors of the Federal Reserve System (Federal Reserve Board) authorized, under section 13(3) of the Federal Reserve Act of 1913, the Federal Reserve Bank of Richmond (FRBR) to provide a lending commitment to Bank of America Corporation (Bank of America). As in the Citigroup Inc. (Citigroup) case, the Federal Reserve Board authorized this assistance as part of a coordinated effort with the Department of the Treasury (Treasury) and the Federal Deposit Insurance Corporation (FDIC) to assist an institution determined to be systemically important. The circumstances surrounding the agencies' decision to provide this arrangement for Bank of America, however, were somewhat different and were the subject of congressional hearings.[147] While the Citigroup loss sharing agreement emerged during a weekend over which the agencies attempted to avert an impending failure of the firm, the agencies' discussions with Bank of America about a possible similar arrangement occurred over several weeks during which Bank of America was not facing imminent failure. According to Federal Reserve Board officials, possible assistance for Bank of America was first discussed in late December 2008 when Bank of America management raised concerns about the financial impact of completing the merger with Merrill Lynch & Co. (Merrill Lynch). Following the January 1, 2009, completion of Bank of America's acquisition of Merrill Lynch, the Federal Reserve Board and the other agencies agreed to provide a loss sharing agreement on selected Merrill Lynch assets to assure markets that unusually large losses on these assets would not destabilize Bank of America. In September 2009, the agencies and FRBR agreed to terminate the loss sharing agreement with Bank of America. As part of the agreement to terminate the agreement-in-principle, Bank of America paid a $57 million fee to FRBR in compensation for out-of-pocket expenses incurred by FRBR and an amount equal to the commitment fees required by the agreement.

Under the agreement-in-principle announced on January 16, 2009, Treasury and FDIC agreed to share in losses on a pool of up to $118 billion pool of assets if they exceeded $10 billion and FRBR agreed to lend against the residual value of this asset pool if losses on these assets exceeded $18 billion. Bank of America agreed to absorb the first $10 billion in cash losses plus 10 percent of any remaining losses incurred. Ninety percent of covered asset losses exceeding $10 billion would be borne by Treasury and FDIC, with maximum guarantee payments capped at $10 billion.[148] Based on analyses by an outside vendor, FRBR determined that it would be unlikely that losses on the Bank of America "ring-fence" assets would exceed the level above which FRBR would be obligated to provide a loan.

Federal Reserve Board staff we spoke with cited two factors that influenced the termination of the agreement-in-principle with Bank of America. First, according to Federal Reserve Board staff, while the Citigroup loss sharing agreement covered only cash losses (such as losses arising from the sale of an asset at a loss), Bank of America requested that its agreement cover mark-to-market losses, which would include accounting losses arising from changes in the market value of the assets. Federal Reserve Board staff said the U.S. government agencies were unwilling to provide protection against such losses and thought making payments to Bank of America based on temporary accounting losses that could reverse if asset prices recovered would be inappropriate. According to Federal Reserve Board staff, the lack of protection on mark-to-market losses made the loss-sharing agreement less appealing to Bank of America. Second, according to Federal Reserve Board staff, because both Federal Reserve System staff and Bank of America Corporation were involved in the Supervisory Capital Assessment Program (SCAP), they agreed to delay negotiations to finalize the loss-sharing agreement. As discussed in detail in a September 2010 report, the purpose of SCAP, as implemented by the Federal Reserve Board and other federal banking regulators, was to determine through a stress test whether the largest 19 U.S. bank holding companies, including Bank of America, had enough capital for the next 2 years (2009–2010) to support their lending activities and survive a second similar economic shock.[149] According to Federal Reserve Board staff, based on the results of the SCAP exercise, Bank of America determined that the loss sharing agreement would not provide enough value to move forward with finalizing an agreement. The Federal Reserve Board agreed with this assessment and began negotiations to terminate the agreement-in-principle.

Table 18. Vendors for Bank of America Lending Commitment that Earned Fees Greater than $1 Million, 2008–2010

Vendor	Services provided	Contract date	Awarded competitively?	Total fees paid (2008–2010)
Pacific Investment Management Company LLC	Valuation services	1/9/2009	No	$12,025,000
Ernst & Young	Due Diligence	1/16/2009	No	$10,593,795

Source: GAO presentation of FRBR information.

Key Vendors for Bank of America Lending Commitment

The key vendors for the Bank of America lending commitment are listed in table 18.

APPENDIX VI. CITIGROUP INC. LENDING COMMITMENT

Key observations
• Authorized under section 13(3) of the Federal Reserve Act of 1913. • The Federal Reserve Bank of New York (FRBNY) provided a lending commitment as part of a larger package of assistance intended to avert a disorderly failure of Citigroup Inc. (Citigroup). • FRBNY did not lend to Citigroup under this agreement and received a $50 million fee from Citigroup following termination of the agreement in December 2009.

Source: GAO summary of Board of Governors of the Federal Reserve System documents and data.

Background

On November 23, 2008, the Board of Governors of the Federal Reserve System (Federal Reserve Board) authorized the Federal Reserve Bank of New York (FRBNY) to lend to Citigroup Inc. (Citigroup), if necessary, under section 13(3) of the Federal Reserve Act of 1913. This lending commitment was approved as part of a package of coordinated actions by the Department of the Treasury (Treasury), the Federal Deposit Insurance Corporation (FDIC), and the Federal Reserve Board to avert a disorderly failure of Citigroup. This package of assistance to Citigroup included an additional $20 billion of capital from Treasury's Troubled Asset Relief Program and a loss sharing agreement intended to assure market participants that Citigroup would not fail in the event of larger-than-expected losses on certain of its assets. On December 23, 2009, Citigroup announced that it had entered into an agreement with FDIC, FRBNY, and Treasury to terminate the loss sharing agreement. As part of the termination agreement, Citigroup agreed to pay a $50 million termination fee to FRBNY. FRBNY did not make any loans to Citigroup under the loss-sharing agreement.

As discussed in our April 2010 report on Treasury's use of the systemic risk determination, Treasury, FDIC, and the Federal Reserve Board said they provided emergency assistance to Citigroup because they were concerned that a failure of a firm of Citigroup's size and interconnectedness would have systemic implications.[150] As of September 30, 2008, Citigroup was the second largest banking organization in the United States, with total consolidated assets of approximately $2 trillion.

Figure 22 illustrates the structure of the loss sharing agreement with Citigroup. Under the final agreement executed on January 15, 2009, Treasury and FDIC agreed to share in losses on a $301 billion pool of Citigroup assets if they exceeded pre-set thresholds and FRBNY agreed to lend against the residual value of this asset pool if losses on these assets exceeded the limits on loss sharing by Treasury and FDIC. Specifically, Citigroup agreed to absorb the first $39.5 billion in cash losses plus 10 percent of any remaining losses incurred. Ninety percent of covered asset losses exceeding $39.5 billion would be borne by Treasury and FDIC, with maximum guarantee payments capped at $5 billion and $10 billion, respectively.[151] Based on stress analyses by an outside vendor, FRBNY determined that it would be unlikely that losses on the Citigroup "ring-fenced" assets would exceed $56.17 billion—the level above which FRBNY would be obligated to provide a loan. FRBNY's loan would have been a one-time, all-or-nothing loan secured by a first priority perfected security interest in all of the remaining assets at the time that the loan was triggered. In addition, interest on the loan would have been with recourse to Citigroup and Citigroup would have had an ongoing obligation to pay 10 percent of the losses (with recourse to Citigroup).

At the time, Citigroup was a major supplier of credit in the U.S. and one of the largest holders of bank deposits in the world.

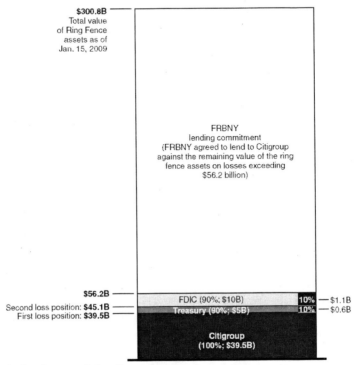

Source: GAO analysis of terms of ring-fence agreement.

Figure 22. Structure of Loss Sharing Agreement with Citigroup.

Table 19. Vendors for Citigroup Inc. Lending Commitment that Earned Fees Greater than $1 Million, 2008–2010

Vendor	Services provided	Contract date	Awarded competitively?	Total fees paid (2008–2010)
BlackRock	Valuation services	12/14/2008	No	$12,700,000
PricewaterhouseCoopers	Valuation services	12/1/2008	No	$7,833,199

Source: GAO presentation of FRBNY information.

Key Vendors for Citigroup Lending

FRBY used vendors to analyze the assets that were identified as part of the ring-fencing effort. The two key vendors were BlackRock and PricewaterhouseCoopers (see table 19).

APPENDIX VII. COMMERCIAL PAPER FUNDING FACILITY

Background

On October 7, 2008, the Board of Governors of the Federal Reserve System (Federal Reserve Board) authorized the creation of the Commercial Paper Funding Facility (CPFF) under section 13(3) of the Federal Reserve Act of 1913 to provide a liquidity backstop to U.S. issuers of commercial paper. CPFF became operational on October 27, 2008, and was operated by the Federal Reserve Bank of New York (FRBNY). CPFF was initially set to expire on April 30, 2009. The Federal Reserve Board authorized extensions of the CPFF to October 30, 2009, and subsequently to February 1, 2010.

Commercial paper is an important source of short-term funding for U.S. financial and nonfinancial businesses. There are two main types of commercial paper: unsecured and asset-backed. Unsecured paper is not backed by collateral, and the credit rating of the issuing institution is a key variable in determining the cost of its issuance. In contrast, asset-backed commercial paper (ABCP) is collateralized by assets and therefore is a secured form of borrowing.

Following the failure of Lehman Brothers Holdings Inc. (Lehman Brothers) in September 2008, commercial paper markets generally ceased to function properly. In the weeks leading up to the announcement of CPFF, the commercial paper markets showed clear signs of strain: the volume of commercial paper outstanding declined, interest rates on longer-term commercial paper increased significantly, and increasing amounts of commercial paper were issued on an overnight basis as money market mutual funds (MMMF) and other investors became reluctant to purchase commercial paper at longer-dated maturities. As discussed in appendix II, which provides an overview of the Asset-Backed Commercial Paper Money Market Mutual Fund Liquidity Facility, during this time, MMMFs faced a surge of redemption demands from investors concerned about losses on presumably safe instruments. The Federal Reserve Board concluded that disruptions in the commercial paper markets, combined with strains in other credit markets, threatened the broader economy, because many large commercial paper issuers provided credit for households and businesses.

By standing ready to purchase eligible commercial paper, CPFF was intended to eliminate much of the risk that commercial paper issuers would be unable to "roll over" their maturing commercial paper obligations—that is, they would be unable to repay maturing commercial paper with a new issue of commercial paper. By reducing this roll-over risk, CPFF was expected to encourage investors to continue or resume their purchases of commercial paper at longer maturities.

Figure 24 illustrates the structure of CPFF. The relatively complex structure reflected the added complication of engaging in market transactions outside FRBNY's traditional operating framework. In contrast to other emergency programs that made direct discount window loans to depository institutions or primary dealers that had been traditional FRBNY counterparties, FRBNY created a special purpose vehicle (CPFF LLC) to facilitate discount window lending to the commercial paper market. FRBNY hired State Street Corporation to perform custodial, accounting, and administrative services. In addition, to execute CPFF transactions, FRBNY relied on primary dealers as transaction agents to coordinate issuance requests brought to the facility. The use of primary dealers as transaction agents leveraged the existing role these dealers played in underwriting, placing, and making markets in the commercial paper market.

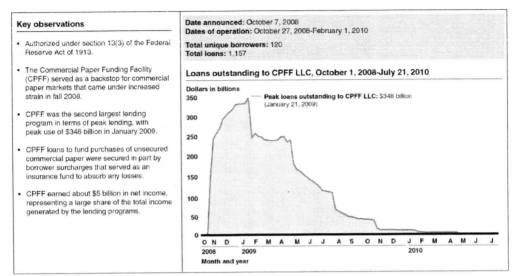

Source: GAO analysis of Board of Governors of the Federal Reserve System documents and data.

Figure 23. Overview of CPFF.

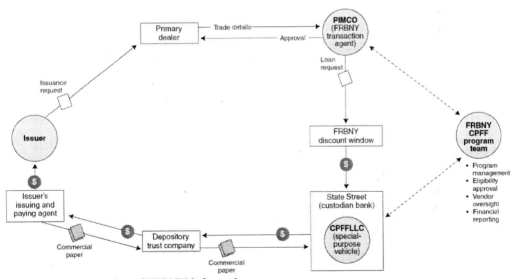

Source: GAO presentation of FRBNY information.

Figure 24. Structure of CPFF.

A typical CPFF transaction included the following steps:

1. An issuer brought a CPFF issuance request to a primary dealer, who then brought this request to FRBNY's transaction agent, Pacific Investment Management Company LLC (PIMCO).

2. PIMCO would review the request and if the issuer met FRBNY's predetermined eligibility requirements, the transaction would be approved.
3. CPFF LLC was authorized to purchase the issuer's commercial paper. Each day, CPFF purchases were matched by a loan from FRBNY's discount window to the custodian, and the custodian bank would transfer the loan amount to CPFF LLC to fund the purchases. CPFF LLC purchased commercial paper through the Depository Trust Company, the market's standard clearing institution.
4. At maturity, the issuer paid the CPFF LLC the loan principal and interest, and the special purpose vehicle (SPV) paid FRBNY the interest on the discount window loan. CPFF LLC retained interest, surcharges, and fees paid in excess of the interest paid on the discount window loan. This excess income was intended to stand ready to absorb potential losses on unsecured paper held by CPFF LLC. As investment manager, PIMCO invested this excess income in permitted investments as directed by FRBNY.

Terms and Conditions for CPFF

Assets Eligible for Purchase

CPFF purchased 3-month U.S. dollar-denominated commercial paper from eligible issuers. Commercial paper (including ABCP) purchased by CPFF was required to be rated not lower than A-1/P-1/F-1 by a major Nationally Recognized Statistical Rating Organization (NRSRO) and if rated by multiple NRSROs was required to have this highest rating from at least two or more major NRSROs.

Issuer Eligibility Requirements

All U.S. issuers (including U.S. issuers with a foreign parent) with eligible unsecured commercial paper or ABCP were eligible for CPFF. The maximum amount a single issuer could have outstanding at CPFF was limited to the greatest amount of U.S. dollar-denominated commercial paper the issuer had had outstanding on any day between January 1 and August 31, 2008. This limit was intended to prevent excessive use of the facility that would be inconsistent with its role as a backstop. On January 23, 2009, the Federal Reserve Board changed the eligibility requirements to prohibit access by ABCP conduits that had been inactive prior to the time CPFF was announced. This change was intended to avoid reviving ABCP conduits that had closed as a result of market discipline.

Table 20 lists the top 25 largest borrowers, which accounted for approximately 88 percent of the commercial paper purchased through CPFF. Total dollar amounts issued through CPFF are aggregated at the level of the parent company for the entities that issued unsecured commercial paper or sponsored ABCP conduits that issued ABCP to CPFF.

Table 20. Top 25 Largest CPFF Borrowers

Dollars in billions

Rank	Issuer of unsecured commercial paper or sponsor of ABCP issuer	ABCP	Unsecured commercial paper	Issuer total	Percent of total CPFF issuance
1	UBS AG (Switzerland)	$0.0	$74.5	$74.5	10.1%
2	American International Group	36.3	24.0	60.2	8.2
3	Dexia SA (Belgium)	0.0	53.5	53.5	7.2
4	Hudson Castle	53.3	0.0	53.3	7.2
5	BSN Holdings (United Kingdom)	42.8	0.0	42.8	5.8
6	The Liberty Hampshire Company	41.4	0.0	41.4	5.6
7	Barclays PLC (United Kingdom)	0.0	38.8	38.8	5.3
8	Royal Bank of Scotland Group PLC (United Kingdom)	24.8	13.7	38.5	5.2
9	Fortis Bank SA/NV (Belgium)	26.9	11.6	38.5	5.2
10	Citigroup Inc.	12.8	19.9	32.7	4.4
11	Natixis (France)	4.7	22.3	27.0	3.7
12	General Electric Co	0.0	16.1	16.1	2.2
13	Ford Credit	15.9	0.0	15.9	2.1
14	Bank of America Corporation	0.0	14.9	14.9	2.0
15	State Street Corporation	14.1	0.0	14.1	1.9
16	GMAC LLC	13.5	0.0	13.5	1.8
17	KBC BANK NV (Belgium)	9.0	2.3	11.3	1.5
18	ING Groep NV (Netherlands)	0.0	10.9	10.9	1.5
19	Dresdner Bank AG (Germany)	5.1	4.9	10.0	1.4
20	Northcross (United Kingdom)	8.6	0.0	8.6	1.2
21	WestLB (Germany)	8.2	0.0	8.2	1.1
22	Merrill Lynch & Co	0.0	8.0	8.0	1.1
23	Allied Irish Bank (Ireland)	0.0	6.6	6.6	0.9
24	Bayerische Motoren Werke AG (Germany)	0.0	6.2	6.2	0.8
25	Handelsbanken (Sweden)	0.0	6.0	6.0	0.8
	All Others	24.9	61.8	86.7	11.8%
Total		$342.3	$395.9	$738.3	100.0%

Source: GAO analysis of Federal Reserve Board data.

Note: In the above figure, total amounts borrowed represent the sum of all loans. Total borrowing is aggregated at the parent company level and generally includes borrowing by branches, agencies, subsidiaries, and sponsored ABCP conduits that we could identify. Total borrowing for each parent company consolidates amounts borrowed by acquired institutions as of the date the acquisition was completed. The country of domicile is shown in parentheses for companies based outside the United States.

Interest Rates and Credit Surcharges

CPFF controlled for changes in short-term interest rates by setting the price of commercial paper issuance to CPFF at a fixed spread above the daily 3-month overnight indexed swap (OIS) rate, a rate that tracks investor expectations about the future federal funds rate. Consistent with market practice, commercial paper issued to CPFF was sold at a discount from face value based on the interest rate. Table 21 summarizes the pricing structure for CPFF. The higher funding costs for ABCP relative to unsecured paper backed by the full faith and credit of the issuer reflected the riskiness and illiquidity of the underlying collateral in ABCP conduits.[152] To secure loans against purchases of unsecured paper, CPFF required issuers of unsecured paper to pay a credit surcharge. FRBNY intended for these surcharges to absorb potential losses and based the level of the surcharge on historical loss rates for highly rated commercial paper. Issuers of unsecured paper did not have to pay a surcharge to CPFF if their paper was guaranteed by the Federal Deposit Insurance Corporation through its Temporary Liquidity Guarantee Program (TLGP).[153]

Registration Fees

To sell commercial paper to CPFF, an issuer was first required to register in advance of the initial issuance. Issuers were required to pay a registration fee of 10 basis points charged on the maximum amount an issuer could sell to CPFF. This fee also served as an insurance premium that could absorb potential losses. The registration process allowed FRBNY to verify eligibility criteria, review the issuer's credit quality, and process the registration fee.

Table 21. Interest rates for CPFF

Rates and fees	Unsecured commercial paper	ABCP
Interest rate	3-month OIS + 100 basis points	3-month OIS + 300 basis points
Credit surcharge	100 basis points	None
All-in-cost	3-month OIS + 200 basis points	3-month OIS + 300 basis points

Source: CPFF program terms and conditions.

Table 22. Vendors for Commercial Paper Funding Facility That Earned Fees Greater than $1 Million

Vendor	Services provided	Contract date	Awarded competitively?	Total fees paid (2008–2010)
PIMCO	Investment manager, transaction agent	10/20/2008	No	$33,608,841
State Street Corporation	Administrator, custodian	10/20/2008	No	$8,809,904

Source: GAO presentation of FRBNY data.

Key Vendors for CPFF

Table 22 lists the key vendors FRBNY used to help administer the CPFF.

APPENDIX VIII. DIRECT MONEY MARKET MUTUAL FUND LENDING FACILITY

Key observations	
• Authorized under section 13(3) of the Federal Reserve Act of 1913. • The Direct Money Market Mutual Fund Liquidity Facility (DMLF) was authorized to help money market mutual funds to provide additional liquidity support following the failure of Lehman Brothers Holdings Inc. • The program's authorization was rescinded on October 10, 2008 and never became operational.	**Date announced:** n/a **Dates of operation:** Never became operational **Total unique borrowers:** n/a **Total loans:** n/a **Loans outstanding under DMLF:** n/a

Source: GAO summary of Board of Governors of the Federal Reserve System documents.

Background

On October 3, 2008, the Board of Governors of the Federal Reserve System (Federal Reserve Board) authorized the creation of the Direct Money Market Mutual Fund Lending Facility (DMLF) under section 13(3) of the Federal Reserve Act of 1913 to provide loans to money market mutual funds (MMMF) to help them address liquidity challenges that emerged following the failure of Lehman Brothers Holdings Inc. in September 2008. Following the launch of the Asset-Backed Commercial Paper Money Market Mutual Fund Liquidity Facility (AMLF) on September 22, 2008, DMLF was approved to provide additional liquidity support to MMMFs facing redemption pressures from their investors and to help prevent forced sales of high-credit quality assets by MMMFs.

However, after consultation with market participants about the program's feasibility, the Federal Reserve Board decided against implementing it. An October 9, 2008, Federal Reserve Board staff memo noted that market participants expressed the view that DMLF could be counterproductive as increased leverage among MMMFs through DMLF borrowing could undermine confidence in the MMMF industry. On October 10, 2008, the Federal Reserve Board rescinded its approval of DMLF and the program never became operational.

If DMLF had been implemented and used, the Federal Reserve Banks of Atlanta and Chicago would have extended DMLF loans to eligible MMMFs against eligible collateral and applied a standard schedule of haircuts. The Federal Reserve Board anticipated that DMLF eligibility would have been limited to 2a-7 MMMFs participating in the Department of Treasury's (Treasury) Temporary Guarantee Program for Money Market Funds.[154] The initial program authorization limited eligible collateral to all U.S. dollar-denominated securities, excluding Treasury or agency securities, rated A-1/P-1 or the equivalent with maturities from 1 to 28 days. DMLF loans would have been extended with recourse to the MMMFs' assets.

APPENDIX IX. DOLLAR SWAP LINES WITH FOREIGN CENTRAL BANKS

Background

In 2007 and 2008, the Federal Open Market Committee (FOMC) authorized the Federal Reserve Bank of New York (FRBNY) to open temporary dollar swap lines with 14 foreign central banks to enhance the ability of these foreign central banks to provide U.S. dollar funding to financial institutions in their jurisdictions. Table 23 lists the dates the FOMC announced swap lines with these central banks. The swap lines expired on February 1, 2010. In May 2010, in response to the reemergence of strains in short-term dollar funding markets abroad, the FOMC reauthorized dollar liquidity swap lines with five foreign central banks through January 2011.[155] On December 21, 2010, the FOMC announced an extension of these lines through August 1, 2011. On June 29, 2011, the FOMC announced an extension of these lines through August 1, 2012.

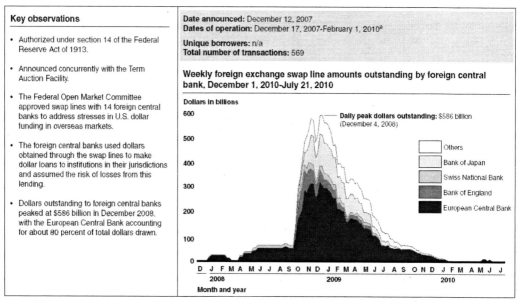

Source: GAO analysis of Board of Governors of the Federal Reserve System documents and data.
[a] As noted in the following section, in May 2010, swap lines were reopened with some foreign central banks.

Figure 25. Overview of Dollar Swap Lines with Foreign Central Banks.

Figure 26 illustrates a typical swap line transaction, in which FRBNY exchanged dollars for the foreign central bank's currency at the prevailing exchange rate and the foreign central bank agreed to buy back its currency (to "unwind" the exchange) at this same exchange rate at an agreed upon future date. The foreign central bank would then lend the dollars to banks in its jurisdiction. Foreign central banks assumed the risk of losses on these dollar loans and paid FRBNY the interest collected on these loans. FRBNY did not pay interest on the foreign currency it received under the swap lines. To avoid difficulties that could arise for foreign central banks in managing the level of their currency reserves, FRBNY agreed not to lend or invest the foreign currency.

Table 23. Announcement Dates for FRBNY's Dollar Swap Lines with Foreign Central Banks

Date	Foreign central bank
December 12, 2007	European Central Bank and Swiss National Bank
September 18, 2008	Bank of Japan, Bank of England, and Bank of Canada
September 24, 2008	Reserve Bank of Australia, Sveriges Riksbank (Sweden), Norges Bank (Norway), Danmarks Nationalbank (Denmark)
October 28, 2008	Reserve Bank of New Zealand
October 29, 2008	Banco Central do Brasil (Brazil), Banco de Mexico, Bank of Korea (South Korea), and Monetary Authority of Singapore

Source: Federal Reserve Board press releases.

The FOMC approved these swap line arrangements to help address challenges in the global market for interbank lending in U.S. dollars. Many foreign banks held U.S. dollar-denominated assets and faced challenges borrowing in dollars to fund these assets. In contrast to U.S. commercial banks, foreign banks did not hold significant U.S. dollar deposits, and as a result, dollar funding strains were particularly acute for many foreign banks. The Board of Governors of the Federal Reserve System (Federal Reserve Board) staff memos recommending that the FOMC approve swap lines noted that continuing strains in dollar funding markets abroad could further exacerbate strains in U.S. funding markets. For example, foreign banks facing difficulties borrowing against U.S. dollar assets may have faced increased pressure to sell these assets at a time of stress, potentially putting downward pressure on prices for these assets. The dollar swap lines allowed foreign central banks to make dollar loans to banks in their jurisdictions without being forced to draw down dollar holdings of foreign exchange reserves or to acquire dollars directly in the foreign exchange market. An FRBNY staff paper noted that the dollar reserves of many foreign central banks at the start of the crisis were smaller than the amounts they borrowed under the swap lines and that efforts by foreign central banks to buy dollars in the market could have crowded out private transactions, making it more difficult for foreign banks to obtain dollars.[156] This paper further noted that the Federal Reserve System (the Federal Reserve Board and Reserve Banks collectively) was in a unique position to provide dollars needed by foreign central banks to provide lender-of-last-resort liquidity to banks in their jurisdictions. The increase in reserves was offset through sales of Treasury securities and increasing incentives for depository institutions to hold excess reserves at FRBNY.

The Federal Reserve Board authorized these swap lines under section 14 of the Federal Reserve Act of 1913. The Federal Reserve Board has interpreted section 14 of the Federal Reserve Act to permit the Federal Reserve Banks to conduct open market operations in foreign exchange markets and to open and maintain accounts in foreign currency with foreign central banks. Section 14 states that "[a]ny Federal reserve bank may…purchase and sell in the open market, at home or abroad, either from or to domestic or foreign banks, firms, corporations, or individuals, cable transfers…"

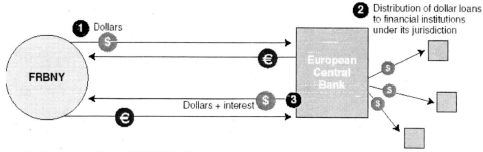

Source: GAO presentation of FRBNY information.

Figure 26. Dollar Swap Line Transaction.

The Federal Reserve Board has interpreted "cable transfers" to mean foreign exchange. Section 14(e) authorizes Reserve Banks to "open and maintain accounts in foreign countries, appoint correspondents, and establish agencies in such countries" and "to open and maintain banking accounts for...foreign banks or bankers." Federal Reserve Board officials noted that the establishment of dollar swap lines with foreign central banks was not unprecedented. In the days following the September 11, 2001, terrorist attacks, the FOMC authorized a similar system of swap lines to help ensure the continued functioning of global financial markets.

Table 24. Foreign Central Banks' Use of Dollar Swap Lines by Aggregate Dollar Transactions

Dollars in billions				
Rank	Central bank	Number of transactions	Aggregate Dollar transactions	Percent of total
1	European Central Bank	271	$8,011	79.7%
2	Bank of England	114	919	9.1
3	Swiss National Bank	81	466	4.6
4	Bank of Japan	35	387	3.9
5	Danmarks Nationalbank (Denmark)	19	73	0.7
6	Sveriges Riksbank (Sweden)	18	67	0.7
7	Reserve Bank of Australia	10	53	0.5
8	Bank of Korea (South Korea)	10	41	0.4
9	Norges Bank (Norway)	8	30	0.3
10	Banco de Mexico	3	10	0.1
Total		569	$10,057	100.0%

Source: GAO analysis of Federal Reserve Board data.
Note: Foreign central banks not included in this table did not draw dollars under their swap line agreement with FRBNY. Aggregate dollar transactions represent the sum of all dollars drawn under the swap line arrangements and have not been adjusted to reflect differences in the terms over which the dollar draws were outstanding.

Use of Dollar Swap Lines by Foreign Central Banks

Table 24 lists the foreign central banks in order of the aggregate amount of dollars drawn under the swap line arrangements with FRBNY. The European Central Bank received the largest amount of dollars under the swap line arrangements. Banco do Brasil, Bank of Canada, Monetary Authority of Singapore, and the Reserve Bank of New Zealand did not draw on their swap lines. The European Central Bank accounted for about 80 percent of total dollars drawn under the swap lines.

APPENDIX X. MONEY MARKET INVESTOR FUNDING FACILITY

Key observations	
• Authorized under section 13(3) of the Federal Reserve Act of 1913.	**Date announced:** October 21, 2008
	Dates of operation: November 24, 2008–October 30, 2009
• The Money Market Investor Funding Facility (MMIFF) was created to provide additional liquidity support to money market mutual funds (MMMF), but was never used.	**Total unique borrowers:** 0
	Total loans: 0
• Through MMIFF, the Federal Reserve Bank of New York (FRBNY) would have extended loans to special purpose vehicles (SPV) created in collaboration with the private sector to purchase eligible financial instruments held by MMMFs.	**MMIFF loans:** n/a
• MMMFs selling assets to an MMIFF SPV would have had to fund 10 percent of the purchase price in the form of a subordinated note issued by the SPV; any initial losses on an SPV's assets would have been absorbed by MMMFs holding the subordinated note.	
• Feedback FRBNY received from MMMFs indicated that they would have accessed MMIFF only under a significant deterioration of market conditions that did not occur during the life of the MMIFF program.	

Source: GAO summary of Board of Governors of the Federal Reserve System documents.

Background

On October 21, 2008, the Board of Governors of the Federal Reserve System (Federal Reserve Board) authorized the Federal Reserve Bank of New York (FRBNY) to work with the private sector to create the Money Market Investor Funding Facility (MMIFF) under section 13(3) of the Federal Reserve Act of 1913 to provide additional liquidity support to money market mutual funds (MMMF). MMIFF became operational on November 24, 2008. Of the Federal Reserve Board's broad-based emergency programs that became operational,

MMIFF was the only program that was never used. MMIFF was initially set to expire on April 30, 2009, but did not close until October 30, 2009.

As discussed in appendix II, which provides an overview of the Asset-Backed Commercial Paper Money Market Mutual Fund Liquidity Facility (AMLF), beginning in mid-September 2008, MMMFs faced considerable liquidity pressure from increased redemption demands from investors. To meet these redemption demands, MMMFs faced pressure to sell assets into stressed markets, and the Federal Reserve Board observed that MMMFs became increasingly reluctant to purchase new debt obligations of financial institutions, particularly at longer-dated maturities. The Federal Reserve Board became concerned that liquidity pressures on MMMFs were exacerbating difficulties for financial institutions in borrowing in short-term debt markets, further impairing these institutions' capacity to meet the credit needs of households and businesses.

MMIFF was intended to complement AMLF by standing ready to purchase a broader range of short-term debt instruments held by MMMFs. AMLF, which began operation in September 2008, financed the purchase of MMMFs' highly rated asset-backed commercial paper (ABCP). In addition to ABCP, MMMFs were significant investors in other short-term debt instruments of financial institutions, such as certificates of deposit, bank notes, and commercial paper. Federal Reserve Board and FRBNY staff noted that the ability of AMLF to address MMMFs' liquidity problems was limited by the amount of eligible ABCP held by MMMFs and that not all MMMFs had significant holdings of eligible ABCP. By allowing MMMFs to sell a broader range of debt instruments at amortized cost—rather than at losses into the markets—MMIFF was intended to reduce the liquidity risks faced by MMMFs and to encourage them to continue or renew purchases of these instruments. FRBNY staff with whom we spoke observed that even if an MMMF did not sell assets through MMIFF, knowing that these assets could be sold to MMIFF if needed provided a form of insurance to MMMFs choosing to continue to hold them.

MMIFF's design featured a relatively complex lending structure intended to facilitate additional liquidity support for MMMFs while building in additional loss protection through a subordinated note feature. Unlike AMLF, which made loans to intermediary borrowers to finance purchases of ABCP, MMIFF created five special purpose vehicles (SPV) that could use FRBNY loans to help finance purchases of eligible assets from MMMFs. MMIFF-eligible assets included short-term debt obligations of 50 financial institutions that FRBNY determined were broadly held by many MMMFs. FRBNY planned to fund 90 percent of each SPV's purchases of eligible MMIFF assets with a senior loan. The remaining 10 percent of MMIFF purchases would have been funded by a subordinated note issued by the MMIFF SPV to the selling MMMF. The first 10 percent of any losses on assets held by a MMIFF SPV would have been absorbed by the subordinated note holders. This would have mitigated some of FRBNY's risk on loans to the SPV. The Federal Reserve Board authorized FRBNY to lend up to $540 billion to the MMIFF SPVs, which could have facilitated the purchase of up to $600 billion of assets from eligible funds.

In contrast to SPVs created by other Federal Reserve Board programs, the MMIFF SPVs were set up and managed by the private sector in collaboration with FRBNY. According to FRBNY staff, JP Morgan Chase & Co. (JPMC), in collaboration with other firms that sponsored large MMMFs, brought the idea for an MMIFF-like facility to FRBNY in early October 2008. FRBNY worked with JPMC to set up the MMIFF SPVs but did not contract directly with JPMC or the firm that managed the MMIFF SPVs. The deployment of multiple

Federal Reserve System

SPVs was intended, in part, to better ensure that MMIFF could continue to provide funding support in the event that one of its SPVs was required to cease purchases.[157]

Because 2a-7 funds could only purchase and hold highly rated debt instruments, the Federal Reserve Board and FRBNY designed MMIFF terms and conditions to help ensure that the subordinated notes issued by each SPV would receive the highest rating from two or more major Nationally Recognized Statistical Rating Organizations (NRSRO). MMIFF SPVs were required to hold any assets purchased until the assets matured, and proceeds from these assets were to be used to repay FRBNY's senior loan and the subordinated note. Minimum yield requirements for assets eligible for purchase and terms for the interest rate to be paid to FRBNY were set to help ensure that SPVs would accumulate sufficient excess income (the positive difference between the yield on purchased assets and interest owed) to absorb potential losses.

MMIFF was never used. Feedback FRBNY received from MMMFs indicated that they viewed MMIFF as a backstop that they would access only in dire circumstances. According to FRBNY, JPMC, as structuring advisor, bore the expenses associated with operating the MMIFF, including payments to the vendors hired by the MMIFF SPVs.

Terms and Conditions for MMIFF

Assets Eligible for Sale through MMIFF

MMIFF SPVs were prepared to purchase U.S. dollar-denominated certificates of deposit, bank notes, and commercial paper issued by selected financial institutions and having a remaining maturity of 7 to 90 days. The selected financial institutions initially included 50 institutions chosen by representatives of the U.S. MMMF industry, according to the Federal

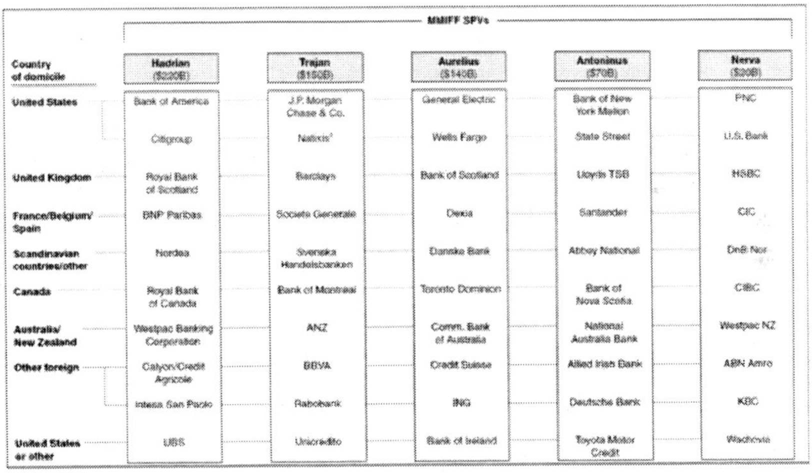

Country of domicile	Hadrian ($220B)	Trajan ($150B)	Aurelius ($140B)	Antoninus ($70B)	Nerva ($20B)
United States	Bank of America	J.P. Morgan Chase & Co.	General Electric	Bank of New York Mellon	PNC
	Citigroup	Natixis[a]	Wells Fargo	State Street	U.S. Bank
United Kingdom	Royal Bank of Scotland	Barclays	Bank of Scotland	Lloyds TSB	HSBC
France/Belgium/Spain	BNP Paribas	Societe Generale	Dexia	Santander	CIC
Scandinavian countries/other	Nordea	Svenska Handelsbanken	Danske Bank	Abbey National	DnB Nor
Canada	Royal Bank of Canada	Bank of Montreal	Toronto Dominion	Bank of Nova Scotia	CIBC
Australia/New Zealand	Westpac Banking Corporation	ANZ	Comm. Bank of Australia	National Australia Bank	Westpac NZ
Other foreign	Calyon/Credit Agricole	BBVA	Credit Suisse	Allied Irish Bank	ABN Amro
	Intesa San Paolo	Rabobank	ING	Deutsche Bank	KBC
United States or other	UBS	Unicredito	Bank of Ireland	Toyota Motor Credit	Wachovia

Source: GAO presentation of FRBNY program documentation for MMIFF.

Note: According to FRBNY staff, a few of the 50 institutions initially selected experienced ratings downgrades that made their short-term debt obligations ineligible for MMIFF purchase. In January 2009, following a ratings downgrade of Dexia, FRBNY approved the suggestion by JPMC, the MMIFF referral agent, to replace Dexia with Bank of Tokyo Mitsubishi. According to FRBNY staff, the other downgraded institutions were not replaced because it appeared unnecessary given the projection for limited use of the MMIFF.

[a]Natixis is based in France.

Figure 27. Five MMIFF SPVs and Approved Financial Institutions for Each.

Reserve Board and FRBNY. MMIFF program terms required each of the 50 financial institutions to maintain the highest short-term debt rating (A-1/P-1/F-1) from two or more major NRSROs. As illustrated in figure 27, each of the five SPVs was authorized to purchase obligations of 10 of the 50 designated institutions. FRBNY staff said that the 50 institutions selected were determined to be among the largest issuers of MMIFF-eligible assets held by MMMFs. In addition, FRBNY staff said that the selected group reflected the need to achieve geographical diversification in each of the five SPVs that could help reduce the risk of the pool of assets held by any given SPV. In addition, to be eligible for MMIFF purchase, assets had to meet minimum yield requirements set by the Federal Reserve Board to help ensure that SPVs would earn a sufficient spread between assets purchased and the interest rate on the senior loan to FRBNY.

Seller Eligibility

Initially, all U.S. 2a-7 MMMFs were eligible to sell assets through MMIFF.[158] On January 7, 2009, the Federal Reserve Board expanded MMIFF eligibility to include other funds that were managed or owned by a U.S. bank, insurance company, pension fund, trust company, Securities and Exchange Commission-registered investment advisor, or a U.S. state- or local-government entity.[159]

Concentration Limits

At the time of an MMIFF SPV's purchase from an eligible investor of a debt instrument issued by 1 of the 50 financial institutions, debt instruments issued by that financial institution could not exceed 15 percent of the assets of the SPV (except during the initial ramp-up period, when the limit was 20 percent).

Interest Rates

FRBNY committed to lend to the MMIFF SPVs at the primary credit rate in effect at the time of the loan. To protect subordinated note holders from increases in the primary credit rate to be paid to FRBNY, which could reduce SPV income available to pay the subordinated note holders, FRBNY agreed to subordinate its right to receive certain amounts of potential interest payments if the primary credit rate rose above specified levels. The interest rate earned by subordinated note holders was expected to be at least 25 basis points below the interest rate on the assets they sold to the MMIFF SPV.

Accumulated Interest Income

Accumulated interest income remaining after full repayment of the senior loan and subordinated note would be distributed to subordinated note holders and FRBNY. According to MMIFF terms and conditions, a small fixed amount of any accumulated income remaining in a MMIFF SPV after completion of a wind-down process would have been allocated proportionally among funds that sold assets to the SPVs. FRBNY would have received any remaining income.

Program Structure

Figure 28 illustrates the structure of MMIFF. Five SPVs were created as limited liability companies incorporated in Delaware to purchase eligible money market instruments from eligible investors using financing from FRBNY and from the issuance of ABCP. JPMC, the referral agent, stood ready to solicit sales of eligible assets from eligible sellers. These assets would then have been purchased at amortized cost using a loan from FRBNY for 90 percent of the purchase price. For the other 10 percent, the SPV would have issued to the seller of the eligible asset subordinated ABCP equal to 10 percent of the asset's purchase price.

Key Vendors for MMIFF

All of the MMIFF service providers were hired directly by the SPVs. FRBNY engaged a single law firm to act as deal counsel, but otherwise did not participate in any direct hiring of vendors for this program. However, FRBNY reviewed all relevant contracts to ensure their interests as the senior lender were protected.

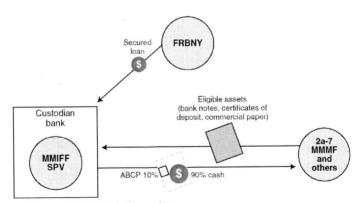

Source: GAO presentation of FRBNY information.

Figure 28. Structure of the MMIFF.

APPENDIX XI. PRIMARY DEALER CREDIT FACILITY AND CREDIT EXTENSIONS FOR AFFILIATES OF PRIMARY DEALERS

Background

On March 16, 2008, the Board of Governors of the Federal Reserve System (Federal Reserve Board) authorized the creation of the Primary Dealer Credit Facility (PDCF) under section 13(3) of the Federal Reserve Act of 1913 to provide overnight secured loans to primary dealers facing strains in the repurchase agreement markets. PDCF was initially set to expire on January 30, 2009. The Federal Reserve Board authorized three extensions of the PDCF in response to market conditions. PDCF was administered by the Federal Reserve Bank of New York (FRBNY) with operational assistance provided by the Federal Reserve Banks of Atlanta and Chicago. PDCF expired on February 1, 2010.

On March 11, 2008, the Federal Reserve Board had announced the creation of the Term Securities Lending Facility (TSLF) to ease these strains, but the first TSLF auction would not be held until March 27, 2008. Challenges obtaining overnight secured funding had contributed to the near failure of Bear Stearns in the preceding days, and Federal Reserve Board officials were concerned that other primary dealers could face runs on their liquidity. Federal Reserve Board and FRBNY staff worked over the weekend of March 15–16, 2008, to prepare PDCF for its launch on Monday, March 17, 2008.

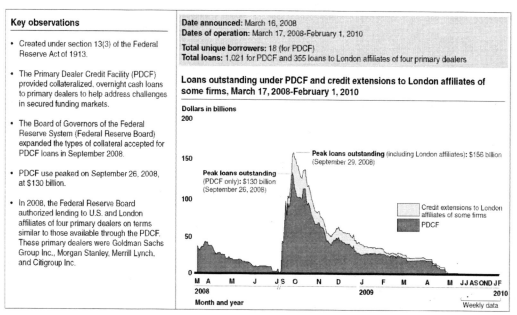

Source: GAO analysis of Board of Governors of the Federal Reserve System documents and data.

Figure 29. Overview of PDCF and Credit Extensions for Affiliates of Primary Dealers.

Although PDCF and TSLF were both created to help address funding challenges faced by the primary dealers, the programs had key differences, including the following:

- PDCF provided cash loans rather than loans of Treasury securities, and it provided them against a broader range of collateral than those eligible for TSLF. By providing funding support for a broader range of collateral, PDCF was intended to further reduce the potential that primary dealers might be forced to sell assets into stressed markets to meet their funding needs.
- While TSLF held scheduled weekly auctions, PDCF was a standing facility that primary dealers could access as needed.
- While TSLF loaned Treasury securities for terms of about 1 month, PDCF made overnight loans. Because primary dealers relied on overnight secured funding through the repurchase agreements markets, they were vulnerable to potential runs on their liquidity if they were unable to borrow in those markets, as illustrated by the rapid deterioration in Bear Stearns' liquidity position. The Federal Reserve Board intended for PDCF to provide assurance to market participants that primary dealers would be able to obtain overnight funding against PDCF-eligible collateral.

As with TSLF, FRBNY used the tri-party repurchase agreement system in relying on the two major clearing banks—JP Morgan Chase & Co. and Bank of New York Mellon—to perform collateral custody and valuation services for PDCF loans.

Figure 30 illustrates the clearing bank's role in a PDCF transaction. To request a PDCF loan, a primary dealer typically communicated its loan request to its clearing bank before 5 p.m. on business days. The clearing bank was responsible for pricing the collateral pledged by the primary dealer and verifying that a sufficient amount of eligible collateral had been pledged to secure the requested loan. Once FRBNY received notice that a sufficient amount of eligible collateral was assigned to its account, it transferred the loan amount to the clearing bank for credit to the primary dealer. The clearing banks priced pledged collateral using a range of pricing services, and applied haircuts to the collateral based on a schedule set by FRBNY.

In September 2008, strains in credit markets intensified following the bankruptcy of Lehman Brothers Inc., the parent company of one of the primary dealers. On September 14, 2008, to help alleviate these strains, the Federal Reserve Board expanded the types of collateral eligible for PDCF beyond investment grade securities to include all collateral eligible for tri-party repurchase agreements through one of the two major clearing banks. New types of collateral that became eligible for PDCF included noninvestment grade bonds and equities.

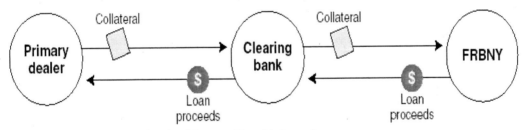

Source: GAO presentation of Federal Reserve Board information.

Figure 30. Structure of the PDCF.

On September 21, 2008, the Federal Reserve Board announced that it would extend credit on terms similar to those of PDCF to the U.S. and London broker-dealer subsidiaries of Merrill Lynch & Co. (Merrill Lynch), Goldman Sachs Group Inc., and Morgan Stanley to provide support to these subsidiaries as they became part of bank holding companies that would be regulated by the Federal Reserve System. In November 2008, as part of a package of federal government assistance to stabilize Citigroup Inc. (Citigroup), the Federal Reserve Board authorized an extension of PDCF assistance to the London affiliate of Citigroup's primary dealer. While the Federal Reserve Board considered these credit extensions to be separate from the PDCF program, the interest rates and collateral requirements for these loans were based on PDCF program requirements. A key difference was that FRBNY accepted collateral denominated in foreign currencies from the London-based affiliates, and it applied higher haircuts to this foreign-currency denominated collateral.

Table 25. Largest PDCF Borrowers by Total Dollar Amount of Loans

Dollars in billions			
Rank	Primary dealer	Total PDCF loans	Percent of total
1	Citigroup Global Markets Inc.	$1,756.8	23.8%
2	Morgan Stanley & Co. Inc.	1,364.4	18.5
3	Merrill Lynch Government Securities Inc.	1,281.8	17.3
4	Bear Stearns & Co., Inc.	850.8	11.5
5	Banc of America Securities LLC	845.6	11.4
6	Goldman Sachs & Co.	433.6	5.9
7	Barclays Capital Inc.	410.4	5.6
8	J. P. Morgan Securities Inc.	112.3	1.5
9	Lehman Brothers Inc.	83.3	1.1
10	Countrywide Financial Corporation	75.6	1.0
11	BNP Paribas Securities Corp.	66.4	0.9
12	Mizuho Securities USA Inc.	42.3	0.6
13	UBS Securities LLC.	35.4	0.5
14	Cantor Fitzgerald & Co.	28.1	0.4
15	Credit Suisse Securities (USA) LLC	1.5	0.0
16	Deutsche Bank Securities Inc.	0.5	0.0
17	Daiwa Securities America Inc.	0.4	0.0
18	Dresdner Kleinwort Securities LLC	0.1	0.0
Total		$7,389.4	100.0%

Source: GAO analysis of Federal Reserve Board data.

Note: Total borrowing for JP Morgan Securities reflects consolidation of total borrowing by Bear, Stearns & Co., Inc. after the acquisition was completed. Amount shown for Bank of America Corporation reflects consolidation of total borrowing by Merrill Lynch and Countrywide following the completion of those acquisitions.

Table 26. Total Amounts Borrowed by London-based Affiliates of Primary Dealers

Dollars in billions			
	Primary dealer	Loans to London affiliates	Percent of total
1	Morgan Stanley & Co. Inc.	$548.2	35.1%
2	Merrill Lynch & Co.	493.1	31.6%
3	Citigroup Global Markets Inc.	263.5	16.9%
4	Goldman Sachs & Co.	155.7	10.0%
5	Banc of America Securities LLC	101.2	6.5%
Total		**$1,561.6**	**100.0%**

Source: GAO analysis of Federal Reserve Board data.

Note: Amount shown for Banc of America Securities reflects borrowings by the London affiliate of Merrill Lynch Government Securities subsequent to completion of Bank of America Corporation's acquisition of Merrill Lynch.

Terms and Conditions for PDCF

Borrower Eligibility

PDCF was available only to the primary dealers.

Table 25 ranks the primary dealers by the total dollar amount of their borrowing through PDCF. The largest five borrowers accounted for approximately 82.5 percent of the total dollar amount of PDCF loans.

As discussed above, the Federal Reserve Board authorized FRBNY to extend credit to the London broker-dealer affiliates of four primary dealers. Table 26 lists the total borrowings by these affiliates.

Term to Maturity for Loans

PDCF made overnight cash loans. FRBNY disbursed PDCF loan proceeds to the clearing banks on the evening of the loan request and the transactions were unwound the following morning when the clearing bank would return the cash to FRBNY's account and the collateral to the borrowing primary dealers' accounts.

Collateral Eligibility

Initially, the Federal Reserve Board restricted eligible collateral for PDCF to collateral eligible for open-market operations as well as investment-grade corporate securities, municipal securities, and asset-backed securities, including mortgage-backed securities. In September 2008, the Federal Reserve Board expanded the set of eligible collateral to match closely all of the types of instruments that could be pledged in the tri-party repurchase agreement system, including noninvestment grade securities and equities.

Loan Size

The Federal Reserve Board did not impose a borrowing limit that applied to each individual primary dealer. The total amount a primary dealer could borrow from PDCF was limited by the amount of haircut-adjusted eligible collateral it had pledged to its clearing bank.

Interest Rate

The interest rate on PDCF loans was equal to the primary credit rate, the interest rate the Reserve Banks charged on discount window loans to depository institutions through its primary credit program.

Frequency-Based Fee

FRBNY charged a frequency-based fee to dealers who accessed the facility on more than 45 business days out of 180 business days. The frequency fee increased according to the following schedule:

- No fee, loans granted on 45 days or less during the first 180 days of the program.
- 10 basis points, annualized rate, 46–90 days.
- 20 basis points, annualized rate, 91–135 days.
- 40 basis points, annualized rate, 136–180 days.

Recourse

PDCF loans were made with recourse beyond the pledged collateral to the primary dealer's other assets.

APPENDIX XII. TERM ASSET-BACKED SECURITIES LOAN FACILITY

Background

On November 24, 2008, the Board of Governors of the Federal Reserve System (Federal Reserve Board) authorized the creation of the Term Asset-Backed Securities Loan Facility (TALF) under section 13(3) of the Federal Reserve Act of 1913 to increase credit availability and support economic activity by facilitating renewed issuance in securitization markets. TALF became operational on March 17, 2009, and was operated by the Federal Reserve Bank of New York (FRBNY). TALF was initially set to expire on December 31, 2009. The Federal Reserve Board authorized one extension of TALF to allow lending against newly issued asset-backed securities (ABS) and legacy commercial mortgage-backed securities (CMBS) through March 31, 2010, and lending against newly issued CMBS through June 30, 2010.

Securitization is a process by which similar debt instruments—such as loans, leases, or receivables—are aggregated into pools, and interest-bearing securities backed by such pools are then sold to investors. These ABS provide a source of liquidity for consumers and small businesses because financial institutions can take assets that they would otherwise hold on their balance sheets, sell them as securities, and use the proceeds to originate new loans, among other purposes.

During the recent financial crisis, the value of many ABS dropped precipitously, bringing originations in the securitization markets to a virtual halt. Problems in the securitization markets threatened to make accessing the credit households and small businesses needed to, among other things, buy cars and homes and expand inventories and operations more difficult. The Federal Reserve Board determined that the continued disruption of the ABS markets, when combined with other ongoing stresses in the credit markets, presented a significant risk to financial stability.

Through TALF, FRBNY provided nonrecourse 3- or 5-year loans to any eligible borrower owning eligible collateral. TALF borrowers served as intermediaries that used TALF loans from FRBNY to purchase ABS, which served as collateral for TALF loans. Borrowers requested TALF loans through primary dealers and a few other firms that served as TALF agents. To increase the support that TALF borrowers could provide to the securitization markets, the Federal Reserve Board set borrower eligibility requirements to permit broad participation by U.S. entities. TALF loans were made without recourse to borrowers' assets beyond the ABS collateral.[160] TALF contained multiple layers of loss protection:

- First, the Federal Reserve Board required TALF collateral to be rated AAA or its equivalent by two of the rating agencies that it deemed eligible to provide credit ratings for TALF.[161] The rating requirement helped to ensure that the securities TALF accepted as collateral presented minimal credit risks. Due diligence performed

on securities to be purchased served as another pillar of loss protection. FRBNY, with the support of vendors, reviewed the credit risks related to individual ABS FRBNY might consider accepting as TALF collateral.[162]
- Second, the Federal Reserve Board required TALF loans to be overcollateralized through haircut requirements. These haircut requirements determined the amount of a TALF borrower's equity in the ABS collateral. This equity represented the amount of money that a TALF borrower would lose by surrendering the collateral and not repaying the loan.

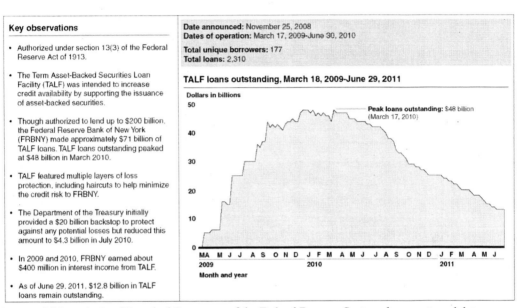

Source: GAO analysis of Board of Governors of the Federal Reserve System documents and data.

Figure 31. Overview of TALF.

- Third, a special purpose vehicle created by FRBNY—TALF LLC—received a portion of the interest income earned by FRBNY on TALF loans and if a TALF borrower chose to not repay its loan, this accumulated excess interest income could be used to purchase collateral surrendered by the borrower.
- Finally, if the excess interest income accumulated in TALF LLC was insufficient to purchase the surrendered collateral, the Department of the Treasury (Treasury) initially committed to lend up to $20 billion of Troubled Asset Relief Program funds to TALF LLC for any such purchases. The Federal Reserve Board authorized FRBNY to lend up to $180 billion for any purchases exceeding this maximum TARP commitment.[163] Both loans would be secured by the assets of TALF LLC, and FRBNY's loan, if made, would be senior to Treasury's loan.[164]

Terms and Conditions for TALF

Borrower Eligibility Requirements

TALF was open to any eligible U.S. company that owned eligible collateral. Eligible TALF borrowers included a broad range of institutions ranging from depository institutions to U.S.-based investment funds. Federal Reserve Board officials told us that broad participation in TALF would facilitate the program goal of encouraging the flow of credit to consumers and small businesses. To prevent participation by borrowers that might pose fraud or reputational risk, FRBNY required all prospective TALF borrowers to approach the program through one of the primary dealers or other firms that acted as TALF agents.[165] FRBNY directed TALF agents to conduct due diligence on prospective TALF borrowing institutions and "material investors" in these institutions.[166] While TALF eligibility rules allowed participation by U.S.-domiciled institutions with foreign investors, it prohibited participation by entities controlled by a foreign government.

Table 27 lists the top 20 largest TALF borrowers (aggregated at the level of the fund family), which accounted for more than 75 percent of TALF loans.

Eligible Collateral Assets Classes

To be eligible for TALF, ABS had to have a long-term credit rating in the highest investment-grade rating category (for example, AAA) from two or more nationally recognized statistical rating organizations. All or substantially all of the credit exposure underlying eligible ABS must have been exposure to U.S.-domiciled obligors. TALF-eligible collateral included U.S. dollar-denominated ABS with one of the following underlying credit exposures:

- auto loans,
- student loans,
- credit card loans,
- equipment loans,
- "floorplan" loans,
- insurance premium finance loans,
- small business loans fully guaranteed as to principal and interest by the U.S. Small Business Administration,
- receivables related to residential mortgage servicing advances (servicing advance receivables), or
- commercial mortgage loans.

Interest Rates

Interest rates for TALF loans were either fixed or floating and varied according to the collateral securing the loan, as determined by FRBNY. For example, the interest rate on loans secured by certain fixed-rate ABS, other than SBA and student loan-related ABS, was 100 basis points over the one-year LIBOR swap rate for securities with a weighted average life less than one year. As another example, TALF loans secured by ABS backed by federally guaranteed student loans had an interest rate of 50 basis points over one-month LIBOR.

Table 27. Top 20 Largest TALF Borrowers

Rank	Asset management parent or borrowing entity	Total TALF loans	Percent of total
1	Morgan Stanley	$9.3	13.0%
2	PIMCO	7.3	10.2
3	California Public Employees' Retirement System	5.4	7.6
4	Arrowpoint Capital	4.0	5.7
5	Angelo Gordon & Co.	$3.7	5.2%
6	Metropolitan West Asset Management, LLC	3.1	4.4
7	Belstar Group	2.8	4.0
8	Wexford Capital	2.8	4.0
9	BlackRock, Inc.	2.8	3.9
10	AllianceBernstein	1.7	2.5
11	One William Street Capital	1.7	2.4
12	Seer Capital	1.3	1.9
13	Prudential Financial Inc.	1.2	1.6
14	Ladder Capital	1.1	1.6
15	Apollo Global Management, LLC	1.1	1.6
16	Teachers Insurance and Annuity Association of America	1.1	1.6
17	OppenheimerFunds, Inc.	1.1	1.5
18	Magnetar Capital LLC	1.1	1.5
19	Atlantic Asset Management, LLC	1.0	1.4
20	Treesdale Partners, LLC	0.9	1.3
	All Others	16.5	23.2
Total		**$71.1**	**100.0%**

Source: GAO analysis of Federal Reserve Board data.

Note: In this table, TALF loans are aggregated across multiple entities for the following companies: Pacific Investment Management Company LLC (PIMCO), Arrowpoint Capital, Belstar Group, BlackRock Inc., AllianceBernstein, Seer Capital, and Ladder Capital. This table aggregates loans only for borrowing entities bearing the name of the same investment fund manager. Morgan Stanley funds include TALF borrowing by funds managed by FrontPoint LLC, which was owned by Morgan Stanley at the time TALF operated.

Haircuts

FRBNY officials said that TALF haircuts were designed to approximate multiples of stressed historical impairment rates for ABS. Table 28 summarizes the haircuts for TALF loans.

Administrative Fees

FRBNY did not charge a registration fee to use TALF although it did charge an administrative fee equal to 10 basis points of the loan amount for nonmortgaged-backed ABS collateral and 20 basis points for CMBS collateral.

Table 28. TALF Haircuts by Asset Class

Sector	Subsector	0 to less than 1	1 to less than 2	2 to less than 3	3 to less than 4	4 to less than 5	5 to less than 6	6 to less than 7
Auto	Prime retail lease	10%	11%	12%	13%	14%	-	-
	Prime retail loan	6	7	8	9	10	-	-
	Subprime retail loan	9	10	11	12	13	-	-
	Motorcycle or other recreational vehicles	7	8	9	10	11	-	-
	Commercial and government fleets	9	10	11	12	13	-	-
	Rental fleets	12	13	14	15	16	-	-
Credit Card	Prime	5	5	6	7	8	-	-
	Subprime	6	7	8	9	10	-	-
Equipment	Loans and leases	5	6	7	8	9	-	-
Floor plan	Auto	12	13	14	15	16	-	-
	Nonauto	11	12	13	14	15	-	-
Premium finance	Property and casualty	5	6	7	8	9	-	-
Servicing advances	Residential mortgages	12	13	14	15	16	-	-
Small business	SBA loans	5	5	5	5	5	6	6
Student loan	Private	8	9	10	11	12	13	14
	Government guaranteed	5	5	5	5	5	6	6
New-issue CMBSs		15	15	15	15	15	-[a]	-[a]
Legacy CMBSs		15	15	15	15	15	-[b]	-[b]

Source: GAO presentation of information gathered from FRBNY's web site.

Note: For ABSs benefiting from a government guarantee with average lives of 5 years and beyond, haircuts were to increase by 1 percentage point for every 2 additional years (or portion thereof) of average life at or beyond 5 years. For all other ABSs with average lives of 5 years and beyond, haircuts were to increase by 1 percentage point for each additional year (or portion thereof) of average life at or beyond 5 years.

[a] For newly issued CMBSs with average lives beyond 5 years, collateral haircuts were to increase by 1 percentage point of par for each additional year of average life. No newly issued CMBS could have an average life of more than 10 years.

[b] For legacy CMBSs with average lives beyond 5 years, haircuts were to increase by 1 percentage point of par for each additional year of average life. No legacy CMBS could have an average life of more than 10 years.

Key Vendors for TALF

FRBNY used a number of entities to help administer the TALF program:

- TALF agents, which were primary dealers or designated broker-dealers whose responsibilities included conducting due diligence on TALF borrowers and making representations to FRBNY regarding eligibility of TALF borrowers and their collateral, submitting TALF loan requests and supporting documentation to FRBNY and the TALF custodian on behalf of borrowers, delivering administrative fees and collateral from TALF borrowers to FRBNY, and distributing the TALF borrower's share of principal and interest payments paid on the collateral backing the TALF loan.
- The Bank of New York Mellon, which has served as custodian of the program and has been responsible for administering TALF loans, holding and reviewing collateral, collecting payments and administrative fees, disbursing cash flows, maintaining the program's books and records, and assisting other TALF entities with the pricing of collateral.
- Collateral monitors—Trepp LLC and Pacific Investment Management Company LLC (PIMCO)—which checked the pricing and ratings of securities; provided valuation, modeling, reporting, and analytical support; and advised on related matters.
- CW Capital, which provided underwriting advisory services related to certain commercial mortgage loans backing newly issued CMBSs.

Table 29 lists all TALF vendors that received more than $1 million in fees.

Table 29. Vendors for TALF That Earned Fees Greater than $1 Million

Vendor	Services provided	Contract date	Awarded competitively?	Total fees paid (2008–2010)
PIMCO	Collateral monitor	7/23/2009	Yes	$12,567,458
Bank of New York Mellon	Administrator, custodian	3/16/2009	Yes	$3,983,816
Trepp LLC	Collateral Monitor	6/12/2009	Yes	$3,217,941
Sidley Austin	Legal services	4/13/2009	No	$2,696,831
Davis Polk & Wardwell	Legal services	9/16/2008	No	$1,353,911
BlackRock	Collateral monitor	2/16/2010	Yes	$1,250,000

Source: GAO presentation of FRBNY information.

APPENDIX XIII. TERM AUCTION FACILITY

Background

On December 12, 2007, the Board of Governors of the Federal Reserve System (Federal Reserve Board) authorized the creation of the Term Auction Facility (TAF) to address continuing strains in U.S. term interbank lending markets—markets in which banks lend to one another for terms of 1 month or longer. Section 10B of the Federal Reserve Act of 1913 authorizes Reserve Banks to make discount window loans to depository institutions. The Federal Reserve Board revised regulations governing Reserve Bank discount window lending to allow the Reserve Banks to auction TAF loans to depository institutions that were eligible to borrow from the discount window.[167] The first TAF auction was held on December 17, 2007, with subsequent auctions occurring approximately every 2 weeks. The final TAF auction was held on March 8, 2010. The auction amount was determined by the Chairman of the Board of Governors of the Federal Reserve Board and announced before the date of the auction. All Reserve Banks participated in the operation of TAF as lenders to banks in their respective districts.

In late summer 2007, sudden strains in term interbank lending markets emerged primarily due to intensifying investor concerns about commercial banks' actual exposure to various mortgage-related activities. The cost of term interbank funding spiked, and commercial banks increasingly had to resort to borrowing overnight to meet their funding needs. To address these funding pressures, the Federal Reserve Board first lowered the discount rate at the discount window and extended the term at the discount window from overnight to up to 30 days. These funding pressures subsided in October 2007 but worsened in late November 2007, possibly driven in part by a seasonal contraction in the supply of year-end funding.

The Federal Reserve Board authorized TAF as an alternative to the discount window to provide term funding support to depository institutions. In contrast to the traditional discount window program, TAF was designed to auction loans to many eligible institutions at once at an auction-determined interest rate. The interest rate on loans for each TAF auction was determined using a single-price auction format. For each auction, winning bidders would be awarded loans at the same interest rate. To determine the interest rate, or "stop-out rate" for each auction, the Federal Reserve Bank of New York (FRBNY) staff ordered bids from all Reserve Bank districts from the highest to the lowest interest rate. Bids were accepted starting with the highest interest rate submitted, down to successively lower rates, until the total auction amount was allocated or the minimum bid rate for the auction was reached, whichever occurred first.[168] When the total bid amount exceeded the auction amount, institutions that placed bids at or above this stop-out rate received loans at this rate. When the total bid amount was less than the auction amount, all bidding institutions would receive loans at the minimum bid rate.

Federal Reserve Board officials noted that one important advantage of this auction approach was that it could address concerns among eligible borrowers about the perceived stigma of discount window borrowing. Federal Reserve Board officials and other market observers have noted that an institution might be reluctant to borrow from the discount window out of concern that its creditors and other counterparties might become aware of its discount window use and perceive it as a sign of distress. The auction format allowed banks to approach the Reserve Banks collectively rather than individually and obtain funds at an interest rate set by auction rather than at a premium set by the Federal Reserve Board.[169] Additionally, whereas discount window loan funds could be obtained immediately by an institution facing severe funding pressures, TAF borrowers did not receive loan funds until 3 days after the auction.

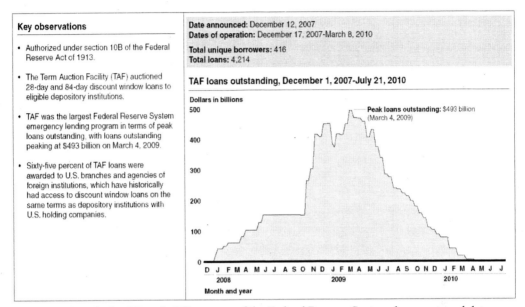

Source: GAO analysis of Board of Governors of the Federal Reserve System documents and data.

Figure 32. Overview of TAF.

Another important advantage of TAF relative to encouraging greater use of the discount window was that the Federal Reserve Board could more easily control the impact of auctioned funds on monetary policy. While the Federal Reserve Board could not predict with certainty the demand for discount window loans, it could control the amount of TAF loans provided at each auction. As a result, the Federal Open Market Committee (FOMC) and FRBNY could more easily coordinate monetary policy operations to offset the impact of TAF auctions. For example, to offset the injection of $75 billion of reserves into the financial system in the form of TAF loans, FRBNY could sell $75 billion of Treasury securities through its open market operations. All else equal, the net effect of these two actions would be to have no impact on total reserves.

Terms and Conditions for TAF

Borrower Eligibility

Depository institutions that were eligible for the primary credit discount window program and that were expected to remain so over the TAF loan term were eligible to participate in TAF auctions. Primary credit is a discount window lending program available to depository institutions judged to be in generally sound financial condition. Institutions with a CAMELS or equivalent supervisory rating of 1, 2, or 3 generally are considered eligible for the primary credit program.[170] U.S. branches and agencies of foreign institutions that met TAF eligibility requirements were eligible to participate.

Term to Maturity for Loans

TAF initially auctioned 28-day loans. The Federal Reserve Board authorized TAF auctions of 84-day loans beginning in August 2008 to provide additional funding support at longer maturities.

Maximum and Minimum Bid Amounts

Eligible depository institutions could submit up to two bids in each TAF auction, and the combined dollar amount of these bids could not exceed 10 percent of the total auction amount. U.S. branches and agencies of the same foreign institution could place separate TAF bids, but their combined bid amount for an auction could not exceed 10 percent of the auction amount. The minimum bid amount for TAF initially was $10 million. In February 2008, the minimum bid amount was decreased from $10 million to $5 million to encourage participation by smaller banks.

Minimum Bid Rate

The Federal Reserve Board initially determined the minimum bid rate based on a measure of the average expected overnight federal funds rate over the term of the loans being auctioned. On December 16, 2008, the FOMC lowered its target federal funds rate from 1 percent to a range of between 0 and 0.25 percent. On January 12, 2009, the Federal Reserve Board announced that the minimum bid rate for TAF auctions would be set equal to the interest rate banks earned on excess reserve balances at the Reserve Banks.[171]

Collateral Eligibility

TAF loans were collateralized based on haircut requirements for the discount window program. For TAF loans, Reserve Banks accepted as collateral any assets that were eligible to secure discount window loans. In addition, a depository institution's TAF loans outstanding with terms greater than 28 days could not exceed 75 percent of the value of collateral it had pledged to the discount window. This requirement was intended to help ensure that depository institutions would retain additional capacity to borrow at the discount window in the event of unexpected funding strains.

Recourse

As with traditional discount window loans, TAF loans were made with recourse to the assets of the borrower beyond the assets pledged as collateral. In the event of a default on a recourse loan, the Reserve Bank would have a claim on the borrower's assets that could allow it to recover all or part of any shortfall arising from the liquidation of the borrower's collateral.

Vendors and Third Parties

The Reserve Banks did not use vendors or third parties for TAF.

TAF Auction Trends

Figure 33 illustrates the bid coverage ratio for all TAF auctions. Bid coverage ratio refers to the ratio of the aggregate bid amount to the auction amount and indicates the level of demand for TAF loans relative to the amount of TAF loans offered at each auction. From December 2007 through September 2008, the bid coverage ratio was more than 100 percent for all TAF auctions, indicating that demand for TAF loans exceeded the amounts auctioned. The Federal Reserve Board increased the TAF auction amount to $150 billion for the October 6, 2008 auction and kept the auction amount at this level until July 13, 2009, when it reduced it to $125 billion. As shown by the blue line in the figure, the level of demand for TAF loans fluctuated from October 2008 through the end of the program and all TAF auctions during this period were not well subscribed, with total bid amounts below the auction amount. For auctions during this period, all bidders received loans at the minimum bid rate rather than at a competitively determined rate.

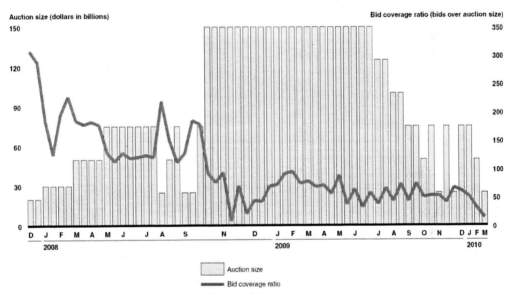

Source: GAO analysis of Federal Reserve System data.

Figure 33. Bid Coverage Ratio for TAF Auctions, December 2007–March 2010.

Table 30 lists the 25 largest borrowers (at the parent company level), which accounted for more than 70 percent of the loans made under this program.

Table 30. Top 25 Largest TAF Borrowers at the Parent Company Level

Dollars in billions			
	Parent company of TAF borrowing institution(s)	Total TAF loans	Percent of total
1	Bank of America Corporation	$280	7.3%
2	Barclays PLC (United Kingdom)	232	6.1
3	Royal Bank of Scotland Group PLC (United Kingdom)	212	5.5
4	Bank of Scotland PLC (United Kingdom)	181	4.7
5	Wells Fargo & Co.	159	4.2
6	Wachovia Corporation	142	3.7
7	Societe Generale SA (France)	124	3.3
8	Dresdner Bank AG (Germany)	123	3.2
9	Citigroup Inc.	110	2.9
10	Bayerische Landesbank (Germany)	108	2.8
11	Dexia AG (Belgium)	105	2.8
12	Norinchukin Bank (Japan)	105	2.8
13	JP Morgan Chase & Co.	99	2.6
14	UniCredit SpA (Italy)	97	2.5
15	Mitsubishi UFJ Financial Group, Inc. (Japan)	84	2.2
16	WestLB AG (Germany)	78	2.1
17	Deutsche Bank AG (Germany)	77	2.0
18	Regions Financial Corporation	72	1.9
19	BNP Paribas SA (France)	64	1.7
20	Sumitomo Mitsui Banking Corporation (Japan)	56	1.5
21	UBS AG (Switzerland)	56	1.5
22	HSH Nordbank AG (Germany)	53	1.4
23	Mizhuo Financial Group, Inc. (Japan)	51	1.3
24	Commerzbank AG	51	1.3
25	Hypo Real Estate Holding AG (Germany)	47	1.2
	All others	1,051	27.5
Total	**$3,818**		**100.0%**

Source: GAO analysis of Federal Reserve Board data.

Note: In the above figure, total amounts borrowed represent the sum of all loans and have not been adjusted to reflect differences in terms to maturity for the loans. Total borrowing is aggregated at the parent company level and generally includes borrowing by branches, agencies, and subsidiaries that we could identify. Total borrowing for each parent company consolidates amounts borrowed by acquired institutions as of the date the acquisition was completed. The country of domicile is shown in parentheses for companies based outside the United States.

Use by Foreign Institutions

Approximately sixty-five percent of the TAF loans were allocated to U.S. branches, agencies, or subsidiaries of foreign institutions in accordance with the auction terms. FRBNY staff identified a few possible reasons for high use by U.S. branches and agencies foreign banks. First, many of them faced liquidity strains arising from the need to bring certain illiquid U.S. dollar assets back on to their balance sheets and could not finance these assets elsewhere. In addition, many of these institutions held U.S.-dollar denominated collateral that could be pledged to TAF but not in their home country.

APPENDIX XIV. TERM SECURITIES LENDING FACILITY

Background

On March 11, 2008, the Board of Governors of the Federal Reserve System (Federal Reserve Board) announced the creation of the Term Securities Lending Facility (TSLF) to help address growing strains in the repurchase agreement markets, which are large, short-term collateralized funding markets that many financial institutions rely on to finance securities. The Federal Reserve Board authorized the Federal Reserve Bank of New York (FRBNY) to operate TSLF under sections 13(3) and 14 of the Federal Reserve Act of 1913. The Federal Reserve Board authorized three extensions of the TSLF in response to market conditions. The program expired on February 1, 2010.

In the repurchase agreement markets, a borrowing institution generally acquires funds by selling securities to a lending institution and agreeing to repurchase the securities after a specified time at a given price. The securities, in effect, are collateral provided by the borrower to the lender. In the event of a borrower's default on the repurchase transaction, the lender would be able to take (and sell) the collateral provided by the borrower. Lenders typically will not provide a loan for the full market value of the posted securities, and the difference between the values of the securities and the loan is called a margin or haircut. This deduction is intended to protect the lenders against a decline in the price of the securities provided as collateral. In early March 2008, the Federal Reserve Board found that repurchase agreement lenders were requiring higher haircuts for loans against a range of less liquid securities and were becoming reluctant to lend against mortgage-related securities. As a result, many financial institutions increasingly had to rely on higher quality collateral, such as Department of the Treasury (Treasury) securities, to obtain cash in these markets, and a shortage of such high-quality collateral emerged.

Through TSLF, primary dealers—a group of securities firms that are traditional counterparties of FRBNY and that were significant participants in the repurchase agreement markets—were able to temporarily exchange illiquid assets for more liquid Treasury securities. The Federal Reserve Board authorized FRBNY to auction up to $200 billion of Treasury securities to primary dealers through competitive auctions that allowed dealers to bid a fee to exchange harder-to-finance collateral for easier-to-finance Treasury securities. These securities then served as high-quality collateral for these dealers to borrow cash against in the repurchase agreement markets. TSLF was intended to promote confidence among lenders and to reduce the need for dealers to sell illiquid assets into the markets, which could have further depressed the prices of these assets and contributed to a downward price spiral.[172]

The Federal Reserve Board and FRBNY structured TSLF as an extension of FRBNY's securities lending program, through which it auctioned overnight loans of Treasury securities to primary dealers.[173] In comparison to the securities lending program, TSLF loaned Treasury securities over a longer term (usually 28 days) and accepted a broader range of collateral. TSLF held separate auctions of Treasury securities against two different schedules of collateral to apply a higher minimum interest rate to riskier assets. Schedule 1 collateral included Treasury securities, agency debt, and agency mortgage-backed securities (MBS) collateral that FRBNY accepted in repurchase agreements as part of its execution of open market operations. Schedule 2 collateral included schedule 1 collateral as well as a broader range of asset types, including highly rated private MBS, against which FRBNY had not traditionally loaned Treasury securities. The Federal Reserve Board determined that providing funding support for private mortgage-backed securities through the schedule 2 auctions fell outside the scope of FRBNY's authority to conduct its securities lending program under section 14 of the Federal Reserve Act. Accordingly, for the first time during this crisis, the Federal Reserve Board invoked section 13(3) of the Federal Reserve Act to authorize the extension of credit to nondepository institutions—in this case, the primary dealers.

For TSLF transactions with participating dealers, FRBNY used a tri-party repurchase agreement system in which both parties to the repurchase agreement must have cash and collateral accounts at the same tri-party agent, which is by definition also a clearing bank. The tri-party agent is responsible for ensuring that collateral pledged is sufficient and meets eligibility requirements, and all parties agree to use collateral prices supplied by the tri-party agent. FRBNY relied on the two clearing banks—JP Morgan Chase & Co. and Bank of New York Mellon—to perform collateral custody and valuation services for TSLF loans. According to FRBNY, using the tri-party system had several advantages. First, the Treasury securities loaned through TSLF remained within the closed tri-party system, helping ensure the safe return of the securities to FRBNY upon maturity of the loan. In addition, the tri-party banks could facilitate the daily repricing and application of haircuts for of a wide range of collateral types. Further, clearing banks were able to facilitate this form of tri-party lending within the tight time constraints.

Figure 35 illustrates the role of the clearing banks in TSLF loan transactions. The clearing banks, which served as the intermediaries between FRBNY and the primary dealers in open market operations, facilitated the clearing, settlement and application of haircuts for TSLF loans. A primary dealer seeking to borrow Treasury securities through TSLF would pledge eligible collateral to its account at its clearing bank. The clearing bank would exchange the Treasury securities and pledged collateral between FRBNY and the primary dealers, transferring collateral to FRBNY's account in amounts needed to collateralize the loan in accordance with TSLF haircut requirements. The loaned Treasury securities remained in the primary dealer's account at the clearing bank, and the eligible collateral remained in an FRBNY account at the clearing bank.

On July 30, 2008, the Federal Reserve Board announced the TSLF Options Program (TOP), in which options to draw shorter-term TSLF loans at future dates were auctioned to the primary dealers. The program was limited to $50 billion and was intended to offer additional liquidity during periods of heightened funding pressures. The Federal Reserve Board approved the establishment of TOP pursuant to its authorization for the TSLF program. The creation of TOP required administrative changes to some TSLF terms, and the Federal Reserve Board did not make a separate authorization for TOP under section 13(3) of the Federal Reserve Act. TOP was suspended effective July 1, 2009.

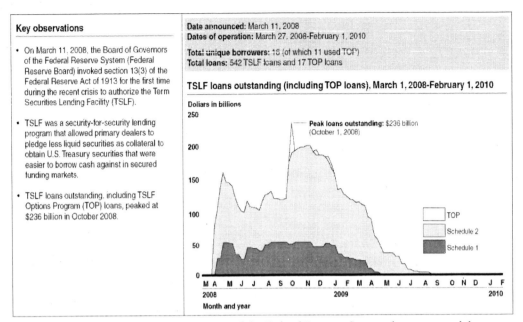

Source: GAO analysis of Board of Governors of the Federal Reserve System documents and data.

Figure 34. Overview of TSLF.

Terms and Conditions for TSLF

Borrower Eligibility

Only primary dealers were eligible to borrow from TSLF.

Table 31 ranks the primary dealers by the total market value (at the time of the loan) of Treasury securities they borrowed through TSLF.

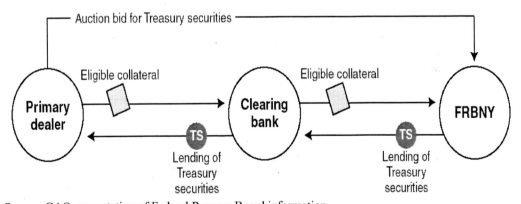

Source: GAO presentation of Federal Reserve Board information.

Figure 35. Structure of the TSLF.

Table 31. Largest TSLF Borrowers by Total Dollar Amount of Loans (Includes TOP Loans)

Dollars in billions

Rank	Primary dealer	Total TSLF loans (market value)	Percent of total
1	Citigroup Global Markets Inc.	$348	15.0%
2	RBS Securities Inc.	291	12.6%
3	Deutsche Bank Securities Inc.	277	11.9%
4	Credit Suisse Securities (USA) LLC	261	11.2%
5	Goldman Sachs & Co.	225	9.7%
6	Barclays Capital Inc.	187	8.0%
7	Merrill Lynch Government Securities Inc.	166	7.2%
8	UBS Securities LLC.	122	5.3%
9	Morgan Stanley & Co. Incorporated	115	4.9%
10	Banc of America Securities LLC	101	4.3%
11	Lehman Brothers Inc.	99	4.3%
12	J.P. Morgan Securities LLC	68	2.9%
13	BNP Paribas Securities Corp.	41	1.8%
14	Countrywide Securities Corporation	8	0.3%
15	HSBC Securities (USA) Inc.	4	0.2%
16	Cantor Fitzgerald & Co.	3	0.1%
17	Bear Stearns & Co., Inc.	2	0.1%
18	Dresdner Kleinwort Securities LLC	1	0.1%
Total		$2,319	100.0%

Source: GAO analysis of Federal Reserve Board data.

Note: Amount shown for Banc of America Securities LLC reflects consolidation of total borrowing by Merrill Lynch after the January 1, 2009, acquisition closing date.

Auction Amount

The amount of Treasury collateral available at each auction was determined by FRBNY and announced one day before the auction date.

Term to Maturity for Loans

The term of securities loans under TSLF was 28 days, unless otherwise stated in the auction announcement.

Maximum and Minimum Bid Amounts

Primary dealers could submit up to two bids in each TSLF auction, and the maximum auction award for each dealer was limited to 20 percent of the offering amount for the auction. The minimum bid size was $10 million.

Interest Rate

The interest rate on TSLF loans of Treasury securities was determined using a single-price auction format. For each auction, winning bidders were awarded loans at the same interest rate. The interest rate bid by a primary dealer represented the interest rate it was willing to pay to borrow a basket of Treasury securities against other pledged collateral. A dealer's bid rate could be considered to be roughly equivalent to the difference that dealer expected between the higher interest rate repurchase agreement lenders could be expected to charge on loans secured by collateral pledged to TSLF and the lower interest rate these lenders could be expected to charge on loans secured by the Treasury securities obtained through TSLF. To determine the interest rate or "stop-out rate" for each auction, FRBNY staff ordered bids from the highest to the lowest interest rate. Bids were accepted in order starting with the highest interest rate submitted until the total auction amount was allocated or the minimum bid rate for the auction was reached, whichever occurred first. The interest rate of the lowest successful bid was the rate applied to all other successful bids for that auction. The minimum bid rates for the TSLF Schedule 1 and Schedule 2 auctions were 10 basis points and 25 basis points, respectively. FRBNY held separate auctions for schedule 1 and schedule 2 collateral to better calibrate the appropriate minimum bid rate.

Collateral Eligibility

TSLF auctioned loans of Treasury securities against two schedules of collateral. Schedule 1 included all collateral eligible for open market operations, including Treasury securities, agency debt securities, and agency MBS. Schedule 2 initially included schedule 1 collateral as well as highly rated MBS. In September 2008, eligible schedule 2 collateral was expanded to include investment grade corporate securities, municipal securities, MBS and asset-backed securities. To mitigate credit risk, FRBNY imposed haircuts on the collateral pledged by dealers. If the pledged collateral fell in value or became ineligible, the dealer would be required to make a collateral substitution over the term of the loan. The initial haircut schedule for TSLF was generally based on FRBNY's existing open market operations practices.[174] According to FRBNY staff, haircuts for assets that were not eligible for open market operations were calculated based in part on discount window margins.

Recourse

TSLF loans were made with recourse beyond the pledged collateral to the primary dealer's other assets. In the event of a default on a recourse loan, the Reserve Bank would have a claim on the borrower's assets that could allow it to recover all or part of any shortfall arising from the liquidation of the borrower's collateral.

Key Vendors and Third Parties

FRBNY did not hire vendors for the program. As mentioned previously, however, clearing banks facilitated the clearing, settlement and margining of the TSLF program.

APPENDIX XV. COMMENTS FROM THE BOARD OF GOVERNORS OF THE FEDERAL RESERVE SYSTEM

BOARD OF GOVERNORS
OF THE
FEDERAL RESERVE SYSTEM
WASHINGTON, D. C. 20551

July 8, 2011

SCOTT G. ALVAREZ
GENERAL COUNSEL

Ms. Orice Williams Brown
Managing Director
Financial Markets and Community Investment
Government Accountability Office
441 G Street, NW
Washington, DC 20548

Dear Ms. Brown:

On behalf of the Federal Reserve System, thank you for the opportunity to comment on the GAO's draft report (GAO-11-696) regarding the Federal Reserve's policies and processes for managing emergency assistance. As you know, we have worked closely with the GAO throughout the fact-gathering portion of its review and have provided extensive technical comments separately. We appreciate the GAO's substantial efforts to review these complex programs and the understanding of these programs that your report demonstrates.

As the report notes, the actions reviewed here took place in times of great economic stress. The Federal Reserve responded with carefully crafted programs, developed rapidly under great pressure. The report shows that the emergency lending programs created during those difficult times were effectively designed and effectively operated. We also appreciate the GAO's recognition that the emergency lending programs have, to date, recouped all funds lent and are expected to recoup all remaining outstanding balances.

The GAO has made seven recommendations regarding procedural changes that would benefit Federal Reserve officials facing times of crises in the future. These recommendations are designed to improve procurement policies in times of crisis, policies for promptly addressing perceived employee conflicts, management of risks related to vendor conflicts of interest, guidance to Reserve Banks about lending to higher-risk borrowers, stress testing across multiple emergency programs, and the level of documentation of Reserve Bank discretion in operating emergency facilities.

These issues are very important to the Federal Reserve and, as the report notes, the Board and Reserve Banks have already identified and taken the initiative to address a number of the report's issues and associated recommendations. To the extent not already addressed, the Board and the Reserve Banks will give each recommendation serious attention, and will strongly consider how best to respond to each. We are confident that this process will further enhance the Federal Reserve's capability to respond effectively in future crises.

Sincerely,

Scott G.

Appendix XVI. Staff Acknowledgments

GAO Acknowledgments

In addition to the contact named above, Paula Rascona and William T. Woods (lead Directors); Cheryl Clark, Karen Tremba, and Katherine Trimble (lead Assistant Directors); Serena Agoro-Menyang, Brandon Booth, Bill Boutboul, Mariana Calderon, Tania Calhoun, Marcia Carlsen, Francine DelVecchio, Rachel DeMarcus, Lynda Downing, Abe Dymond, John Fisher, Chuck Fox, Jason Kelly, Michael Kendix, Caroline Kirby, Jeff Knott, Rob Lee, Aaron Livernois, Gail Luna, Robert Mabasa, Tom McCool, Sarah M. McGrath, Marc Molino, Tim Mooney, Lauren Nunnally, Joseph O Neill, Jennifer Schwartz, Sophie Simonard, Andrew Stavisky, Eva Su, Cynthia S. Taylor, Greg Wilshusen, and Weifei Zheng made significant contributions to this report.

Glossary of Terms

Agency Mortgage-Backed Securities

Mortgage-backed securities issued by the housing government-sponsored enterprises, which are Fannie Mae and Freddie Mac, or guaranteed by Ginnie Mae.

Asset

An item owned by an individual, corporation, or government that provides a benefit, has economic value, and could be converted into cash. For businesses, an asset generates cash flow and may include, for example, accounts receivable and inventory. Assets are listed on a company's balance sheet.

Asset-Backed Commercial Paper

Short-term debt instruments (maturities ranging from overnight to 270 days) issued by corporations and financial institutions to meet short-term financing needs. The instruments are backed by assets, such as credit card receivables.

Asset-Backed Securities

Tradable securities backed by pools of assets, such as loans, leases, or other cash-flow producing assets. The holders of asset-backed securities are entitled to payments that are distributed by the underlying assets.

Bank Holding Company

A company controlling one or more banks. Bank holding companies are supervised by the Board of Governors of the Federal Reserve System (Federal Reserve Board).

Clearing Bank

A financial services company that provides settlement services for financial transactions between two counterparties.

Collateral

Properties or other assets pledged by a borrower to secure credit from a lender. If the borrower does not pay back or defaults on the loan, the lender may seize the collateral.

Collateralized Debt Obligation

Securities backed by a pool of bonds, loans, or other assets. In a basic collateralized debt obligation, a pool of bonds, loans, or other assets are pooled and securities then are issued in different tranches that vary in risk and return.

Commercial Paper

An unsecured obligation with maturities ranging from 2 to 270 days issued by banks, corporations, and other borrowers with high credit ratings to finance short-term credit needs, such as operating expenses and account receivables. Commercial paper is a low-cost alternative to bank loans. Issuing commercial paper allows a company to raise large amounts of funds quickly without the need to register with the Securities and Exchange Commission, either by selling them directly to an investor or to a dealer who then sells them to a large and varied pool of institutional buyers.

Credit Default Swap

Bilateral contract that is sold over the counter and transfers credit risks from one party to another. In return for a periodic fee, the seller (who is offering credit protection) agrees to compensate the buyer (who is buying credit protection) if a specified credit event, such as default, occurs.

Credit Rating

An external assessment of the creditworthiness of corporations and securities. A credit rating is a financial risk indicator used by potential investors. The ratings are assigned by credit rating agencies, such as Standard & Poor's, Moody's, or Fitch Ratings.

Depository Institution

A bank or other entity responsible for holding assets in safekeeping.

Discount Window

A Federal Reserve Board lending program that allows eligible institutions to borrow money, usually on a short-term basis, from the Federal Reserve Board at an above market rate to meet temporary liquidity shortages.

Equity

Ownership interest in a business in the form of common stock or preferred stock.

Fair Value

An estimated value of an asset or liability that is reasonable to all willing parties involved in a transaction taking into account market conditions other than liquidation. For example, the fair value of derivative liability represents the fair market valuation of the liabilities in a portfolio of derivatives. In this example, the fair value provides an indicator of the dollar amount the market thinks the trader of the portfolio would need to pay to eliminate its liabilities.

Haircut

The amount by which a maximum authorized loan amount is below the value of the assets used as collateral for the loan. When a borrower pledges assets as collateral, the lender making the loan treats the assets as being worth less than they actually are, so as to provide the lender a cushion in case the assets' market price decreases.

Liability

A business's financial obligation that must be made to satisfy the contractual terms of such an obligation. Current liabilities, such as accounts payable or wages, are debts payable within 1 year, while long-term liabilities, such as leases and bond repayments, are payable over a longer period.

Liquidity

Measure of the extent to which a business has cash to meet its immediate and short-term obligations. Liquidity also is measured in terms of a company's ability to borrow money to meet short-term demands for funds

London Interbank Offered Rate

The interest rate at which banks borrow unsecured funds in the London wholesale money market.

Margin

A percentage applied to the observed market price or estimated fair market value of an asset to mitigate the risk that the observed market price or estimated market value of an asset will decline over time. The Federal Reserve Board's margins are based on risk characteristics of the pledged asset as well as the anticipated volatility of the fair market value of the pledged asset over an estimated liquidation time frame.

Money Market Mutual Fund

A fund that invests solely in money market instruments, such as government securities, certificates of deposit, commercial paper, and other short-term and low-risk securities. Unlike a money market deposit account at a bank, money market mutual funds are not federally insured. The Securities and Exchange Commission regulates money market mutual funds under the Investment Company Act of 1940.

Mortgage-Backed Securities

Securities or debt obligations that represent claims to the cash flows from pools of mortgage loans, such as mortgages on residential property.
These securities are issued by Ginnie Mae, Fannie Mae, and Freddie Mac, as well as private institutions, such as brokerage firms and banks.

Nationally Recognized Statistical Rating Organizations

Credit rating agencies that provide their opinions on a business entity's or security's creditworthiness. They are registered with the Securities and Exchange Commission. These ratings demarcate investment-grade (quality) and noninvestment grade (lower quality) securities and provide additional risk-based information for investors to make investment decisions.

Open Market Operations

The primary tool used to implement monetary policy. This tool consists of Federal Reserve Board sales, purchases, or repurchase agreements regarding financial instruments, usually securities issued by the Department of the Treasury, federal agencies, and government-sponsored enterprises. Open market operations are carried out by FRBNY's Trading Desk under direction from the Federal Open Market Committee. The transactions are undertaken with primary dealers.

Overnight Indexed Swap Rate

The overnight indexed swap rate is a type of interest rate swap that is based on daily federal funds rates. The rates indicate investor expectations of future interest rates set by central banks, such as the federal funds rate.

Primary Dealers

Firms that are authorized to buy and sell U.S. government securities with FRBNY's Open Market Desk, which operates on behalf of the Federal Open Market Committee, in order to implement monetary policy.

Repurchase Agreement

A financial transaction in which the holder of a security obtains funds by selling that security to another financial market participant under an agreement to repurchase the security at a fixed price on a predetermined future date.

Securitization

The process of pooling debt obligations and dividing that pool into portions (called tranches) that can be sold as securities in the secondary market—a market in which investors purchase securities or assets from other investors. Financial institutions use securitization to transfer the credit risk of the assets they originate from their balance sheets to those of the investors who purchased the securities.

Special Purpose Vehicle

A legal entity, such as a limited partnership that a company creates to carry out some specific financial purpose or activity. Special purpose vehicles can be used for purposes such as securitizing loans to help spread the credit and interest rate risk of their portfolios over a number of investors.

Tri-party Repurchase Agreement

Tri-party repurchase agreements include three parties: the borrower, the lender, and a tri-party agent that facilitates the repurchase agreement transaction by providing custody of the securities posted as collateral and valuing the collateral, among other services.

End Notes

[1] For this report, we use Federal Reserve Board to refer to the federal agency and Federal Reserve System to refer collectively to the federal agency and the Reserve Banks. The background section of this report contains more information about the roles and responsibilities of the Federal Reserve Board and the Reserve Banks.

[2] Lehman Brothers was an investment banking institution that offered equity, fixed-income, trading, investment banking, asset management, and other financial services. According to the bankruptcy examiner appointed by the bankruptcy court, Lehman Brothers originated mortgages, securitized them, and then sold the securitized assets. Although headquartered in New York, Lehman Brothers operated globally. Lehman Brothers had $639 billion in total assets and $613 billion in total debts as of May 31, 2008, the date of its last audited financial statements.

[3] On December 1, 2010, the Federal Reserve Board disclosed detailed information about entities that received loans or other financial assistance from its emergency programs. This information included, but was not limited to, the identity of the entities that received the assistance, the type of financial assistance provided, the value or amount of the assistance, the date on which the assistance was provided, and terms of loan repayment.

[4] Pub. L. No. 111-203, Title XI, 121 Stat. 1376, 2113 (2010).

[5] In addition, this report does not cover the single-tranche term repurchase agreements conducted by FRBNY in 2008. FRBNY conducted these repurchase agreements with primary dealers through an auction process under its statutory authority for conducting temporary open market operations.

[6] The Dodd-Frank Act includes provisions that expand the roles and responsibilities of the Federal Reserve System. First, the act authorizes the Federal Reserve Board to regulate nonbank financial companies designated as systemically significant by a newly created Financial Stability Oversight Council (FSOC). The FSOC is chaired by the Secretary of the Treasury and its membership includes the Chairman of the Federal Reserve Board and the heads of the other federal financial regulators. In addition, the act consolidated many federal consumer protection responsibilities into a new independent Bureau of Consumer Financial Protection within the Federal Reserve Board.

[7] The Dodd-Frank Act also requires us to report on issues related to Reserve Bank governance by October 2011. Among other issues, that report will examine the extent to which the current system of appointing Reserve Bank directors effectively represents "the public, without discrimination on the basis of race, creed, color, sex, or national origin, and with due but not exclusive consideration to the interests of agriculture, commerce, industry, services, labor, and consumers" in the selection of Reserve Bank directors, as such requirement is set forth under section 4 of the Federal Reserve Act.

[8] These excess earnings remitted to Treasury consist of Reserve Bank earnings after providing for operating expenditures, capital paid out in dividends to banks that are members of the Federal Reserve System, and an amount reserved by Reserve Banks to equate surplus with capital paid in.

[9] Capital generally is defined as a firm's long-term source of funding, contributed largely by a firm's equity stockholders and its own returns in the form of retained earnings. One important function of capital is to absorb losses. Each of the 12 Reserve Banks maintains two capital accounts—a paid-in-capital account and a surplus account. The paid-in capital account represents the contributions by member banks of the Federal Reserve System. Under the Federal Reserve Act, members of the Federal Reserve System, which include state-chartered banks that apply for and have been granted membership and all national banks, must subscribe to the stock of their respective Reserve Bank. Dividends paid by the Reserve Banks to the member banks are set by law at the rate of 6 percent on paid-in capital stock. The Reserve Banks' second capital account is the capital surplus account. According to Federal Reserve Board policy, this account is to be maintained at a level equal to the paid-in capital. The capital surplus account is funded from the Reserve Banks' earnings after operating expenses and dividends are paid.

[10] For purposes of the Capital Purchase Program, qualifying financial institutions generally include stand-alone U.S.-controlled banks and savings associations, as well as bank holding companies and savings and loan holding companies.

[11] On October 14, 2008, the Secretary of the Treasury invoked the systemic risk provision in the Federal Deposit Insurance Act to allow FDIC to provide certain assistance to insured depository institutions, their holding companies, and qualified affiliates under TLGP. For more information about Treasury's use of the systemic risk provision, see GAO, *Federal Deposit Insurance Act: Regulators' Use of Systemic Risk Exception Raises Moral Hazard Concerns and Opportunities Exist to Clarify the Provision*, GAO-10-100 (Washington, D.C.: Apr. 15, 2010).

[12] At the time of these authorizations, section 13(3) allowed the Federal Reserve Board, in "unusual and exigent circumstances," to authorize any Reserve Bank to extend credit in the form of a discount to individuals, partnerships, or corporations when the credit was indorsed or otherwise secured to the satisfaction of the Reserve Bank, after obtaining evidence that the individual, partnership, or corporation was unable to secure adequate credit accommodations from other banking institutions. As a result of amendments to section 13(3) made by the Dodd-Frank Act, the Federal Reserve Board can now authorize 13(3) lending only through programs or facilities with broad-based eligibility.

[13] Mortgage-backed securities are securities that represent claims to the cash flows from pools of mortgage loans, such as mortgages on residential property.

[14] The sudden spike in the cost of term funding followed the August 9, 2007, announcement by BNP Paribas, a large banking organization based in France, that it could not value certain mortgage-related assets in three of its investment funds because of a lack of liquidity in U.S. securitization markets. Greater reliance on overnight borrowing increased the volatility of banks' funding costs and increased "roll-over" risk, or the risk that banks would not be able to renew their funding as loans matured.

[15] One basis point is equivalent to 0.01 percent or 1/100th of a percent.

[16] Federal Reserve Board, *Monetary Policy Report to the Congress* (February 27, 2008). This paper observed that the average interest rate in interbank lending markets was almost equal, on average, to the lower discount rate. In addition, because of the perceived stigma associated with borrowing from the discount window, depository institutions may have been reluctant to turn to the discount window for funding support.

[17] Section 10B of the Federal Reserve Act provides the Reserve Banks broad authority to extend credit to depository institutions.

[18] Another important advantage of TAF relative to encouraging greater use of the discount window was that the Federal Reserve Board could more easily control the impact of auctioned funds on monetary policy. While the Federal Reserve Board could not predict with certainty the demand for discount window loans, it could control the amount of TAF loans provided at each auction. As a result, the FOMC and FRBNY could more easily coordinate monetary policy operations to offset the impact of TAF auctions. For example, to offset the injection of $75 billion of reserves into the financial system in the form of TAF loans, FRBNY could sell $75 billion of Treasury securities through its open market operations. All else equal, the net effect of these two actions would be to have no impact on total reserves.

[19] As discussed in appendix XIII, when TAF auction demand was less than the total amount offered for the TAF auction, the interest rate resulting from the auction was the minimum bid rate set by the Federal Reserve Board—not a competitively-determined rate.

[20] In April 2009, the FOMC announced foreign-currency swap lines with the Bank of England, the European Central Bank, the Bank of Japan, and the Swiss National Bank. The foreign currency swap lines were designed to provide the Federal Reserve System with capacity to offer liquidity to U.S. institutions in foreign currency. According to the Federal Reserve Board, the foreign currency swap lines were not used.

[21] For example, an FRBNY staff paper observed that by facilitating access to dollar funding the swap lines could reduce the need for foreign banks to sell dollar assets into stressed markets, which could have further reduced prices for these dollar assets.

[22] The Federal Reserve Board has interpreted section 14 of the Federal Reserve Act to permit the Federal Reserve Banks to conduct open market operations in foreign exchange markets and to open and maintain accounts in foreign currency with foreign central banks. Section 14 states that "[a]ny Federal reserve bank may...

purchase and sell in the open market, at home or abroad, either from or to domestic or foreign banks, firms, corporations, or individuals, cable transfers..." The Federal Reserve Board has interpreted "cable transfers" to mean foreign exchange. Section 14(e) authorizes Reserve Banks to "open and maintain accounts in foreign countries, appoint correspondents, and establish agencies in such countries..." and "to open and maintain banking accounts for...foreign banks or bankers...." The use of swap lines under section 14 of the Federal Reserve Act is not new. For example, FRBNY instituted temporary swap arrangements following September 11, 2001, with the European Central Bank and the Bank of England.

[23] These foreign central banks were the Reserve Bank of Australia, the Banco Central do Brasil, the Bank of Canada, Danmarks Nationalbank (Denmark), the Bank of England (United Kingdom), the Bank of Japan, the Bank of Korea (South Korea), the Banco de Mexico, the Reserve Bank of New Zealand, Norges Bank (Norway), the Monetary Authority of Singapore, and Sveriges Riksbank (Sweden).

[24] When the market value of assets used to secure or collateralize repurchase transactions declines, borrowers are usually required to post additional collateral.

[25] Unusually high demand for certain U.S. Treasury securities resulted in negative yields on these securities at times during the crisis, indicating that investors were willing to accept a small loss in return for the relative safety of these securities.

[26] For more information about the potential causes and impacts of downward price spirals, see GAO, Financial Markets Regulation: Financial Crisis Highlights Need to Improve Oversight of Leverage at Financial Institutions and across System, GAO-09-739 (Washington, D.C.: Jul. 22, 2009).

[27] Before the crisis, FRBNY ran an overnight securities lending facility, the terms of which involved the lending of certain Treasury securities by FRBNY to primary dealers against other Treasury securities as collateral. Certain of the legal infrastructure for the traditional securities lending program was used for TSLF. Other legal and operational infrastructure had to be created specifically for TSLF.

[28] TSLF held separate auctions of Treasury securities against two different schedules of collateral to better calibrate the interest rate on TSLF loans to the level of risk associated with the collateral. The Federal Reserve Board set a higher minimum interest rate for schedule 2 TSLF auctions, which accepted riskier collateral types than schedule 1 auctions. For more information about how interest rates were determined for TSLF auctions, see appendix XIV.

[29] Bear Stearns was one of the largest primary dealers and engaged in a broad range of activities, including investment banking, securities and derivatives trading, brokerage services, and origination and securitization of mortgage loans.

[30] In our prior work on the financial crisis, Securities and Exchange Commission officials told us that neither they nor the broader regulatory community anticipated this development and that Securities and Exchange Commission had not directed large broker-dealer holding companies to plan for the unavailability of secured funding in their contingent funding plans. Securities and Exchange Commission officials stated that no financial institution could survive without secured funding. Rumors about clients moving cash and security balances elsewhere and, more importantly, counterparties not transacting with Bear Stearns also placed strains on the firm's ability to obtain secured financing. See GAO-09-739.

[31] The loan was made through JP Morgan Chase Bank, National Association pursuant to FRBNY's discount window authority under section 10B of the Federal Reserve Act. Recognizing that the ultimate borrower was Bear Stearns, a nondepository institution, the Board of Governors voted on the afternoon of March 14, 2008, to authorize the loan under section 13(3) authority. Federal Reserve Board officials explained that the use of JP Morgan Chase Bank, National Association as an intermediary was not strictly required as section 13(3) permitted a direct loan to Bear Stearns. However, they used the back-to-back loan structure because this was the structure FRBNY lawyers had prepared for in developing required legal documentation late on Thursday, March 13, 2008.

[32] Timothy F. Geithner, testimony before the U.S. Senate Committee on Banking, Housing and Urban Affairs (Washington, D.C., Apr. 3, 2008).

[33] Under the terms outlined in this letter and approved by the Federal Reserve Board, FRBNY agreed to lend up to $30 billion to JPMC against eligible Bear Stearns collateral listed in an attachment to the letter. The types and amounts of eligible collateral under this agreement were broadly similar to the assets ultimately included under the final lending structure, Maiden Lane LLC. The agreed price of the collateral was to be based on Bear Stearns's valuation of the collateral as of March 14, 2008, regardless of the date of any lending to JPMC under this agreement. JPMC would not have been required to post margin in any amount to secure any borrowing under this agreement. The letter also included certain regulatory exemptions for JPMC in connection with its agreement to acquire Bear Stearns. For example, the Federal Reserve Board granted an 18-month exemption to JPMC from the Federal Reserve Board's risk-based and leverage capital requirements for bank holding companies. The exemption would allow JPMC to exclude the assets and exposures of Bear Stearns from its risk-weighted assets for purposes of applying the risk-based capital requirements at the parent bank holding company.

[34] Before the crisis, FRBNY regularly undertook traditional temporary open market operations—repurchase agreement transactions—with primary dealers. The repurchase transactions, in normal times, are used by

FRBNY to attempt to meet the target federal funds rate, as directed by the FOMC, by temporarily increasing the amount of reserves. The repurchase transactions undertaken pursuant to PDCF were not for the purpose of increasing reserves (although they did do that), but rather for extending credit as authorized by the Federal Reserve Board.

[35] For TSLF, previously, only Treasury securities, agency securities, and AAA-rated mortgage-backed and asset-backed securities could be pledged. For PDCF, previously, eligible collateral had to have at least an investment-grade rating. Tri-party repurchase agreements include three parties: the borrower, the lender, and a tri-party agent that facilitates the repurchase agreement transaction by providing custody of the securities posted as collateral and valuing the collateral, among other services.

[36] Concurrently, the Federal Reserve Board announced that it had approved applications by Goldman Sachs and Morgan Stanley to become bank holding companies. In addition, Bank of America agreed to acquire Merrill Lynch, which would become part of a bank holding company pending completion of its merger with Bank of America, a bank holding company supervised by the Federal Reserve System upon completion of the acquisition. On November 23, 2008, in connection with other actions taken by Treasury, FDIC, and the Federal Reserve Board to assist Citigroup Inc., the Federal Reserve Board authorized FRBNY to extend credit to the London-based broker-dealer of Citigroup on terms similar to those applicable to PDCF loans. The other actions taken to assist Citigroup Inc. are discussed later in this section.

[37] A mutual fund is a company that pools money from many investors and invests the money in stocks, bonds, short-term money market instruments, other securities or assets, or some combination of these investments. These investments comprise the fund's portfolio. Mutual funds are registered and regulated under the Investment Company Act of 1940, and are supervised by the Securities and Exchange Commission. Mutual funds sell shares to public investors. Each share represents an investor's proportionate ownership in the fund's holdings and the income those holdings generate. Mutual fund shares are "redeemable," which means that when mutual fund investors want to sell their shares, the investors sell them back to the fund, or to a broker acting for the fund, at their current net asset value per share, minus any fees the fund may charge. MMMFs are mutual funds that are registered under the Investment Company Act of 1940, and regulated under Securities and Exchange Commission rule 2a-7 under that act. MMMFs invest in high-quality, short-term debt instruments such as commercial paper, treasury bills and repurchase agreements. Generally, these funds, unlike other investment companies, seek to maintain a stable net asset value per share (market value of assets minus liabilities divided by number of shares outstanding), typically $1 per share.

[38] Many financial institutions created ABCP conduits that would purchase various assets, including mortgage-related securities, financial institution debt, and receivables from industrial businesses. To obtain funds to purchase these assets, these conduits borrowed using shorter-term debt instruments, such as ABCP and medium-term notes. The difference between the interest paid to the ABCP or note holders and the income earned on the entity's assets produced fee and other income for the sponsoring institution. However, these structures carried the risk that the entity would find it difficult or costly to renew its debt financing under less-favorable market conditions.

[39] A branch or agency of a foreign bank is a legal extension of the foreign bank and is not a freestanding entity in the United States. Foreign bank branches and agencies operating in the United States are subject to Federal Reserve regulations, and the Federal Reserve examines most foreign bank branches and agencies annually.

[40] There are two main types of commercial paper: unsecured and asset-backed. Unsecured paper is not backed by collateral and the credit rating of the issuing institution is a key variable in determining the cost of its issuance. In contrast, ABCP is collateralized by assets and therefore is a secured form of borrowing.

[41] As discussed in appendix VII, the CPFF SPV was needed to allow FRBNY to engage in market transactions (purchases of commercial paper) outside its traditional operating framework for discount window lending.

[42] Commercial paper generally has fixed maturities of 1 to 270 days.

[43] Securitization is a process by which similar debt instruments—such as loans, leases, or receivables—are aggregated into pools, and interest-bearing securities backed by such pools are then sold to investors. These asset-backed securities provide a source of liquidity for consumers and small businesses because financial institutions can take assets that they would otherwise hold on their balance sheets, sell them as securities, and use the proceeds to originate new loans, among other purposes.

[44] Initially, securities backed by automobile, credit card, and student loans, as well as loans guaranteed by the Small Business Administration were deemed eligible for TALF because of the need to make credit in these sectors more widely available. The Federal Reserve Board later expanded TALF eligibility to other ABS classes, including commercial mortgage-backed securities.

[45] TALF loans were made without recourse to the intermediary borrower. However, under the TALF lending agreement, if FRBNY found that the collateral provided for a TALF loan or a borrower who had participated in the program was found to be ineligible, the nonrecourse feature of the loan would have become inapplicable.

[46] Through AIGFP—a financial products subsidiary that engaged in a variety of financial transactions, including standard and customized financial products—AIG was a participant in the derivatives market. The securities

lending program allowed certain insurance companies, primarily the life insurance companies, to lend securities in return for cash collateral that was invested in residential mortgage-backed securities.

[47] Credit default swaps are bilateral contracts that are sold over the counter and transfer credit risks from one party to another. The seller, who is offering credit protection, agrees, in return for a periodic fee, to compensate the buyer if a specified credit event, such as default, occurs. Collateralized debt obligations are securities backed by a pool of bonds, loans, or other assets.

[48] All three Maiden Lane SPVs incorporated a first-loss position for the private sector that was equal to the difference between the total purchase price of the assets and the amount of the FRBNY loan. As discussed later in this report, this first loss position took different forms in the three SPVs.

[49] On January 14, 2011, using proceeds from the initial public offering of AIA Group Limited and the sale of American Life Insurance Company to another insurance company, AIG repaid its outstanding balance on the AIG RCF.

[50] See also GAO, *Troubled Asset Relief Program: Status of Government Assistance Provided to AIG*, GAO-09-975 (Washington, D.C.: Sept. 21, 2009).

[51] As of September 30, 2008, Citigroup was the second largest banking organization in the United States, with total consolidated assets of approximately $2 trillion. Citigroup was and remains a major supplier of credit and one of the largest deposit holders in the United States and the world.

[52] For more information about the basis for the federal government's assistance to Citigroup, see GAO-10-100.

[53] The amount of this "attachment point" for FRBNY was approximately $56.17 billion. Even in stress scenarios, FRBNY did not expect losses to reach this level.

[54] Although FRBNY did not lend to Citigroup under this lending commitment, FRBNY staff confirmed that Citigroup subsidiaries were permitted under the agreement to pledge ring-fence assets as collateral to the Federal Reserve Board's emergency loan programs, such as PDCF, TSLF, and TAF, subject to the terms and conditions for these programs. The Citigroup loss-sharing agreement was clear, however, that if FRBNY ever were to lend to Citigroup under the agreement, all such pledges would need to be removed.

[55] In June and November 2009, the U.S. House of Representatives Subcommittee on Domestic Policy, Committee on Government Oversight and Reform held hearings on the events that led to federal government assistance to protect Bank of America against losses from Merrill Lynch assets. Committee members expressed concerns about the reasons for this intervention when Bank of America had already agreed to acquire Merrill Lynch without government assistance.

[56] Agency MBS include MBS issued by the housing government-sponsored enterprises, which are Fannie Mae and Freddie Mac, or guaranteed by Ginnie Mae.

[57] Section 11B of the Federal Reserve Act, codified at 12 U.S.C. § 248b.

[58] FRBNY consolidated the accounts and results of operations of LLCs into its financial statements, thereby presenting an aggregate look at its overall financial position. FRBNY presents consolidated financial statements because of its controlling financial interest in the LLCs. Specifically, FRBNY has the power to direct the significant economic activities of the LLCs and is obligated to absorb losses and has the right to receive benefits of the LLCs that could potentially be significant to the LLC. While FRBNY's financial statements include the accounts and operations of the LLCs, each LLC also issues its own set of annual financial statements.

[59] As noted previously, on September 21, 2009, the Bank of America program was terminated. As part of the termination agreement, Bank of America paid $57 million in compensation for out-of-pocket expenses incurred by FRBR and an amount equal to the commitment fees required by the agreement.

[60] Pub. L. No. 107-204, §404, 116 Stat. 745, 789 (July 30, 2002) requires management assessment of the effectiveness of their internal control over financial reporting. The Reserve Banks and LLCs are not registered with the Securities and Exchange Commission and therefore are not required to follow this law.

[61] Each of the Reserve Banks is supervised by a board of nine directors who are familiar with economic and credit conditions in the district. Three of the directors represent member commercial banks and six of the directors represent the public. The six directors are elected by member banks in the district, and the three directors are appointed by the Federal Reserve Board.

[62] COSO is a voluntary initiative of private sector organizations. COSO is dedicated to guiding executive management and governance entities toward the establishment of more effective, efficient, and ethical business operations on a global basis. It sponsors and disseminates frameworks and guidance based on in-depth research, analysis, and best practices.

[63] The CPFF LLC issued its final financial statements in August 2010. Deloitte audited these financial statements but did not issue an opinion on internal control over financial reporting because the LLC was dissolved during the year.

[64] The audit committee of each Reserve Bank's board of directors is responsible for assessing the effectiveness and independence of the Reserve Bank's internal audit function. The Federal Reserve Board expects the Reserve Bank's board of directors to appoint at least three independent directors to the audit committee.

[65] OIG, *The Federal Reserve's Section 13(3) Lending Facilities to Support Overall Market Liquidity: Function, Status, and Risk Management* (Washington, D.C., November 2010).

[66] As disclosed in the notes to the Reserve Banks' financial statements, the Reserve Banks possess a unique set of governmental, corporate, and central bank characteristics, and accounting principles for entities with such unique responsibilities have not been formulated by accounting standard-setting bodies. Therefore, the Federal Reserve Board develops and issues specialized accounting principles and practices that it considers appropriate for the nature and function of a central bank. The Federal Reserve Board requires all Reserve Banks to adopt and apply accounting policies and practices and prepare its financial statements in accordance with accounting principles the Federal Reserve Board establishes. The financial statements of each of the LLCs are prepared in accordance with GAAP. Limited differences exist between the accounting principles and practices of the Federal Reserve Board and GAAP. The primary differences are the presentation of securities holdings (Treasury securities, government-sponsored enterprise debt securities, and foreign government debt instruments) at amortized cost and the recording of such securities on a settlement-date basis. The cost basis of the securities is adjusted for amortization of premiums or accretion of discounts on a straight-line basis, rather than using the interest method required by GAAP. The effects on the financial statements of the differences between the accounting principles established by the Federal Reserve Board and GAAP are also described in the notes to the financial statements.

[67] The Public Company Accounting Oversight Board is a nonprofit audit and professional practice standard-setting corporation established by Congress to oversee the audits of public companies in order to protect investors and the public interest by promoting informative, accurate, and independent audit reports.

[68] A material weakness is a deficiency, or a combination of deficiencies, in internal control such that there is a reasonable possibility that a material misstatement of the entity's financial statements will not be prevented or detected and corrected on a timely basis.

[69] A deficiency in internal control exists when the design or operation of a control does not allow management or employees, in the normal course of performing their assigned functions, to prevent or detect misstatements on a timely basis. A significant deficiency is a deficiency, or a combination of deficiencies, in internal control that is less severe than a material weakness yet important enough to merit attention by those charged with governance.

[70] Service auditors' reports refer to reports typically prepared by an independent auditor based on a review of the internal controls over an entity's servicing operations as discussed in the American Institute of Certified Public Accountants' Statement on Auditing Standards No. 70, Service Organizations.

[71] FRBNY also paid 36 subvendors more than $3.3 million for services related to the emergency programs.

[72] The two contracts were with Morgan Stanley and Ernst & Young to provide AIG RCF-related services, for which FRBNY paid $108.4 million and $66.9 million, respectively, from 2008 through 2010. AIG reimbursed FRBNY for these amounts.

[73] FRBB entered into a single $25,000 contract for AMLF and FRBR entered into three contracts totaling $22.8 million for the Bank of America ring-fencing agreement.

[74] Any loans made under the Bank of America or Citigroup ringfencing agreements were to be secured by specified pools of assets belonging to each institution. However, no loans were extended under the programs.

[75] As noted earlier, FRBNY has undertaken repurchase agreement transactions with primary dealers in regular open market operations for some time. These transactions have been executed through a triparty arrangement, with the clearing banks providing execution and collateral-management services. The clearing banks provide this service to dealers that maintain accounts on their books. The resulting system is frequently referred to as "triparty." FRBNY implemented PDCF using the existing triparty legal and operational infrastructure. For TSLF, FRBNY entered into a new triparty agreement with each primary dealer and its clearing bank.

[76] FRBNY officials said the structure of the MMIFF program required that the LLCs be independent of FRBNY. A key to the MMIFF program was the issuance of highly rated commercial paper to program participants. However, the rating agencies required that the LLCs be operated independently of FRBNY so that if losses were sustained, FRBNY could not potentially place its own interests ahead of the interests of program participants.

[77] The Reserve Banks jointly developed acquisition guidance, called the Model Acquisition Guidelines (MAG), based on the American Bar Association's Model Procurement Code for State and Local Governments. Individual Reserve Banks use the MAG framework for their acquisition policies, and FRBNY's Operating Bulleting 10 is an enhanced version of the MAG. Operating Bulletin 10 has been in place since 1986.

[78] Of the noncompetitive contracts we reviewed, FRBNY awarded only three under the sole-source exception, when a service was available from only one vendor.

[79] FAR § 6.301(d).

[80] The American Bar Association's Model Procurement Code for State and Local Governments, on which Operating Bulletin 10 is based, also requires as much competition as is practicable under the circumstances.

[81] FAR § 6.302-2(d)(1). Operating Bulletin 10 describes exigency as follows: "the Bank's need for the property or services is of such unusual and compelling urgency that it would be demonstrably and significantly injured unless it can limit the number of suppliers from which it solicits responses or take other steps to shorten the time needed to acquire the property or services." Exigency as described in Operating Bulletin 10 is called "unusual and compelling urgency" in the FAR. See FAR § 6.302-2.

[82] FRBNY officials noted that multiyear contracts contained termination rights.

[83] PIMCO's 0.25 basis point variable fee only applied to the first $400 billion in outstanding commercial paper so it was capped at $10 million per quarter.

[84] The Reserve Banks do not receive appropriated funds and therefore did not use appropriated funds to pay vendors.

[85] In some cases, vendors were paid directly by the program recipient so the Reserve Banks did not need to be reimbursed. In one case, FRBNY paid a Maiden Lane vendor and was later reimbursed.

[86] For TALF, vendors were paid both directly and through a waterfall.

[87] Under 18 U.S.C. § 208(b)(2), the Director of the Office of Government Ethics, an executive branch agency that provides guidance to federal government agencies on how to prevent and resolve conflicts of interest on the part of government employees, may, by regulation, exempt from the general prohibition financial interests which are too remote or too inconsequential to affect the integrity of the services of the employee to which the prohibition applies. See 5 C.F.R. Part 2635, subpart D, and Part 2640.

[88] FRBNY's Code of Conduct incorporated Office of Government Ethics regulations concerning divestiture, disqualification (recusal), and waivers of or exemptions from disqualification. See 5 C.F.R. § 2635.402(c)-(e). According to FRBNY staff, some employees recused themselves out of an abundance of caution even though a conflict of interest did not exist. In some cases, FRBNY granted a temporary waiver that allowed an employee to continue to perform duties in connection with a financial interest while taking steps to divest the related financial interests.

[89] 5 C.F.R. §2640.301.

[90] While AIG received individual assistance through emergency actions authorized by the Federal Reserve Board, GE received assistance through a broad-based program authorized by the Federal Reserve Board.

[91] As explained in an earlier footnote, COSO is a voluntary initiative of private-sector organizations. COSO is dedicated to guiding executive management and governance entities toward the establishment of more effective, efficient, and ethical business operations on a global basis. It sponsors and disseminates frameworks and guidance based on in-depth research, analysis, and best practices.

[92] However, Office of Government Ethics regulations provide that when an employee acts in accordance with a statutory waiver, the waiver will constitute a determination that the interest of the government in the employee's participation outweighs the concern that a reasonable person may question the integrity of agency programs and operations. 5 C.F.R. §2635.501.

[93] Office of Government Ethics regulations specifically provide that Reserve Bank directors may participate in specified matters, even though they may be particular matters in which they have a disqualifying financial interest. 5 C.F.R. § 2640.203(h). These matters concern the establishment of rates to be charged to member banks for all advances and discounts; consideration of monetary policy matters and other matters of broad applicability; and approval or ratification of extensions of credit, advances or discounts to healthy depository institutions or, in certain conditions, to depository institutions in hazardous condition.

[94] FRBNY's Audit and Operational Risk Committee is appointed by its Board of Directors to assist the board in monitoring, (1) the integrity of the financial statements of the Reserve Bank, (2) the Reserve Bank's external auditor's qualifications and independence, (3) the performance of the Reserve Bank's internal audit function and external auditors, (4) internal controls and the measurement of operational risk, and (5) the compliance by the Reserve Bank with legal and regulatory requirements. The Audit and Operational Risk Committee also assesses the effectiveness of (2), (3), (4), and (5).

[95] Section 1109(b) of the Dodd-Frank Act required us to examine Reserve Bank governance. This report will be issued in October 2011.

[96] Section 1107 of the Dodd-Frank Act amended the Federal Reserve Act to require that the president of a Reserve Bank be appointed not by its board of directors, but only by its Class B and C directors, with the Federal Reserve Board's approval.

[97] Other changes included prohibiting Class A directors from having a role in the appointment of FRBNY's president and first vice president, consistent with the Dodd-Frank amendment, voting for or playing a role in the selection of individuals managing the Financial Institution Supervision Group, and approving the budget for the Financial Institution Supervision Group. In addition, at most, two out of five Class A directors can serve as members on the Reserve Bank's Nominating and Corporate Governance Committee, on which at least five directors must sit.

[98] Security policies refer broadly to policies put in place to secure repayment of loans. Although the Federal Reserve System is not funded by appropriations from Congress, any losses on the Reserve Banks' emergency loans would have reduced the amount of excess earnings that the Federal Reserve System remitted to Treasury.

[99] For the purposes of this report, we use the term "overcollateralized" to refer to Reserve Bank lending for which borrowers were required to pledge collateral in excess of the loan amount. By using this term, we do not intend to suggest that the amount of excess collateral required was inappropriately excessive given the Federal Reserve Board's policy objectives.

[100] The Reserve Banks extend discount window credit to U.S. depository institutions (including U.S. branches and agencies of foreign banks) under three programs, one of which is the primary credit program. Primary credit is

available to generally sound depository institutions, typically on an overnight basis. To assess whether a depository institution is in sound financial condition, its Reserve Bank can regularly review the institution's condition, using supervisory ratings and data on adequacy of the institution's capital.

[101] At each examination of a depository institution performed by federal financial regulators, examiners assign a supervisory CAMELS rating, which assesses six components of an institution's financial health: capital, asset quality, management, earnings, liquidity, and sensitivity to market risk. An institution's CAMELS rating is known directly only by the institution's senior management and appropriate regulatory staff. Institutions with a CAMELS or equivalent supervisory rating of 1, 2, or 3 generally are considered eligible for the primary credit program, unless supplementary information indicates that the institution is generally not sound.

[102] According to TAF terms and conditions, the aggregate sum of all TAF loans outstanding with a term to maturity of more than 28 days could not exceed 75 percent of the value of the collateral available to secure the loan.

[103] In the FRBNY's open market operations repurchase agreement transactions, the collateral pledged by dealers was subject to a haircut schedule. Similar to the discount window and TAF margin tables, these margins were derived using value-at-risk methodology, but the margins were not identical to discount window margin tables. Value-at-risk is a statistical measure of the potential loss in the fair value of a portfolio due to adverse movements in underlying risk factors. The measure is an estimate of the expected loss that an institution is unlikely to exceed in a given period with a particular degree of confidence.

[104] The selected ABCP collateral was highly rated, short-term, secured by an interest in a diversified pool of assets, and was held in significant quantity by MMMFs. In addition, as market conditions improved, the collateral eligibility requirements for AMLF tightened from its initial design to exclude collateral that had an A1/P1/F1 rating but were on negative watch.

[105] Economic incentives for intermediary borrowers to participate were based on the ability to earn returns on eligible ABCP in excess of the interest rate on the AMLF loan.

[106] The use of an SPV allowed FRBNY to leverage existing market infrastructure for the issuance of commercial paper. Using loans from FRBNY's discount window infrastructure, the CPFF LLC would purchase eligible paper in the same way that investors would purchase this paper in the marketplace.

[107] At the time of its registration to use the CPFF, each issuer also had to pay a facility fee equal to 10 basis points of the maximum amount of its commercial paper the SPV could own.

[108] This limit was equal to the sum of the commercial paper an issuer had issued through CPFF and other outstanding commercial paper the issuer had issued in the market. According to FRBNY staff, FRBNY monitored compliance with issuance limits on an ex-post basis due to limitations with the availability of commercial paper issuance data. By reviewing the prior day's data rather than reviewing aggregate amounts in advance of issuance, FRBNY identified a few instances of CPFF issuers exceeding the program's issuance limits. In these cases, FRBNY took steps to either unwind the transaction or encourage the borrower to reduce its exposure to below the limit.

[109] Some MMMFs indicated that the subordinated note feature presented an obstacle to their participating in MMIFF. In particular, MMIFF notes were to be collateralized by all assets held by the SPV and some funds would have had to obtain special approval from their boards of directors to invest in one or more of the 50 institutions whose obligations were to be held by the MMIFF SPVs.

[110] TALF collateral was required to have a AAA rating from a minimum of two rating agencies and was further required to have a AAA rating from all eligible rating agencies that rated the security.

[111] In addition, for legacy CMBS, FRBNY reserved the right to reject a legacy CMBS if the legacy CMBS did not meet the explicit requirements stated in the TALF Terms and Conditions. In addition, FRBNY conducted due diligence on major participants in CMBS transactions, including issuers, loan sellers, and sponsors of mortgage borrowers and reserved the right to reject any legacy or newly issued CMBS based on its assessment of fraud exposure or other risks. FRBNY did not disclose its selection criteria to reduce the likelihood that only the poorest-performing collateral would be put forward for TALF loans.

[112] Treasury and the Federal Reserve Board later reduced these lending commitments to up to $4.3 billion from TARP and up to $38.7 billion from FRBNY, respectively.

[113] In contrast to a cash CDO, which invests in fixed income securities, a synthetic CDO is a form of CDO that invests in credit default swaps or other noncash assets to gain exposure to fixed income securities and then issues synthetic CDO securities to match the underlying exposure.

[114] With a first priority perfected security interest, no other parties would have a claim to the collateral that would supersede FRBNY's claim.

[115] According to FRBNY attorneys with whom we spoke, FRBNY's contracts with some vendors included provisions that would have held the vendor liable for any losses arising from misapplication of program requirements.

[116] For its analysis of stress losses for CPFF, FRBNY defined stress losses as a 1-in-100 years event.

[117] FRBNY staff noted that the Reserve Banks maintain low levels of capital, remitting excess earnings to Treasury, because capital levels do not reflect a central bank's ability to bear losses.

[118] As discussed earlier in this report, the foreign institutions receiving dollar loans through the foreign central banks were not counterparties to FRBNY.

[119] A Federal Reserve Board staff memorandum indicated that not all inquiries from foreign central banks were escalated to the FOMC for a formal FOMC approval or rejection. Staff said they informed some foreign central banks that the FOMC would be unlikely to approve a swap line arrangement.

[120] FRBNY leveraged these existing bilateral legal agreements with the primary dealers by amending them to provide for PDCF and TSLF and also leveraged existing triparty agreements among FRBNY, each primary dealer and its clearing bank to implement tri-party aspects of PDCF. FRBNY negotiated new securities loan agreements to cover the triparty aspects of TSLF.

[121] 2a-7 MMMFs are required to adhere to the restrictions of the maturity, quality, and diversification of their assets defined under the Securities and Exchange Commission rule 2a-7 and held the highly rated ABCP that could serve as collateral for FRBB loans.

[122] According to FRBNY, MMMF industry representatives selected the 50 financial institutions whose short-term debt obligations would be eligible for purchase by the five MMIFF SPVs. Each of the five MMIFF SPVs was authorized to purchase obligations of 10 of these institutions. According to FRBNY staff, achieving geographic diversity for each SPV was one criterion considered in allocating these institutions across the SPVs. More broadly, JPMC and FRBNY considered the obligations of the selected institutions to be broadly held across many MMMFs.

[123] TALF agents were primary dealers or designated broker-dealers whose responsibilities included conducting due diligence on TALF borrowers and making representations to FRBNY regarding eligibility of TALF borrowers and their collateral, submitting TALF loan requests and supporting documentation to FRBNY and the TALF custodian on behalf of borrowers, delivering administrative fees and collateral from TALF borrowers to FRBNY, and distributing the TALF borrowers' share of principal and interest payments paid on the collateral backing the TALF loan.

[124] FRBNY defined material investors as investors with at least a 10 percent ownership stake in the entity borrowing from TALF.

[125] Our scope was limited to review of detailed collateral data for TAF and PDCF.

[126] Section 1101 of the Dodd-Frank Act amended the Federal Reserve Board's section 13(3) authority; such lending can now be made only through programs or facilities with broad-based eligibility. The amendments also require the Federal Reserve Board to establish regulations on the policies and procedures governing its emergency lending under section 13(3).

[127] The TALF program, which was developed last among the broad-based emergency programs, included specific rules for changing any of its extensive documentation that included sign-off from staff at the Federal Reserve Board, FRBNY, and Treasury. In addition, according to Federal Reserve Board staff, there were regular daily calls between the lead staff from the Federal Reserve Board, FRBNY, and Treasury where all issues related to the program were discussed, including any issues that fell outside the program documentation. Federal Reserve Board staff regularly briefed members of the Board of Governors about the program, and material changes to the program were formally authorized by the Federal Reserve Board.

[128] When the turmoil in the markets began in 2007, some banks had to finance the assets held by off-balance-sheet entities when those entities were unable to refinance their expiring debt due to market concerns over the quality of the assets. In some cases, these off-balance-sheet entities relied on financing commitments that banks had extended to them. In other cases, financial institutions supported troubled off-balance sheet entities to protect their reputations with clients even when no legal requirement to do so existed. For more information about liquidity problems that emerged in connection with off-balance-sheet entities, see GAO-09-739.

[129] A "material investor" is an investor who owns, directly or indirectly, an interest in any class of securities of a borrower that is greater than or equal to a 10 percent interest in such outstanding class of securities.

[130] On September 6, 2008, the Federal Housing Finance Agency (FHFA) placed Fannie Mae and Freddie Mac into conservatorship out of concern that the deteriorating financial condition of the two enterprises threatened the stability of financial markets. According to FHFA's former Director, James B. Lockhart III, at the time the conservatorships were established, Fannie Mae and Freddie Mac had worldwide debt and other financial obligations totaling $5.4 trillion, and their default on those obligations would have significantly disrupted the U.S. financial system. For more information about the enterprises, see GAO, *Fannie Mae and Freddie Mac: Analysis of Options for Revising the Housing Enterprises' Long-Term Structure*, GAO-09-782 (Washington, D.C.: Sept. 10, 2009).

[131] Prices of fixed income securities such as agency MBS move in the opposite direction of the yield. When the yield on the Fannie Mae securities dropped, the price that investors were willing to pay for agency MBS securities increased. One basis point is equivalent to 0.01 percent or 1/100th of a percent.

[132] The Department of the Treasury (Treasury) agreed to provide substantial financial support to the enterprises so that they could continue to support mortgage finance during the financial crisis. On September 7, 2008, Treasury agreed to provide up to $100 billion in financial support to each enterprise through the purchase of their preferred stock so that the enterprises maintain a positive net worth. In February 2009, Treasury agreed to increase this commitment to $200 billion per enterprise. Treasury also agreed to purchase the enterprises' mortgage-backed securities and establish a lending facility to meet their borrowing requirements if needed.

[133] When mortgage interest rates fall, homeowners that had borrowed at a higher rate may be able to refinance to lower rates. Proceeds from the new loan are used to pay off the existing loan in the process.

[134] ABCP refers to commercial paper issued by a special purpose vehicle, or conduit, created to purchase asset-backed securities, such as mortgage-backed securities or securities backed by other types of receivables. Many financial institutions created ABCP conduits that would purchase various assets, including mortgage-related securities, financial institution debt, and receivables from industrial businesses. To obtain funds to purchase these assets, these conduits borrowed using shorter-term debt instruments, such as ABCP and medium-term notes. The difference between the interest paid to the ABCP or note holders and the income earned on the entity's assets produced fee and other income for the sponsoring institution. However, these structures carried the risk that the entity would find it difficult or costly to renew its debt financing under less-favorable market conditions.

[135] A mutual fund is a company that pools money from many investors and invests the money in stocks, bonds, short-term money market instruments, other securities or assets, or some combination of these investments. These investments comprise the fund's portfolio. Mutual funds are registered and regulated under the Investment Company Act of 1940, and are supervised by the Securities and Exchange Commission. Mutual funds sell shares to public investors. Each share represents an investor's proportionate ownership in the fund's holdings and the income those holdings generate. Mutual fund shares are "redeemable," which means that when mutual fund investors want to sell their shares, the investors sell them back to the fund, or to a broker acting for the fund, at their current net asset value per share, minus any fees the fund may charge.

[136] For more about this stress test exercise, see GAO, *Troubled Asset Relief Program: Bank Stress Test Offers Lessons as Regulators Take Further Actions to Strengthen Supervisory Oversight*, GAO-10-861 (Washington, D.C.: Sept. 29, 2010).

[137] According to Federal Reserve Board officials, the maximum term allowed for commercial paper was 270 days, and depository institutions were restricted to a loan of 120 days because of limitations that section 10B of the Federal Reserve Act places on the term of loans Reserve Banks can make to depository institutions.

[138] AIG is an international insurance organization serving customers in more than 130 countries. As of March 31, 2011, AIG had assets of $611.2 billion and revenues of $17.4 billion for the 3 preceding months. AIG companies serve commercial, industrial, and individual customers through worldwide property-casualty networks. In addition, AIG companies provide life insurance and retirement services in the United States.

[139] Through AIGFP—a financial products subsidiary that engaged in a variety of financial transactions, including standard and customized financial products—AIG was a participant in the derivatives market. The securities lending program allowed certain insurance companies, primarily AIG's life insurance companies, to lend securities in return for cash collateral that was invested in investments such as residential mortgage-backed securities.

[140] Credit default swaps are bilateral contracts that are sold over the counter and transfer credit risks from one party to another. The seller, who is offering credit protection, agrees, in return for a periodic fee, to compensate the buyer if a specified credit event, such as default, occurs. Collateralized debt obligations are securities backed by a pool of bonds, loans, or other assets.

[141] GAO, *Troubled Asset Relief Program: The Government's Exposure to AIG Following the Company's Recapitalization*, GAO-11-716 (Washington, D.C.: Jul. 18, 2011); *Troubled Asset Relief Program: Third Quarter 2010 Update of Government Assistance Provided to AIG and Description of Recent Execution of Recapitalization Plan*, GAO-11-46 (Washington, D.C.: Jan. 20, 2011); *Troubled Asset Relief Program: Update of Government Assistance Provided to AIG*, GAO-10-475 (Washington, D.C.: Apr. 27, 2010); *Troubled Asset Relief Program: Status of Government Assistance Provided to AIG*, GAO-09-975 (Washington, D.C.: Sept. 21, 2009); and *Federal Financial Assistance: Preliminary Observations on Assistance Provided to AIG*, GAO-09-490T (Washington, D.C.: Mar. 18, 2009).

[142] In contrast to a cash CDO, which invests in fixed income securities, a synthetic CDO is a form of CDO that invests in CDS or other noncash assets to gain exposure to fixed income securities and then issues synthetic CDO securities to match the underlying exposure.

[143] In our work on the financial crisis, Securities and Exchange Commission officials told us that neither they nor the broader regulatory community anticipated this development and that SEC had not directed the five large broker-dealer holding companies to plan for the unavailability of secured funding in their contingent funding plans. SEC officials stated that no financial institution could survive without secured funding. Rumors about clients moving cash and security balances elsewhere and, more importantly, counterparties not transacting with Bear Stearns also placed strains on the firm's ability to obtain secured financing. See GAO, *Financial Markets Regulation: Financial Crisis Highlights Need to Improve Oversight of Leverage at Financial Institutions and across System*, GAO-09-739 (Washington, D.C.: Jul. 22, 2009).

[144] The loan was made through JPMC under FRBNY's discount window authority under section 10B of the Federal Reserve Act. However, recognizing that the ultimate borrower was Bear Stearns, a nondepository institution, the Board of Governors voted on the afternoon of March 14, 2008, to authorize the loan under section 13(3) authority. Federal Reserve Board officials explained that the use of JPMC as an intermediary was not strictly required as section 13(3) permitted a direct loan to Bear Stearns. However, they used the back-to-back loan

structure because this was the structure FRBNY lawyers had prepared for in developing required legal documentation late on Thursday, March 13, 2008.

[145] Timothy F. Geithner, testimony before the U.S. Senate Committee on Banking, Housing and Urban Affairs (Washington, D.C., Apr. 3, 2008).

[146] Under the terms outlined in this letter and approved by the Federal Reserve Board, FRBNY agreed to lend up to $30 billion to JPMC against eligible Bear Stearns's collateral listed in an attachment to the letter. The types and amounts of eligible collateral under this agreement were broadly similar to the assets ultimately included under the final lending structure, Maiden Lane LLC. The agreed price of the collateral was to be based on Bear Stearns's valuation of the collateral as of March 16, 2008, regardless of the date of any lending to JPMC under this agreement. JPMC would not have been required to post margin in any amount to secure any borrowing under this agreement. The letter also included certain regulatory exemptions for JPMC in connection with its agreement to acquire Bear Stearns. For example, the Federal Reserve Board granted an 18-month exemption to JPMC from the Federal Reserve Board's risk-based and leverage capital requirements for bank holding companies. The exemption would allow JPMC to exclude the assets and exposures of Bear Stearns from its risk-weighted assets for purposes of applying the risk-based capital requirements at the parent bank holding company.

[147] In June and November 2009, the House of Representatives Subcommittee on Domestic Policy, Committee on Government Oversight and Reform, held hearings on the events that led to federal government assistance to protect Bank of America against losses from Merrill Lynch assets. Committee members expressed concerns about the reasons for this intervention when Bank of America had already agreed to acquire Merrill Lynch without government assistance.

[148] Bank of America agreed to issue FDIC and Treasury $4 billion in preferred stock with an 8 percent dividend rate and warrants with an aggregate exercise value of 10 percent of the total amount of preferred stock issued.

[149] See GAO, *Troubled Asset Relief Program: Bank Stress Test Offers Lessons as Regulators Take Further Actions to Strengthen Supervisory Oversight,* GAO-10-861 (Washington, D.C.: Sept. 29, 2010).

[150] See GAO-10-100.

[151] Citigroup issued FDIC and Treasury approximately $3 billion and $4 billion of preferred stock, respectively, for bearing the risk associated with the guarantees.

[152] Adrian, T., K. Kimbrough, and D. Marchioni. "The Federal Reserve's Commercial Paper Funding Facility." FRBNY Economic Policy Review (2010).

[153] FDIC charged a fee for its guarantee that depended on the term of the unsecured commercial paper. FDIC's fee for 3-month unsecured commercial paper initially was 50 basis points.

[154] On September 19, 2008, Treasury announced the Temporary Guarantee Program for Money Market Funds, which temporarily guaranteed certain investments in money market funds that decided to participate in the program. Treasury's Temporary Guarantee Program for Money Market Funds expired on September 18, 2009. Treasury guaranteed that upon liquidation of a participating money market fund, the fund's shareholders would receive the fund's stable share price of $1 for each fund share owned as of September 19, 2008. Participating funds were required to agree to liquidate and to suspend shareholder redemptions if they broke the buck. Most money market funds elected to participate in the program.

[155] These foreign central banks were the Bank of Canada, the Bank of England, the European Central Bank, the Bank of Japan, and the Swiss National Bank.

[156] Michael Fleming and Nicholas Klagge, "The Federal Reserve's Foreign Exchange Swap Lines," *Federal Reserve Bank of New York Current Issues,* vol. 16, no. 4 (New York, NY, April 2010).

[157] If the debt instruments of a financial institution held by an SPV were no longer eligible assets due to a debt rating downgrade, the SPV would have been required to cease all asset purchases until all of the SPV's assets issued by that financial institution had matured. Upon a payment default of any asset held by an SPV, the SPV would have been required to cease all asset purchases and repayments on outstanding ABCP; proceeds from maturation of the SPV assets would be distributed to FRBNY and subordinated note holders according to program terms and conditions.

[158] 2a-7 MMMFs are required to adhere to the restrictions of the maturity, quality, and diversification of their assets defined under the Securities and Exchange Commission rule 2a-7.

[159] Additional newly eligible investors included U.S. dollar-denominated cash collateral reinvestment funds, portfolios, and accounts associated with securities lending transactions that were managed or owned by a U.S. bank, insurance company, pension fund, trust company, or a Securities and Exchange Commission-registered investment advisor.

[160] TALF loans were made without recourse to the intermediary borrower. However, under the TALF lending agreement, if FRBNY found that the collateral provided for a TALF loan or a borrower who had participated in the program was found to be ineligible, the nonrecourse feature of the loan would become inapplicable.

[161] TALF collateral was required to have a AAA rating from a minimum of two rating agencies and was further required to have a AAA rating from all eligible rating agencies that rated the security.

[162] In addition, for legacy CMBS, FRBNY reserved the right to reject any ABS if the legacy ABS did not meet the explicit requirements stated in the TALF terms and conditions. In addition, FRBNY conducted due diligence

on major participants in CMBS transactions, including issuers, loan sellers, and sponsors of mortgage borrowers and reserved the right to reject any legacy or newly issued CMBS based on its assessment of fraud exposure or other risks. FRBNY did not disclose its selection criteria to reduce the likelihood that only the poorest-performing collateral would be put forward for TALF loans.

[163] Treasury and the Federal Reserve Board later reduced these lending commitments to up to $4.3 billion from TARP and up to $38.7 billion from FRBNY, respectively.

[164] For more information about how FRBNY administered the TALF program, see GAO, *Troubled Asset Relief Program: Treasury Needs to Strengthen Its Decision-Making Process on the Term Asset-Backed Securities Loan Facility*, GAO-10-25 (Washington, D.C.: Feb. 5, 2010).

[165] TALF agents were primary dealers or designated broker-dealers whose responsibilities included conducting due diligence on TALF borrowers and making representations to FRBNY regarding eligibility of TALF borrowers and their collateral, submitting TALF loan requests and supporting documentation to FRBNY and the TALF custodian on behalf of borrowers, delivering administrative fees and collateral from TALF borrowers to FRBNY, and distributing the TALF borrower's share of principal and interest payments paid on the collateral backing the TALF loan.

[166] FRBNY defined material investors as investors with at least a 10 percent ownership stake in the entity borrowing from TALF.

[167] Extensions of Credit by Federal Reserve Banks, 72 Fed. Reg. 71202 (Dec. 17, 2007).

[168] The Federal Reserve Board set the minimum bid rate and initially determined the minimum bid rate based on a measure of the average expected overnight federal funds rate over the term of the loans being auctioned.

[169] For all TAF auctions from October 2008 through the end of the program, the TAF interest rate awarded was the minimum bid rate set by the Federal Reserve Board because demand for TAF loans was below the amount offered at auction.

[170] At each examination of a depository institution performed by federal financial regulators, examiners assign a supervisory CAMELS rating, which assesses six components of an institution's financial health: capital, asset quality, management, earnings, liquidity, and sensitivity to market risk. An institution's CAMELS rating is known directly only by the institution's senior management and appropriate regulatory staff.

[171] On October 6, 2008, the Federal Reserve Board announced that pursuant to new authority granted by the Emergency Economic Stabilization Act of 2008, Reserve Banks would begin to pay interest on required and excess reserve balances depository institutions held at the Reserve Banks. In a January 2009 speech, the Chairman of the Federal Reserve Board said, "In principle, the interest rate the Fed pays on bank reserves should set a floor on the overnight interest rate, as banks should be unwilling to lend reserves at a rate lower than they can receive from the Fed. In practice, the federal funds rate has fallen somewhat below the interest rate on reserves in recent months, reflecting the very high volume of excess reserves, the inexperience of banks with the new regime, and other factors. However, as excess reserves decline, financial conditions normalize, and banks adapt to the new regime, we expect the interest rate paid on reserves to become an effective instrument for controlling the federal funds rate. Ben S. Bernanke, lecture given at the London School of Economics (London, England, Jan. 13, 2009).

[172] For more information about the potential causes and impacts of downward price spirals, see GAO-09-739.

[173] Before the crisis, FRBNY ran an overnight securities lending facility, the terms of which involved the lending of certain Treasury securities by FRBNY to primary dealers against other Treasury securities as collateral. Certain of the legal infrastructure for the traditional securities lending program was used for TSLF. Other legal and operational infrastructure had to be created specifically for TSLF.

[174] In FRBNY's open market operations repurchase agreement transactions, the collateral pledged by dealers was subject to a haircut schedule. Similar to the discount window and TAF margin tables, these margins were derived using value-at-risk methodology, but the margins were not identical to discount window margin tables. Value-at-risk is a statistical measure of the potential loss in the fair value of a portfolio due to adverse movements in underlying risk factors. The measure is an estimate of the expected loss that an institution is unlikely to exceed in a given period with a particular degree of confidence.

INDEX

A

abatement, 48
access, 2, 6, 10, 15, 16, 18, 36, 37, 41, 42, 55, 65, 77, 98, 99, 101, 103, 104, 106, 108, 109, 110, 111, 117, 128, 129, 131, 132, 134, 135, 136, 137, 139, 147, 148, 149, 151, 182, 191, 194, 221
accommodations, 9, 221
accountability, 56, 60, 138, 140, 150
accounting, vii, 22, 40, 42, 53, 54, 59, 60, 63, 67, 82, 85, 86, 87, 88, 93, 156, 177, 180, 225
acquisitions, 143, 144, 196
adaptations, 2
administrative efficiency, 87
adverse effects, 4
agencies, 20, 22, 64, 66, 67, 76, 80, 94, 110, 111, 132, 133, 138, 141, 143, 144, 157, 176, 177, 183, 188, 206, 208, 219, 222, 223, 226, 227, 230
agriculture, 107, 220
AIG, vii, 1, 2, 3, 9, 18, 19, 20, 21, 22, 23, 24, 25, 26, 27, 28, 29, 32, 33, 35, 36, 37, 38, 42, 46, 48, 49, 50, 51
allocating, 43
alters, 18
amortization, 225
appropriations, 67, 130, 226
arbitrage, 136
assessment, 7, 82, 83, 84, 87, 106, 111, 177, 217, 224, 227, 231
asset-backed commercial paper, 13, 56, 58, 61, 76, 156, 180, 190
Asset-Backed Commercial Paper Money Market Mutual Fund Liquidity Facility (AMLF), 13, 66, 156, 185, 190
asset-backed securities, vii, 1, 3, 5, 7, 11, 47
atmosphere, 36
attachment, 222, 224, 230

audit, vii, 2, 3, 40, 41, 42, 46, 47, 53, 54, 60, 63, 64, 66, 81, 82, 84, 85, 86, 87, 88, 89, 93, 105, 118, 120, 122, 148, 174, 224, 225, 226
audits, 3, 40, 51, 54, 63, 82, 84, 85, 86, 87, 88, 225
authorities, 27, 42, 46, 107, 150
authority, 1, 2, 3, 6, 8, 9, 14, 15, 17, 18, 19, 34, 36, 38, 39, 40, 46, 49, 51, 54, 60, 69, 73, 78, 80, 83, 101, 108, 132, 135, 138, 139, 140, 150, 151, 152, 171, 172, 210, 221, 222, 228, 229, 231
auto dealers, 11
automobiles, 4
awareness, 99

B

background information, 95
balance sheet, 1, 3, 10, 17, 24, 26, 27, 29, 30, 31, 33, 34, 36, 43, 44, 47, 52, 74, 87, 108, 129, 130, 144, 173, 198, 209, 215, 220, 223, 228
bank failure, 37
bank lending, 16
Bank of Canada, 71, 81, 187, 189, 222, 230
Bank of England, 71, 81, 187, 188, 221, 222, 230
bankers, 188, 222
banking, vii, 1, 2, 4, 6, 9, 10, 16, 33, 37, 38, 51, 60, 66, 67, 68, 140, 158, 164, 177, 178, 188, 220, 221, 222, 224
banking sector, 60
banking system, vii, 1, 2, 4, 6, 10, 16, 33, 37, 38
bankruptcy, 2, 13, 23, 29, 37, 51, 73, 74, 75, 78, 163, 172, 173, 195, 220
banks, vii, 1, 2, 4, 5, 6, 7, 9, 10, 13, 15, 16, 17, 18, 20, 27, 29, 30, 31, 33, 36, 38, 39, 40, 42, 43, 44, 45, 46, 47, 48, 51, 66, 67, 68, 70, 71, 92, 107, 113, 122, 123, 125, 129, 132, 135, 144, 147, 153, 186, 187, 188, 195, 197, 204, 206, 210, 213, 216, 218, 220, 221, 222, 224, 225, 226, 228, 231
barriers, 98, 99, 105, 106

base, 30, 31, 34, 44, 45, 49, 50, 52, 162
basis points, 70, 96, 115, 116, 154, 165, 167, 169, 184, 192, 197, 200, 201, 213, 227, 230
BBB, 111
Bear Stearns, vii, 1, 2, 9, 10, 18, 19, 20, 21, 24, 26, 27, 28, 32, 35, 36, 37, 38, 42, 46, 48, 49, 51
Belgium, 142, 143, 183, 208
Ben Bernanke, 34, 44, 48, 50, 51, 52
beneficiaries, 23, 145
benefits, 16, 17, 28, 46, 95, 130, 224
bias, 44, 108, 135
board members, 74, 173
Board of Governors of the Federal Reserve System, vii, 9, 48, 51, 53, 59, 153, 155, 156, 158, 160, 161, 163, 166, 168, 171, 176, 178, 180, 181, 185, 186, 187, 189, 193, 194, 198, 199, 204, 205, 209, 211, 214, 216
bonds, 12, 14, 34, 35, 36, 43, 112, 113, 169, 195, 216, 223, 224, 229
bonuses, 22
borrowers, 2, 3, 7, 15, 16, 27, 29, 39, 40, 41, 43, 46, 47, 48, 55, 60, 65, 71, 76, 92, 105, 108, 109, 110, 111, 113, 114, 115, 116, 117, 120, 123, 125, 127, 128, 129, 131, 132, 133, 134, 135, 136, 137, 140, 141, 143, 144, 145, 146, 147, 149, 151, 155, 157, 159, 182, 185, 189, 190, 197, 198, 200, 203, 204, 207, 216, 222, 226, 227, 228, 231
Brazil, 187
budget deficit, 17, 34, 45
business model, 136
businesses, 9, 57, 60, 62, 68, 70, 76, 77, 79, 96, 141, 145, 161, 180, 190, 215, 223, 229
buyer, 216, 224, 229
buyers, 216

C

capital account, 221
capital gains, 24, 26, 29
cash, 8, 16, 18, 20, 21, 22, 23, 34, 35, 36, 37, 51, 56, 57, 61, 62, 68, 72, 75, 76, 78, 79, 97, 99, 112, 118, 119, 133, 153, 156, 162, 165, 167, 168, 169, 174, 177, 178, 194, 197, 203, 209, 210, 215, 218, 221, 222, 224, 227, 229, 230
cash flow, 21, 23, 37, 57, 62, 97, 99, 153, 168, 169, 203, 215, 218, 221
central bank, vii, 1, 3, 4, 5, 10, 15, 16, 28, 29, 30, 33, 40, 44, 49, 52, 56, 61, 66, 69, 71, 75, 81, 132, 140, 186, 187, 188, 219, 221, 222, 225, 227, 228, 230
certificates of deposit, 77, 190, 191, 218
certification, 136

challenges, 22, 36, 60, 110, 121, 148, 150, 185, 187, 194
Chicago, 185, 193
circulation, 30
Citigroup, vii, 1, 2, 3, 24, 26, 28, 29, 38, 40, 46, 50
city, 49
class, 12, 39
classes, 10, 11, 42, 107, 119, 174, 223
classification, 37, 128
clients, 103, 222, 228, 229
collaboration, 77, 189, 190
collateral, 2, 5, 7, 8, 9, 10, 11, 12, 13, 18, 19, 20, 21, 22, 27, 28, 29, 36, 39, 40, 41, 42, 47, 48, 51, 55, 56, 61, 64, 72, 73, 74, 75, 77, 78, 79, 81, 84, 91, 92, 94, 96, 106, 109, 110, 111, 112, 113, 114, 115, 116, 117, 120, 122, 123, 127, 134, 135, 136, 144, 145, 147, 157, 159, 160, 162, 163, 165, 172, 173, 180, 184, 185, 194, 195, 197, 198, 199, 200, 201, 202, 203, 206, 209, 210, 212, 213, 216, 217, 220, 222, 223, 224, 225, 226, 227, 228, 229, 230, 231
collateralized debt obligation, 21, 58, 78, 161, 168, 216
collusion, 87
color, 220
commerce, 107, 220
commercial, vii, 1, 3, 6, 8, 11, 12, 13, 14, 18, 28, 29, 30, 36, 38, 40, 42, 43, 46, 47, 48, 49, 51, 56, 58, 61, 69, 71, 75, 76, 96, 99, 108, 111, 115, 116, 118, 119, 133, 135, 136, 140, 144, 148, 156, 162, 174, 180, 182, 183, 184, 187, 190, 191, 198, 200, 203, 204, 216, 218, 223, 224, 225, 226, 227, 229, 230
commercial bank, 6, 36, 38, 51, 69, 71, 187, 204, 224
commercial paper, vii, 1, 3, 13, 14, 28, 29, 30, 40, 42, 43, 46, 47, 48, 49
Commercial Paper Funding Facility (CPFF), 13, 68, 180
commodity, 31, 45
communication, 83, 98, 103, 104, 137
communication systems, 98
community, 222, 229
compensation, 12, 80, 90, 92, 96, 176, 224
competing interests, 103
competition, 17, 54, 89, 93, 94, 95, 148, 150, 225
competitive process, 120
competitors, 42
complement, 68, 190
complexity, 88, 154, 167
compliance, 55, 64, 84, 98, 102, 103, 105, 106, 107, 115, 116, 122, 123, 136, 151, 157, 226, 227
composition, 27, 29, 33, 88, 130

computer, 65
conference, 3
confidentiality, 40, 103
conflict, 54, 64, 84, 97, 98, 99, 100, 101, 102, 103, 104, 105, 106, 107, 148, 150, 151, 226
conflict of interest, 54, 64, 84, 97, 98, 100, 102, 105, 107, 148, 226
congress, 1, 2, 3, 16, 17, 22, 27, 29, 31, 36, 39, 40, 41, 42, 46, 47, 48, 49, 50, 51, 60, 66, 68, 85, 130, 138, 221, 225, 226
Congressional Budget Office, 25, 29, 50, 63
congressional hearings, 80, 176
consciousness, 83
consensus, 45
consolidation, 196, 212
construction, 4
consulting, 84, 124
consumer price index, 30
consumer protection, 3, 220
consumers, 11, 60, 77, 107, 134, 198, 200, 220, 223
consumption, 11
controversial, 102
conversations, 103, 105, 146
corporate governance, 108
cost, 15, 17, 26, 27, 66, 67, 70, 90, 95, 106, 122, 156, 180, 184, 190, 193, 204, 216, 221, 223, 225
counsel, 193
covering, 106
creativity, 46
credit facilities, vii, 1
credit market, 43, 60, 69, 77, 110, 114, 180, 195, 198
credit rating, 5, 7, 8, 11, 18, 20, 21, 22, 42, 47, 48, 55, 78, 111, 115, 117, 135, 136, 147, 158, 161, 163, 180, 198, 200, 216, 217, 223
creditors, 23, 35, 36, 37, 38, 51, 71, 204
creditworthiness, 39, 111, 217, 219
crises, 9, 53
critics, 9, 33, 45
CRM, 59, 124, 127, 129
currency, 3, 4, 15, 16, 27, 28, 30, 56, 61, 71, 85, 118, 167, 170, 174, 186, 187, 195, 221
customers, 147, 229

D

database, 122
debts, 218, 220
decision makers, 139
deduction, 72, 209
deficiency, 87, 225
deficit, 17, 34, 45
deflation, 43
Denmark, 187, 188, 222

depository institutions, 5, 10, 36, 37, 46, 56, 60, 61, 67, 69, 71, 76, 88, 89, 98, 99, 100, 101, 110, 116, 122, 127, 128, 129, 132, 133, 134, 135, 137, 145, 149, 151, 156, 157, 159, 180, 187, 197, 200, 204, 205, 206, 221, 226, 229, 231
deposits, 13, 17, 30, 33, 39, 40, 71, 179, 187
depreciation, 19
depth, 46, 105, 224, 226
derivatives, 15, 26, 217, 222, 223, 229
detection, 82
directives, 67, 83, 130
directors, 22, 41, 54, 60, 61, 64, 65, 66, 82, 83, 84, 97, 107, 108, 220, 224, 226, 227
disclosure, 2, 3, 39, 40, 41, 46, 99, 100, 105, 138, 150
discount rate, vii, 1, 2, 5, 6, 7, 10, 18
discrimination, 220
disposition, 82, 120
distortions, 43
distress, 71, 204
divergence, 7
diversification, 192, 228, 230
divestiture, 22, 91, 100, 101, 226
Dodd-Frank Wall Street Reform and Consumer Protection Act, vii, 3, 53, 60
Dollars at risk in Event of Need to Terminate under Stress, 59, 127
draft, 9, 95, 138
drawing, 23, 156

E

earnings, 16, 27, 29, 35, 65, 67, 129, 130, 131, 220, 221, 226, 227, 231
economic activity, 4, 44, 198
economic crisis, 3
economic downturn, 11
economic growth, 45
economic incentives, 114, 157
economic recovery, 40, 46
economic theory, 34
economy, 1, 3, 4, 5, 15, 17, 28, 30, 31, 33, 34, 37, 38, 41, 43, 44, 45, 47, 50, 52
eligibility criteria, 108, 147, 184
e-mail, 104
emergency, vii, 1, 2, 3, 6, 8, 9, 10, 15, 24, 27, 28, 29, 36, 38, 39, 40, 42, 46, 51, 53, 54, 55, 56, 60, 63, 64, 65, 66, 67, 68, 69, 72, 73, 76, 79, 81, 82, 84, 85, 87, 88, 89, 90, 91, 92, 93, 94, 95, 96, 97, 99, 100, 101, 102, 105, 106, 107, 108, 109, 110, 112, 121, 124, 125, 126, 127, 128, 129, 130, 131, 132, 134, 135, 137, 138, 139, 140, 141, 147, 148, 149,

150, 151, 171, 172, 178, 180, 189, 220, 224, 225, 226, 228
Emergency Assistance, v, 53
Emergency Economic Stabilization Act, 16, 39, 49, 68, 138, 149, 231
emergency facilities, vii, 1, 3
emergency loan programs, vii, 53, 81, 109, 129, 224
employees, 54, 61, 64, 97, 98, 99, 100, 101, 102, 103, 104, 107, 124, 125, 148, 225, 226
employment, 4, 43, 67, 130
enforcement, 98
England, 52, 132, 231
environment, 35, 38, 83, 88, 106
environment factors, 83
equipment, 4, 11, 200
equities, 10, 75, 195, 197
equity, 19, 22, 23, 25, 26, 35, 36, 38, 39, 79, 90, 97, 99, 100, 101, 117, 118, 163, 168, 169, 170, 199, 220, 221
ethical standards, 98
ethics, 98, 99
European Central Bank, 15, 71, 81, 187, 188, 221, 222, 230
evidence, 7, 9, 40, 44, 52, 66, 86, 108, 221
examinations, 37, 84
excess demand, 50
exchange rate, 15, 71, 186
exclusion, 136
execution, 4, 67, 80, 139, 154, 210, 225
executive branch, 226
executive compensation, 12
executive pay, 22
exercise, 55, 109, 128, 131, 135, 136, 138, 149, 151, 177, 229, 230
expenditures, 82, 129, 130, 220
expertise, 41, 60, 90, 95, 124, 148, 154
exports, 4
exposure, 13, 21, 22, 55, 79, 109, 115, 127, 135, 139, 161, 163, 200, 204, 227, 229, 231
externalities, 43

F

faith, 8, 184
fear, 2, 45, 51, 162
fears, 1, 6, 11, 14
federal agency, 59, 66, 220
federal assistance, 23
federal funds, vii, 1, 2, 4, 5, 6, 7, 12, 16, 17, 24, 31, 34, 43, 44, 47, 49, 67, 70, 183, 206, 219, 223, 231
federal government, 3, 8, 17, 24, 25, 26, 64, 138, 155, 160, 163, 195, 224, 226, 230

Federal Open Market Committee, 40, 59, 66, 151, 152, 186, 205, 219
Federal Reserve (Fed), vii, 1, 2
Federal Reserve Bank of Richmond, 59, 63, 176
Federal Reserve regulations, 223
fencing, 179, 225
filters, 118, 174
financial condition, 3, 5, 17, 31, 33, 35, 36, 43, 55, 68, 73, 79, 99, 111, 112, 115, 128, 129, 135, 172, 205, 227, 228, 231
financial crisis, vii, 6, 30, 39, 41, 45, 47, 50, 53, 60, 63, 68, 75, 77, 84, 98, 107, 127, 130, 145, 147, 160, 198, 222, 228, 229
financial data, 64
financial institutions, 2, 4, 7, 8, 14, 31, 33, 37, 43, 46, 60, 65, 68, 72, 74, 76, 102, 110, 115, 133, 162, 172, 186, 190, 191, 192, 198, 209, 215, 221, 223, 228, 229
financial markets, 3, 4, 6, 8, 13, 19, 20, 22, 38, 43, 46, 54, 58, 62, 66, 68, 69, 74, 78, 80, 81, 111, 134, 138, 147, 152, 156, 162, 163, 173, 188, 228
financial performance, 122
financial reporting, vii, 40, 42, 53, 54, 60, 63, 82, 86, 87, 88, 89, 224
financial sector, 2, 5, 27, 30, 31, 44, 46, 52, 60, 76
financial shocks, 148
financial soundness, 110
financial stability, 43, 64, 88, 109, 120, 130, 134, 198
financial support, 168, 228
financial system, vii, 1, 2, 4, 5, 6, 10, 29, 30, 31, 33, 34, 35, 37, 38, 42, 47, 60, 68, 162, 205, 221, 228
flexibility, 36, 47, 102
flight, 50
force, 31, 45, 46
Ford, 183
foreign banks, 16, 71, 76, 110, 132, 133, 141, 144, 157, 187, 209, 221, 222, 226
foreign companies, 134
foreign exchange, 16, 187, 221
foreign exchange market, 16, 187, 221
foreign firms, 141
fragility, 33
France, 142, 143, 144, 183, 191, 208, 221
fraud, 84, 105, 134, 145, 200, 227, 231
full employment, 43
funds, vii, 1, 2, 4, 5, 6, 7, 12, 13, 14, 16, 17, 18, 19, 20, 21, 22, 23, 24, 31, 34, 36, 37, 38, 40, 42, 43, 44, 46, 47, 49, 51, 56, 57, 61, 64, 67, 68, 71, 72, 75, 76, 77, 78, 96, 114, 117, 128, 132, 133, 134, 136, 138, 140, 141, 144, 145, 147, 156, 161, 162, 164, 165, 167, 170, 172, 180, 185, 186, 187, 189, 190, 191, 192, 194, 199, 200, 201, 204, 205, 206,

209, 210, 216, 218, 219, 221, 222, 223, 226, 227, 229, 230, 231

G

GDP, 34, 44
General Accounting Office (GAO), vii, 2, 3, 40, 42, 46, 47, 51, 53, 54, 55, 56, 63, 81, 83, 86, 91, 93, 111, 113, 116, 119, 121, 125, 126, 136, 143, 144, 145, 146, 153, 154, 155, 158, 159, 160, 163, 164, 166, 167, 168, 169, 170, 171, 173, 175, 176, 177, 178, 179, 181, 183, 184, 185, 186, 188, 189, 191, 193, 194, 195, 196, 199, 201, 202, 203, 205, 207, 208, 211, 212, 215, 221, 222, 224, 228, 229, 230, 231
Germany, 142, 143, 183, 208
goods and services, 43, 52, 90, 93, 94
governance, 41, 65, 84, 107, 108, 121, 220, 224, 225, 226
government intervention, 35
government securities, 67, 99, 218, 219
government spending, 31
governments, 34, 40
governor, 44
grants, 38
graph, 93
Great Depression, vii, 1, 37, 40, 60, 68
Greece, vii, 1, 3, 16, 49
growth, 17, 30, 31, 34, 45, 52
growth rate, 52
GSE debt, 3, 9, 15, 29, 43
guidance, 54, 55, 56, 63, 64, 89, 93, 94, 95, 97, 98, 99, 100, 101, 102, 103, 107, 109, 122, 123, 126, 128, 129, 131, 134, 135, 136, 137, 138, 139, 140, 148, 149, 150, 151, 224, 225, 226
guidelines, 34, 98, 99, 100, 104, 111, 135, 148

H

health, 37, 227, 231
hedging, 170
height, 42, 145
hiring, 148, 193
holding company, 23, 138, 141, 157, 222, 223, 230
homeowners, 154, 229
homes, 77, 198
house, 3, 9, 39, 41, 51, 151, 152, 224, 230
House of Representatives, 51, 151, 152, 224, 230
housing, 3, 4, 14, 15, 33, 54, 58, 62, 68, 69, 80, 152, 162, 215, 224
Housing and Urban Development, 153
housing markets, 33

I

identification, 64, 83, 122
identity, 39, 99, 138, 220
illiquid asset, 8, 35, 36, 42, 51, 72, 140, 209
improvements, 125
income, 2, 19, 20, 24, 26, 27, 28, 29, 39, 50, 54, 64, 67, 79, 81, 90, 97, 114, 115, 117, 118, 129, 130, 131, 161, 174, 182, 191, 192, 199, 220, 223, 227, 228, 229
independence, 41, 46, 51, 82, 84, 224, 226
individuals, 45, 68, 77, 104, 187, 221, 222, 226
industry, 65, 83, 96, 101, 107, 185, 191, 220, 228
inflation, 1, 17, 30, 31, 33, 45, 46, 47, 52
information technology, 84
infrastructure, 75, 84, 94, 124, 154, 222, 225, 227, 231
insider trading, 108
institutions, 2, 4, 5, 7, 8, 9, 10, 14, 19, 27, 31, 33, 36, 37, 38, 39, 42, 43, 46, 51, 54, 55, 60, 61, 65, 68, 69, 71, 72, 73, 74, 76, 78, 89, 90, 96, 98, 100, 101, 107, 108, 109, 110, 111, 112, 113, 116, 119, 125, 127, 128, 131, 132, 133, 134, 135, 136, 137, 140, 141, 143, 144, 147, 148, 149, 150, 151, 153, 162, 172, 173, 183, 190, 191, 200, 204, 205, 208, 210, 217, 218, 219, 221, 226, 227, 228, 229
integrity, 40, 42, 66, 83, 102, 148, 226
interest rates, 4, 5, 8, 27, 28, 33, 34, 43, 44, 50, 52, 77, 80, 130, 131, 152, 153, 155, 156, 180, 195, 219, 222, 229
intermediaries, 117, 146, 198, 210
internal controls, vii, 40, 42, 53, 54, 63, 82, 84, 87, 88, 89, 101, 104, 107, 225, 226
International Monetary Fund, 50
intervention, 21, 35, 42, 46, 224, 230
investment, 2, 4, 8, 10, 14, 18, 20, 33, 35, 38, 51, 75, 78, 80, 88, 90, 91, 92, 94, 95, 96, 98, 99, 100, 101, 105, 111, 112, 113, 115, 133, 134, 154, 155, 156, 162, 165, 168, 169, 182, 192, 195, 197, 200, 201, 213, 219, 220, 221, 222, 223, 230
investment bank, 2, 10, 18, 38, 51, 220, 222
investments, 13, 20, 54, 68, 88, 98, 99, 100, 101, 102, 115, 118, 156, 165, 174, 182, 223, 229, 230
investors, 2, 12, 13, 14, 34, 35, 38, 40, 42, 43, 50, 51, 57, 61, 68, 76, 77, 133, 134, 145, 153, 156, 180, 185, 190, 193, 198, 200, 217, 219, 220, 222, 223, 225, 227, 228, 229, 230, 231
Ireland, 183
issues, 2, 3, 4, 46, 50, 54, 55, 56, 61, 64, 70, 74, 77, 85, 87, 88, 97, 99, 101, 108, 115, 116, 126, 173, 220, 224, 225, 227, 228, 229
Italy, 208

J

Japan, 15, 43, 45, 50, 52, 71, 81, 132, 144, 187, 188, 208, 221, 222, 230
jurisdiction, 40, 41, 186
justification, 10, 39, 56, 94, 95, 131, 138, 149, 151

K

Korea, 145, 187, 188, 222

L

laws, 101, 108
lawyers, 222, 230
lead, 4, 31, 37, 38, 39, 43, 87, 101, 131, 215, 228
Leahy, 50
learning, 95
legislation, 3, 31, 34, 37, 39, 42, 63
Lehman Brothers Holdings Inc, 59, 60, 142, 162, 163, 180, 185
lender of last resort, 4, 6, 10, 17, 36, 37, 38, 39
light, 162
limited liability, 20, 36, 48, 54, 59, 193
liquid assets, 8, 43
liquidate, 18, 57, 62, 128, 230
liquidity, vii, 1, 2, 3, 4, 5, 7, 8, 10, 13, 16, 17, 18, 20, 22, 29, 31, 33, 34, 35, 36, 42, 43, 44, 45, 46, 47, 49, 51, 52, 68, 73, 75, 76, 78, 79, 91, 110, 114, 115, 129, 132, 134, 138, 141, 144, 147, 156, 157, 158, 161, 162, 163, 165, 166, 169, 172, 180, 185, 186, 187, 189, 190, 194, 198, 209, 210, 217, 221, 223, 227, 228, 231
liquidity swap lines, vii, 1, 3
liquidity trap, 43, 45, 52
loan principal, 121, 182
loan repayment, vii, 53, 220
low risk, 13, 105

M

magnitude, 54
majority, 6, 23, 90, 94, 123, 135, 145, 153
management, vii, 26, 29, 38, 42, 53, 55, 64, 73, 74, 80, 82, 83, 84, 85, 87, 89, 90, 96, 97, 99, 101, 103, 104, 105, 106, 107, 108, 109, 118, 121, 122, 123, 124, 125, 126, 127, 132, 139, 148, 149, 151, 170, 172, 173, 174, 176, 201, 220, 224, 225, 226, 227, 231
management of conflicts of interest, vii, 53
market capitalization, 35

market discipline, 182
market share, 96
marketplace, 6, 29, 227
mass, 132
materials, 99
matter, 98, 102, 107
measurement, 226
membership, 2, 37, 66, 67, 126, 220, 221
merger agreement, 26, 74, 173
mergers, 26
methodology, 65, 227, 231
Mexico, 187, 188, 222
Minneapolis, 10, 49
mission, 67, 153
misuse, 135
monetary expansion, 47
monetary policy, 3, 4, 40, 41, 43, 44, 45, 50, 66, 67, 69, 98, 99, 100, 130, 131, 205, 219, 221, 226
Money Market Investor Funding Facility, 14, 57, 59, 61, 76, 77, 189
money markets, 38, 157
money multiplier, 31
money supply, 8, 30, 31, 33, 45, 47, 52
moral hazard, 2, 26, 37, 38, 39, 46
mortgage-backed securities, 3, 5, 8, 11, 12, 21, 32, 33, 48, 54, 57, 58, 59, 62, 69, 72, 75, 80, 96, 118, 152, 162, 197, 198, 210, 223, 224, 228, 229
motivation, 7
multiples, 117, 201
multiplier, 31

N

national origin, 220
Nationally Recognized Statistical Rating Organization, 59, 111, 159, 182, 191, 219
negotiating, 91
Netherlands, 183
newsgroup, 51
Norway, 50, 187, 188, 222

O

objectivity, 89
Office of the Inspector General, 59, 63
officials, viii, 51, 53, 63, 64, 66, 67, 71, 73, 74, 75, 76, 80, 85, 92, 94, 95, 96, 98, 100, 107, 108, 117, 124, 125, 127, 130, 132, 133, 134, 137, 138, 139, 140, 141, 144, 145, 147, 150, 151, 156, 172, 173, 176, 188, 194, 200, 201, 204, 222, 225, 226, 229
one-time audit, vii, 53, 60
opacity, 35

open market operations, vii, 1, 4, 5, 6, 8, 14, 30, 31, 35, 40, 41, 49, 67, 72, 80, 92, 112, 113, 122, 124, 132, 137, 152, 187, 205, 210, 213, 220, 221, 222, 225, 227, 231
operating costs, 19
operational independence, 41
operations, vii, 1, 4, 5, 6, 8, 10, 14, 30, 31, 33, 35, 40, 41, 49, 50, 62, 66, 67, 75, 77, 79, 81, 84, 85, 100, 104, 108, 112, 148, 162, 197, 198, 205, 213, 219, 221, 224, 225, 226
opportunities, vii, 54, 55, 90, 94, 97, 106, 109, 126, 149
organ, 83
outreach, 99, 108
oversight, 2, 3, 39, 40, 41, 46, 60, 63, 84, 85, 102, 107, 123, 124, 126, 148
ownership, 20, 97, 99, 113, 163, 223, 228, 229, 231

P

Pacific, 59, 90, 155, 177, 181, 201, 203
parallel, 45
participants, vii, 6, 38, 40, 53, 55, 61, 65, 73, 76, 92, 94, 95, 99, 108, 109, 110, 131, 132, 133, 134, 135, 141, 144, 146, 147, 149, 172, 178, 185, 194, 209, 225, 227, 231
payment of vendors, vii, 53, 60, 63
permit, 37, 82, 117, 140, 150, 187, 198, 221
playing, 108, 226
policy, vii, 1, 2, 3, 4, 5, 6, 17, 19, 34, 37, 38, 39, 40, 41, 43, 44, 45, 46, 50, 52, 55, 60, 65, 66, 68, 78, 93, 94, 97, 99, 103, 106, 107, 114, 118, 123, 124, 126, 129, 130, 133, 136, 138, 139, 140, 147, 148, 149, 150, 151, 157, 174, 205, 221, 226
policy issues, 2, 3
policy options, 44
policy rate, 44
policy responses, 60
policymakers, 38, 39, 40, 41, 46, 131, 140
pools, 11, 90, 198, 215, 218, 221, 223, 225, 229
poor performance, 35
portfolio, 18, 21, 22, 49, 50, 57, 62, 96, 100, 117, 118, 119, 120, 121, 123, 124, 161, 162, 165, 166, 167, 168, 169, 170, 174, 217, 223, 227, 229, 231
portfolio management, 124
positive externalities, 43
precedent, 38, 39
preferential treatment, 134
preparation, 78, 82, 87
preparedness, 37
president, 19, 66, 67, 68, 74, 101, 126, 172, 173, 226
prevention, 82
price index, 30

price stability, 4, 31, 67
principles, 59, 82, 85, 86, 88, 98, 225
private banks, 109
private firms, 15, 42
private investment, 14
probability, 45, 132, 136
profit, 19, 99, 120
program staff, 99, 124
progress reports, 74, 172
project, 55, 65, 109, 120, 124, 130, 131, 160
protection, 3, 26, 46, 73, 74, 111, 114, 115, 117, 118, 127, 149, 159, 162, 172, 173, 174, 177, 190, 198, 199, 216, 224, 229
prudential regulation, 3
Public Company Accounting Oversight Board, 86, 87, 225
public interest, 225
public markets, 111
publishing, 130

Q

qualifications, 226

R

race, 220
ramp, 95, 192
rate of return, 19, 50
ratification, 226
rating agencies, 20, 111, 112, 115, 117, 162, 198, 217, 219, 225, 227, 230
rating scale, 111
rational expectations, 34
reading, 36
real estate, 15, 119, 174
real terms, 44
reality, 28, 33
reasoning, 43
recession, 43, 45
recommendations, 53, 64, 84, 85, 87, 100, 101, 121, 124, 138, 148
recovery, 19, 40, 46
recreational, 11, 202
recurrence, 3
reform, vii, 3, 39, 41, 48, 53, 59, 60, 224, 230
regulations, 46, 54, 67, 71, 84, 97, 98, 100, 102, 107, 111, 149, 151, 204, 226, 228
regulatory changes, 38
regulatory oversight, 2
regulatory requirements, 226
reimburse, 97

rejection, 228
reliability, 65
remediation, 97, 104, 105, 151
remittances, 17, 27, 28, 35, 67
replacement, 49
repo, 50
reputation, 42
requirements, 6, 8, 11, 28, 37, 39, 54, 55, 63, 64, 82, 94, 95, 97, 98, 100, 103, 105, 108, 109, 110, 112, 115, 116, 117, 122, 123, 132, 133, 134, 135, 138, 139, 140, 148, 149, 150, 151, 157, 159, 182, 191, 192, 195, 198, 199, 206, 210, 222, 227, 228, 230
Reserve Bank of New Zealand, 187, 189, 222
Reserve Bank Operations and Payment Systems, 59, 84
reserves, vii, 1, 2, 4, 5, 7, 10, 16, 17, 30, 31, 33, 34, 40, 43, 44, 45, 47, 49, 50, 52, 67, 156, 162, 187, 205, 221, 223, 231
resistance, 33
resources, 17, 49, 51, 96, 106, 124, 125, 129, 154
response, vii, 1, 9, 11, 16, 17, 22, 33, 39, 41, 43, 44, 46, 53, 84, 88, 98, 105, 121, 124, 128, 135, 148, 186, 193, 209
restrictions, 2, 3, 12, 22, 40, 46, 54, 55, 65, 94, 98, 100, 101, 102, 104, 106, 128, 129, 131, 134, 135, 136, 137, 149, 151, 156, 228, 230
restructuring, 21, 25, 78, 88, 163, 169
retail, 11, 162, 202
retained earnings, 35, 221
retirement, 229
revenue, 17, 67, 120
revolving credit facility, 23, 59, 78, 160, 161, 162
rights, 92, 110, 226
risk, 2, 3, 7, 8, 11, 12, 13, 15, 19, 20, 29, 37, 38, 42, 43, 44, 46, 50, 55, 59, 61, 64, 74, 77, 84, 87, 88, 89, 102, 103, 104, 106, 107, 108, 109, 110, 111, 112, 114, 115, 117, 118, 120, 121, 122, 123, 124, 125, 126, 127, 128, 129, 131, 134, 135, 136, 137, 139, 140, 145, 148, 149, 150, 151, 154, 157, 158, 159, 169, 173, 174, 180, 186, 190, 192, 198, 200, 213, 216, 217, 218, 219, 220, 221, 222, 223, 226, 227, 229, 230, 231
risk assessment, 84, 106, 136
risk factors, 227, 231
risk management, 29, 55, 109, 121, 123, 124, 126, 128, 129, 135, 137, 148, 149
risks, 11, 19, 28, 29, 38, 53, 55, 64, 65, 74, 83, 85, 88, 99, 102, 103, 105, 106, 107, 108, 109, 111, 115, 117, 119, 121, 124, 126, 127, 128, 129, 133, 137, 138, 148, 149, 150, 151, 173, 174, 190, 198, 216, 224, 227, 229, 231
rules, 67, 99, 122, 134, 139, 200, 228

S

safety, 11, 37, 46, 222
Sarbanes-Oxley Act, 82
savings, 156, 221
savings account, 156
scope, 8, 63, 65, 73, 84, 85, 88, 94, 95, 106, 139, 150, 210, 228
SEC, 8
Secretary of the Treasury, 220, 221
securities borrowing facility, 59, 78, 160, 161
securities firms, 68, 209
security, 29, 61, 64, 74, 76, 83, 106, 109, 110, 113, 114, 119, 122, 163, 179, 219, 222, 227, 229, 230
seigniorage, 16
seller, 99, 162, 193, 216
sellers, 92, 99, 114, 132, 133, 159, 160, 193, 227, 231
senate, 3, 9, 39, 41, 49, 50, 66, 151, 222, 230
sensitivity, 102, 148, 227, 231
service organizations, 88, 89
service provider, 92, 96, 106, 193
services, 43, 52, 54, 63, 67, 80, 82, 88, 89, 90, 91, 93, 95, 96, 97, 100, 102, 103, 104, 105, 106, 107, 133, 147, 148, 154, 157, 164, 171, 175, 177, 179, 180, 195, 203, 210, 216, 220, 222, 223, 225, 226, 229
sex, 220
shape, 68
shareholder value, 38
shareholders, 26, 38, 74, 114, 157, 173, 230
shock, 177
shortage, 72, 209
shortfall, 111, 127, 206, 213
short-term interest rate, 4, 50, 52, 67, 183
signs, 77, 180
simulations, 130
Singapore, 187, 189, 222
small businesses, 11, 77, 134, 145, 198, 200, 223
solution, 79, 171
South Korea, 187, 188, 222
special purpose vehicle (SPV), 13, 74, 161, 174, 182
speech, 48, 51, 52, 231
spending, 4, 11, 31, 43, 44, 52, 54, 89, 90
stability, 4, 31, 41, 43, 60, 66, 228
staff members, 94, 98
staffing, 124, 125
stagflation, 45
stakeholders, 126
state, 12, 66, 101, 102, 111, 192, 221
state laws, 111
states, 94, 187, 221
statutory authority, 2, 3, 19, 36, 150, 220

stigma, 6, 40, 71, 204, 221
stimulus, 31, 43, 44, 52
stock price, 14, 19, 24, 35
stock value, 35
stockholders, 221
stress, 7, 127, 149, 156, 177, 178, 187, 224, 227, 229
structure, 11, 21, 64, 74, 77, 83, 97, 114, 115, 118, 123, 124, 126, 133, 138, 157, 173, 174, 178, 180, 184, 190, 191, 193, 222, 225, 230
style, 83
subjective judgments, 101
subprime loans, 68
subsidy, 28, 29, 50
substitution, 213
supervision, 67, 85
supervisors, 133
supplier, 179, 224, 225
surplus, 27, 129, 220, 221
surveillance, 175
Sweden, 183, 187, 188, 222
Switzerland, 132, 142, 143, 183, 208
systemic risk, 2, 3, 37, 38, 78, 79, 162, 178, 221

T

takeover, 26, 27
target, 2, 4, 5, 16, 17, 31, 44, 47, 70, 115, 132, 156, 206, 223
taxpayers, 10, 20, 29, 39, 67
team members, 104
teams, 84, 124
tension, 21, 70, 71, 72, 77
tensions, 71, 73, 172
Term Securities Lending Facility, 8, 28, 48, 56, 59, 61, 72, 172, 194, 209
testing, 63, 89, 106, 107, 127
time commitment, 164
time constraints, 76, 121, 210
time frame, 83, 154, 218
trading partners, 132
training, 64, 98, 107
tranches, 11, 216, 219
transactions, 8, 16, 19, 23, 28, 39, 40, 41, 47, 67, 82, 85, 88, 89, 92, 104, 118, 119, 120, 129, 132, 138, 165, 170, 180, 187, 188, 197, 210, 216, 219, 222, 223, 225, 227, 229, 230, 231
transparency, 46, 56, 60, 88, 130, 131, 138, 140, 150
treasury, 1, 2, 4, 5, 8, 9, 10, 11, 12, 13, 14, 15, 17, 18, 19, 21, 22, 24, 25, 26, 27, 28, 30, 32, 33, 34, 35, 36, 37, 39, 42, 44, 46, 47, 48, 49, 50, 51, 59, 64, 65, 67, 68, 72, 78, 79, 80, 104, 105, 112, 114, 117, 119, 129, 130, 131, 149, 153, 155, 162, 163, 176, 178, 185, 187, 194, 199, 205, 209, 210, 211, 212, 213, 219, 220, 221, 222, 223, 225, 226, 227, 228, 230, 231
Treasury Department, 19
Treasury Secretary, 10
treatment, vii, 53, 55, 61, 65, 88, 131, 134, 137
treatment of program participants, vii, 53
Troubled Asset Relief Program (TARP), 11, 12, 22, 23, 24, 25, 26, 29, 36, 39, 40, 46, 48, 50, 51
turbulence, 22, 48

U

U.S. economy, 42
U.S. Treasury, 4, 21, 22, 25, 35, 42, 49, 50, 56, 61, 72, 110, 113, 114, 222
unacceptable risk, 149
underwriting, 153, 181, 203
unemployment, 35, 45
unforeseen circumstances, 36
united, v, 16, 53, 68, 142, 143, 151, 178, 183, 208, 222, 223, 224, 229
United Kingdom, 142, 143, 183, 208, 222
United States, v, 16, 53, 68, 151, 178, 183, 208, 223, 224, 229
USA, 196, 212

V

valuation, 88, 123, 148, 195, 203, 210, 217, 222, 230
variables, 65
vehicles, 11, 136, 189, 190, 202, 220
volatility, 17, 218, 221
vote, 9, 74, 173, 226
vulnerability, 133

W

wages, 218
waiver, 64, 100, 101, 102, 107, 226
Washington, 35, 48, 51, 66, 221, 222, 224, 228, 229, 230, 231
weakness, 6, 87, 225
wealth, 68
wholesale, 218
withdrawal, 165
World War I, 34
worldwide, 228, 229

Y

yield, 13, 34, 44, 191, 192, 228